in Therapy We Trust

iN **THERAPY** WE TRUST

America's Obsession
with Self-Fulfillment

EVA S. MOSKOWiTZ

The Johns Hopkins
University Press
Baltimore & London

9 8 7 6 5 4 3 2 1

The Johns Hopkins University Press
2715 North Charles Street
Baltimore, Maryland 21218-4363
www.press.jhu.edu

Library of Congress Cataloging-in-Publication Data
Moskowitz, Eva S.
    In therapy we trust: America's obsession with self-fulfillment
/ by Eva S. Moskowitz.
        p.   cm.
Includes bibliographical references and index.
    ISBN 0-8018-6403-8 (hard : alk. paper)
    1. Social problems—United States—History—19th century. 2. Social
problems—United States—History—20th century. 3. United States—
Social conditions. 4. Psychotherapy—Popular works. 5. Happiness.
6. Self-actualization (Psychology) I. Title.
HN64 .M872 2001
361.1'0973—dc21   00-008987

A catalog record for this book is available from the British Library.

To Eric J. Grannis

Contents

Acknowledgments

In the course of writing this book I have accumulated many debts. My editor, Bob Brugger, helped me clarify key ideas and offered very helpful suggestions. Columbia University's Seminar Office, under the direction of Aaron Warner, provided an invaluable grant that allowed me to acquire the photographs for this book. Radcliffe's Mary Lizzie Clapp Fund scholarship provided me with travel money that allowed me to look at key documents at the Schlesinger Library. I would like to acknowledge the help and support I received from professors at the Johns Hopkins University, including Ron Walters, Louis Galambos, Mary Poovey, and Walter Michaels. I would also like to thank several colleagues at Vanderbilt University, including Hugh Graham, Lew Perry, and Arlene Tuchman.

Over the years my friends from graduate school Brian Balogh and Cathy Kerr have continued to stimulate my thinking about twentieth-century American culture and life. Sarah Nazimova-Baum has offered me unique insights and has always been willing to have one more round of discussions concerning the therapeutic gospel. I also want to thank Judy Beggs and Kathryn Gregorio, who lived through the more difficult aspects of this project. My research assistant, Kris Houlton, deserves special credit for slogging through an enormous amount of material, especially on virtual support groups. She also kept me going while I madly tried to finish the research for this book before my baby was born.

My family deserves my deepest gratitude. Eric Grannis, my husband, read every page of this manuscript innumerable times, and I simply cannot thank him enough for his help. My son, Culver Grannis Moskowitz, in his first two years of life cheerfully lived through not only his mother's election to the

New York City Council but also the completion of this book. I am most grateful for his patience. I would also like to thank my mother, Anita Moskowitz, who herself undertakes intellectually ambitious projects. I extend my heartfelt thanks to Alex Grannis, my mother-in-law, Marty Moskowitz, my father, and Teresa and Roman Witkowski, without whose help with childcare I could not have finished the book.

In Therapy We Trust

INTRODUCTION

The Therapeutic Gospel

We live in an age consumed by worship of the psyche. In a society plagued by divisions of race, class, and gender we are nonetheless bound together by a gospel of psychological happiness. Rich or poor, black or white, male or female, straight or gay, we share a belief that feelings are sacred and salvation lies in self-esteem, that happiness is the ultimate goal and psychological healing the means.

Today Americans turn to psychological cures as reflexively as they once turned to God. But our relationship to the psyche appears to have exceeded that of believers and become more like that of cult members. An almost slavish devotion to psychological health and emotional problems dominates our culture: in *Geraldo, Oprah,* and *Ricki Lake;* in self-help books, from *Negaholics* to *Your Sacred Self;* in high-brow tales of psychological woe, like Elizabeth Wurtzel's *Prozac Nation;* and in books catering to every possible niche market, including black women *(In the Company of My Sisters: Black Women and Self-Esteem)*, gays and lesbians *(Double Duty: Help for the Adult Child Who Is Also Gay or Lesbian)*, and even Christian fundamentalists *(Eternal Security and Healing Grace)*.

If talk shows and self-help books were the only churches for this faith, it would still be a phenomenon of only limited importance. In fact, its reach is far greater. Our world outlook has been profoundly shaped by this faith. Not only our personal lives but the entire landscape of human events, from sports to geopolitics, has been reduced to psychological terms, as the following newspaper headlines attest: "Chronic Pessimism Haunts Germans," "Stunned Islanders Fight Off Despair," "Bush Choice Fails to Upset Top Aide." Even how people feel *about* how they feel is news: "Gloom at Saatchi Spawns Anger," "Clinton Is Leery of Premature Joy," "G.O.P. Fears Overconfidence in South."[1]

This philosophy is not, however, merely a perspective, a means of understanding the world, but a faith, a program for individual and social development. There are three central tenets to this "therapeutic gospel." The first is that happiness should be our supreme goal. Wealth, public recognition, high moral character—each of these achievements is held valuable only to the extent that it makes us happy. Success, in the final analysis, must be measured with a psychological yardstick.

This preoccupation with achieving happiness is reflected in popular magazines proffering tests to measure every aspect of the psyche—happiness, loneliness, depression. Nor are psychological barometers only for the individual. Alongside gross national product is a new measure of national success: the happiness index. Fortunately, according to a researcher at the University of Illinois, Americans are winners in this category too: while the citizens of the rest of the world skulk around with a disheartening happiness level of 6.85, Americans stand buoyantly above the rest with a cheery 7.0.[2] Not to be outdone, New York City recently established its own Mental Health Index.

So concerned are Americans with psychological outlook that it provides a new standard even for questions of public policy. The *Wall Street Journal* praised the Gulf War in an editorial. The basis for its praise? Not realpolitik but therapolitik: the Gulf War was helping us recover from our Vietnam War inferiority complex.

The second tenet of our therapeutic faith is the belief that our problems stem from psychological causes. Problems that were once considered political, economic, or educational are today found to be psychological. Consider, for example, the following evaluation from the realm of education: "Grammatical or punctuation errors within sentences, poor paragraph organization, multiple spelling errors, and poor handwriting." Or this evaluation: "Difficulty understanding or naming mathematical terms, operations, or concepts, and decoding written problems into mathematical symbols." These sound like descriptions of students poorly educated in writing and math, but in fact they are clinical diagnoses for disorder of written expression and mathematics disorder. And just as our failures are psychologized, so are our successes. One's IQ is no longer believed to be the predominant factor in success; it has been displaced by EQ, emotional quotient, or a measure of emotional intelligence.

The third and final tenet of the therapeutic gospel is the most important, but it is so universally accepted, so seemingly self-evident, that we hardly notice its existence. This tenet is that the psychological problems that underlie our failures and unhappiness are in fact treatable and that we can, indeed *should,* address these problems both individually and as a society. This is the essence of the therapeutic gospel. It is practiced in every conceivable institution, from professional sports to prisons, from businesses to schools. In New York City, for example, students who lack basic emotional skills, such as handling feelings of anger, frustration, and loneliness, are assigned to a program of "remedial emotional education" to address their "emotional illiteracy." Similarly, business executives with inadequate "emotional skills" may be sent to the Center for Creative Leadership for "emotional retooling."

And more and more, the application of the therapeutic is not confined simply to emotional underachievers at the margins of society but has infused its very fabric. In schools the therapeutic is no longer limited to counselors' work with troubled children. All students are found to be in need of psychological help, to such an extent that self-esteem has become a central element of the curriculum. Michigan promotes self-esteem to elementary students through programs like POP, or the Power of Positive Thinking, and Massachusetts does so through its "I Am a Good Person" curriculum. Teachers must not only learn how to teach self-esteem but also improve their own. This emphasis on feeling good has spawned a new industry, with organizations such as Go For It Unlimited, Inc. providing lectures and workshops on self-esteem for children, parents, and teachers.

It seems that no segment of American society is exempt from the duty to improve the self-esteem of children. Pity the toy company that neglects this obligation. When Mattel, for example, made the mistake of programming its talking Barbie to say "Math class is tough," the American Association of University Women demanded her recall because she was a danger to girls' self-esteem. Unlike many consumer protests, however, this one did not represent a fundamental breach with the business world, which has been eager to plug into the self-esteem market. Witness *Positively Mother Goose,* penned by certified "self-esteem consultants," the Happy to Be Me Doll, made by Self-Esteem Toys, and the Shining Star, a black talking doll designed to foster self-esteem among black girls.

The education of children is but one avenue for Americans' worship of the psyche. Psychological idolatry knows no bounds; it permeates everything, from the social-welfare system to the criminal-justice system. In the court-room, psychological defenses multiply: the adopted-child syndrome, the battered-wife syndrome, the distant-father syndrome, the American Dream syndrome, and the Super Bowl Sunday syndrome. Our therapeutic faith dictates that whatever the social problem, it can be solved psychologically. New York City, for example, found itself confronting the problem of poor families' doubling up in single apartments and fighting because of cramped living conditions. The city's solution was not to alleviate the overcrowding but to have therapists trained in conflict resolution work with the families to help them cope. Los Angeles spent $6 million on counseling in response to the riots there in 1992. Interestingly, the subjects of all this therapeutic attention appear to pray to the same God. When Ohio held statewide hearings on socially disadvantaged black males, the poor black teenagers who testified on their condition fingered the same culprit: poor self-esteem.

Nor is the private sector immune from the psychological siren song. Major companies, including General Electric, Ameritech, and DSC Logistics, bring "the couch" into executive suites to quell personality clashes among senior managers. Even ordinary workers are increasingly eligible for employee assistance programs that provide counseling. Labor too has gotten into the act, providing counseling to union members and their families.

If we are to believe what we are told by newspapers, popular magazines, and television talk shows, emotional ailments have reached epidemic proportions. Perhaps this is in part because there are so many of them. In the fifteen years that the *Diagnostic and Statistical Manual of Mental Disorders* has been available the number of mental disorders listed has grown from 100 to more than 300. Old favorites such as schizophrenia and manic depression have been joined by such newcomers as oppositional defiant disorder, suffered by children who do at least four of the following for a period of six months: lose their temper, argue with adults, refuse to comply with adults' rules, annoy people, blame others for their misbehavior, or act touchy, angry, or spiteful; religious or spiritual disorder, involving a loss or questioning of faith, a problem associated with conversion to a new faith, or an emotional disturbance related to questioning of spiritual values; and premenstrual dysphoric disorder (basically crabbiness).

To help Americans figure out where they fit in, there are special therapeutic holidays. During National Depression Screening Day and National Anxiety Disorder Day, for example, Americans across the country can go to their local mall or shopping center for psychological diagnosis. Even if your problems do not qualify as a true disorder, you may find out that you are "subsyndromal." You may also find out that if you frequently get angry at, are excessively solicitous of, or in general interact too much with a person who is afflicted, you are codependent.

Today, disorders, addictions, and syndromes can involve any conceivable activity. In addition to substances, we are addicted to behaviors like eating, collecting, driving, shopping, sports, sex, even talk shows. Do you find solace in religion? If so, ask yourself whether you are just using it to escape or avoid painful feelings; if you are, you may have a "religious addiction." Even following public events may be psychologically dangerous, as those hapless individuals who watched too much of the O. J. Simpson trial found out when they developed "Simpson fatigue." As for mental-health professionals, they are so busy treating the rest of us that they are developing "compassion fatigue."

Perhaps no psychological condition better illustrates the foolishness of trying to avoid being diagnosed with some form of mental disorder than "happiness anxiety." This condition frequently afflicts those (presumably rare) people who are actually happy. Though temporarily content, they are tortured by the awareness that they may someday become unhappy, an awareness undoubtedly heightened when they look around and see what a miracle it is that they are still psychologically healthy.

Those who suffer from these assorted afflictions and disorders are commanded by the therapeutic gospel to seek treatment. Four in ten Americans fulfill this therapeutic obligation by becoming members of support groups, which exist for every possible problem, including codependency (Codependents Anonymous), weight (Overeaters Anonymous), alcoholism (Rational Recovery), drugs (Pills Anonymous, Potsmokers Anonymous), sexuality (Sex and Love Addicts Anonymous or Regeneration, a Christian support group for gays who are giving up homosexuality), or being related to any of the foregoing (Adult Children of Alcoholics). For those who do not want to recover with the hoi polloi there are more exclusive groups, such as International Lawyers in Alcoholics Anonymous and International Doctors in Alcoholics Anonymous. Or if you prefer to recover with persons who are outside of your profession but share your group identity, you can do that too. You can recover with other Jews, Catholics, Blacks, gays, Hispanics, even other motorcyclists.

America's quest for emotional health has resulted in what is today a $69 billion industry. Not only are total expenditures large but mental health is a growth industry. During the last ten years expenditures in this area grew at an annual rate of 7 percent. The growth in psychopharmacology, however, is nothing short of phenomenal. In less than ten years, for example, the number of Prozac users reached 25 million. Antidepressants alone account for $11 billion. Each year more than 15 percent of adults and 21 percent of children visit mental-health professionals.[3] In the United States today there are more than 40,000 psychiatrists, 65,000 family therapists, 125,000 psychologists, 10,000 psychoanalysts, and 150,000 social workers. And then there are art, music, recreational, drama, and dance therapists, transactional analysts, Jungian analysts, occupational counselors, multicultural counselors, pastoral counselors, rehabilitation counselors, peer counselors, geriatric counselors, correction counselors, milieu therapists, reality therapists, existential therapists, Gestalt therapists, behavioral therapists, cognitive therapists, phototherapists, poetry therapists, bibliotherapists, activity therapists, pharmacotherapists, remotivational therapists, rational-emotive therapists, flotation therapists, phone therapists, van therapists, Cybershrinkers, and Internet counselors.

* * *

America's faith in the psyche is easily mocked. Perhaps this is because it has crossed the line between religion and cult, between faith and obsession. It may also be because so often promoters of the therapeutic gospel offer vapid therapies that only the naive or desperate could take seriously. But whatever the reason, there is a danger in this mockery. It permits us to distance ourselves, to imagine the therapeutic gospel as a bizarre fad with few real consequences. But the story of the therapeutic gospel is the story of modern America. Its history is intimately bound up with the major developments of the twentieth century—the rise of the welfare state, the transformation of the public and private realms, the emergence of the military-industrial complex, and the increasing influence of television in American culture. Today a psychological point of view dominates our political, economic, and cultural life. Clearly, we cannot simply dismiss the therapeutic gospel as strange and amusing. It is too important, too pervasive, and ultimately the consequences are too far-reaching.

Time and again the history of the nation's obsession with the psyche indicates that Americans have embraced simple, quick, and easy therapeutic solutions to complex and difficult problems. Lacking psychological rigor, the therapeutic gospel proposes that every problem be solved by positive thinking. In the early twentieth century this way of looking at the world began to be institutionalized in the emerging welfare state. The schools, courts, and hospitals embraced feeling management as a key part of their mission. During World War II and the cold war, pop psychology, with its emphasis on identity and self-esteem, became an important instrument of domestic and foreign policy.

Historically, our obsession with the psyche and quick-fix solutions has crowded out other ways of thinking. It has blinded us to underlying economic and political realities. The case of the housing shortage in New York City is typical. Instead of addressing the far more complex problem of people who need housing but are too poor to pay for it, the city sends in therapists to do conflict resolution with families living in overcrowded apartments. This tendency can be seen over and over again in American history. Psychological interpretations displace or somehow trump economic ones. The therapeutic gospel obscures the realities of class and the flaws of the market economy.

The therapeutic gospel also robs us of the ability to make serious moral judgments. In this religion there is no place for right and wrong. As one late-nineteenth-century booster of the therapeutic gospel explained, there was now a radical new standard by which everything should be judged: "Let this be our test: the indulgence of any feeling that causes unhappiness to ourselves is always wrong."[4] Outside of the therapeutic there is no good and evil. The therapeutic gospel celebrates all that promotes self-realization and condemns all that promotes psychological harm. This therapeutic morality, of course, focuses our attention on the private life, blinding us to the larger, public good. Indeed, the therapeutic gospel collapses any distinction between the two. Oprah Winfrey summed up this conflation of the personal and the political when she announced the goal of one of her shows: "What we are trying to change in this one hour is what I think is at the root of all the problems in the world—lack of self-esteem."[5] Boiling all problems down to feelings of inferiority, the therapeutic gospel shows itself utterly incapable of leading us out of today's devastating social, economic, and political quagmires.

Despite the therapeutic gospel's substantial shortcomings, at this point its repudiation, even if universally desired, would not work: it has taken root too deeply in our culture. We can, however, become aware of its origins. We can closely examine its history and its effects upon our society. Given the therapeutic gospel's importance to understanding modern American history, it is surprising that more thought has not been devoted to this story.[6] Even though we confront this faith in the psyche every day and are intimately familiar with it, the full story of America's devotion has not been told. This book seeks to explain America's investment in personal problems and psychological happiness. At stake are questions that go to the heart of our personal and civic lives. How did a whole nation get caught up in the goal of fulfillment? Why and how did our personal lives and public debate become infused with a psychological agenda? Perhaps more important, what difference has this investment in the therapeutic made? What has society gained or lost by placing so much emphasis on self-esteem, psychological happiness, and emotional growth?

Though we recognize the therapeutic gospel's grip on our culture, we have little idea how we came to this point. Perhaps this is because the therapeutic has snuck up on us. Perhaps it is because we are only dimly aware that America has not always been obsessed with the psyche. But our therapeutic faith is neither timeless nor universal. Our nation has not always been so preoccupied with personal dilemmas and emotional cures, nor are other nations so preoccupied today. The citizens of Asia, Africa, and Europe do not share Americans' proclivity for the couch. There are fewer psychological professionals in China, Israel, and Korea combined, for example, than there are sex and art therapists in America.

But other cultures differ from our own not only in the absence of therapists but also in their attitude toward the psyche and toward their personal lives. In Poland, for example, when Ignacy Gogolewski, a famous actor and director who had disappeared from the cultural scene, revealed that he had been sidelined by alcoholism, he was denounced for making this personal revelation. The Poles considered his personal problems and recovery inappropriate topics of public discussion.[7]

Even in America the therapeutic gospel has not always reigned. We have not always had youth programs like STOP (Stand Tall on Positiveness), churches called the Temple of I AM, organizations like the National Council for Self-Esteem, reference materials like *The Feeling Good Handbook*,[8] and ads for therapy on public transportation beckoning riders to call 1-800-Feeling. Even the advice given to one another about personal matters has not always emphasized the psyche. In the nineteenth century, for example, those dispensing advice on marriage emphasized physiology. As one marital adviser explained, "The first great requirement necessary in those whose desire is for a happy and loveable married life" is a familiarity with "physiological princi-ples." For men, this meant familiarizing themselves with sexual anatomy, while for women it meant proper food preparation since marital troubles could be caused by "badly cooked and unhygienic food."[9]

Clearly, America has come a long way since such advice. Yet if America's faith in the therapeutic gospel is not as old as our nation, neither has it sprung up overnight with twelve-step programs or *The Oprah Winfrey Show*. Rather, this faith has a long and strange history that begins in the 1850s in Belfast, Maine, with an obscure clockmaker with the curious name Phineas P. Quimby.

1 ILLNESS

1850–1900

Phineas Pankhurst Quimby was born in Lebanon, New Hampshire, in 1802. He spent most of his life in Belfast, Maine, where he worked as a watch- and clockmaker. One day in 1838 Quimby went to hear Charles Poyen, a French mesmerist, who happened to be passing through Belfast. Mesmerism was a theory first proposed by Franz Anton Mesmer (1734–1815), who apparently had "discovered" the principle of animal magnetism and had become well known in Europe for his "marvelous cures."

Upon hearing Poyen, Quimby immediately became a convert and took up mesmerism on a part-time basis. With the help of a man named Lucus Burkmar, Quimby began giving exhibitions of mesmerism throughout New England. Over the years—exactly when is not clear—Quimby renounced mesmerism. By 1859, when he set up his medical practice in Portland, Maine, Quimby had dissociated himself from mesmerism and a host of other healing movements. Announcements specifically billed him as "opposed to Deism or Rochester Rapping Spiritualism." He was said to offer instead "Spiritual Science."[1]

Newspapers throughout New England came to cover what was reported as a startling development, the discovery of "a new principle of treatment of diseases." Apparently, Quimby's novel medical practice involved "investigations in psychology." The press reported that Quimby's "new theory of disease" was "so contrary to the commonly received opinions" that people "hardly dare believe there can be any truth in it." Quimby would treat his patients simply by "sit[ting] down beside [the patient], and put[ting] himself en rapport with him." He did "not use medicine or any material agency, nor call to his aid mesmerism or any spiritual influence whatever." Rather, observers maintained, "his power over disease arises from his subtle knowledge of the mind."[2]

What mid-nineteenth-century Americans found strangely fascinating—Quimby's reliance upon psychology to diagnose and heal—has become commonplace today. So thoroughly infused are we with psychological conceptions of health that it is almost impossible to imagine that such a conception might be new or even nonexistent. Yet, in Quimby's story we see a snapshot of America's journey to the therapeutic altar. Several decades before Freud came on the scene, Quimby proclaimed the mind's role in producing illness. He also announced that the psyche had curative powers if only man knew how to harness them. Quimby claimed to have the secret to such a therapeutics. The secret lay in science and in faith. Quimby's "mental therapeutics"—or mind cure, as it came to be called—preached a "therapeutic ethos," a new psychological gospel.

Quimby's New Moral Calculus

After Quimby's death many of his followers sought to explain the essence of his methods and philosophy; however, the best source is his own writings. Quimby's four-hundred-page tome *Science of Health and Happiness* explores a wide range of topics, including language, mind, patriotism, the cause of man's troubles, the rich and the poor, music, parables, death, imagination, the efficacy of prayer, shadow and substance, superstitious beliefs, the identity of man and God, right and wrong, the senses, knowledge and wisdom, odor, the standard of law, character, happiness, conservatism, intelligence, aristocracy and democracy, and false reasoning.

Despite the book's many subjects, Quimby's interest, at least in his own eyes, was actually quite singular: "I frequently introduce subjects into my articles which do not seem to have any bearing on the subject of disease, but they do."[3] Writing before the era of specialization but at a time when science was acquiring enormous prestige, Quimby related all topics to disease. Indeed, he criticized his contemporaries for failing to recognize the centrality of health and happiness to all aspects of life. In particular, he took the religion, medicine, and the morality of his day to task for embracing an untherapeutic agenda.

Quimby denounced religion as it was currently practiced for contributing to sickness and distress. Indeed, he went so far as to argue that "religion and disease is synonymous" (235). According to Quimby, religion promoted disease by idealizing suffering. He insisted that most people "believe . . . if they suffer, it is for their good to convince them of the weakness of man's wisdom and his dependence on a superior power and if they suffer for his sake they will receive a reward in heaven that shall recompense them for all their suffering" (177). Mocking his contemporaries, Quimby rejected a logic that connected deprivation and reward.

Quimby objected to religion's convincing believers that denial in this world would result in salvation in the next: he lambasted those who "tell you, you are in danger of losing your soul" and those who "offer great inducements for you to enlist in the army of the Lord and fight for their own particular creed, promising you a crown of glory at the end of the war or when you die, so you are deprived of every pleasure you might otherwise enjoy, and torment yourself to death, merely for what you are promised at the end of your lives." Quimby viewed his contemporaries' obsession with punishment and the afterlife as both sacrilegious and unhealthful.[4]

By contrast, Quimby imagined his "spiritual science" as a religion that was therapeutic. It sought to help man understand himself. Quimby's God not only had no need for punishment but had done everything in his power to help man achieve health and happiness in this world. According to Quimby, postponement of happiness was a false idea, a form of idolatry that man practiced at his own peril. Indeed, Quimby argued that man had both a moral and a medical obligation to get out from under such falsehoods. He preached that spiritual science would lead the way out.

It would do so by curing the sick of their false beliefs. Quimby maintained that such an approach was one that Jesus himself had practiced. He sought to save his followers "from the misery of belief, and introduce a new science of kingdom, where there would be no offering up of prayer or forgiving of sins, but a consciousness or science that would put them in possession of a knowledge of themselves." Quimby imagined religion as a science that helped man gain self-knowledge and find happiness. His therapeutic vision of religion was one in which self-consciousness released man from ideas that bound him to his troubles.

Quimby believed that to be cured, man had to cast off false ideas promoted not only by religion but also by medicine. He accused doctors of promoting the false idea that disease was physiological in origin and material in nature. He scoffed at such falsehoods, ridiculing physicians who asserted that disease was "a certain something that comes in various shapes and on various accounts or causes, and attacks people in various parts of the body." A consideration of the evidence demonstrated the absurdity of this medical principle: "If [the disease] is a thing of itself, did anyone ever see it? In all postmortem examinations and dissections of bodies which have taken place, had the thing dissected been found in the body?" Confident that the answer to both questions would be no, Quimby concluded, "You know yourself that it [is] not a material thing of itself." For Quimby the problem with the medicine of his age was not simply that it did not hold up to Victorian standards of evidence—a faith in the visibility or readability of truth—but that it was lethal.

Quimby viewed the medicine of the age as superstition with deadly consequences. It deserved not respect but contempt. "For instance a physician, from his theory, which is based on the lowest grade of ignorance and superstition produces a chemical change in your friend and blows him up or kills him from his science, and your friend gives him credit for being a scientific man. Now to kill a person by the theory of science of the faculty is one of the easiest things in the world." Quimby attributed medicine's murderous record to its emphasis on physiology. In Quimby's view, doctors failed to cure because they neglected the mind; they mistakenly believed the body to be all important.

According to Quimby, even when medicine did not kill, it did more harm than good. He gave as an example the case of a woman with "a very fine piano." The woman in question placed "a great value" upon the piano. She "feel[s] annoyed by everyone coming in and thrumming on the keys." Indeed, when anyone approaches the piano the patient becomes nervous. Eventually a physician is sent for. "He comes in as ignorant of music as the rest, goes to the piano and begins to look at it." As the doctor fiddles with the piano the patient becomes increasingly agitated. The doctor says, "You look sick and your blood is low. You need some little tonic. . . . I will leave you some powders." On his way out the doctor strikes the piano keys once more, and the patient's condition worsens.

In a few days the doctor returns: "The sight of the doctor reminds [the patient] of the instrument and [the patient] grows nervous." This process is repeated until "they have run through the medical faculty." So consumed with the body are the doctors that they fail to understand the patient's possessive attitude toward her piano. They also fail to comprehend the power of imagery and association, for even the sight of the doctor recalls the patient's feelings of possessiveness and nervousness. Because medicine focused on the corporal and neglected the patient's mind, it did not succeed. In this case, material interventions were bound to fail, according to Quimby, because the woman's sickness stemmed from an emotional association, a set of feelings about the piano.

Few today would dispute Quimby's theory of association. Psychotherapists believe that images can trigger emotional as well as physical reactions and that therapists need to be sensitive to the patient's psychological history. Quimby's appreciation of psychodynamics makes him strikingly modern. Yet, his account of going through the entire medical faculty and even his description of the piano lady's problem is thoroughly nineteenth-century. Quimby's vision of psychodynamics is utterly mechanical and literal. The doctor's presence calls up unpleasant experiences, and "the sight" of him makes the piano lady ill.

Quimby maintained that despite the damage done by doctors in such a case, his "true" or "spiritual" science could cure. It was an effective medicine, for it took account of the role of beliefs in producing sickness. Quimby placed ideas and the mind at the heart of his medicine. What his contemporaries called disease, Quimby saw as the external manifestation of internal error or ignorance. Disease existed in the mind "in the form of belief, and the body being under the control of the mind, and subject to its influence is molded and affected just in proportion to the state of mind, in its belief." The trick to therapeutics, according to Quimby, was to set the mind in the "true direction." A sick person, "deceived by error" and "in trouble," needed to be shown his "false direction." He needed to be put "in possession of a science" that taught "that thought is matter governed by another power and that his own belief is the cause of his trouble, and that to correct his belief is his cure." According to Quimby, his spiritual science was such a science.

With his spiritual science Quimby forged not only a fundamentally new vision of religion and medicine but indeed a new morality. Dismissing self-denial as untherapeutic, immoral, and sacrilegious, Quimby's new moral calculus emphasized the ideal of self-fulfillment. His science, or medicine, was designed to secure happiness. In fact, he argued that contentment and growth were the standards by which his healing methods could be judged. As his book, *Science of Health and Happiness*, indicated, all interventions that resulted in the patient's feeling better were clearly successful. This new perspective links Quimby to the modern therapeutic project. Independent of Freud, Americans chartered their own therapeutic course.

Quimby's therapeutic morality was created out of a Victorian vocabulary of moral absolutism and self-improvement. It relied heavily on the dichotomies of truth and falsehood, right and wrong, knowledge and ignorance. It defined these absolutes, however, in terms of subjective feelings of health and well-being. The goal of Quimby's medicine was to put man in possession of truth so that he could be cured of his false ideas. Quimby admitted only two kinds of ideas, true and false ones. False ideas made people sick. As Quimby explained it, "The effect of error is discord, disease, and death." Conversely, truth "takes matter in a deranged state, giving a true direction, and the effect is harmony, happiness, and peace." Quimby's emphasis on acquiring truth and banishing falsehoods links him to the Victorian culture from which he came. Victorians devoted considerable energy to the elimination of falsehoods, viewing their prevalence as one of the major problems of the age. But whereas most other Victorians mobilized for the purpose of enhancing the chances for salvation and improving character, Quimby did so to improve health and happiness in this world.

Quimby also put Victorian techniques of self-improvement to new uses. Victorians embraced self-consciousness as a technique for overcoming moral turpitude. Rejecting the corporal punishment of their forebears, they substituted the mind for the body as the site of social control. They advocated extreme self-consciousness as the way to guard against sinful or evil tendencies. Indeed, the Victorians made self-control and self-policing a favored pastime. Quimby drew upon this legacy to advance therapeutic goals. He advocated self-consciousness as the way to keep happy and achieve a state of perfect health. For Quimby, policing the mind for wrong ideas was a technique not of salvation but of self-fulfillment.

With such a vision, Quimby exceeded the bounds of mid-nineteenth-century American culture and laid the ground for modern therapeutic culture. Indeed, he put himself directly at odds with the "self-improvement" literature of his age. Whereas the didactic energies of the Victorians went into promoting diligence, perseverance, and self-denial, Quimby's went into promoting personal contentment. He repeatedly insisted that "happiness being man's aim, it is what we are all striving for" (90) and that "every idea going to destroy the progress of happiness must perish" (149). He defined his therapeutic mission in terms of eliminating unhappiness: "My method is based on a science . . . which destroys opinions on all subjects which tend to disturb man's happiness" (5). Condemning his contemporaries for promoting a morality of grief and discouragement, Quimby proposed a morality of happiness.

It is perhaps Quimby's concern with unhappiness and personal troubles that marks him most conspicuously as an important precursor to the therapeutic gospel of modern America. In his practice Quimby saw patients who suffered from what he called false ideas, what today would be called emotional problems. Reviewing his years of medical service, Quimby described his patients as consumed with troubles stemming from incorrect beliefs and mental distortions: "I have sat with more than 300 individuals every year for 20 years, and for the last 5 years I have averaged 500 yearly, people with all sorts of diseases in every possible state of mind, and with hypochondriacs and insanity brought on by all kind of ideas that people believed in" (90). It was to these ideas and inner problems that Quimby directed his therapeutic attention. As Quimby himself continually put it, "My practice is unlike all medical practice. I give not medicine or outward applications. I tell the patient his troubles."[5]

Like a modern-day therapist or counselor, Quimby addressed himself to the mind and its role in hindering happiness and development. He was committed to what today would be called emotional growth. As he explained this interest, "That which gives me the most satisfaction is to develop a mind capable of development."[6] Quimby devoted himself to excavating those mental constructions that prevented self-development and distorted man's view of himself. He blamed feelings for skewing man's image of both himself and the world: "Your feelings as far as I have gone are witnesses that testify against you. You have none to appear on your behalf and you are cast into prison by these false witnesses" (56). Quimby imagined himself in the role of a lawyer, defending the patient against his own feelings and ideas, He sought to expose the mind's role in misrepresentation. Quimby was convinced that if man understood himself, he could correctly interpret himself: "If man knew what he was composed of, that is the identity called man, then his wisdom would put a different construction on his acts" (116). Doctors could help patients by getting at their true identity, by helping them correctly interpret their acts and feelings. Within a thoroughly Victorian vocabulary, Quimby, like a modern-day therapist, called upon his clients to obtain self-knowledge.

His actual medical practice also links him to modern-day therapy. While

Quimby treated and analyzed a variety of cases, he was particularly excited about the role of spiritual science in what we today would call interpersonal relations. He was convinced, for example, that mental treatment could have a profound effect on troubled marriages, for he thought marital problems stemmed from "ignorance of ourselves." Quimby extolled the practical implications of spiritual science for marital troubles: "I have also found that I can change the mind so that a person that is hated can be loved . . . and also that the person that is changed can respect what he never had any respect for" (149). Recognizing the power of the therapeutic gospel to shape personal relations, Quimby lamented its limited use.

Quimby describes one case, for example, that could have been solved if only it had been brought to him early enough. In the case of the "Divorced Lady" the husband and wife had loved each other when they married and continued to do so until the lady "took cold and was very sick." Once sick, "she lost all patience, had no confidence in her husband, forsook his bed, and would not have anything to do with him." The rejected husband got a divorce. Looking behind the behavior of the couple, Quimby finds a wealth of subtle psychological motivations that explain how their love turned into hatred.

According to Quimby, the lady's "sickness caused her husband to fear for her life." But she "put a false construction on his fears; for his love when she was well did not excite her fears." Apparently, she was unable to recognize her husband's love for her at least in part because when she was well he did not express his love through fear. In addition, her fear that her husband did not love her "attached to her trouble, made her worse so that the more he would try and please her, the more he tormented her till each one's love turned to hatred, and at last they were divorced." Quimby blames fear for distorting the true situation. He is certain that if she could have been made aware of the "insane idea" that was causing the "discord," she could have been cured. Generalizing, Quimby concludes that "insanity consists in some little discord that might be corrected, if the person knew it" (40–41). But most people, Quimby sadly reports, remain completely ignorant of the psychological method of treatment.

Quimby, of course, was right to view his therapeutics as marginal. Few of Quimby's contemporaries believed that most problems had psychological origins or that mental sources of illness and discontent were as important as physical sources. They did not agree with Quimby that if man was "as careful as to what he does believe as he will be about what he eats or drinks," travel could resume on the "true scientific highway" and happiness and health could be reestablished. They did not see consciousness as the key to health and happiness, even though they saw it as the key to salvation and virtue. During Quimby's lifetime, the therapeutic gospel he forged out of the religion and medicine of his day, a gospel that emphasized happiness and demanded faith in psychological cures, remained on the sidelines of American culture.

In the 1890s, however, approximately forty years after Quimby articulated his core therapeutic principles, mind cure, or mental therapeutics, became the rage. The movement that embraced mental healing became known as New Thought. Its devotees could be found in large urban areas as well as smaller cities and towns. For example, major centers of New Thought included Hartford, Connecticut, San Jose, California, Walla Walla, Washington, Pueblo, Colorado, Fort Worth, Texas, Eliot, Maine, Jackson, New Hampshire, and Oscawana, New York. There were local New Thought organizations, like the League for the Larger Life, whose mission was "to spread a knowledge of the fundamental principles that underlie healthy and harmonious living" and "to assist the individual in the solution of personal problems,"[7] and the Church of the Higher Life, "where words of cheer and friendly fellowship might be given and exchanged." It had a corps of fifty-two letter writers who wrote "cheerful words" to anyone who for any reason felt "shut in from fellowship with the outside world."[8] In addition to local organizations, New Thought had a national organization, the National New Thought Alliance, and even an international organization, the International Divine Science Association.

Most New Thought activity, however, was not directed toward those who had personal contact with the movement's instructors, organizations, or healers. Rather, it was directed toward the anonymous readers of books and periodicals. In many ways New Thought was a movement of the printed word, promoting its ideas through a broad range of publications, including philosophical treatises, novels, and practical-advice literature. It was really New Thought's self-help books that captured the public imagination. Ralph Waldo Trine's *In Tune with the Infinite*, for example, sold more than 1.5 million copies. Elizabeth Towne's books, which included *Practical Methods for Self-Development* and *How to Use New Thought in Home Life*, sold more than 100,000 copies each. Henry Wood's *Ideal Suggestions through Mental Photography*, Helen Bigelow Miriam's *What Shall Make Us Whole*, and Annie Payson Call's *The Power of Repose* were also New Thought bestsellers.

New Thought reached its broadest audience through magazines. During the late nineteenth and early twentieth centuries more than a hundred New Thought magazines reached a mass audience. *Nautilus,* for example, had an estimated 45,000 subscribers and a circulation of 150,000. *Unity* magazine achieved a similarly large circulation. Other important New Thought magazines include *Fulfillment* (later *Aspire*), *Wayside Lights,* the *Universal Truth Monthly, Success Magazine, Realization, Mind, Mental Science Magazine,* the *Journal of Practical Metaphysics, Immortality, The Higher Law, Harmony,* and *Now,* "a monthly journal of positive affirmations devoted to mental science and the art of living." New Thoughters even boasted a magazine for German Americans, *Das Wart,* and one for children, *Wee Wisdom.* At the height of its popularity New Thought had an advice column published in the mainstream women's magazine *Good Housekeeping.*

New Thought and the Modernization of Self-Help

Between 1866, when Quimby died, and the 1890s American society underwent vast changes. In many spheres of life, including leisure, economics, politics, and religion, Victorian culture was under attack. Economically, the rise of the corporation forever changed the country. Politically, the administrative state, with its web of regulatory agencies, came into existence. Culturally, America gave birth to new forms of entertainment, including the amusement park, film, and dance halls. This transformation, described by cultural historians as nothing less than a reorientation in American values, entailed a reaction against gentility, decorum, and passivity. In the words of one historian, the 1890s brought forth a "new activist mood."[9] It also brought forth a new penchant for organization. Municipalities organized themselves, expanding services. Universities grew, establishing new schools and new departments. Civic and cultural groups re-created themselves on a national and even international level.

It was in this context of frenetic organization building and a rejection of Victorian values that Quimby's principles of mind cure became immensely popular. Indeed, in unprecedented numbers Americans flocked to New Thought, a movement of religious medicine based loosely on Quimby's teachings.

The term *New Thought,* first used in 1887, had achieved widespread acceptance by 1889. Before the late 1880s, it was known as mind cure, mental science, metaphysical healing, or Christian Science. The establishment of Mary Baker Eddy's Christian Science Church in Boston in 1881 and Eddy's vigorous effort to retain this term for her own brand of metaphysical healing led others to embrace the term *New Thought,* which had no specific denominational meaning. New Thoughters insisted that anyone who desired "to know the truth, regardless of creed or other affiliations whether members or non-members" could join their movement.[10]

The popularity of New Thought clearly lay in its message about modern life: modernity required a faith in psychological cures as well as a knowledge of special therapeutic techniques. According to New Thoughters, the problem that threatened to overwhelm American society was not poverty per se but poverty of the mind. They worried not about material shortages but about shortages of positive thinking. The proliferation of such problems as melancholia, anxiety, and unhappiness roused them to action. New Thought sought to expose those responsible for low therapeutic standards. They identified the fields of religion, science, and metaphysics as particularly culpable in this regard, accusing them of damaging "millions of sensitive and responsive souls" each year.[11]

New Thoughters castigated religion for its role in creating anxiety and promoting pessimism. They accused their contemporaries of fostering a belief in a revengeful God and a belief that "things are against us." Such pessimistic ideas not only kept God "at arm's length" but also ruined the health of believers. By contrast, the "new" system of thought favored a view of God and the power of man that was radically optimistic. At the core of New Thought's religious vision were the ideas that everything was possible and that man through the power of his mind could control his health and his happiness. Condemning the view of God as unforgiving, New Thoughters imagined him instead as "an ever-present Help." They believed that God was always ready to aid "us in our attempts to overcome our difficulties." He was man's own personal problem solver. Since on God's "part all is done even before we ask it," religion was neither about honoring God as the great architect nor about man's duty to achieve virtue and avoid sin. It concerned man's positive feelings about himself and freeing himself from pessimistic notions.

This reconceptualization of religion had important implications for its practice. In New Thought, for example, prayer became a therapeutic, almost secular device. It was used to attain complete health and harmony and was considered something that "chiefly concerns ourselves and others like us in whom ignorance, doubt, and self-will hinder the workings of that perfect love and perfect wisdom to which we appeal." New Thoughters conceived of prayer as a technique for overcoming the problems of doubt and achieving self-fulfillment. They recommended using prayer to find that "divine spark within yourself." They viewed it as the means to become "self-conscious— that is aware of our lack of adjustment to God, the Real." For New Thoughters, prayer, if successfully practiced, enabled man to adjust internally to the positive in this world.

Such a project of adjustment, New Thoughters complained, was absent not only from religion but also from science and metaphysics. While people were dying from melancholia, metaphysics persisted in its overly abstract inquiry, and science in its overly material one. As one character in Henry Wood's New Thought novel *Edward Burton* explains, the problem with science is that "no development of science, aerial navigation, perfected photographs, nor telephones, technical education, improved legislation, sanitation, medication, nor all combined can enhance human happiness." Similarly, philosophy had failed to address the fundamental question of life: "How can a weary traveller on the highway of life, who is carrying a burden of mental and physical inharmony, anxiety, and discouragement leave them behind and gain veritable harmony and illumination?"[12] By contrast, New Thoughters imagined their mental science as the fundamental answer to the problem of "making the world as happy as it should be." They saw their audience as composed of "every striving soul with longings within that will not be satisfied."[13] It was to these individuals and to this problem of unhappiness that New Thought directed the bulk of its attention.

New Thought's effort to call attention to the problem of unhappiness was unprecedented in both its extent and its quality. Never before had Americans' poor state of mind received so much scrutiny. Alarmed by the "ocean of morbidity" engulfing Americans, New Thoughters felt compelled to alert the public. The increase in bad feelings, they warned, threatened to put "an end to all healthful activity." It had already made man's "whole mentality" become "cramped, limited, and depressed."[14] With the aim of providing a true, unsentimentalized picture of the variety of unhealthful feelings that plagued the nation, New Thoughters categorized and described forms of discontent. Their documentation of bad feelings went beyond that provided by Quimby, for New Thoughters named specific states of mind and described their psychological effects. In doing so they introduced considerable specificity to America's therapeutic gospel.

The bad feelings that most troubled New Thoughters were anxiety, worry, and fear. They found that "a large part of mankind is in bondage to that state of mind which is apprehensive of some sort of trouble or misfortune." Observing that "we are afraid of poverty, afraid of accident, afraid of public opinion," New Thoughters lamented the prevalence of dread. They also found that sorrow and self-doubt had afflicted a disturbing number of people. Great sadness, according to New Thoughters, often became "magnified out of all proportion," engaging "the whole attention of the miserable sufferer."[15] Self-doubt had a similar effect. New Thoughters regretted that there were so many "who narrow their lives through want of confidence." Finding that there were many who did not treat themselves with respect, New Thoughters condemned this lack of charitableness, or what today would be called low self-esteem: "Should not a man have the same charity for himself that he would feel toward another? Would we bear it for a moment if another should condemn us as rudely as we sometimes condemn ourselves?"[16] Applying Victorian conceptions of etiquette and charity to the self, New Thoughters endorsed a new therapeutic morality. Finding rudeness and uncharitableness in self-condemnation, they rejected these attitudes as inappropriate building blocks for a psychologically healthy self.

New Thought's psychologized vision of life exceeded the bounds not only of the era's morality but also of its medicine. Its medicalization of a whole range of feelings set it apart from late Victorianism. In conceiving of anger and doubt as diseases, New Thought challenged late-nineteenth-century medical debate. In the 1880s and 1890s American medicine was still committed to a somatic interpretation of mental diseases. Thus, for example, George Beard in his famous book *American Nervousness,* of 1881, insisted that nervousness was "a physical and not a mental state."[17] By contrast, New Thought embraced a far more psychological interpretation. Its promoters argued that debilitating emotions were a form of illness that required a special therapeutics, one that addressed the forces of mental causation. In medicalizing a whole range of feelings, New Thought legitimized a new kind of treatment for a new kind of problem.

Their vision of therapeutics, however, was not a secular one. In New Thought, religion and medicine were deliberately blended. New Thoughters, like Quimby, believed that there was no distinction between health, the Divine, and psychological well-being. Often in the same breath, New Thoughters would discuss depression and the remedy of thinking positively or allowing the mind to become "the channel of the Infinite."[18] They viewed wrong thinking or feeling bad as not only unhealthy but also a subversion of the will of God. Ultimately, they traced all mental problems to the ignorance of God: "Ignorance of man's God given dominion over all things is the basic cause of incorrect thought."[19] They maintained that to feel good one needed only to learn that God had given man the power to control his thoughts and feelings. While man supposedly had this power, he rarely exercised it. More often than not his thoughts controlled him. Through a tour of the mind and its powers, New Thoughters hoped to reverse this trend.

New Thoughters viewed the mind as a powerful but simple conduit that controlled every aspect of life. Completely beholden to the mind, they insisted that "nothing carries more weight for good or ill to body or mind than the thoughts of people."[20] New Thoughters believed that thoughts had a direct, immediate effect. "If we are fractious, depressed or discordant, we find all things in the same condition about us, while if we glance with clear insight at things we see no antagonism in them." Because of the direct and controlling nature of thoughts, it was imperative that the mind be set in a positive direction. It was in the mind's power to ward off depressing thoughts and attain contentment that New Thoughters found salvation. They took comfort in the fact that the mind, if properly exercised, could act as the conduit for positive feelings and bear immediate results. New Thoughters strove to convince others that "one can in the early morning set his mental focus for the day by dwelling a few moments on a right thought and by practice hold this mood so that everything has a healthy tinge."[21]

New Thoughters believed that health and happiness also depended upon psychological investigation. They embraced excavation, which entailed uncovering the "universe of ideas" in which each individual lived, as an important part of the therapeutic project.[22] "You will never be perfectly well," they insisted, "until you have brought forward to light" those thoughts and "dispositions as lie quiescent in the past and even buried in oblivion."[23] Making visible and conscious one's mental processes and deep-seated emotions is a key aspect of the modern therapeutic agenda. The therapeutic gospel assumes that mental health and happiness require that we become aware of the underlying and often hidden emotions that determine our outlook.

In addition to establishing the basic rationale for the therapeutic gospel, New Thoughters also anticipated resistance to it. They worried about the reluctance to probe the psyche. New Thoughters explained that "many shrink from such a searching inward": they are willing "to look out ward, but cannot abide introspection" because such an examination might "reveal them to themselves." Others would not want to initiate such an undertaking because they believe they are already healthy and would therefore not benefit from it. But New Thoughters insisted that "you need not fear that you are so good that you will not be able to find your error. You need not fear that you will find nothing to correct in yourself; for after intelligent introspection of an hour, you will be aghast at the host of errors, in the form of weaknesses and indulgences—to speak of nothing worse—that you will bring to the front."[24] Drawing upon the Victorian era's vision of a flawed human nature, New Thoughters justified the modern project of psychological investigation and intervention.

New Thoughters also justified their therapeutic project by pointing to the flawed nature of society and the particular opportunities presented by modern life. The trials and tribulations of the times required a mental reservoir of self-knowledge: "Man's greatest need is a knowledge of himself."[25] Modern life had made it possible for man to acquire self-knowledge and put it to effective use. The discovery of the principles of mental treatment would allow man to finally fulfill his purpose in life, which New Thought defined as "self-manifestation, or realization of our essential nature through the evolution of consciousness."[26] The laws of psychology and the new goal of self-consciousness made possible a new morality. As one New Thoughter succinctly explained, "Let this be our test: the indulgence of any feeling that causes unhappiness to ourselves is always wrong."[27] Armed with this moral calculus, New Thoughters found a society deeply flawed and in much need of practical guidance.

The advice offered by New Thought was its most important activity not only because the movement wanted above all to make its ideals practical but also because it was New Thought's self-help materials that most interested consumers. New Thought sought to address the problems "within" and to offer counsel. It addressed those who wanted to know what to do if they were feeling depleted or plagued by mental disorder. Its purpose was to save readers from their own thoughts. New Thoughters found the answer to the problems of mental discouragement and disorder in organization, discipline, concentration, and self-control. They also advocated the techniques of *mental sugges-tion, mental photography,* and *psycho-gymnastics.* Thus, they recommended the application of conventional Victorian ideals as well as the new techniques of *scientific thought-training* with the hope that readers would feel positive and realize themselves. In creating a new set of practical techniques, New Thoughters drew upon concepts of Victorian self-help but fundamentally modernized them.

Like the Victorians, New Thoughters demanded that individuals take re-sponsibility for their thoughts. They believed that man could control his mental outlook and ought to improve it. Insisting that no external circum-stances limited man, New Thoughters maintained that the "barriers, checks, and limitations are self-erected consciously or subconsciously and have only the power we give them."[28] They claimed that even those who had been weighed down by bad thoughts for years "need only the rousing of their dor-mant thought to life to lift them to the grandeur of their God-given state."[29] Indeed, this emphasis on the individual's role in both creating and solving his problems was the central rationale for offering practical guidance. New Thoughters believed that man was the architect of his outlook and that it was therefore essential that he learn the principles of mental design. While they conceded that individuals needed training in mental treatment and con-sciousness-raising, they insisted that everyone was accountable for their own mental progress.

New Thought advice retained not only the Victorian commitment to per-sonal responsibility but also its emphasis on discipline. Hard work produced mental success. New Thoughters criticized the person who failed to apply himself in this area: "Pray when has he made any systematic effort? He will spend years of time and no end of effort to educate himself on the surface, but can hardly afford hours to scientific thought-training."[30] While New Thoughters recognized the difficulty of bringing forth healthy thoughts, they nonetheless insisted that individuals must devote concerted effort to improv-ing their mental atmosphere. Those who would not strive for "mental focus" suffered from the effects of "scattered, ungoverned thinking"—anxiety weak-ness, disintegration, and sometimes even death. Concentration, on the other hand, if properly directed, led to the elimination of inimical thoughts: "Con-centration, rightly directed leads to knowledge born of intuition thus un-folded. . . . The perplexities of the work-a-day world disappear, and the wisest and best thing to do in any given circumstance comes to us; anxieties flee away; the soul realizing its Divine self serenely watches for its own heavenly vision."[31] New Thoughters encouraged those with mental disorder to reach into the recesses of their mental atmosphere to root out discouragement and concentrate on good thoughts. Unfortunately, there was much resistance to such work. As one New Thoughter explained, "Many shrink from such a searching inward reconstruction" because they lacked courage and commitment.[32] Much of New Thought's practical activities were directed toward overcoming such hesitancy.

New Thought also strove to convince readers that incorrect thought or bad feelings did not have to rule their lives, that there were techniques for subduing them. One such method of mind control was psycho-gymnastics, in which the mind was trained to shut out all negative thoughts and ideas of self-condemnation. Mental exercise ensured that "the ills, spectres, beliefs of evil, and disorders of the mind and body may be crowded out of the consciousness, and finally as a natural result, vanish from outward expression." To the would-be exerciser New Thoughters promised that a positive "attitude of mind, firmly held" would "gradually change his consciousness concerning himself."[33]

Other recommended techniques for thinking therapeutically included mental suggestion and mental photography. Both techniques involved imagining or verbally repeating ideal thoughts so that bad feelings became finally unreal. As one advocate of "mental suggestion" explained, when you are feeling bad, you suggest or "make the statement that you are in a harmonious condition of mind and equal to the duty of the hour." If properly practiced, the suggestion will lead to "its corresponding condition of mind."[34]

Mental photography, most fully developed by Henry Wood, a businessman turned New Thoughter, worked in a similar manner. Wood laid down the principles of this technique in his famous *Ideal Suggestions Through Mental Photography, A Restorative System for Home and Private Use* (1893). As its name implies, this technique involved taking mental pictures of good and positive thoughts. The person whose "mental chambers" were filled with a "host of indefinable fears, spectres, imaginings, forebodings, and morbid depressions" was supposed to fix his gaze on a thought, which for convenience was printed on a placard, and stare at it for ten to twenty minutes. Sufferers were advised to prop the placard up "at a suitable distance from the eyes" and "rivet the mind" on it. As Wood explained it, "Through the medium of the eye, by exposure, their truth becomes photographed upon the deep, living, consciousness."[35]

Though much New Thought advice consisted of general maxims regarding how to think therapeutically, the movement also added considerable specificity to therapeutic discourse by counseling individuals on their particular problems. This form of advice was promoted through mass magazines. Of special interest is the "Family Counsel" column established by *Nautilus* in the first decade of the twentieth century and *Good Housekeeping*'s "Happiness and Health" column, organized by the famous New Thoughter Horatio Dresser. These columns sought to help readers achieve fulfillment.

"Family Counsel" was a "department of consultation and suggestion" conducted by the editor of *Nautilus*, Elizabeth Towne. Towne explained her aims as follows: "I will try to reply to the 1001 odds and ends of life-problems and home interests which are presented to me. . . . Every reader is welcome to what advice and suggestion I can give, and I sincerely hope that with the aid of this department we can reach and help many more people."[36] Since only Towne's responses were printed in the magazine, the kind of advice readers sought from "Family Counsel" must be inferred from the responses. While readers appear to have suffered from a wide range of difficulties, many sought help with their feelings of loneliness, anxiety, self-doubt, and anxiety.

Whatever the problem was, Towne offered therapeutic advice. Thus, to R.E.G., for example, Towne explained, "I believe that a cheerful right-thinking attitude of mind along with fasting properly and persistently applied will cure any kind of disease except broken bones." To this she added positive reinforcement: "You are on the right track. Keep cheerfully along." To F.P.R., Towne recommended, "Always hold the thought awhile, and then let your mind slip off into the Infinite without any definite aim to listen to anything. Just float in the Infinite." Not all of "Family Counsel"'s advice was quite so abstract. Towne advised W.L., who it can be inferred was plagued with doubt and ambivalence, to "follow your own soul, your own highest ideal. When in doubt be still. And don't try too hard to settle in your own mind a decision for which you have no immediate use. Things come to us as we need them." To H.L.B., who also may be inferred to have suffered from a lack of self-confidence and loneliness, Towne advised:

Accustom yourself to meeting people and you will outgrow self-consciousness. And when you are alone at work, think of yourself as working before lots of people and not caring a darn whether they admire your actions or not. . . . Be proud of yourself; consider yourself as good as the best. . . . Be your own angular, positive, knotty self, and know that those who are bright enough will value you for your selfness, and the rest aren't worth bothering about. . . . Under such self training the habit of bashfulness will soon disappear.[37]

"Family Counsel" offered psychological advice to readers who appear to have been relatively familiar and comfortable with the project of divulging personal and mental conflicts and receiving counsel from a mass-circulation magazine.

By contrast these basic premises of modern therapeutic discourse were alien to readers of the mainstream magazine *Good Housekeeping.* Its New Thought advice column, "Happiness and Health," presumed a modesty about sharing problems of mental discomfort with a mass public. Sensitive to the difficulties of divulging personal problems and receiving advice from an unknown adviser, "Happiness and Health" presented itself to readers not as an advice column but as a personal insurance company. It aimed to "insure, as far as possible, health and happiness to each of our policyholders." While in other types of insurance companies, the column explained, a financial payment was required, in Health and Happiness "the medium of exchange is not money, but mutual service." The column appears to have assumed that would-be advisees had to be coaxed into presenting their problems. It made a special appeal "to readers of this department to ask questions and make known their needs." Assuaging readers' fears of public self-revelation, it encouraged them not to "be afraid to make the most realistic description of your life and your needs or afraid to reveal your ignorance, your conflicts, and heart-hungers." Introducing familiar Victorian concepts to obscure the new, therapeutic nature of the project, it told readers that they might find it easier if they "write as you might to a friend or brother, freely and frankly."[38] But of course readers were being asked to thrust their personal troubles into full public view. They were being asked to become participants in the therapeutic gospel. That there was reluctance to do so suggests that the modern therapeutic project had a way to go before it was completely accepted by the public at large.

* * *

Responding to what were perceived as the inadequacies of religion and medicine, mind cure and then New Thought promoted a new kind of thinking. These movements of religious medicine advocated consciousness-raising as the key to mental reform. They expanded Americans' conception of the mind and created a new vision of the circumstances that legitimated therapeutic intervention. Unhappiness became reason enough. This reorientation toward the psychological also involved the promotion of new techniques of catharsis.

While New Thoughters brought a new ideal of organization to the personal sphere, most Americans and many members of the psychological and medical professions remained wary of the therapeutic gospel. Professionals often rejected religious medicine's distinctively modern form of advice and conception of mental illness. In fact, doctors in Massachusetts during the 1890s attempted to limit the practice of mind cure and New Thought through licensing. Others labeled it a form of insanity. In "A Pathological View of the 'New Thought' as a Form of Mania," for example, Dr. George M. Gould explained that a healthy mind "cannot read the so-called New Thought journals for an hour or two without the overwhelming conviction that these people are really insane." Categorizing the spread of New Thought as an epidemic, Gould stated, "In the worst cases . . . the magazine's editor becomes one with God, and his sentences for pages are entirely meaningless drivel and word-wash, and one wonders how soon there must be a writ de lunatico inquirendo and a commitment to the asylum."[39]

Although many professionals were unsympathetic to the movement, some did acknowledge its influence. Dr. Richard Cabot, for example, went so far as to assert that "a great deal which physicians have not taken into their practice they really owe to Quimby and Christian Science." And Hugo Munsterberg, writing several years after the enthusiasm for mental healing had subsided, said that if "physicians will at last make use of the psychical factors in their regular practice, they ought not to forget that the important step forward was taken under the pressure of popular religious movements."[40] Not until after World War I did the professions of psychology and psychiatry in fact gain a measure of control over the therapeutic gospel. When professionals entered the fray in substantial numbers, they eliminated many of its religious and Victorian elements. They also put the therapeutic gospel to use in the service of Progressive era social reform. In the second decade of the twentieth century key aspects of the modern therapeutic agenda were adopted by the rapidly expanding state. In the 1920s experts working in the fields of psychiatry, social work, criminology, and education became not only strong advocates of therapeutic rhetoric but also managers of its institutionalization in the courts, schools, and welfare agencies.

2 POVERTY

1890–1930

In 1913 John Mitchell, the reform-minded mayor of New York, asked Katharine Davis to become the city's commissioner of correction. Davis had been the superintendent of the innovative Bedford Reformatory for Women, considered the cutting edge of American criminal justice. Bedford hired psychologists and psychiatrists to "treat" rather than merely punish its female charges. Having successfully administered this bold, new approach to criminology, Davis gained a national reputation. Mitchell offered Davis the opportunity to modernize the city's criminal-justice system, which comprised fifteen prisons housing 125,000 inmates, the largest jail system in the world. Davis's acceptance made her the first woman to hold a cabinet-level position in New York City.

What made headlines, however, was her first act of office: the abolishment of traditional prison garb. A bemused press reported that "convict stripes are going to be abolished as soon as Commissioner Davis can get rid of 18,000 yards of stripes." With complete seriousness, however, Davis insisted that a woman "always has more self-respect when she has on her best clothes . . . you cannot reform a woman who is wearing bed-ticking." Davis declared, "I believe strongly in the psychology of clothes."[1] For Davis, the psyche was a critical factor in both causing and rehabilitating deviance.

Katharine Davis's psychological vision of reform was part of a broader cultural phenomenon. During the early twentieth century an entire group of reformers began to psychologize the social problems of the day. These reformers, whom I call therapeutic reformers, "looked within" for the sources of social pathology. They maintained that neither the environment nor economic conditions could explain the social blight around them. They also maintained that contemporary reform methods had failed. In their view, only by applying new psychological principles could the nation hope to solve the problems of crime, education, and home life. This therapeutic theory of reform had a lasting effect on America's welfare state. It profoundly affected not only the nation's conception of poverty but also its provision of social services.

Despite the attention devoted to the Progressive era and its program of social reform, the importance of the therapeutic gospel in the period has not been understood. Few have appreciated that psychological notions were critical to the reform movement and growth of the welfare state. Yet, the "discovery" of maladjustment as a national social problem played a key role in the extraordinary expansion of the state during the early decades of the twentieth century. Between 1900 and 1930, new professionals who handled the poor successfully advocated for the provision of psychological services in prisons, courts, hospitals, and schools.

The story of the birth of this new therapeutic theory of welfare begins in the 1870s with scientific charity. This movement applied so-called scientific principles to the dispensing of aid to the poor. Scientific charity laid the ground for a fundamentally new approach to poverty, one that relied on investigation. Through Scientific charity, knowledge and eventually "psychological" knowledge became a central part of America's antipoverty strategy.

Welfare before the Therapeutic, 1870–1910

On a cold winter morning in 1888 twenty-seven-year-old Mary Richmond, who was to become a leading figure in the social-work profession, scoured the "help-wanted" ads in the newspaper. For eight years Mary had worked as a bookkeeper, but she wanted something more out of life. In the late nineteenth century it was not easy for women to fulfill grander professional ambitions. So when Richmond's eye caught an ad put out by a poor-relief organization, she became excited. Perhaps, she thought, this was the opportunity she had been looking for:

> THE CHARITY ORGANIZATION SOCIETY desires the services of an educated Lady or Gentleman of good social position and well-acquainted in the city to COLLECT ITS SUBSCRIPTIONS AND EXTEND ITS MEMBERSHIP AND KNOW OF ITS METHODS AND AIMS with knowledge of ALL CLASSES OF THE COMMUNITY.[2]

Richmond got the job, the beginning of a lifelong career.

Charity organization societies first appeared in London in the 1860s and spread to the United States during the 1870s, a response to the enormous waves of poverty that hit the country during the last decades of the century. These relief organizations drew upon the new principles of social science. They argued that pauperism could only be eliminated by determining its exact causes and placing all relief efforts on a scientific basis. By the 1890s cities large and small had adopted the fundamental principles of scientific charity and established charity organization societies.

Mary Richmond played a critical role in their development. Highly energetic and organizationally talented, Richmond transformed the Baltimore Charity Organization Society. She took a small, financially starved organization and turned it into a national model of charity. She increased the number of volunteers to more than three hundred and undertook a major development campaign, raising more than five thousand dollars in her first year. Richmond also standardized procedures for both volunteers and paid district agents. In fact, she wrote one of the earliest handbooks on charity work, in which she articulated a new antipoverty strategy. According to Richmond, to solve the problem of poverty one needed knowledge and information. And indeed in only a few years the walls at the Baltimore Charity Organization Society were lined with file cabinets containing records for thirty thousand cases.[3]

These file cabinets indicate a fundamental change in American history, a critical shift in approach to the problem of poverty. Before scientific charity, poor people simply received food, shelter, fuel, occasionally funds, or nothing at all. Sometimes provisions were given in exchange for work, and sometimes they were given outright. But with the rise of scientific charity came a brand-new approach to poverty.

To scientific-charity leaders, the problem of poverty was a problem of relief-roll expansion. They feared that pauperism was becoming "a permanent institution, a positive profession."[4] Seeing that "poverty and suffering are increased," they found the difficulty to be "how to help those who are poor, without adding to their numbers." Finding that "the larger the funds given in relief in any community, the more pressing is demand for them," advocates of scientific charity sought to devise ways to resist such expansion.[5] They imagined their movement as a struggle to "root out" pauperism by repressing both need and requests for aid. Their antipoverty strategy emphasized "repression," or keeping the number of poor people down and preventing them from rising up.

Scientific charity held sentimental almsgiving responsible for unleashing new demands for relief. It blamed those motivated by feelings of pity for increasing the number people needing relief. According to proponents of scientific charity, benevolence led people to give without thinking. Those who responded to beggars on the street apparently were most guilty of sentimental almsgiving. By contrast, advocates of scientific charity saw themselves as "empirical givers": they gave based on knowledge. Not only did they know from experience which antipoverty strategies worked in general but they knew the particular circumstances of individual families and therefore exactly what kind of help would most benefit them.

It was therefore anonymous and indiscriminate help that most troubled scientific-charity workers. To them, the dole exemplified this kind of help. They described the dole as a "crime against society, a crime against good citizenship, and a crime against morality." Direct handouts were thought to be criminal because they created the conditions of moral and financial ruin. One scientific-charity leader compared them to the effects of alcohol: "I know nothing which does so much damage to encourage pauperism and educate paupers for the next generation, as this system [of outdoor relief]. . . . There is nothing except intemperance in the use of alcoholic liquors which is more demoralizing to the head of the family or more ruinous to children than to become imbued with the idea that the public is bound to provide for them." Proponents of scientific charity argued that the moral cost of relief often outweighed its benefit. They presumed that direct aid without any prior knowledge of the situation had a corrupting effect.[6]

Scientific-charity workers continuously documented these negative effects. For example, Mary Richmond described in her charity manual a case in which more harm than good was done by help. A friendly visitor finds a poor woman out of work and in desperate need. The friendly visitor decides to temporarily employ her. As it turns out, Richmond tells us, "once or twice it happened that the woman had to go to court in the morning and came at ten instead of eight or again the visitor let her off early, but she always paid her for the whole day." After a few months the friendly visitor finds the woman a job with neighbors. But "they complained that she came at ten instead of eight and expected pay for the whole day and they would employ her no longer." The moral of the story is that "the careless, patronizing charity of the thoughtless almsgiver" had to be stopped. Relief "without plan or purpose" was worse than no aid at all.[7]

Direct handouts made poor people believe that the public had a responsibility to care for them, thereby undermining their will to be independent. Until those in charge of dispensing relief had a better understanding of their
clients, their efforts would be at best wasteful and at worst criminal. In Buffalo, New York, site of the first charity organization society in the United
States, this principle was put into bold relief. A large sign over the society's
door read "NO RELIEF GIVEN HERE."[8] It must have been difficult for the poor
to understand what a charity organization did if it did not materially help the
poor.

Contemporary commentators did not fail to note scientific charity's bizarre, mixed goals. At times its work was mocked. The Boston Irish poet John
Boyle O'Reilly poked fun at scientific charity's invoking science to refuse relief:

> The Organized Charity scrimped and iced.
> In the name of a cautious, statistical Christ."[9]

George Washington Plunkitt, of Tammany Hall, the famous New York City
political machine, stated his criticism by way of contrast: "If a family is
burned out . . . I don't refer them to the charity organization society, which
would investigate their case in a month or two and decide that they were worthy of help about the same time they are dead from starvation. I just get
quarters for them . . . and fix them up till they get things runnin' again. It's
philanthropy, but its politics too—mighty good politics. . . . The poor are the
most grateful people in the world."[10]

Scientific-charity advocates opposed not only relief with political
strings attached but also relief dispensed anonymously, that is, without really
knowing the recipients. They believed that if relief was to be effective, it had
to be individual and personal. They believed that those who gave out aid had
no desire "to know them [the poor] as they really are."[11] Knowing the poor
meant, first and foremost, understanding their faults. Scientific-charity leaders insisted that no matter how "lavish may be the relief, unless self-restraint
and providence be conferred upon those who receive it, all that is bestowed
will often be wasted in riotous living."[12] For scientific-charity leaders, a poverty policy that did not take into account the poor's tendency to be profligate
was bound to fail. To prevent both riotous living and plain old riots, they
argued, indiscriminate or unscientific giving had to be abandoned.

Scientific-charity leaders urged instead that scientific systems for dispensing relief be adopted. Investigating the applicant's background was the cor-

nerstone of this project. As one leader explained, "We are diametrically opposed to all systems, all institutions, all charities, all forms of relief what-
soever which avowedly or tacitly adopt 'give and ask no questions.' . . . The
fundamental law of its [scientific charity's] operation is expressed in one
word: INVESTIGATE."[13] Another leader in the scientific-charity movement,
Edward Devine, explained that when it came to investigation of the poor, the
probe "cannot be too thorough or extensive or painstaking or the record too
careful."[14]

But the knowledge scientific-charity workers sought to derive from their
investigations was not psychological knowledge. Rather, it was moral knowledge that interested them. Scientific-charity workers believed that whether
they were dealing with a tendency toward "unrestrained novel reading" or intemperance, knowledge of such characteristics was relevant to dispensing
aid. That character flaws were a major concern was made abundantly clear
with the creation of the term asthenontology for the study of human weak-
ness. The term was created in 1897 by Alexander Johnshon, president of the
National Conference of Charities and Corrections, the professional organization for charity workers, to describe what scientific charity was all about.[15]
Scientific-charity advocates likened themselves to doctors studying disease:
"Experience in the examination of families will give a visitor the same readi-
ness in looking for all these items which a physician has in inquiry after the
symptoms of disease." Unlike the medical patient, who presumably had nothing to hide, the poor person often sought to hide both his economic and his
moral condition. The visitor had to be on the lookout for both. Charity experts therefore recommended that "visits to a house be at irregular periods"
so that the poor could be observed as they really were.[16]

Manuals for friendly visitors advised that they ask very specific questions.
Often these revolved around the family's financial circumstances. Richmond, for example, advised that the following questions be asked by each visitor: "Can anything be done to increase the family income? can number of
wage earners be added to?, can anything be done to make the existing income
go further? Is too much being paid away in rent? could the family do with less
accommodation? is money being wasted on medicine, habitual pawning, or
in purchasing from tallymen or buying things not wanted? Do husband or
children keep back an undue share of earnings?"[17] Another expert advised
visitors to obtain a slightly broader range of information, including (1) the
number of persons in the family, (2) who earned anything and what the in-

come was, (3) whether there were any other able-bodied workers, (4) the trade and avocation of each worker, (5) what other things they could do, (6) why any were out of work, (7) the amount of the rent, (8) whether anything had been saved in prosperous times, (9) whether the family was in debt, (10) whether anything had been pawned, (11) habits, and (12) the state of the family's health. This charity worker also recommended obtaining information pertaining directly to relief. He advised finding out what type of assistance was most needed, what assistance, if any, have been given and by whom, the family's nationality, whether the family had any relatives or references, and whether any family members attended church or school.

Imagining swarms of "imposters" ready and willing to prey on innocent or even experienced almsgivers, proponents of scientific charity sought to devise measures that would enable charity workers to distinguish between the deserving and the undeserving poor. With the goal of ending "indiscriminate giving" and the fraud it engendered, scientific charity articulated an elaborate science of detection.[18]

This science consisted of procedures to keep track of relief applicants and judge the legitimacy of their claims. Techniques of surveillance thus became a key part of scientific charity's antipoverty program. These techniques were deployed to ensure that the undeserving did not receive aid and so that charity workers could more easily decide "what it is wise to give and what not to give so as not to pauperize" those eligible for relief. The scientific-charity movement hoped to eliminate indiscriminate giving by creating an extensive paper trail. The "personal inquiry" form was the linchpin of this effort. Scientific charity required that every applicant for relief "make answers to a printed form." Its proponents claimed that "not a clue is left which may shed light upon the question of how or by what steps the man has come to a state of want and been compelled to ask for aid." However, in practice only certain types of information were solicited. The "facts" that interested scientific-charity leaders were those that revealed the applicant's credibility and moral character. The applicant was required to supply "references" who could vouch for his or her honesty.[19]

This antipoverty strategy of verification depended heavily upon the police. As various handbooks on scientific charity explained, the personal inquiry form was to be sent to the superintendent of police, who would give it to the precinct captain, who in turn "details an officer to make an investigation of the case and report back." All relief, scientific-charity leaders explained, was to be given "in accordance with police recommendations."[20] Contemporary critics of scientific charity did not fail to note this reliance on the forces of law and order. One clergyman from Cleveland, Ohio, for example, said, "I doubt as I read the New Testament whether the twelve disciples would have been able to qualify as worthy according to your system. And Christ himself might have been turned over by you to the police department."[21]

Complementing and offsetting the role of the police was that of the friendly visitor. Scientific-charity leaders maintained that the poor needed to "be in the possession of a real friend, whose education, experience, and influence, and . . . whose special knowledge of domestic economy are placed at the service of those who have neither the intelligence, the tact, nor the opportunity to extract the maximum good from their slender earnings." The friendly visitor was imagined as one who would not give out "doles of food and clothing and money which only pauperize" but would inculcate "a loving, friendly spirit." This was to be accomplished by sending women of the wealthier classes to the homes of the poor.[22]

This strategy of combating poverty through systematized "friendly visiting" was perhaps the most therapeutic aspect of scientific charity's reform agenda. The friendly visitor was imagined as having an effect that was both "civilizing and healing." Individual paupers were to be "cured" through "personal contact" with their social betters. Rich women and their daughters, "coming from bright and happy homes," would impart "to the cheerless tenement or wretched hovel, a little of their own happiness." Friendly visitors would teach the poor "unconsciously a practical lesson" and "awaken in them at times a little ambition for home life."

The practical lessons taught by friendly visitors were not, however, psychological lessons. Scientific-charity workers envisioned learning about "the conditions of the cellar walls, yard plumbing and outhouses" and the family's method of garbage disposal. Other topics considered of critical importance were sunshine, carpets, and food. They believed that the poor had to be taught, for example, that "no person can be preserved in health without being exposed to the sun" and that "the morning sunshine is more desirable than that of the afternoon." Charity workers found ventilation harder to teach. But perhaps most difficult of all was to convince the poor of the evil of carpets, which "are intolerable in many homes of the poor. Persuade these people to part with them; if you can to burn them." As for diet, "certain foods . . . should never find their way to the tables of the poor. Pork is one of these."

And veal and lamb "should be vetoed." Even funeral homes were considered an important subject for instruction. Friendly visitors were advised to carry with them information about reputable cemeteries, for they viewed the poor as gullible and profligate when it came to death: "Have in your book of memoranda, a list of cemeteries which are under good management with the prices asked for graves in each, the cost of opening a grave."[23]

Whether a charity worker advised that you teach "your poor to give up frying," to use pea coal, to keep the fire clean "not by violent shaking but by a straight poker used on the back of the fire," or that small children should "never have stimulants, greasy food, green fruit, or cakes, nuts, and candies,"[24] the advice they gave was not personal in the way we think of that term today; that is, it was not of a psychological nature.

Although advocates of scientific charity alluded to the psychological mechanisms by which the poor would be uplifted and emphasized cheerfulness, the therapeutic agenda of scientific charity was limited in both scale and scope. Health and happiness did not constitute a primary or direct objective. Friendly visitors were explicitly told not to comfort and console but rather to "strengthen [the poor's] resolve" to resist poverty. Scientific charity emphasized that harsh, even painful methods often had to be adopted to achieve moral and healthful results. "The cause of want and suffering are to be removed" even "if the process be as painful as plucking out an eye or cutting off a limb."[25] Even friendly visiting, perhaps the most therapeutic aspect of scientific charity, relied upon a vision of reform as repression. This contrasts directly with the antipoverty efforts of the Progressive era, which relied on "sublimation." As one Progressive era reformer said of one of the most pressing social problems of the day, "Prostitution and promiscuity will be eliminated not by force but through sublimation."[26] Not until the rise of social science and the creation of the helping professions would poverty workers adopt an explicitly therapeutic agenda. But scientific charity laid the ground for a new "scientific" and ultimately psychological approach to poverty.

The Psychologization of Poverty and a New Theory of Welfare, 1910–1930

During the Progressive era, the period between 1890 and 1920, there developed an intense interest in reform. Fundamental changes were proposed in practically every sphere of American life. Reformers tackled a wide range of issues, including factory conditions, political patronage, birth control, and trade regulation. The push for change came from labor and business, writers and activists, legal scholars and genteel women.

This was an era of big proposals and larger-than-life reformers. The labor movement produced such well-known leaders as Big Bill Haywood, Mother Jones, and Elizabeth Gurley Flinn. In the area of political reform there was Robert La Follette, the governor of Wisconsin, and Teddy Roosevelt. The women's movement gave us Margaret Sanger, Jane Addams, and Carrie Chapman Catt. The story of the Progressive era, as this intense period of reform is called, has been rehearsed many times, though there is continued debate about its significance in American history.

But what remains largely unexamined is a strand of reform that enlisted the help of the therapeutic gospel. The reformers involved, whom I call therapeutic reformers, came out of the social-reform movements of the era. These reformers, mostly women, had taken advantage of the new educational opportunities offered by the growth of postgraduate education. They argued for fundamental change at a time when the emergence of philanthropic foundations made new sources of funding available. They used these funds and the influence they gave them to demand changes in the welfare state. More often than not, they worked behind the scenes in hospitals, courts, schools, and prisons. But what most distinguished therapeutic reformers were their ideas.

Therapeutic reformers, like other reformers of the era, understood that harsh economic conditions were the background against which the poor struggled, and references to the poor's economic difficulties fill their writings. However, they challenged what they perceived as an exclusively economic view of reform. As one reformer put it, it was not enough to make the poor child "healthy or to provide him with immaculate teeth or tonsils." The question society had to address was, "Do we provide him with anything which shows that he himself is worthwhile?"[27] Not satisfied with providing food, clothing, and basic medical care, therapeutic reformers sought also to address the question of self-worth.

With this radical extension of reform came a redefinition of the poor's characteristics. Instead of imagining the poor as not doing well economically, therapeutic reformers viewed them as not doing well "from the standpoint of conduct."[28] They saw them as suffering not from financial bankruptcy but from "imbalance," "impulsiveness," "suggestibility," "emotional inadequacy," "emotional excess," and "egotism." Psychologizing their charges, therapeutic reformers defined them as emotionally rather than economically deprived.

Around this population, which was poor but whose defining characteristic ceased to be poverty, therapeutic reformers created a new conception of the state. In this new view the state, with help from experts, was obligated to provide for those with "abnormal" psychologies. It had to establish minimum psychological standards of living. In addition to imposing new responsibilities on the state, reformers also had new expectations for the poor. In their view, the poor had the responsibility to "develop the desire to grow up," "face situations," and "abandon the infantile mechanisms on which they have learned to rely."[29] In proposing that citizens be responsible for ridding themselves of their abnormalities and that the state be responsible for managing personality reconstruction, therapeutic reformers radically extended notions of both public and private responsibility.

Therapeutic reformers deemed approaches to reform that did not engage in such an extension as woefully inadequate. They condemned, for example, the popular technique of mental testing, viewing its version of "mental inquiry" as narrow and superficial.[30] In their view, it was naive at best to assume that simply administering intelligence tests would allow society to contain the problem of maladjustment. Therapeutic reformers believed that only a clinical investigation of the whole mental life of those who were poorly adjusted and individual programs of rehabilitation would enable society to curb social deviance.

Therapeutic reformers also condemned caseworkers for engaging in "snapshot diagnoses." Mary Richmond, who had become more therapeutically oriented, denounced others in her field for poor investigatory work. Citing the transcript of an interview that reads, "Assistance Asked? Coals and Groceries; Cause of Need? Out of Work; Any Relatives Able to Assist? No," Richmond wrote, "This stupid compilation of misleading items does not get at the cause of the problem."[31] Nor did it reveal "what course of procedure will place this client in his right relationship to society." No longer satisfied with simply providing coals and groceries to those who had none, therapeutic reformers wanted the poorly adjusted to attain psychological health by means of therapeutic procedures.[32]

First and foremost this new approach necessitated collecting information that had never been collected before. It also meant viewing all information, whether consciously or unconsciously provided, as relevant. Therapeutic reformers warned that since personality displayed itself "ordinarily not in a few conspicuous acts, but in a trend of behavior evidenced by innumerable trifling remarks or by a succession of decisions and impulses each unimportant in itself," they would have to be prepared to identify those impulses. The task of comprehending the personalities of their charges also necessitated gaining a new kind of knowledge about individuals, including their "mental content and imagery," "inner conflicts, complexes, inhibitions, or resistances," and "hopes and fears."[33]

From this knowledge reformers fashioned a special treatment program, "talking." In this new treatment, the key was to lay bare the patient's psychological patterns and logic. If the patient was allowed to talk about his past and current feelings, the source of his maladjustment could be uncovered. As one therapeutic reformer explained, "No conditions should interfere with our efforts to lead [the client's] mind back to the events that will reveal the deeper-seated difficulties."[34] Another advised clinicians to "let your patient talk: do not interrupt him even when he becomes prolix and diffuse. It is to your interest as well as his to study his psychology and to lay bare his mental defects."[35] Therapeutic reformers understood that unveiling the client's psyche was their most difficult and important task and that special procedures had to be followed to ensure that such revelation occurred. It was at hospitals specially designed to handle those with "mental defects" that "talking" as a new method of cure was first institutionalized.

Mental Hospitals

In 1904 Clifford Beers had a mental breakdown and was admitted to a Connecticut hospital. He entered the horror that mental institutions were in his day. He would overhear "the dull thuds of blows" against his fellow inmates, who would "cr[y] for mercy until there was no breath left the man with which he could even beg for his life."[36] Unlike most of his fellow inmates, Beers decided to write about his experience. In 1908, encouraged by William James, who wrote an introduction for him, Beers published his account under the title *A Mind That Found Itself.* The book was quite successful, running through four printings in the decade that followed.

Beers's book came at a crucial moment, as the seeds for reform in treating the psychologically ill had only recently been planted. In 1896 the Pathological Institute of the New York State Hospitals had been founded, the first of its kind in the country, and in 1902 Adolph Meyer had become its director. In 1906 the University of Michigan followed suit, erecting its own psychopathic hospital. Dr. Albert Barrett, a student of Meyer's, was made its director.

Meyer envisioned psychopathic hospitals' playing a far different role from that of the mental institutions of the day. Meyer's psychopathic hospitals would seek to create "a remedial rather than a merely custodial environment for the patient." Moreover, he perceived a much broader range of patients for the hospitals, including what today might be called the "clinically depressed" but which Meyer referred to as the "not insane" and the "not-yet-insane."[37] Meyer envisioned psychopathic hospitals' helping the community at large by treating all those suffering from maladjustments and other psychological abnormalities. In effect, he saw those hospitals as the solution to the problem of social deviance. They would treat those responsible for the problems plaguing the nation's schools, homes, and prisons.

Meyer was at the New York Psychopathic Institute when Beers sent him his manuscript. In many ways Beers's book fit perfectly with Meyer's vision. What was striking about *A Mind That Found Itself* was that it attempted to explain insanity to the public, to make the insane seem comprehensible. The book illustrated how the sane could become insane and then return to sanity. Moreover, Beers's impeachable credentials—he was a Yale graduate—seemed designed to induce a "there but for the grace of God go I" reaction in the reader. In short, Beers's book served to decrease the otherness of mental illness.

After Beer's book was published, he and Meyer met. Discovering that they had a mutual interest in reforming the way the mentally ill were treated, in 1909 they founded the National Committee for Mental Hygiene. The committee soon attracted numerous benefactors from a stellar list: Henry Phipps, Mrs. William K. Vanderbilt, Joseph Choate, Marshal Field III, the Rockefeller Foundation, the Commonwealth, Milbank Memorial, and Julius Rosenwald Funds, and of course Jane Addams. The committee took on the task of first investigating how the mentally ill were treated and then lobbying state and local governments to make improvements in their treatment.

In the succeeding decade and a half, psychopathic hospitals sprouted up in several cities around the country: in Boston in 1912, in Baltimore in 1913, in Chicago and Denver soon thereafter. Even the U.S. government jumped on the bandwagon, transforming its insane asylum, St. Elizabeth's, into a state-of-the-art psychopathic pavilion.

These new hospitals made psychological investigation and therapeutic treatment an important component of institutional life. Patients entering psychopathic hospitals, for example, first were assessed at the admitting office (30 min.) and then underwent the following exams: physical (20 min.), neurological (15 min.), mental (1 hr.), x-ray (45 min.), and psychological (2.5 hr.). All these exams culminated in an hour-long staff meeting at which the hospital psychiatrists, psychologists, and social workers (sometimes as many as fifteen), as well as the hospital stenographer, were present. In this meeting the highlights of the largely psychological information gathered by individual staff members were rehearsed and a course of treatment recommended.

Between 1912 and 1930 many hospitals introduced a form of treatment quaintly called "talk." The Boston Psychopathic Hospital, for example, hired the Freudian psychologist L. Eugene Emerson to conduct talk therapy. As Emerson explained his method, these "talks" were designed to help patients reorganize "certain of their psychic materials [so] that they can take hold of life again and meet it." A patient described talk as a meeting in which she talked "with the doctor about experiences that happened to me in the past, things that troubled me the last two years." Patients at the psychopathic hospitals, who were generally unfamiliar with therapeutic methods, often reacted to talk much as a patient today might react to being sent to a psychic. When Florence Edwards, a forty-two-year-old teacher with suicidal impulses, was asked whether her treatment at Boston Psychopathic Hospital was helping her, she responded, somewhat surprised, that "I cannot truthfully say that I feel that as yet, because all that you have done with me so far, as you know, has been to question me very closely." Another patient responded simply that "talking don't do me any good," and yet another said that it made her feel worse.[38]

Nor were patients accustomed to the idea, readily accepted today, that they should disclose intimate personal facts to perfect strangers. Agnes Moran, a twenty-seven-year-old patient at Boston Psychopathic Hospital, objected to being asked questions that were, in her words, of a "very personal character," particularly since, as she learned, her answers were shared with others at staff meetings. "Our own doctor read off everything we ever told him, how we came out in all the tests, and in fact, every single thing you have said or done is read off before these doctors and they pass views as to your sanity."[39] However invasive the new psychological methods were, it was not the sanity of their patients that doctors were passing judgment on. Indeed, the doctors using the case method and practicing the "talking cure" at the new psycho-pathic hospitals were trying desperately to move away from the care of pa-tients considered insane. These new doctors were interested in patients who had psychological problems that with treatment could be ameliorated.

Their interest lay in treating the "abnormalities" of everyday life. Early mental-health advocates saw a need for a hospital that dealt with the "psy-chopathic personality" responsible for many of the social problems of the day. They also increasingly lent their services to such institutions as the courts, prisons, and schools.

The Therapeutic Gospel and the Criminal-Justice System

In 1898 newspapers in Chicago reported a story that provoked outrage among many citizens. A policeman had caught a four-year-old-boy "stealing" cakes and had told the child, "If you git into my hands again, I'll cut your ears off close ter yer head, and I'll sew your mouth up so's yer can't eat no cakes, an' then I guess yer won't want to steal 'em. Now git! Yer little bastard."[40]

The story put wind into the sails of reformers who had been trying for nearly a decade to establish a juvenile court. Among these was Jane Addams, who had witnessed firsthand through her work at Hull House how children were treated by the justice system: "Children over ten years of age were ar-rested, held in police stations, tried in police courts. If convicted, they were usually fined and if the fine was not paid sent to the city prison." Moreover, since "no exchange of court records existed," the same children "could be in and out of various police stations an indefinite number of times, more hard-ened and more skillful with each experience."[41]

When the story of the boy who came to be known as the "baby crook" ap-peared in 1898, social reformers and social scientists happened to be gathered in Chicago for one of the early conferences on social work. Among those in attendance was Horace Fletcher. Fletcher, with the encouragement of Ad-dams and Julia Lathrop, the first director of the Children's Bureau, wrote a tract publicizing the incident as an example of the justice system's treatment of children. The reformers believed that the incident illustrated their point that a juvenile should not be considered a crook. It was plain that "baby crook" was an oxymoron, and reformers hoped to convince Chicagoans that "juvenile crook" was an oxymoron as well.

A broad coalition of women's groups, settlement-house workers, and social scientists from the newly expanding University of Chicago lobbied the Chicago legislature to create a juvenile-court system. Legislators soon found another motivation, however, for creating a juvenile-justice system: since nothing was as expensive as institutionalization, perhaps the legislative changes proposed by the reformers, such as probation and treatment, might lead to cost savings.

In 1899 the Juvenile Court Act was passed and Chicago's Cook County became the first government entity in the United States to establish a special court for young offenders. For the reformers, the Juvenile Court Act was a great strategic victory. They had argued for the need to deal with the problems of urban youth, yet funding for such programs had always been a problem. But there was no doubt that lawmakers would fund courts and jails, which were recognized as a necessity. Nor would there be any question about eligibility and who really needed to be treated: the police were bringing in a fresh supply of candidates on a daily basis.

Thus, there were resources and candidates and the need for people to organize this new court system. The reformers, who were bent on changing the fundamental approach to child delinquency, readily took charge. They attacked the very cornerstone of the justice system—the concept of punishment—which they viewed as "the most dangerous of all methods," a "corollary of vengeance, vindictiveness and hate."[42] They wanted the very "idea of punishment" banished from the criminal-justice system.[43]

Chicago's reformers began by eliminating all of the trappings of the criminal-justice system at the juvenile court—warrants, handcuffs and other mechanical restraints, even criminal terminology, such as *complaint, trial, sentence,* and *criminal.*[44] The truant boy, the runaway girl, and the child thief all were treated in a room where there was "no forbidding legal air" and where "something of the clinic, something of the confessional is present."[45] Injecting a clinical atmosphere into the courtroom was designed to underscore the new therapeutic approach to juvenile justice. The focus of traditional courts was on what criminal acts had taken place, what laws had been violated. However, "the whole theory on which the [juvenile] court is established [is] that the act committed by the child is, from the point of view of the court in determining what is to be done, of slight importance." Rather, the important question was, "How did he or she happen to commit this offense?"[46] Juvenile courts thus radically redefined jurisprudence, turning it into a system of diagnosis and treatment rather than punishment.

Jane Addams described the contribution of the new court system this way: "There was almost a change in mores when the juvenile court was established. The child was brought before the court with no one to prosecute him— the judge and all concerned were merely trying to find out what could be done on his behalf. The element of conflict was absolutely eliminated and with it all notions of punishment as such."[47] In the new therapeutic theory the only viable response of the court to the offending child was diagnosis and treatment.

Soon there were juvenile courts in other cities. One of the earliest cities to establish a juvenile court was Denver, Colorado, in 1901. The Denver Juvenile Court was presided over by Judge Ben Linsey. Judge Linsey developed a curious criminal proceeding that he called a "snitching bee." In it, boys were encouraged to tell all about themselves and what wrongs they had committed. Lindsey explained, "Usually I find I am the first person who has ever afforded them this essential relief—unless they happen to be Roman Catholics, in which event the Confessional, which is in many respects one of the most profoundly wise of human institutions, has helped them." He said that a juvenile court "should more nearly approximate a doctor's office or hospital than the court of the present." He likened his court to "a hospital, a moral hospital. It deals with the sick and crippled in spirit. Its function is therefore psychologically one of extreme delicacy."[48]

Yet, not surprisingly, while the legislature was readily willing to set up the juvenile court, with its promise of less money expended on incarceration, it was less eager to pay for the more intensive therapeutic treatment envisioned by the reformers. It was here that a fundamental change in America came to play a role.

In the late nineteenth century, as a result of America's industrial revolution, there were enormous concentrations of wealth in America, larger than ever before in the country's history. In 1880 fewer than a hundred Americans were worth a million dollars (at the time a considerable sum of money). By 1916 there were more than 40,000 millionaires.[49] Eight percent of American families controlled 75 percent of the country's wealth.

Many of these newly wealthy individuals decided that instead of simply doling out their money to a variety of traditional charitable organizations, they should place it in a lump sum in a foundation. John D. Rockefeller argued that "if a combination to do business is effective in saving waste and in getting better results, why is not combination far more important in philanthropic work?"[50] The result was charitable foundations, a new type of institution at the turn of the century, with sums that vastly exceeded those of traditional charitable organizations.

Foundations such as the Rockefeller Foundation, the Julius Rosenwald Fund, the Commonwealth Fund, the Russell Sage Foundation, and the Laura Spellman Fund wished not simply to help the poor but to change the way they were helped. Thus, these organizations were more receptive to the idea of extending the mission of charitable organizations beyond simply providing food for the destitute and homes for orphans.

One of these philanthropists was Ethel Dummer, the wife of a successful Chicago banker. She was relatively inactive in Chicago social reform until 1905, when she read an article about the need for child protection in *Outlook*, one of the leading Progressive journals. After reading that article, she joined the National Child Labor Committee and the Chicago Juvenile Justice Protection Association, where she fell in with Jane Addams, Julia Lathrop, and a professor of medicine by the name of William Healy.

Healy, born in England, had emigrated to the United States as a boy. Because of his family's modest circumstances, he was forced to leave school after the eighth grade. His first job was at a Chicago bank, and within ten years he had become head bookkeeper. His career path would change, however, after he joined Chicago's Ethical Culture Society, whose minister was William Slater. Slater recognized that Healy had a lively and inquisitive mind. He recommended him for admission as a special student to Harvard, where Slater's brother-in-law, William James, was a professor. Healy entered Harvard in 1893 at twenty-four years of age. For financial reasons, however, he was forced to return to Chicago, where he completed his medical studies at Rush Medical School in 1900 and went on to specialize in gynecology.

While he was successful in his medical practice—he wrote one of the leading texts in his field and became a professor at Northwestern University—he found himself drawn to the social reforms of the day, in particular to Hull House. In fact, it was through Hull House circles that he met his wife, Mary Tenney. Gradually, Healy became increasingly interested in psychology and psychiatry. He convinced Northwestern to let him teach in the field of nervous and mental diseases.

It was through his association with Ethel Dummer, however, that Healy was able to gain real credentials and knowledge in the field of psychiatry. In 1906 Drummer provided Healy with a grant to do postgraduate work in Berlin, London, and most importantly Vienna, where Healy first encountered the ideas of Freud by attending his lectures.

When Healy returned to Chicago, the Juvenile Justice Protection Association was trying to realize the therapeutic goals of the juvenile court. In addition, therapeutic reformers wanted to understand why a child engaged in delinquent conduct. As Ethel Dummer explained her support for a court clinic, "There were certain children who without rhyme or reason repeated some one symptom of delinquency, either stealing, lying, or sex offense. These were so abnormal that I urged scientific research concerning the causes."[51]

Dummer and members of the Juvenile Justice Protection Association consulted Adolph Meyer, director of New York's first mental clinic and a pioneer of the case method of psychiatric treatment, and William James, who founded academic psychology in America and was involved in every major reform project of the early twentieth century. James counseled that "it was the dynamic aspect which he thought was important—in other words, the general, clinical, personal study of the individual child." And he advised that "if you're going to start something, why don't you get Healy to do it himself?"[52]

For funding Dummer once again stepped up to the plate. Healy recalls her saying to him, "None of us knows what should be done and what to find out. I'll give you the funds for five years to pay for the research and study of the material that comes into the juvenile court." The result was the founding of the Juvenile Psychopathic Institute in 1909.[53]

Becoming director of the Juvenile Psychopathic Institute meant a financial sacrifice for Healy. Moreover, despite the seeming grandeur of its title, the institute consisted of a psychologist, a secretary, and Healy himself, who were housed in offices at the juvenile court building. However, perhaps because he had himself been born on the wrong side of the tracks, he considered the opportunity to serve the less fortunate an important one. Thus, Healy undertook his task with relish. Healy's mandate was to make possible the juvenile court's goal of diagnosis before treatment. Between 1909 and 1914 Healy "diagnosed" and "treated" eight hundred juvenile delinquents.

In order to recommend a course of action, Healy tried to understand the delinquent's conduct. He found that the most effective way to do this was simply to encourage the delinquent to tell his story. While common today, this simple approach, which he came to call the "own story" approach, was relatively novel at the time: "It was just a friendly inquiry with the youngster, if you are friendly with them and ask them, 'Do you know why you do this?'

A good many times they say they don't. 'Can't we find out why you're delinquent in these ways?' And so on. The child likes to talk it out, much the same
as a person who goes into psychoanalysis who gets the idea that it's lots of fun
talking about yourself. . . . That's how it began and that's how you still do it
with youngsters." Healy explained that "some of the material is so deeply
buried that it requires considerable skill on the part of the inquirer to overcome inhibitions and forgetfulness so that the underlying fundamental
truths of the situation may be brought to the surface."[54] But with such skill
the method produced not only material of an academic interest but also
material that offered practical guidance in treating individual cases of juvenile delinquency.

But whether or not Healy was in fact talented at treatment, he was undoubtedly tireless and influential. Using his "own story" approach, Healy
identified 823 major causes of juvenile delinquency and 2,097 minor causes,
which he placed in fifteen different categories. He published his work in a
textbook, *The Individual Delinquent*, that was used in social-work classes
across the country. Reformers from all over the nation came to the Psychopathic Institute to examine his work, including Augusta Bronner, Jane Wei-
senthall, and Edith Spaulding, all of whom would become leading figures in
therapeutic reform work.

In 1917, Healy's final year as director of the Chicago Psychopathic Institute,
a young woman named Miriam Van Waters, who ran a detention home in
Oregon, feared that her career had come to an abrupt and premature end: she
had been diagnosed with tuberculosis, a disease for which there was no cure.
When not fatal—it accounted for more than 10 percent of all deaths at the
time—the disease was tremendously debilitating, requiring prolonged bed
rest. It seemed a cruel blow to a young woman who until then had refused to
let any obstacle stand in the way of her ambitions. In 1913, when few women
pursued postgraduate education, she had earned a Ph.D. in anthropology
from Clark University. She had gone on to become the first female probation
officer in Massachusetts and then the first female superintendent of a detention home in Oregon. Van Waters held this latter position when she was diagnosed with tuberculosis, and she was forced to resign.

The only treatment for tuberculosis was rest. For the highly energetic and
ambitious Van Waters, such a prescription was particularly difficult. Moreover, unmarried and from a middle-class family, she worried about money.

Fortunately, after a year of convalescence Van Waters gradually regained her health and began to think about returning to work. Following the advice of her friend Sara Fischer, she took the Los Angeles civil-service exam and applied for a job with the city. Landing squarely on her feet, she was appointed superintendent of Los Angeles's Juvenile Hall, where youths were detained before and after court hearings.

One of her first acts as superintendent was to decorate her office with a large portrait of G. Stanley Hall, the founder of academic psychology in the United States. Hall, author of a two-volume study entitled *Adolescence* (1904), provided the theory for the child-study movement during the late 1880s and 1890s. As president of Clark University, Hall had invited Freud to present a series of lectures in 1909, Freud's first and only visit to the United States. Van Waters had studied first with Henry Sheldon, a student of Hall's, at the University of Oregon and then with Hall himself at Clark.

Van Waters was troubled by what she found at the Los Angeles Juvenile Hall. She detested the "repressive spirit" that dominated work with delinquent youths.[55] This spirit was embodied in the physically oppressive atmosphere of the place, with its "cells, bars, toiling bells, wooden floors reeking of soap-suds, curious stocks, strait-jackets, leathren straps, and other aids of penitence."[56] These accouterments reflected the origins of the juvenile court in criminal law, which rested "upon the proposition that to vindicate society and the law, the accused must be punished."[57] The criminal law could not achieve her mission, however, for "criminal law cannot ask if the sentence inflicted will make the criminal or any group of human beings better or happier." Van Waters believed that no progress could be made until she had "banished the idea of punishment."[58]

Van Waters began by firing Juvenile Hall staff who "run with the lash." In their place she hired trained psychologists or social workers. With a new staff in place, she sought to remove the "taint of the repressive spirit" that dominated work with delinquent youths.[59] Solitary confinement was eliminated. And most important, a "mental clinic" was established.

Van Waters's goal was to shift the focus away from questions of guilt or innocence and toward discovering the psychological context of social deviance and prescribing its treatment. This approach is reflected in the assessment of Clarence, a twelve-year-old boy who had been arrested for truancy and burglary and had run away from home. His circumstances were found not to be fundamentally flawed: while his parents were divorced, his mother had kept the neat house and owned a confectionery store, and Clarence himself was found to be physically "sound" and of "good average intelligence." His criminal behavior therefore was on the surface a mystery. It became less so with probing. Apparently, Clarence had been seeing "he-man" movies and reading newspapers with headlines like "Girl and Lawyer Drunk at Party" and "Daring Downtown Robbery by Masked Bandits." These outlets were "his only chance to stretch his muscles or to use his imagination, to satisfy his biological cravings." Clarence "did not wish to kill, but he deeply wished to feel excitement and heroism." Clarence needed treatment to redirect his desires for wish fulfillment.

In other cases, the solution to the problem involved some form of institutionalization. Take Evelyn, an eighteen-year-old girl who had a history of stealing and a troubling tendency toward lesbianism. Like Clarence, Evelyn was physically in "perfect health"; she had "pretty, regular features" and "hair carefully done" and was of "a superior normal intelligence." Once again, her delinquent behavior did not have an obvious explanation. With probing, one was found. The problem, the court found, was that Evelyn was "emotionally arrested" and lacked self-esteem: "Underneath her suave manner is a haunting fear that she is really not superior, that after all she is inadequate." So long as she remained in this state, "her emotional life will be self-centered or flow toward those of her own sex." The solution, plainly, was not punishment but treatment: "To punish an infantile personality is not only cruel, but useless." She was sent to a state training school for girls that had a mental-hygiene clinic.

Van Waters dramatically changed the Juvenile Hall, but she believed that she could not fully realize her ambitions at Juvenile Hall itself. The problem with many juvenile delinquents was the city itself, where there was "not a tree or yard for a square mile" but instead opportunities for the "wrong kind of stimulation," offered by movie palaces, dance halls, and automobiles. In these circumstances it was not surprising that young girls turned to the amusements at hand. The Juvenile Hall removed the harmful stimulation, but it failed to provide the stimulation children needed.[60]

The solution, Van Waters believed, was to create a facility for delinquent girls outside the city. Van Waters found a former tuberculosis sanitarium in the San Fernando Valley that was owned by the state. Made up of cottages on a pleasant rural sight surrounded by olive groves, it was just what she was looking for. Van Waters managed to enlist Dummer's support to remodel the sanatorium. She added tennis courts and a swimming pool and staffed the facility with psychologists, social workers and, again with Dummer's help, a psychiatrist. Van Waters gave the facility the charming name El Retiro.

El Retiro would house twenty-five to sixty girls for six-month visits. The staff used the casework-conference method, drawing upon Healy's methods. The round-table discussions brought to light a wealth of information about each girl and allowed the staff to formulate an appropriate treatment plan. The cases handled at El Retiro varied, but psychological principles were applied in each. Reformers from around the country with an interest in the therapeutic, including such luminaries as Grace and Edith Abbott, Sophonisba Brekinridge, Adolf Meyer, Jessie Taft, Martha Falconer, Edna Mahan, Emma Lundberg, Jessie Binford, and even William Healy himself, visited El Retiro or the juvenile court to witness Van Waters's work firsthand.

Although reformers clearly saw the need to reform the criminal-justice system's treatment of children, they also believed that it was important to reach these children before this stage. Moreover, they came to believe that many pressing social problems could be avoided by addressing the difficulties of "problem children." The obvious place to reach these children was in school. "The public school possesses central strategic advantages," one reformer explained. "It reaches practically all children, and it has them under observation and to a certain extent under its control during their plastic period."[61]

The Therapeutic Gospel and the School

Reformers believed that schools, much like the courts, were dominated by the penal point of view. Truant officers, for example, would use "scare tactics" and corporal punishment to compel attendance; in some cities warrants were issued for the arrest of truants. Repeated truants were sent to parental schools, where, in the words of one reformer, "some handy young teacher, intellectually and socially not far advanced beyond the delinquent, herds him with 'bad boys' and young 'rough necks' and ignorantly administers 'swats' with a paddle to make him manly . . . without the slightest reference to the needs of childhood."[62]

To address this problem, reformers invented the idea of the "visiting teacher." The visiting teacher was to use her special "skill in meeting personal problems."[63] She was to draw on her knowledge of psychological principles to work with children who were arrested emotionally and suffered from other school and home problems. In addition, as the only person in the school with psychological training and "with genuine insight into child life" the visiting teacher was expected to "aid teachers discover and understand the emotional and personality problems of the pupils and institute classroom treatment."[64] Her mission was to help "the school give the individual child the fullest possible growth as a personality."[65]

The visiting-teacher movement began in New York City. In 1907 the New York City Public Education Association hired its first visiting teacher, Miss Jane Day, to work with Miss Julia Richmond, the first female superintendent in the country. By 1913 the board of education had taken over this function, employing about seventeen visiting teachers and adding more each year. By 1920 schools in cities across the country had hired visiting teachers; some had even established entire departments of visiting teachers. In 1921 visiting teachers established their own professional organization, the National Committee on Visiting Teachers. That same year the Commonwealth Fund initiated a five-year program to expand the work of visiting teachers. In addition to offering fellowships for the training of visiting teachers, it agreed to fund a series of three-year pilot projects in schools in thirty communities. The idea was to give visiting teachers the opportunity to demonstrate to the state and the public the value of their therapeutic services in the hope that such programs would then be entirely publicly funded.

The visiting-teacher movement was a beachhead of a broader assault on punitive measures in school. Visiting teachers were deeply critical of the lack of psychological sensitivity to students, such as mentally deficient and disruptive children, who were assigned to schools run by the Bureau of Ungraded Classes. According to the visiting teachers, the principals of such schools believed their only role was to tell teachers "you are behind in spelling or in number work, give more drill" and possessed no understanding "of complexes and the hidden sources of emotional difficulties."[66]

Particularly troubling to visiting teachers was the lack of concern for children's feelings of embarrassment and humiliation. Visiting teachers found that regular teachers often lacked a basic understanding of how children felt and thought and perhaps out of ignorance did everything in their power to damage students' self-respect. Esther Long Richards, for example, who worked at the Johns Hopkins University Phipps Clinic, went to observe a boy at P.S. 76 in Baltimore who was doing poorly in school. When she arrived, the teacher reportedly announced: "I'm glad you've come to examine John! He can't seem to learn a thing. I don't know what's the matter with him. John Jones! Stand up and let the doctor see you."[67]

Visiting teachers sought to combat this insensitivity to students' feelings by launching a major campaign to introduce a different vision of school to the general public, one in which "success or failure will be determined not by the intelligence of students nor by the richness of the course of study, but in the degree of skill with which it develops the emotional life of children." It was the educational system's ability to "develop or mar, the personality of the child" that made schools a critical battleground for therapeutic reformers.

Visiting teachers came to the view that not just they but all teachers should have psychological training, including at least a basic familiarity with the leading psychological experts of the time. Furthermore, they believed that all teachers should be members of the local mental-hygiene association.

But therapeutic reformers did not stop at knowledge when listing a teacher's ideal qualifications. At bottom teachers needed to respect the personality of the child. In order to be able to do that, the teacher "should have made adequate adjustments to life, should not look to children to supply her with opportunities for outlet . . . she should not use affect of children to gratify her need of love and approval." Once she herself had achieved a level of psychological maturity, she could then minister to the needs of children.[68]

More than anything else, therapeutic reformers believed that children needed to be understood. The Commonwealth Fund, which underwrote the initial expansion of the visiting-teacher movement, made this point clear: "To the Commonwealth Fund it has appeared that for the child who is tending toward delinquency, who fails to 'get along' in his school, . . . the greatest single need is that he be accurately and adequately understood."[69] If the visiting teachers had had their way, this process of understanding would have begun at the beginning and enormous school resources would have been devoted to such understanding. One day, they envisioned, "at the earliest age at which a psychiatric examination is possible, the child will be examined psychologically and psychiatrically so that his habit training may be planned properly."[70] Planning and managing the psychological development of students had become a key educational goal.[71]

The Therapeutic Gospel and the Home

While visiting teachers were attempting to remake the public school into "our greatest child welfare agency," other reformers were tackling the American home itself.[72] Like their Victorian forebears, Progressive era reformers viewed the domestic realm as a critical area of intervention. But in direct contrast to their forebears, they saw the home, not as a haven, but as a source of social pathology. In the new therapeutic theory, the home warped the psychologies of its members. Therapeutic reformers explained the effects of the home and family on its members this way: "The child picks up emotional flavor as effectively as a glass of milk in the ice-chest acquires the flavor of the onions that might be lying near by."[73] In the new therapeutic theory of the home, poor domestic conditions produced poorly adjusted members of society.

Believing that problems at home led to problems in schools, courts, and hospitals, therapeutic reformers launched a major effort to identify the domestic conditions that led to maladjustment and delinquency. They identified homes ruled by "anxiety," "low esteem," and "anger" as dangerous, perverse, and defective. They condemned homes dominated by irritation, jealousy, rationalization, overindulgence, repression, and self-righteousness. On the other hand, therapeutic reformers considered homes in which family members possessed maturity, mental order, and the ability to healthily adjust to be normal.

These new psychological standards for judging the home led to a new conception of parental responsibilities. Parents were now expected to provide a psychologically healthy home environment, and failure to provide children with psychological training and guidance constituted neglect. Thus, therapeutic reformers criticized parents for failing to organize their homes according to the principles of mental hygiene.

These failures, which took several forms, frequently resulted from tensions between spouses. As one reformer explained, "Jealousy, hypocrisy, and antagonisms between parents may cause in their children mental retardation, physical disease, or delinquency."[74] Therapeutic reformers established a link between the intimate relations of spouses and various forms of delinquency. In the new therapeutic theory, problems between their parents might lead children to commit antisocial acts. To prevent such a descent into abnormality and criminality, spouses needed to possess psychologically healthy attitudes toward each other and toward their children.

Reformers devoted the bulk of their attention to families lacking such attitudes, who were therefore likely to send their members to the courts, hospitals, or special ungraded schools. Not surprisingly, the homes reformers found most in need of treatment were those of the poor. In the new therapeutic theory, the poor came from troubled homes and produced psychopathic personalities. In addition to class, of course, gender also informed discussions of abnormal homes. In the new therapeutic theory, men and women contributed to the abnormality of the home in different ways. Men negatively affected the home by unsteady work, desertion, or harsh punishment of children. They were guilty of "occupational faults" and "industrial defects." Fathers and husbands contributed to the degeneration of families by "leaving home" and refusing to fulfill their "family duties."[75] They created delinquent children by beating them instead of trying to understand them. Women, on the other hand, contributed to problems in the home by being too lenient with the children or by working. Therapeutic reformers also found that many mothers of delinquent children expressed too much sexual interest. One reformer said that the conduct of girls who came before the court was "largely imitative of the sex-behavior of their mothers."[76]

Class considerations also inform discussions of "normal" homes. Therapeutic reformers defined as normal a home in which parents focused on the psychologies of its members. It was also one in which men and women found psychological satisfaction in their separate roles. Therapeutic reformers imagined homes as normal if infants were sheltered and nourished "in comfort without inflicting damage of premature anxiety," the "father is dominant, but not cruel or mean," the "mother is a satisfied woman . . . that is she is not restlessly seeking her life gratification apart from mate and children," and both parents "have respect for their [children's] unfolding personalities." To the extent that any family could fulfill such ideals, it was a middle-class family. This was made explicit by one reformer who explained that the children of such homes "never come before the Juvenile Court, but as healthy young people, they become excellent parents, social workers, or leaders on intellectual frontiers." That middle-class children often embodied normality by choosing to become social workers and that only children from poor homes found themselves charged with abnormality reveals the class lens through which therapeutic reformers saw the world.[77]

More surprising and perhaps much more interesting than the fact that reformers found poor homes to be abnormal and middle-class homes to be
normal is that information about the social conditions of such families
emerged but then was neglected. The so-called abnormal homes therapeutic
reformers dealt with were characterized by economic privation. References to
crowded living conditions and unsteady work abound. Therapeutic reformers
often devoted their clinical attention to families that lived in "congested,
dirty district[s] near the mills and railroads"[78] or families in which the wage
earner had "been thrown out of work." They sought to help families in which
the husband could "not provide the necessities of life" or unwed mothers
who had "no opportunity to learn a trade."[79] The families requiring rehabilitation were those that lived in "great squalor" and "crowded homes." Therapeutic reformers addressed themselves to the families whose members were
"employed irregularly at unskilled work," families in which husbands were
"out of work much of the time" or wives worked in factories "earning a very
small wage."[80] Most families that therapeutic reformers came into contact
with faced economic hardships and had few economic opportunities.

Despite therapeutic reformers' explicit references to the economic context
of their clients' lives, this perspective is ultimately excluded from their interpretation of the problem. Although they refer to the poor living conditions,
they describe the homes in need of help as those characterized primarily by
"strife, disharmony, or unsatisfied longings of either parent."[81] In cases where
men are out of work or can only find intermittent employment, the problem
comes to be described as a matter of the man's "subconscious feeling of failure" or "mortification and sense of inferiority."[82] With their eye on the clinical ball, therapeutic reformers made their clients' psychologies the most important piece of information and the dominant factor in their analysis. Of
course, therapeutic reformers viewed the surpassing of economic interpretations as progress. In the old days, said one reformer, the "emphasis would
have been placed on the more simple and obvious problems of financial need
and physical health," whereas now "the chief consideration was always the
interplay of personalities."[83] Therapeutic reformers suggested not simply that
reformers must broaden their conception of health and well-being but that
physical or economic interpretations of need were necessarily inadequate. In
the new theory of reform, the therapeutic frequently trumped all other para-
digms. It did not always do so in practice, however.

Therapeutic Theory and Practice

Convinced that earlier modes of reform had been supplanted by a psychological approach, therapeutic reformers rejoiced in their new-found authority. They believed that Spinoza's dictum "Neither condemn nor ridicule but try to understand" had finally been institutionalized. Juvenile courts, psychopathic hospitals, prisons, reformatories, and schools all had embraced the therapeutic gospel. Mental hygiene had become an important guiding principle for these diverse institutions. Even the army had utilized the new principles in World War I: the Mental Hygiene War Work Committee claimed to have helped the army reject seventy-two thousand men with mental disorders.[84] Private industry too seems to have embraced the therapeutic gospel. What was called "industrial psychology" captured the imagination of many leading businesses.

Popular culture also seems to have embraced key elements of the therapeutic gospel. The popular *Woman's Home Companion,* for example, had a column, "Tower Room Talk," that psychologically analyzed women readers' problems.[85] Psychoanalysis also featured in fiction, such as *Mrs. Marden's Ordeal* (1918), a popular crime novel in which it is the key forensic tool. This novel contains all of the tenets of the therapeutic gospel of the early twentieth century. Plagued by depression, jealousy, and anxiety, Mrs. Marden consults Dr. Doyle, or DR, as she comes to call him, who is a psychoanalyst. As Mrs. Marden tells the story, "I have agreed to bare my soul to the scrutiny of another . . . there is to be neither mental reservation nor deception . . . only agony can drive one to such exposure of one's real self."[86] Ultimately, through dream analysis the psychoanalyst uncovers the "mental mechanism" responsible for the crime.

But despite the fictionalizing of the triumph of the therapeutic perspective, the reality of reformers' success was far more complex. The therapeutic regime's power was not as extensive as either reformers at the time or historians subsequently have imagined. Not only that, but there was a significant gap between therapeutic theory and practice. The case of female deviance illustrates the limits of the new therapeutic regime of power.

* * *

In 1915 William Healy, then director of Chicago's Psychopathic Institute and a leader of the therapeutic reform movement, denounced the emphasis on vaginal exams for wayward girls. He asserted that "examinations of girls for their virginity as a basis for their moral classification is, from our observation in many cases, to be greatly depreciated and I have urged parents against it." Insisting that "the evidence of actual penetration" should not be given "great weight," Healy condemned what he viewed as an overly "materialistic" perspective that did not pay sufficient attention to the "psychological or spiritual life."[87] In Healy's view, vaginal exams illuminated neither the cause of a girl's delinquency nor her prognosis. He maintained that there were some girls with "a record of scores of physical contacts" who responded to treatment; on the other hand, there were girls "who had not experienced complete sexual contact, whose minds nevertheless were so charged with mental imagery and desires concerning sexual things" that they would not have responded to treatment. Echoing Healy, many early-twentieth-century reformers argued that effective treatment of female delinquency and maladjustment required not physical examinations but in-depth psychological investigation and therapeutic intervention.

During the early decades of the twentieth century the state, philanthropic organizations, and reformers devoted substantial resources to defining and treating female deviance. *Female deviance* was a vague term in therapeutic reformers' vocabulary that often was used synonymously with *aberrant, unadjusted, maladjusted, pathological, delinquent, incorrigible, psychopathic,* and *disorderly.* Despite the range of terms used to describe such young women, therapeutic reformers agreed that they were clearly distinguishable from the mentally diseased. The reformers insisted that while these women were "disturbers wherever they were placed," they did not suffer from "hallucinations or delusions."[88] Neither insane nor necessarily feeble-minded, the female deviant had what was commonly considered a "perverted" sense of values. Her defective psychology led her to commit antisocial acts.

Not surprisingly, women suffering from "abnormality" and "maladjustment" shared a number of nonpsychological characteristics that reformers omitted or relegated to the margins of their interpretations. Most of the women sent to penal institutions for their deviance came from poor families, and many were immigrants. Their low standard of living manifested itself in several ways. First, many of the women came from large families in which the father was dead or incapacitated, leaving the family bereft of the worker with the greatest earning capacity. In some cases the mother also had died. Among those with living parents, sickness was a common threat to the household.

Take, for example, Theresa B: "Theresa's father died of nephristis and her mother diabetes. There were ten siblings, of whom the patient was the youngest. The first three died in early childhood, two girls died in a state hospital during attacks of depression, one also having tuberculosis."[89]

The socioeconomic class of female deviants was reflected in their work histories as well as in their education level. Female deviants tended to leave school early and to start work at a young age. Their employment, however, usually in factories, was often intermittent. Tilly J., for example, worked at a paper box-factory.[90] Elsie C. worked in a cigar factory or helped her mother, who took in washing. Female deviants slipped in and out of legal employment. Stints of prostitution complemented factory work or housework. Clara W., for example, ran away to Boston, where she became a prostitute: "She then began to prostitute . . . and to induce young girls to go into prostitution. Occasionally she worked for short periods in factories or at housework, which she did not like."[91] In addition to their similar work histories, young women punished by the courts also had in common their relationship to men. Their sexual encounters with men left them in conflict with the authorities. Taken advantageous of sexually or left economically vulnerable, female deviants faced many circumstances that were highly gender-specific. Stories of rape, abortion, and desertion are common in the case records. The women were also sometimes accused of child neglect. Finally, many of them had venereal disease.

Though reformers documented the social circumstances of female deviants' lives, it was their psychological characteristics that interested them. They described the women brought to court as having "inadequate emotional control" or "self-assertion" that took the form of exhibitionism. They found "evidence of distinctly pathological processes in their mental life," for example, when they "dolled-up" or felt that they must have "the latest craze in dress."[92] Reformers also interpreted running away or staying out late at night as signs of pathology. And of course sexual relations, either for pay or for pleasure, especially with other women, were regarded as indications of psychopathology.

Whatever the signs of their perversions, female deviants were charged with a specific but limited number of offenses, including stealing, perjury, child neglect, bigamy, abortion, disorderly conduct, contracting venereal disease, running away, associating with dissolute persons, soliciting, vagrancy, loitering, and possession of narcotics. Most often, however, women between the ages of thirteen and thirty were charged with some form of sex delinquency. Reformers themselves noted the gendered nature of the charge of deviance. One reformer stated that "among girl delinquents, sex offenses predominate, while among boys the violation of property rights is the most frequent cause for commitment."[93] Another reformer explained that the adjectives *disorderly* and *incorrigible* mean entirely different things when applied to boys than they do when applied to girls. The meaning in the case of girls is sexual: "In general, the incorrigible girl or disorderly girl is one who 'has a bad reputation in the neighborhood,' one who has been going with bad company and staying away at night." Eighty percent of delinquent girls were brought to court because their virtue had been threatened. Grafting the Victorian ideology of separate spheres onto the new psychological discourse of deviance, therapeutic reformers created a new area of gender difference.[94]

But reformers' psychological perspective also tempered a source of gender difference by recognizing women's sexual appetites. In the Victorian period women were not viewed as possessing a strong sexual instinct. On the other hand, men, while rational and intelligent, were considered inherently lustful. In the therapeutic theory of female deviance, however, women lost their sexlessness and hence some of their difference from men. Indeed, it was their robust sexual instincts that brought women before the law. Rejecting the wages-and-sin theory of fallen women, therapeutic reformers did not attribute female deviance to either economic exploitation or some moral flaw. Rather, they maintained that women became deviant because they failed to properly channel their normal sexual instincts into healthy and wholesome activities. In defining sexual instincts as universal, even normal, therapeutic reformers embraced a gender-neutral (though class-based) theory of psychosexual development but a gendered theory of criminal justice. Women, of course, were considered delinquent and therefore were arrested when they failed to sublimate their sexual impulses, whereas men were not.

Therapeutic reformers, believing that the sexual double standard was right and appropriate, did not dwell on the inconsistency of simultaneously arguing that everyone had to sublimate their sexual impulses but only women committed sexual delinquency. Indeed, they were in general far less interested in the external circumstances of a girl's arrest than in the internal motivations and mental content of her transgression. Their goal was to get at the "inwardness of the girl's waywardness."[95] When therapeutic reformers "looked within," they found that it was the girls' "enthusiastic response to life's instinctive urges which seem to have brought them into conflict with authority." They uncovered a "total lack of sex repression" and women suffering from a "freedom from advantageous inhibitions." Such women, reformers believed, needed emotional training and therapeutic guidance.[96]

If girls were to avoid deviance, they needed to be shown their emotional needs and to be helped to sublimate them. Therapeutic reformers therefore hoped to help the female deviant "meet her needs" and "interpret" life. They sought to get "in touch with the women" and "help them with their personal problems." Their aim was "to build new habits and a new outlook on life."[97] They hoped to accomplish this by introducing wayward girls to their own mental processes and to the basic principles of mental hygiene. They also believed that intensively studying each girl's psyche and finding suitable "emotional outlets" were a fundamental part of treating such women. Therapeutic reformers set out to unravel "the intricacies of the various complexes and resistances of the personality," helping patients move beyond a "fixation at an infantile level.[98] Despite such grandiose visions of their mission and their well-laid plans, therapeutic reformers were unable to implement many of their goals. The experience at the Bedford Reformatory's psychopathic hospital for women provides one example of the limits of the new therapeutic regime of power.

While therapeutic reformers at Bedford hoped to provide the most up-to-date and scientific methods of individual treatment, they ended up providing routinized custodial care. The promised "atmosphere of therapy" never materialized. Each girl did not "receive the special attention she required." She was not taught the principles of mental hygiene or provided with individual or group therapy. While there was tetherball, gardening, and weaving, the girls spent a good deal of their time locked up, put in the isolation room, or being bathed or given wet packs. Indeed, the physical space of the hospital suggests that the treatment of female deviants fell far short of the goals. The Bedford Psychopathic Hospital had several types of spaces, none of which were for the purpose of helping the young offender "to get a better hold on herself and to understand what has led to her being brought to court." There were no rooms that allowed for the frank discussion of problems or where "the simplest principles of mental hygiene are discussed with her."

The Bedford Psychopathic Hospital comprised sixteen single rooms (8 ft. by 12 ft.) and a dormitory that held four beds for patients, 3 bedrooms for nurses and two bedrooms for matrons (12 ft. square), and three bathrooms, one for patients, one for nurses, and one for matrons. In addition, there was a reception room, a sitting room, a recreation room, a dining room, a pantry, and a kitchen on the first floor. On the second floor there was a sleeping porch, a sterilization room, a soundproof isolation room, an operating room, and a hydrotherapy room. The physical plant also included a library and a laboratory. Despite their goal of providing "the greatest number of therapeutic and occupational resources possible, with a staff sufficiently large and experienced to give each of the patients the special attention she required," these rooms either were not designed to fulfill therapeutic goals as in the case of the sterilization room or in practice were not used in therapeutic ways. Indeed, reformers themselves recount their frustrations with their inability to use space as they had intended.

It was common at Bedford for activities viewed as therapeutic to be discontinued. When the Psychopathic Hospital first opened, for example, women at Bedford put on plays. This ended, however, after the first several productions. "This type of entertainment was finally abandoned" one reformer explained, because "it was the cause of too much strain and was followed by an undesirable emotional reaction." The gymnastic teacher (who after being at Bedford for a short time was replaced by a matron who better disciplined the patients) also frequently put an end to recreational activities, sending the women back to their rooms. Her notebooks were filled with such remarks as "Due to the quarreling etc, the plans for the afternoon had to be discontinued." Abandoning activities with therapeutic value and settling for discipline and punishment occurred frequently at Bedford. The goal of controlling patients continually displaced the goal of treating them. Gaining such control extended even to the dining room, where a nurse or matron monitored the women's conversation in order "to guide the conversation and prevent if possible, topics or incidents which might lead to trouble." Keeping patients out of trouble and in line became the major preoccupation at Bedford.[99]

Given what occurred at Bedford, which was widely recognized as one of the most innovative and well-endowed Progressive era experiments in criminal justice, it is not surprising that the therapeutic agenda remained an elusive goal at most more ordinary institutions. Indeed, historian David Rothman has shown that although many institutions brought on board psychologists and psychiatrists, "invariably these would-be therapeutic innovations had little effect on prison routines." Rothman maintains that the "presence of psychiatrists and psychologists on the prison pay roll was of more symbolic value that real importance, their credentials lending legitimacy to incarceration, without their services altering routines." The numbers alone confirm Rothman's contention that inmates did not get therapeutic care. In 1926, for example, there were only twenty-nine full-time psychiatrists working at prisons in thirteen states (five of them in New York). Most of these institutions had at most one psychiatrist and one or two psychologists.[100]

But it wasn't only at prisons that practice fell far short of therapeutic ideals. The reality of the juvenile-court movement, for example, does not live up to the rhetoric. A Children's Bureau study revealed that "no more than 7% of the juvenile courts sought psychological advice before making decisions, even though every bill authorizing a special court justified its existence on the basis that each offender's mental condition would be studied and appropriate 'treatment' prescribed." A study of the juvenile court in Minneapolis found an alarming gap between theory and practice. This study found that out of more than a thousand cases handled in 1923 only two children per week received psychological exams.[101]

Both in the courts and at schools it appears to have been difficult to actually put into practice the therapeutic principles reformers had worked so hard to articulate. The high hopes of the visiting-teacher movement, for example, pale in comparison with the reality. Although the visiting teacher was supposed to get a handle on each child's "psychic paternity," it proved difficult when there was one visiting teacher for every two thousand students. And although therapeutic reformers wrote about and lobbied for work on "wish fulfillment," more often than not custodial care of one form or another characterized the prisons, schools, and hospitals. For example, the annual report for the year 1926 at New York Hospital's psychiatric facility in Westchester indicates that considerable time was spent on patient treatments that were nonpsychological. The hospital, which had about three hundred patients that year, proudly reported that it had dispensed 6,787 massage treatment and 8,274 hydrotherapeutic treatments in addition to "the 12,003 prolonged baths." It appears that not much time was left for individual counseling.[102]

But worse from the therapeutic reformers own perspective was that in many cases punishment returned as the major institutional response to "deviance." At a reformatory in Maine built for the express purpose of rehabilitating female prisoners a "punishment building" was constructed in the late 1920s. At Bedford the superintendent, Helen Hobbs, was actually dismissed because of her use of force and coercion. The New York Times reported that an investigation at Bedford had revealed that "certain punishments have been inflicted which were cruel and unusual." Women were "handcuffed with their hands behind their backs and fastened to the cell grating by another pair of handcuffs attached to those on their wrists so that in some cases their toes or the balls of their feet only touched the floor and while thus suspended their faces were dipped into pails of water until subdued."[103]

Even a juvenile-justice reformer as successful as Miriam Van Waters found herself fighting against the forces of punishment. At El Retiro, in many ways the model of therapeutic reform, the pro-punishment forces managed to gain the upper hand. Van Waters had appointed therapeutically minded Alma Holzschuh as superintendent of El Retiro. One of the things that made El Retiro unique was that there were no guards. Girls believed to be too difficult to handle were simply sent to Ventura, the more conventional state-run reformatory for women. The staff was female and therapeutically oriented. In the mid-1920s the Probation Committee of the state of California summarily dismissed Holzschuh for allowing "too much freedom without thought of necessary discipline." In reaction to Holzschuh's dismissal, the girls at El Retiro protested. Male guards were sent in to quiet the disturbance. Van Waters was furious and vowed to fight the destruction of everything she had worked for. Turning to the women of Los Angeles, she mobilized the forces. The League of Women Voters, local women's clubs, and parent-teachers groups all got involved. Van Waters achieved a temporary stay of the return to punishment, but she later conceded that while she had won the battle, she had lost the war. Eventually El Retiro was redesigned with "new all-like residences with high windows covered with slit like bars." According to Van Waters, both the attitude and the machinery of punishment returned.[104]

There are several reasons for the return of punishment or, in many cases, the simple absence of therapeutic treatments. First, the gap between theory and practice was partially a result of financial constraints. The resources that would have enabled undoing "fixation" or "an ego-centric personality" were not provided. The implementation of therapeutic reformers' regimens of rehabilitation was also stymied by other experts. The agenda of persons running and staffing hospitals, reformatories, and prisons was radically different from that of therapeutic reformers. Forced to deal with the day-to-day business of managing wards of the state, these men and women found it easier to warehouse and strictly discipline rather than treat their charges. Their main concerns were security and order. Ultimately, these experts ensured that the custodial triumphed over the therapeutic. Finally, resistance from wards of the state themselves contributed to the gap between therapeutic theory and practice.

Therapeutic reformers most frequently called upon this last interpretation to explain the abandonment of therapeutic ideas and the return of punishment and discipline. They insisted that inmates themselves were responsible for the failure to fulfill therapeutic goals. At Bedford, for example, administrators blamed "the quarrelsome tendencies of the girls and their strong sex attraction for one another" for the elimination of the use of the sleeping porch for rests. They found girls like L.S. responsible for making Bedford's "educational therapy" less than effective. L.S., according to Mrs. Eleanor Clarke Slagle, Bedford's "authority on educational therapy," was not interested in the therapeutic value of weaving baskets. She was "always more interested in the prices she was going to get for them than in doing good work." At one point L.S. lost patience and threw her basket to the floor, exclaiming, "There, take your damned old basket. I never want to see it again."[105] Therapeutic reformers maintained that such outbursts caused institutions to fall short of their therapeutic goals. With characteristic condescension, they imagined female deviants as the source of failure.

Their assessment, however, was not completely off the mark. Female deviants' resistance to the therapeutic agenda partially explains reformers' inability to fulfill their therapeutic goals.[106] Female delinquents rejected both the terms and the practices of therapeutic intervention. Their resistance to the therapeutic thinking took a variety of forms and occurred in a variety of settings. On the streets, female delinquents sought to escape entrapment. For example, one woman on probation who had been sent to Bedford recounted how she had managed to avoid possible entrapment: "I met one nice man and he want to go with me for a good time but I realized maybe he some kind of detective, so I told him 'What do you want, I can't understand you.' 'Oh you know what I mean,' he said. I told him 'you big slob, you leave me alone' and he left me. He was very nice and blonde."[107] Once arrested, girls charged with delinquency frequently refused to talk to psychologists or psychiatrists appointed by the court. One reformer reported, for example, that the delinquent she was interviewing "had intercourse at sixteen while intoxicated, but she refused to tell much about the experience." When the girls did submit to the battery of tests and psychological interviews, reformers did not get the answers they wanted. Edith, for example, who was charged with prostitution, responded to a psychiatrist's query about "pervert practices" by denying that she had engaged in any. But she quickly added, to the psychiatrist's horror, "Many women have chased after me. I'll have to try that next." Therapeutic reforms also complained that in addition to their brazen responses, the girls "excused their sex delinquency." Their justifications were many, including intoxication, men's promises to marry them, rape, that they had been innocent until they began to work, and their need for money.[108]

Female delinquents also "excused" their behavior, and thereby resisted the terms of the therapeutic agenda, by insisting that it was natural and normal for a young girl to want to have a good time. Indeed, the phrase *good time* comes up again and again in case records. The term *Sunday school* was frequently used by female delinquents to refer to their probation officer or case worker; it was a derogatory term used to describe someone who was always good, never independent or adventurous. A series of letters from a girl named Esther (who spent time at Bedford) to a female friend with whom she had been arrested for stealing two pair of stockings and one belt illustrates how young female delinquents construed their own behavior. From these letters we learn that Esther continually tried to escape the surveillance of her "lady," that is, her probation officer. She revels in mass entertainment and the opportunity it provides for sexual pleasure. She writes to her friend that on Sunday "we can go in a place where we can have a good time and lots of kissing." In another letter she writes: "Friend come to me, I am not allowed to go to see you. You come over and we going to have a good time together. Here its lots of nice young men. Listen dear, my lady ask me if I'm going to school and I told her that I go to visit girls which I knows from school, but I'm going to moving picture and I three nice young mens." Many delinquent women saw nothing wrong with exchanging sexual favors for entertainment or just kissing and flirting for the fun of it. Recounting her relationship with the egg man, Esther described the pleasure this way: "Always when he comes we kiss each other, but he isn't rich; that's nothing for us, but when you can get a kiss from a man, its nice isn't it?" What reformers called "exhibitionism" or "attempts at compensation by an ego that has failed to express itself constructively," young, poor women often called pleasure. Whether on probation, on the streets, or in prison, "unadjusted" girls and female "psychopaths" frequently resisted therapeutic interpretations of their lives.[109]

* * *

When social scientists and social reformers launched their campaign to "look within" in the early decades of the twentieth century, they focused their attention on "abnormal" homes and other problems of social deviance, including the problem of "unadjusted" girls and female "psychopaths." They began with high hopes, believing that it was possible to eliminate "maladjustment" in all its forms. To do so merely required educating the public about the dangers of punitive approaches to reform and the virtues of therapeutic approaches. And therapeutic reformers did indeed have a significant impact on the emerging welfare state. They can be credited with creating juvenile courts, psychopathic hospitals, and the system of probation and introducing the principles of mental hygiene into such diverse institutions as schools, maternal homes, and prisons. But although therapeutic reformers succeeded in creating these institutions, they did not always control them. Even when they did, therapeutic practice often fell far short of their goals. Resources, other experts, and those they sought to treat all interfered with the new therapeutic regime of power.

Though institutionally therapeutic reformers' success was limited, they succeeded in creating a powerful new morality that had a lasting effect on American society. This morality condemned punishment and idealized treatment. It argued that the solution to social problems lay in psychological remedies. The new therapeutic morality promoted understanding and introspection as the most effective reform strategies. While this new therapeutic morality was sensitive, at least in theory, to the potentially negative effects of punitive approaches to reform and the ethic of making moral judgments, it remained largely blind to the politics of clinical categorization or the ideological consequences of its own morality. Imagining normality and abnormality as self-evident psychological categories, therapeutic reformers rarely reflected on the social processes by which these categories were constructed. Nor did they concern themselves with the costs of placing a therapeutic morality at the center of reform work.

The social and political implications of therapeutic thinking were not questioned because the framework adopted by therapeutic reformers did not allow it. Their therapeutic framework only permitted clinical justifications for intervention. It regarded all other justifications as not only ethically suspect but clinically damaging. Therapeutic reformers also believed that their own psychological morality had no social costs, only benefits. While they were always willing to admit, and indeed frequently complained, that the application could be improved, as a morality it was the best, the most scientific, the financially most efficient, the most therapeutic, and from an ethical perspective the most justifiable one around.

Reformers' therapeutic ethos justified extraordinary intervention into the lives of poor persons by the state and middle-class reformers. But this kind of intervention obscured and ignored the economic condition of the poor. The clinical frame adopted by reformers excluded nonpsychological information as ultimately irrelevant. It also offered no solutions outside of treatment. Indeed, reformers believed that they were morally prohibited from doing so by their subscription to clinical ideals. Although therapeutic reformers of the Progressive era undoubtedly had a genuine desire to help the poor, they psychologized difficulties that were structural and social.

3 MARRIAGE

A Science of Personal Relations

1920–1940

On 28 October 1935, in the midst of the nation's most severe economic depression, the *New York Times* reported that another disaster had hit: America's divorce rate had increased by more than 2,000 percent. Apparently, a wave of marital breakdowns was sweeping the country, threatening its very social fabric. But divorce statistics did not tell the whole story. The discord rate added to the divorce rate revealed that 50 percent of American couples were unhappy. As one expert explained, "An appalling number of husband and wives are not really married but simply undivorced: they live in a sort of purgatory."[1]

To marriage experts, the high divorce rate, while perhaps less conspicuous than the economic depression, was no less important. Indeed, they saw it as a crisis the country could ill afford to ignore. In their view, marriage failure was not merely a private affair, an individual misfortune, but "an imperfection in the whole social fabric."[2] Failure to nip a marriage problem in the bud could mean divorce, children with warped personalities, and in the long run, psychologically damaged citizens. It was for this reason that marriage experts ridiculed a society that was willing to plan for the building of bridges but not for marriage. They believed that America needed a specific social policy dealing with domestic relations. Laissez-faire would not do.

Never before had so many professionals so loudly proclaimed that marital harmony was a matter of grave public import. It was not merely that the institution of marriage was deemed important, for earlier generations had certainly felt that way. In the Victorian era, for example, there had been a special emphasis on domesticity. What distinguished the 1920s and 1930s was that era's psychological valuation of marriage. No longer was the home simply the conduit for good character and a respite from the commercial world. Rather, marriage was expected to be the fount of all human happiness. And happiness was a matter of being free from emotional complexes and possessing a fully integrated personality. For a couple to be happy, both parties had to know themselves psychologically. They also had to experience emotional growth together. With this psychological definition of marriage, marriage experts imposed a new and from one perspective particularly high standard for marital success.

Between 1920 and 1940 experts dedicated to a psychological vision of marriage banded together to form the new profession of marriage counseling. This profession developed both a substantial body of knowledge and an extensive clinical practice. Investigating every aspect of the marriage problem, researchers made domestic discord and happiness a serious subject of inquiry. Universities, colleges, and even high schools developed new marriage courses. And a new type of expert created marriage clinics, where a kind of first aid was offered to those facing domestic trouble. Their technique was simple and straightforward. In the words of one of the leading doctors of matrimony, "There is nothing mysterious about it, any more than there is about the overhauling of an automobile that is not working properly. The mechanic investigates one possibility at a time: he checks the ignition, the carburetor, the transmission, the valves, and so on; finds where the trouble lies; and removes the cause if possible. We do the same with a marriage."[3] With simple rules and step-by-step solutions, marriage counselors applied the principles of the therapeutic gospel to a new sphere of American life.

They also applied the therapeutic gospel to a brand-new constituency. Before the rise of marriage counseling, therapeutic reformers had directed their attention almost exclusively toward the poor. By contrast, marriage counselors preached their therapeutic gospel to so-called fine young men and women. In doing so, they not only expanded the therapeutic base but also redefined the therapeutic agenda. No longer concerned with physical unity and domestic organization marriage counselors sought for their clients fulfillment, growth, and happiness. With the birth of marriage counseling, achieving domestic happiness for the middle class replaced eliminating social deviance among the poor as the central therapeutic aim.

Domestic-Relations Courts and the Therapeutic Gospel

During the Progressive era those who dealt with marriage and family problems became increasingly dissatisfied with the courts, indeed with the whole
legalistic frame of mind. Therapeutic reformers believed that regular courts
not only were ineffective in "treating" marital discord but sometimes made
matters worse. One critic stated that "lawyers all too often foment rather
than reduce irritation." Another stated that until marriage "ceased to be controlled by legalistic minds—not until those whose training and experience
qualify them to enter this human laboratory will we make the desired progress—better human beings, better homes."[4] In the meantime, the courts were
making marital reconciliation all but impossible.

In the case of the newlyweds Mary and Henry, for example, we learn how a
salvageable marriage was destroyed by the court. One domestic-relations
court advocate referred to it as a typical example of "another romance
wrecked," leaving us with "two more disillusioned embittered souls." Young
and ignorant of the subtleties of marriage, the couple did not know how to
handle tensions when they arose. Indeed, they were better prepared to maintain their new car than they were to maintain their new marriage: "When
they bought their automobile the salesman told them to drive it slowly and
bring it in for an adjustment after they had driven 500 miles. No such common sense advice was given to them at the time they married." Mary and
Henry had no idea what to do when they experienced marital discord. At the
first sign of trouble, they went to see lawyers. In court "the issues were to be
decided by reading affidavits," and "motions and countermotions were made
all without the judge seeing or talking to Mary or Henry." It was such failures
to investigate individual stories that led to the call for a new kind of court.

Maintaining that "broken" homes damaged the nation's economic, educational, and cultural progress, reformers lobbied for the creation of special
courts to handle the growing marriage problem. They said that regular courts
could only provide "impersonal justice," a justice not capable of dealing with
the personal and psychological matter of marriage. After all, those who had
experienced marital strife "were not criminals"; therefore, "the customary legal procedure, its rules of evidence, its insistence on categorical answers of
'yes' and 'no' have no place here." Courts of domestic relations sought to
abolish the guilty/not guilty paradigm at the center of jurisprudence and replace it with the therapeutic gospel.[5]

The first domestic-relations courts were established in Buffalo and in New York City in 1910. By 1932 there were twenty-six such courts nationwide. In Dayton, Ohio, for example, the domestic-relations court was founded by Judge Arthur Mackey because of the number of cases in his courtroom having to do with marital conflict. In response, he decided to establish additional office hours at his home in the evenings. At these less formal sessions "many people came to him asking his help and advice in their marriage problems." It seemed that the court might play a more productive role if it spent its time reconciling cases rather than simply punishing the party responsible for marital dissolution.

Domestic-relations courts were designed to be fundamentally different from regular courts. They depended "not upon the abstract learning of lawyers but upon case-history data secured by probation officers, case workers, psychiatrists, or psychologists . . . . There are no juries and decisions are private." Moreover, the aim was not to punish those who came before the court but to rehabilitate them. To fulfill this broad therapeutic mission, the domestic-relations court often had a "reconciliation" department or a "domestic relationship adjustment bureau" attached to it.[6]

That experts trained in psychology, psychiatry, or social work were to play a critical role in the new courts was often mandated by law. In New York State, for example, the law establishing domestic-relations courts required that "each division and part of the court shall be served by a bureau for physical, mental, and psychiatric examination. . . . Such a psychiatric bureau shall be organized and staffed as an adjunct of the court, with a competent and sufficient staff of psychiatrists and others."[7] Maintaining that those who came before it had committed no crime but suffered from marital maladjustment, therapeutic reformers discarded many of the procedures and rules of evidence that had dominated court procedure in the past.

Therapeutic reformers cited many cases as evidence for their view that better homes could be produced if, and only if, legalistic methods were relinquished and therapeutic ones adopted. One such typical case was that of Mr. and Mrs. John Morely, who had been married for more than twenty years. Recently the couple had found themselves plagued by terrible tension. Mrs. Morely had rather suddenly taken to "fault finding." She also had ceased to show affection for her husband. In response, Mr. Morely had begun drinking, yelling and screaming, and even hitting Mrs. Morely. Utterly perplexed by the case, the court had asked for the assistance of Dr. Fred Tilney, head of a local neurological institute. After an hour or two of in-depth interviews with the husband and wife separately, the doctor cracked the case. It turns out that Mrs. Morely was going through menopause. Case solved! To therapeutic reformers it was obvious that "a court cannot handle the problem of menopause with 'objection sustained' and 'objection overruled.'" Legal jockeying had no place in the struggle to preserve marital harmony.[8]

Domestic-relations courts sought to replace legalistic procedures with therapeutic ones. As one expert explained, "The crucial step in the treatment of domestic discord cases, accordingly is the interview," at which both husband and wife could tell their stories. Domestic-relations courts encouraged all procedures that encouraged talk and discouraged those that led to reserve. Getting the "psychological" facts of the case, however, was only the first step and probably the easiest. The real trick was "emotional re-education."[9]

Domestic-relations courts partially satisfied therapeutic reformers. The regular courts, with their punitive orientation, were clearly not the place to repair frayed marital relations. On the other hand, the domestic-relations courts were not ideal either. They continued to take a penal point of view, and treatment never became their primary mission. Fundamentally the problem was one of orientation. The criminal-justice system, even reorganized, catered to a legal mentality that was not conducive to therapeutic principles. Lawyers, one marriage counselor complained, are "primarily concerned with legal requirements and only secondarily with adjustment and the happiness of individuals."[10] Without such an emphasis, domestic-relations courts would remain unsatisfactory in the eyes of therapeutic reformers.

This intense focus and concern with happiness marked a fundamental shift away from the therapeutic vision of Progressive-era social reformers, though it hearkened back to the emphasis in mind cure and New Thought. But unlike this earlier incarnation of the therapeutic gospel, the investment in happiness was not merely as an ideal but as a practical, measurable reality. Moreover, the focus on marriage as uniquely suited to producing personal happiness was new. In the view of an emerging group of experts who dealt with marriage and family problems, no other social institution had the potential to provide so much pleasure or pain. In the words of one marriage counselor, marriage has "an emotional quality belonging to no other relationship and one that makes the most demands on the character of the person and brings him the greatest satisfaction or the largest disappointment."[11] Indeed, one writer went so far as to argue that "control of maladjustment in marriage would probably eliminate most of the endogenous part of human misery within a century."[12] Wildly optimistic about their potential contribution, the new experts could not accept the domestic-relations courts' inadequacies, and they instead built brand-new institutions designed to handle what they saw as a looming national marriage problem.

Marriage Repairmen and Their Clinics

Paul Popenoe, the founder of the first marriage clinic in the United States, was born in Topeka, Kansas, in 1888. He grew up in California, where his father was a leader in the avocado industry. After studying briefly at Stanford, he became an agricultural explorer, traveling around the world. A few years later he returned to the United States with sixteen thousand date specimens, and in 1913 he published his first book, *Date Growing in the New and Old Worlds.* But tired of his work on dates, Popenoe pursued his interest in lineage and reproduction in an entirely new arena. Popenoe became fascinated with eugenics, the "science" of human breeding.

Combining his eugenical interests with his writing skills, he secured a position as the editor at the *Journal of Heredity.* The United States' entry into World War I, however, cut short Popenoe's stint as editor. Popenoe joined the staff of the United States Army Sanitary Corps, where he worked on the problem of "social hygiene." After the war, with the help of contacts he had made during wartime, Popenoe became the director of research for the Human Betterment Foundation in Pasadena, California, where he became a national expert on eugenics and published three books, *Problems of Human Reproduction* (1926), *Sterilization for Human Betterment* (1929), and *The Practical Applications of Heredity* (1930).

Profoundly disturbed by the lack of eugenic consciousness, he devoted himself to raising it. "Among the 1,000 leading American men of science," an exasperated Popenoe noted, "there is not one son of a day laborer. It takes 48,000 unskilled laborers to produce one man distinguished enough to get in *Who's Who,* while the same number of Congregational ministers produces 6,000 persons eminent enough to be included."[13] Utterly blind to the realities of class, Popenoe blamed bad stock for such statistics. Like other eugenicists, his interest in conserving the family of the so-called better stock led him to call for a radical expansion of state authority. Espousing a belief in the "common protoplasmic good," Popenoe advocated governmental regulation of

marriage, birth control, and sexual adjustment so that the "fit" would out-
breed the "unfit."

But no sooner had Popenoe jumped on the eugenic bandwagon than its
underlying premises came under attack. Experts in both the social sciences
and the hard sciences subjected it to a steady stream of criticism. Finally, the
proposals of the National Socialist Party in Germany also contributed to the
loss of enthusiasm for eugenics in the United States.

One key aspect of the eugenics movement in Germany, however, caught
Popenoe's attention: the idea of increasing the number of offspring of the fit
through marriage-consultations centers. During the second and third decades of the twentieth century Europe experienced devastating destruction
and death from war and disease. World War I resulted in 18 million European
deaths. An additional 15 million died from the postwar smallpox epidemic.
During the immediate postwar period European states became intensely focused on nation building through procreation. *Race hygiene* and *race betterment* became key watchwords. It was in this context that the first matrimonial health consultation center opened in Vienna in 1922.[14] In 1926 the
Prussian Social Welfare Ministry ordered that marriage-consultation centers
be established in every Prussian city. By 1934 more than a thousand centers
provided everything from eugenical to psychological advice.

Inspired by these new centers, Paul Popenoe opened the first "marriage
clinic" in the United States in Los Angeles in 1930. His pioneering Institute of
Family Relations developed new approaches to "getting at the root of difficulties that come to mar and sometimes ruin marital happiness." Popenoe believed that the tragedy of marital discord was that it was treatable: "There is
plenty of scientific information in existence to prevent most failures in marriage, and even to stop many of them after they have started, if people only
knew where to get it."[15] To provide such a place was Popenoe's goal. He envisioned the institute as "a human laboratory where marriage problems were
classified, studied, and solved."[16] His success in putting marriages under a
clinical microscope and offering clients practical help gained him worldwide
attention.

Popenoe's mission was to provide "mental fitness for marriage" and help
couples through a "confidential clinic where patients suffering from any of
the hundred and one causes of matrimonial frictions and fracases might go
to have their ills diagnosed by real scientists." Every day at the institute experts confronted the effects of matrimonial frictions: "open warfare or

armed truce, sexual reprisals, and reprisals on children, financial extravagance in pleasure seeking, extra-marital adventure, venereal infection, divorce or desertion, exploitation through alimony, chronic bitterness, defeated and disintegrated personality." Essentially, those who came to Popenoe's clinic were unhappy.[17]

Popenoe insisted that for this population the key was "talking it out." And Popenoe's talents at listening were becoming renowned. One journalist reported that the secret to Popenoe's "extraordinary career" was that he insisted on "hearing the rest of it."[18] Apparently, it was by prodding the interviewee to go on that Popenoe was able to lay bare the source of the marital trouble. From there it was necessary to derive a course of action, for which Popenoe and his colleagues relied on certain basic principles.

First, marital success could not be left to chance. As Popenoe explained, "Our greatest difficulty is to make [clients] realize that they can not escape from their trouble without prolonged effort."[19] Those who came to the clinic were not familiar with the emotional work involved in avoiding marital discord and achieving marital happiness. They did not necessarily understand that managing the "interplay of personalities" often took considerable work. It also took the skills and expert knowledge of the counselor. A trained counselor could help save a marriage because he knew how to get below the surface.

Counselors had to psychologize the marital problems they confronted because their clients often did not. Indeed, many resisted acknowledging that they had come to the clinic with a personal problem; often clients purported to be doing educational research. But, says Popenoe, "after getting data for an essay or debate, the high school girl will remark as casually as she can, 'By the way, I know a girl who, etc., etc., What do you advise in such a case?'"[20] That most clients came for psychological advice does not mean that the institute publicly advertised its role as a provider of psychological services. Indeed, it initially appeared quite hesitant to do so.

The institute anticipated a poor public reaction to its psychological orientation and therefore took steps to avoid bad publicity. This involved placing a gynecologist at the head of medical services. Popenoe explained that having "a psychiatrist in charge might lead some of the public to conclude that anyone who sought advice concerning marriage was considered to be mentally diseased."[21] The resident gynecologist and his staff, however, were not in great demand: "apart from physical examinations in connection with pre-

marital conferences, the medical staff has little to do."[22] Although the institute was hesitant to call attention to its therapeutic agenda, it nonetheless
devoted the bulk of its attention to "adjustment" problems.

The institute's Department of Personal Service handled private consultations for those "seeking adjustment of conjugal disharmony."[23] By today's
standards these consultations comprised extraordinarily few sessions, at
most six but usually only two or three. Also by today's standards, the cases
were not very psychological. Take the case, for example, of the man who could
not dance with his wife. The couple had been married for twenty years and
had four children. The husband was a professional man, and his wife was a
housewife. He loved dancing; she hated it. His dancing had brought their
marriage to the brink of disaster. He visited the clinic because "he wants to be
told definitively by Dr. Popenoe whether a man can go dancing and leave his
wife at home—if not he says he'll have to get a divorce." The trained counselor
suggested a "playtime budget." Just like the family income, leisure time had to
be negotiated and budgeted so that each marriage partner satisfactorily spent
his or her free time. The solution to this particular marriage problem was
simple: the husband could go dancing but "must balance that time with an
equal number of nights taking his wife out to the movies or driving."[24] Problem solved. Divorce avoided!

Eighty percent of cases were brought to the clinic by wives. This did not,
however, lead counselors to sympathize with the women. For example, in the
case of a young, college-educated woman who had alienated her husband,
causing marital strife, Popenoe discovered that not only did she make meals
"with a can-opener" but she suffered from a "superiority complex." Popenoe
told her "that few men are interested in listening to fragments of a senior
course in philosophy, and most males preferred a well-cooked dinner to a discourse on economics from a wife who happened to be a Bachelor of Arts."
Fortunately, because the wife was bright, the "re-education" process went
very smoothly. Once she learned more about "the psychology of the sexes," in
particular men's ego needs and emotional priorities, she understood why her
marriage was in danger and how she could salvage it.[25]

The psychology of sex itself, and its particular implications for women, was
a common theme in consultations at the marriage clinic. In one case of a
marriage in which the husband adored his wife but she rebuffed his sexual
advances, Popenoe's thorough investigation revealed that the source of the
trouble lay in the wife's childhood. As a young girl the wife had been psycho-

logically damaged by "an inflammatory illustrated book" she had accidentally come across, and "she carried the shock of discovery, deep-seated in her sub-conscious mind, into her marriage." Every time her husband approached her sexually, "the book rose as a barrier between them." Using a version of the recovered-memory technique, the counselor cured her in just a half-dozen sessions.[26]

At Popenoe's clinic, clients learned that marital problems could be solved if they were willing to investigate their marriages. Indeed, Popenoe strongly recommended that investigation begin even before marriage. "To live happily ever after," those about to be married had to take certain precautions. Pope-noe advised, for example, that those seeking marriage partners "stay out of the West," for divorce rates were higher there. It turns out that geography matters: "The riskiest place, geographically, to contract a marriage is on the Pacific slope; the safest place, the Middle Atlantic seaboard. The Mississippi valley provides an average gamble." Education also mattered: "The educated part of the American population furnishes a small proportion of the unhappy marriages." Socioeconomic class had a direct bearing on marital success. Popenoe advised that one of the ways to avoid marital breakdown was to "own things" since couples with personal attachments to material things were less likely to divorce.[27]

Popenoe's ideas about mate selection were highly gendered. Despite his general claims about education, for example, Popenoe found that wives' be-ing better educated than their husbands was a key cause of marital break-down since "men want to be superior to women." In his view, well-educated women were at high risk not only for marital failure but also for not marrying at all. This conclusion led Popenoe, in the name of marital happiness and success, to oppose loans for college women: "One of the most diabolical ways of preventing 'superior' women from marrying is through scholarship loan funds." He argued that graduating from college already placed women at "the margins of greatest marriageability" and loans further eroded their chances of marrying. According to Popenoe, for a woman a B.A. and debt were a recipe for marital disaster.[28]

With such simple rules as these Popenoe helped more than five thousand persons with marital problems in just three years. Not one couple who had been given premarital guidance had divorced, so that he had met his eugen-ical goal of conserving the family. Popenoe believed that his clinic had saved thousands of marriages not only because he and his counselors were "adept at human relations" but also because they applied the latest scientific wisdom to the most intimate of human experiences. Popenoe found that 2,208 different factors affected marital happiness. But he also found that there were several simple rules that couples about to be married or already married could follow to avoid trouble. This can-do attitude about marriage repair soon spread.

Within a couple of years of the institute's founding, other marriage-consultation centers opened their doors. "Nowadays," one observer claimed in 1932, "a new marriage clinic opens its doors every month."[29] There was, for example, the Marriage Advice Center in New York City, founded by Drs. Abraham and Hannah Stone, who had been active in the birth-control movement. Emily Mudd's Marriage Counsel of Philadelphia came out of her work in maternal health. Mudd found that all too often the women her clinic treated suffered from poor marriage hygiene. As she later recalls, we were increasingly "spending time and effort to patch up, figuratively speaking, human wrecks."[30] To address this problem, in 1932 Emily Mudd and her colleagues opened the Marriage Counsel, which promised its clients "complete privacy and lack of interruption" in a "cheerful, somewhat informal office setting" containing a "carefully selected lending library of technical books and fiction" designed to facilitate the therapeutic process of "free talk." For one dollar clients received a one-hour, confidential "consultation."[31]

Psychologically trained experts were not the only professionals involved in the establishment of brand-new institutions to stop the spread of marital unhappiness. During the 1920s and 1930s religious leaders took an active role. Their actions stemmed from their belief that they had a special responsibility to address the marriage problem since they were intimately involved with administering the marriage vows. They also strongly believed that religious institutions could not cede the field of marriage counseling to secular institutions. "It would be a calamity if the marriage clinic should be taken over by secular agencies," said one minister.[32] With instructions from the highest echelons, communities of faith became proactive on the marriage front.

In six large denominations commissions and committees were established to deal with topics of marriage, home, and divorce. In April 1933, for example, the Federal Council of Churches of Christ's Committee on Marriage and the Home issued a report that "urged pastors to act as marital guides." The report indicated that ministers' responsibilities included helping couples "adjust views" and "assist later if home difficulties arise."[33] To help ministers, rabbis, pastors, and priests fulfill this role, theological seminaries expanded their curricula. Many seminaries required ministers to take a course in psychology or psychiatry. Single semester courses in "the art of helping people out of trouble" and even clinical training increasingly became available. The Craigie Foundation, of Cambridge, Massachusetts, for example, in 1931 provided funding for supervised training in mental hospitals for fifty young ministers.[34]

Seminaries, dioceses, and church federations increasingly paid special attention to the problem of marital discord. Between 1930 and 1935 more than a hundred conferences on the subject were organized. The leaders of such conferences often came from the large urban churches, which had just begun to take up "marriage repair" work. In the early 1930s a number of churches in Washington, Philadelphia, Boston, and New York established marriage clinics. By 1932 fifteen such clinics offered classes and private consultations.[35]

Whether religious or secular in origin, the new marriage clinics spread the therapeutic gospel. They promoted the idea that marriage problems had psychological origins and that advisers had to get at "the hidden or inner processes of which the client or patient himself is not aware."[36] To do so, the counselor needed not only formal training in psychiatry, psychology, or mental hygiene but also clinical experience in "re-education" or modification of attitudes. Finally, the clinician also needed to be free from personal problems; as one marriage counselor explained, effective marriage counseling is difficult if the counselor's "own emotional conflicts are far from solved." But marriage counselors were confident that as long as they met the above requirements the marriage problem could be solved. To the founders of marriage clinics it was simply a matter of resources: "Successful marriage is distinguished from unsuccessful marriage not by the number of problems or the kind of problems which the married people need to face, but rather by the presence or absence or resources for dealing with the common problems at hand. The successful and unsuccessful alike have problems. The resourceless people are overcome by their problems; the resourceful overcome them."[37]

By 1937 there were more than 150 centers devoted exclusively to providing such resources and another 100 or so that provided marriage guidance along with a host of other sorts of services.[38] Marriage experts founded these centers because they believed that the real problems of marriage "must be dragged out into the open.[39] Their private consultations were part of a fight against silence and reticence. Marriage counselors believed that frank and open discussion of marital discord was critical if the nation was to ensure mastery over drift.[40]

Marriage and Education

During the 1920s and 1930s marriage counselors looked to higher education as a fruitful area of expansion. In so doing, they denounced its lack of leadership on the marriage front. Marriage experts denounced a "higher education system [that] is so squeamish that marriage training is ignored."[41] They ridiculed colleges and universities for claiming to educate students for citizenship when "young men and women enter upon the most fundamental relationship of human society with practically no training at all." Hopeful that "some day the colleges will wake up" to the folly of such neglect, they noted that "in the meantime we're graduating thousands of fine young men and women every year to lives of unhappiness." What galled them was that the knowledge and tools to prevent "matrimonial illiteracy" existed.[42]

To ensure marital happiness, students needed to be taught the "science" of personal relations; they needed to know "how to make wise choices," "how to recognize and reject fantasies," and how to live "under conditions promoting growth, security, and integration."[43] The new "professors of marriage" recommended not only that students take courses dealing specifically with marriage but that all courses in history, art, and literature be "broadened to deal with the various phases of marriage."[44] Of course, they conceded that the success of such an expanded curriculum would depend upon "an enlightened faculty made up of persons who themselves have reached an adult level emotionally."[45]

This expansive vision of higher education, with its emotionally mature faculty, therapeutic lessons neatly incorporated into the liberal-arts curriculum, and graduates with fully integrated personalities, today seems both strangely inappropriate and overly ambitious. Many who now teach in the academy still struggle to teach students reading, writing, and arithmetic. And they expect their students to deal with their psychological issues at the counseling center.

The professor most responsible for introducing marriage to the higher-education curriculum was Ernest R. Groves. Not only did he teach the first course on marriage as a practical problem of daily living but he started the first graduate program in marriage counseling.[46] Known as the "professor of marriage" or the "doctor of troubles," Groves began his career in sociology after obtaining a divinity degree from Yale. Between 1920 and 1927 he chaired the sociology department at Boston University. His first major intellectual interest was revealed in an article on the implications of Freud for sociology, "Sociology and Psycho-analytic Psychology." He wrote the first textbook on social psychiatry, *Introduction to Mental Hygiene* (1930) and also the first textbook on marriage entitled *Marriage* (1933).[47]

But Groves's academic work occupied only a portion of his time. As early as 1915, when he was a dean at the University of New Hampshire, Groves saw patients. One reporter for a popular magazine described Groves as follows: "He is nationally recognized as an authority on these subjects, is the author of widely read and studied books on them, and a lecturer of note. But this man, Ernest R. Groves, is far more than a teacher, a writer or a speaker. He is a builder, and the edifices which he builds are human lives." At first students and then, as his reputation spread, ordinary men and women suffering from personal difficulties came to Groves for advice and help. Groves's secret, apparently, was that he "cast no stones, nor did he attempt to judge." Rather, with sympathy and compassion he helped people get at the root cause of their trouble. When asked if he charged for his help, Groves explained that he had once after a wealthy client insisted. But after that he had determined not to charge again because "it seemed like taking pay for throwing a drowning man a rope." Obviously, the profession has since come to a different conclusion.

Through his work with these early "clients," Groves made the remarkable discovery that people could be helped simply by teaching them to face their problems. Groves's mantra became, "Tell it, down to the last detail which you have confided to no man and which nearly chokes you to bring out. Don't stop with this year, or the year before, but keep digging back into your life. It will be hard. It will hurt." But Groves promised that it would be cathartic.

In these early years, Groves saw a range of people, but most were married couples who thought they could no longer live together or men and women whose love had thrown them into "all sorts of chaos." In one case, for example, a well-educated man with a bright economic future came to him on the verge of suicide. Filled with worry, anxiety, and negative feelings, he had "for no apparent cause, gone to pieces." The trouble had started a year earlier. In response to Groves's question whether anything in particular had happened to him that year the man replied that he had fallen in love. As Groves probed deeper, he discovered that the man had fallen so deeply in love "that the young lady seemed too good for him, that he was unworthy." His mood was one of "despair"; he was convinced that if the woman really knew him, she would disapprove of him. The man apparently had "a good position in a professional office" but really wanted to grow apples. Once Groves discovered the cause of the problem, the solution was easy:

> I shoved him a telegraph blank and commanded him to write to her a message that he was on his way to see her that very day. Before he hardly realized what was up, I had dispatched it by a messenger. "First of all," I instructed him, "you will see that lady you love and ask her to marry you. Second, you are going to tell her, with all the enthusiasm you possess, why you want to grow apples, and where you want to grow apples, and of the future you see in apples." "But what if she says no?" he gasped. "She won't, I assured; "but if she does, grow apples anyway! . . . If you lose her, you can still grow apples. If you lose the apples, you will still have her. And you may win both!"

The man followed Groves's advice, and the couple lived happily ever after in apple country, "growing not alone fine apples, but two fine sturdy boys as well." Groves learned from a letter from the young man that the woman loved him so much that she would have gone to China with him to grow rice if that had been what he wanted.[48]

It was the exhilarating experience of helping people like the apple grower that led Groves to take on the whole issue of training and preparation for marriage, for he came to believe that it was "folly" for colleges and universities to provide "no opportunity to gain insight into the meaning of domestic experience upon which they [students] stake so much of their happiness." He criticized colleges for their "laissez-faire attitude" and warned that "the time had come when no institution of higher learning can fully meet its social obligations without including education for marriage."[49] By the mid-1920s Groves had become a tireless advocate for marriage education. His work on behalf of marriage preparation not only resulted in the radical expansion of the mission of higher education but also redefined social obligation as the responsibility to free graduate students of personal problems. Groves's campaign to get colleges to meet their new responsibilities was largely successful. In 1924 he taught the first service course on marriage, dealing with the practical and personal problems of domestic life, at Boston University. By 1935, 225 colleges offered 234 courses that dealt "in whole or in part. . . with preparation for marriage and family life."[50]

At the University of Iowa, for example, taught, appropriately, by a professor named Jung, the course was offered to both men and women. The *New York Times* reported that the course on marriage was finally introduced in 1935 because educators realized that the "prudish conspiracy of silence regarding marriage problems has constituted a questionable, even shameful morality." Professor Jung brought in a variety of guest lecturers, including psychiatrists who discussed "the mental hygiene and psychopathology of marriage, interpreting from the psychiatric point of view the mental and emotional disturbances peculiar to marriage and suggesting practical solutions." But teachers of such courses hoped to have their students master not only why marriage went awry but also all facets of the therapeutic gospel related to marriage. Teachers of marriage held that premarital education must involve "emotional preparation." Students were expected to have "a firm grip upon the psychology of intimacy" after taking a marriage course. Their goal was to make students "good marriage risks" by teaching the fundamentals of the "science of personal relations."[51]

Students were taught that marriages were not made in heaven, that marital happiness resulted from "intelligent idealism based on the knowledge of the principles of human adaptation." Without marriage training, professors of marriage insisted, couples were marrying blindfolded; "once the bandage is off, trouble [was] likely to follow." It was for this reason that Butler University in Indianapolis began offering an extension course on marriage in 1932 ($7.50 for married couples, $5.00 for celibates). The course was designed to teach "the art and science of happy marriage." Anyone could register for it, be they "maritally unskilled," "unhappy practitioners" of marriage, or even "divorced persons seeking late wisdom." The evening lectures covered the physical, psychological, economic, social, and religious aspects of marriage. Students could also expect "the interchange of experiences." Administrators who embraced the course hoped that it would "oppose and in time presumably suppress" the number of couples heading to Reno for divorce.[52]

What is interesting about these new additions to the higher-education curriculum is their practical and psychological orientation. The courses on marriage not only dealt with such intimate and new subjects as masturbation, frigidity, intercourse, homosexuality, the self, the unconscious, childhood memories, and self-esteem but also blurred the boundaries between education and therapy. Professors who taught marriage courses conducted small group discussions and private consultations with their students. As Ernest R. Groves himself explained, "Work as a consultant on personal problems became more and more a part of the program of preparation for marriage and family life carried on at the University of North Carolina."[53] Another professor said that the conferences "held with each student provided one of the most important opportunities for emotional education and for greater understanding of the students' needs."[54] Indeed, it appears that the early teachers of marriage functioned as both educators and therapists. Professors opened clinics with the approval and sometimes the official backing of their universities.

Even when this was not formally the case, the courses on marriage were organized in such a manner that the student's own psychology became a central concern. One professor said that he sought to teach each student how to analyze "himself as a personality, a psychological entity, and a member of a family group."[55] Another aimed to increase the student's "ability to communicate his feelings."[56] Professors of marriage strove to get their students "to recall from their own childhood and adolescent memories various problems that arose in their own homes."[57] In marriage courses the student's experience of psychological pain and pleasure became an important building block in this process, psychological excavation a critical method. Through these courses professors became involved in the new business of solving their students' personal problems.

The drive for marriage education was not limited to higher education. During the 1920s and 1930s high schools too were seen as a critical agency in the war against marital failure and unhappiness. Charles Philbower, the supervising principal of the Westfield, New Jersey, schools, for example, spoke for many when he insisted that "boys and girls should be given courses having a regular place in the high school curricula which would teach them what to expect and look for in their life mates." Philbower wanted to "remove the selection of husbands and wives from its present emotional basis" and "place it on a more scientific plane."[58] Philbower's call for marriage education in high schools was echoed by teachers and administrators at the 1934 conference entitled "Education for Social-Family Relationships, Marriage, and Parenthood at the Secondary Level."[59] At this conference participants called the lack of marriage education "one of the real tragedies of modern secondary education."[60]

To avoid such tragedies, schools sought to offer courses on "home relations." The main objective of these courses, largely oriented toward girls, was to give them "the guidance and experience that will help them develop as persons and to become happy cooperative and contributing members to their families."[61] Experts on marriage recommended teaching students about the causes of marital conflict and factors leading to marital success. They also recommended that students be required to study the development of a well-adjusted personality. One teacher who had institutionalized these new educational goals covered "obstacles, such as undesirable personality traits, the differences in emotional suitability to one another, lack of common ideals, wide differences in social background, that will most likely prevent the attainment of happiness and satisfaction in marriage."[62] While some educators wanted marriage education to begin in high school, others wanted it to begin earlier. One marriage-education advocate went so far as to argue that schooling in marriage should be made "an integral part of the education of every child beginning at the kindergarten age of 4 years."[63]

Marriage Research and the New Science of Personal Relations

During the 1920s and 1930s research universities embraced marriage as a legitimate subject of inquiry. They lent financial and disciplinary support to the new field. As a result there was an explosion of studies. Scholars from the fields of sociology, psychiatry, and social work produced a substantial body of knowledge on marriage. Out of these efforts came hundreds of books, such as *Psychological Factors in Marital Happiness, Emotional Adjustment in Marriage, Foundations of Happiness in Marriage, Chart for Happiness,* and *Predicting Success or Failure in Marriage,* and thousands of journal articles. Indeed, whole new journals specifically devoted to marriage appeared, including *Marriage Hygiene* and *Marriage and Family Living.* Students of marriage took postgraduate courses with titles like "Factors in Marital Success," "Marital Incompatibility," and "The Distribution of Success in Marriage" and even began to write dissertations on various facets of the marriage problem.

This new breed of academics was part of a larger trend, the expansion of higher education and the growing prestige of the social sciences. Riding the wave of enthusiasm, marriage researchers defined marriage in scientific terms, arguing that the marriage problem could be questioned, studied, graphed, and mapped. Their exhaustive studies convinced them that what made marriage succeed or fail could be determined. Both the nature of marriage and the laws that it followed could be discerned by breaking marriage down into its discrete elements. For students of marriage, the domestic relation was a series of "interaction patterns."

Such patterns were sometimes described in highly mathematical terms. For example, one researcher described marriage this way, using M for men and W for women: "Personalities M and W, starting at a certain social distance, become ultimately transformed into Mn and Wn, either more intimate than at the beginning of their marriage or now separated by a vast gulf of resentment and bitterness." When symbolically represented, marriage worked as follows: "With marriage, the interaction of M and W begins or continues, with each person in a new role. Assuming a gesture of stimulus from M to W, or in more general terms an impact of M's personality upon W, this influence may be either friendly or hostile. Assuming that the gesture is hostile, W withdraws from M and is transformed into personality W1, which is predisposed to make a hostile gesture which will alienate M and convert him to M1, now predisposed to a certain kind of behavior toward W1, which tends to be cumulative."[64] Such diagramming was typical of the marriage research of the period.

The payoff of this new scientific approach to marriage was supposedly the predictability of success. Marriage researchers promised that they would be able to predict which couples would experience negative interactions and for which couples marriage would result in "disorganized" personalities. "Recent American researches on this subject . . . prove conclusively that success in marriage can be predicted within a modest range of error," wrote one researcher.[65] Taking their science even further, researchers claimed to be able to accurately measure and predict marital happiness. "Increasingly successful attempts have been made to measure the degrees of happiness attained by various persons in marriage, to ascertain the symptoms by means of which the happiness or unhappiness of a proposed marriage can be predicted and to ascertain the causes by which the happiness of a marriage and of the resulting members of the family can be increased."[66] Such grandiose claims make even those of the New Thoughters of the late nineteenth century seem modest by comparison.

But it gets worse, for researchers claimed to be able to predict not only marital success or failure but also the exact amount of happiness any two parties could expect. Their "science" of personal relations revealed "by what observable combinations of characteristics can two individual contemplating possible marriage with each other predict the probable degree of happiness which would be experienced by them in such a marriage."[67] This feat was accomplished by a variety of means. First, massive surveys were taken to measure individuals' temperament and attitude toward their spouses. Second, marriage researchers worked out formulas and equations that identified the key ingredients in marital happiness. The following formula, for example, was worked out for the relationship between marriage and satisfaction:

$$\text{Happiness} = \frac{Achievement}{Expectation}$$

This formula expressed the idea that "satisfaction with marriage may be increased by expecting less or achieving more."[68] Finally, marriage researchers quantified the factors associated with marital satisfaction by the development of "happiness tests," including the Humm-Wadsworth Temperament Scale, the Bernreuter Personality Inventory, the Willoughby Emotional Maturity Scale, and the Bernard Scale for Marital Happiness.[69]

One of the most popular such tests was the Euphorimeter. This test developed in response to the question whether happiness could be measured "operationally and validly, on one commensurate scale, where units will have the same meaning for every intelligent person." The researchers at Duke University who invented the Euphorimeter concluded that it was possible if "Euphor" units were used. The Euphorimeter actually represented three different tests: the Long-Run Euphorimeter, the At-the-Moment Euphorimeter, and the Diagnostic Euphorimeter. The Long-Run Euphorimeter measured the "general level of happiness at which the individual ordinarily lives"; the At-the Moment Euphorimeter measured the "level of happiness of the individual when he is taking the test"; and the Diagnostic Euphorimeter actually "located the aspect of the personality from which unhappiness arises." Apparently, no amount of precision was beyond the grasp of marriage researchers.[70]

Based on the results of happiness tests like the Euphorimeter researchers offered the public a new science of mate selection. This science promised to help the middle class avoid choosing the wrong marriage partners. Not too surprisingly, marriage researchers found that those with the best chances of marital happiness were those who led a racially and ethnically insular life. They recommended that the members of the middle class stay away from partners of a different race, religion, or ethnicity. They found, for example, that interracial marriages experienced "added stresses"; partners' "feelings of inferiority or failure connected with being ostracized" made it "especially difficult for marriages across racial lines to be successful."[71] Indeed, happiness tests showed that any differences in the spouses' social background presented a real threat to the marriage. These findings led marriage researchers to conclude that "both prospective partners should have a similarity in race, religion, economic and social status, outlook on life, age, and education."[72] Proving what they already believed, marriage researchers put their "science" of personal relations in the service of protecting middle-class insularity.

Marriage researchers believed that colleges had a potentially critical role to play in this regard. The university campus was a propitious setting for finding a mate, for at college men and women could only find mates of a relatively similar socioeconomic background. Based on their findings that only one in seventy-five couples who met in college divorced, marriage researchers suggested that "if you think perhaps you are in love with a person of inadequate education, but are not quite sure, your future happiness will probably be increased by breaking off this relationship." These researchers found a close association not only between education and marital happiness but also between economic position and marital happiness: "The lowest-paid and economically least secure occupations have the least happy marriages."[73]

Other sociological factors found to have a direct and immediate bearing on a happy marriage and, not coincidentally, on the preservation of a middle-class lifestyle were age at marriage and age when children were born. Marriage researchers recommended that young people wait until after college to marry. They continually found that persons who married at a young age experienced marital trouble. One counselor reported that six independent studies had confirmed this finding. Researchers' findings concerning the relationship between having children and marital happiness—that childless couples were unhappier—also promoted middle-class ideals: "couples who desired children (whether they had them or not) averaged 151 Euphor-units in their marital happiness, while those who did not desire children averaged -20."[74] Conveniently, conformity to marriage researchers' "family values" meant high happiness scores.

This was particularly true when it came to homosexuality. Refraining, however, from earlier purely moral arguments against it, marriage researchers rejected homosexuality on the basis of happiness. After thorough investigation, they found that homosexuality appeared to adversely affect marital happiness. They found that those with homosexual experience were less happily married than those without. Apparently, it did not occur to marriage researchers that homosexuals in homosexual relationships might have scored high on the Euphorimeter test. Mistaking a correlation for a cause, marital counselors concluded that homosexuality reduced one's chances of marital happiness.

Marriage researchers thus argued against homosexuality less because they viewed it as abnormal than because failing to conform to a middle-class lifestyle would create an unhealthy degree of emotional conflict within the homosexual. They warned that the psychological effects of the ostracization resulting from homosexuality could be overwhelming. As one counselor explained, the homosexual "finds himself or herself confronted therefore with an intense mental conflict between the desire to be thought of with admiration and approval and the auto-erotic or homosexual pattern which has become established in the personality." In an odd kind of argument then, marriage researchers suggested that homosexuals should resist homosexuality because it would result in unhappiness.[75]

In addition to the sociological characteristics that made for happy marriages or preserved the homogeneity of the middle-class lifestyle, marriage researchers also found that specific psychological characteristics fostered or undermined happy marriages. Marriage researchers discovered, for example, that there was a direct correlation between a "cooperative" personality and marital happiness. Warm, friendly persons made good spouses. One counselor recommended that when contemplating marriage, one should "watch the other person's reactions toward the sick, crippled, beggars, and old people. Watch particularly, their behavior toward little children and the reactions of children toward them. Watch them when they are in authority over other people." The assumption was that mean and unempathetic persons made poor spouses and were less likely to make their partners happy. One student of marriage reported that "those who are irritable and quarrelsome tend to be less than half as happy as normal in marriage and frequently sink below the zero point to active unhappiness."[76]

In their search for guiding principles for wise mate selection, marriage researchers "discovered" widespread sexual dissatisfaction. Finding it to be a significant factor in marital unhappiness, they investigated it with a vengeance. Operating under the assumption that sexual expression was normal, they concluded that sexual repression was one of the major sources of marital dissatisfaction. In fact, the dangers of sexual repression went beyond the conjugal relationship. Researchers found, for example, that "sexually repressed men and women are dangerous influences to their children." Indeed, marriage researchers identify sexual repression as a major source of marital trouble: "The thwarting of sexual activity is often among the etiological factors of mental disorders and of unhappiness in general. The most unwholesome feature of the existing social order is that it renders difficult for the majority of individuals and impossible by great numbers the attainment of a satisfactory adjustment of their sexual lives." In direct contrast to early-twentieth-century therapeutic reformers, who defined wholesome activities as those that were free of sexuality, marriage researchers of the 1920s and 1930s identified sexual repression as unwholesome.[77]

Marriage researchers found dissatisfaction with the sexual side of marriage to be an important source of tension and conflict. "As we search for causes which are disrupting an increasing number of homes each year, we find again and again the failure to adjust on the physiological plane as one of the deep and underlying factors."[78] That sexual maladjustment was indeed a fundamental factor was indicated in couples' happiness scores: the higher the sexual satisfaction, the higher the Euphor score. Unfortunately, researchers found that positive sexual interaction was a surprisingly elusive goal for many women. Estimates ranged, but most researchers concluded that 25–33 percent of married women never achieved sexual satisfaction.[79]

Applying new therapeutic standards, marriage researchers viewed women's inability to obtain sexual pleasure as a problem of national significance.[80] They spent considerable energy analyzing and diagnosing the problems of frigidity. In keeping with their view of sexual problems in general, marriage researchers believed that frigidity was largely a psychological problem. They insisted that sexual incompatibilities were merely "the external signs of an inner emotional conflict."[81] Frigidity was no different. What was distinctive about frigidity, however, was that it represented one of the few instances in which marriage researchers at least partly blamed men. Their sexual narcissism and retrograde notions about women were two important causes of women's inability to enjoy sex. As one of the leading experts on frigidity explained, "The husband may be largely at fault; he may have formed selfish and infantile habits, thinking mainly of his own gratification."[82] Students of frigidity also found that "in a surprisingly many cases the husband later makes the fact of pre-marital sex relations a basis for recrimination against his wife."[83] Guilt and anger at the husband for making her feel bad could lead to a lack of sexual responsiveness on the part of the wife. If these feelings of shame, bitterness, and insecurity were not brought to light, they might handicap her permanently.

Though marriage researchers conceded that men played an important role in the problem of frigidity, they often focused on changing women's state of mind. Marriage researchers saw emotional conflict behind women's frigidity and sought to uncover it. They believed that this conflict stemmed from some sort of emotional shock caused by some past experience, most likely a sexual one. Ultimately, it was women who were expected to resolve the emotional conflict behind frigidity. Whether a woman suffered from "occasional frigidity," "relative frigidity," or "pathological frigidity," her lack of sexual responsiveness was believed to be a symptom of a larger personality problem. Marriage researchers believed that frigidity was a neuroticism that took its toll on women. Women's fears and anxieties manifested themselves in an inability to experience sexual satisfaction:

> It is often found that her trouble dates back, if not to childhood, at least to the early days of marriage. She discovered that her husband was likely to fail her at the crucial moment; that his premature ejaculation prevented her from attaining acme. She entered each successive intercourse, therefore, with the fear that she would be defrauded and this fear completely prevented her from satisfaction. . . . Even though her husband later attained self-control and could prolong coitus indefinitely, the results of the early fear remained.[84]

Researchers believed that deep-seated fears stemming in part from the experience of being unable to achieve sexual arousal were responsible for women's frigidity.

Marriage researchers' investigations of frigidity indicate how the therapeutic gospel reconfigured the ideals of womanhood. In the early twentieth century therapeutic reformers viewed poor women's refusal to be modest or their eagerness for sexual satisfaction as a problem. By the 1930s marriage researchers found the major sexual problem to be women's lack of sexual satisfaction. Though marriage researchers viewed women's sexual discontent as a significant problem and advocated a measure of sexual equality, the problem was still conceived in terms of gender difference. Women were construed as fundamentally different from men in ways that produced a lack of sexual responsiveness. Or they were seen as too similar to men in their desire for sexual satisfaction, in which case they could also experience frigidity. "Pathologically frigid" women, for example, suffered from this problem. Such women thought about sex continually and wanted intercourse "as often as possible" but apparently failed to reach climax because "the barriers [to sexual satisfaction] are within." Such women, one marriage researcher warned, "may now be started on the road toward nymphomania."[85] Apparently, for women frigidity was a slippery slope.

The sexual double standard pervades the research literature on marriage. What is interesting, however, is not so much the existence of the double standard, which has a long and venerable history, but how marriage researchers harness the double standard to their new quantitative and therapeutic agendas. Marriage researchers' double standard is distinguished by their use of statistical evidence in their investigations into marital happiness and the idea that women must be sexual but not too sexual. Indeed, the category "sexual approachableness" is seen as positively correlated with marriageability and marital happiness.[86] Conversely, marriage researchers saw as "the most disturbing condition" a woman's being "more passionate than the husband."[87] Researchers said that their studies proved conclusively that women who were sexually expressive but also modest were the happiest wives.

Marriage researchers devoted considerable attention to gender difference. Just as women were securing a measure of political equality and entering into the professions in increasing numbers, marriage counselors identified a whole new area of difference: men and women had different priorities when it came to choosing spouses. What made wives unhappy in marriage was considered to be fundamentally different from what made men unhappy.

Not surprisingly, researchers found that women with key "feminine" characteristics, women who were "attentive to details," "kindly, cooperative, and charitable," and "self-confident" but were "not offended by being required to take subordinate roles" tended to be happily married women.[88] Conversely, women who were afraid of sex or were emotionally immature were likely to be unhappy in their marriages. Finally, women were advised that marital success depended on their ability to minister to a man's psyche: "A girl to be attractive as a wife must appeal to the man's emotion, she must be able to enhance his ego."[89] Creating a new area of domestic competence, marriage researchers ascribed to women a new therapeutic role: they were to be men's confidantes, and it was through their understanding of men's psychologies that their bond with them would form: "A fundamental principle which almost all successful women understand and apply is that the sympathetic and understanding listener is credited, by the talker, with having keen intelligence and an admirable personality. Some girls have learned the not very difficult art of welcoming the confidences which young fellows are often so eager to make about their own ambitions, their work, their struggles. . . . Such girls are sometimes astonished to find how readily boys become attached to them."[90] According to marriage researchers, women who developed therapeutic skills would enhance not only their marriageability but also their chances of marital happiness.

Marriage researchers were neither reticent nor self-conscious about the qualities they believed women needed if they were to be happily married. Indeed, there is something refreshingly honest, if ultimately terribly distasteful, about their views. Pulling no punches, for example, marriage researchers stated that women who submitted to their fathers' authority were happier: "We find that wives who have loved their fathers dearly and never quarreled with them [score] more than twice as much happiness in their own marriages (117 Euphor-units) as do wives who have been antagonistic to their fathers (50 Euphor-units)."[91] The basic message for women being that patriarchy pays.

Researchers' findings on weight are no less shocking to the contemporary feminist, for they found a "striking relationship" between weight and happiness for women and between health and happiness for men: "Health is a more important predictor of happiness in choosing husbands, while underweight is a more important prediction for happiness in choosing wives, but both should be taken into consideration."[92] Further, they found that women who were fifteen pounds underweight achieved Euphorimeter scores of 137, whereas those who were fifteen pounds overweight scored only 23.

While marriage researchers found evidence that the qualities that made women good spouses differed from those that made men good spouses, the issue of marriageability was directed solely toward women. It was women's work to get married, and it was up to men to protect themselves from marrying unwisely. Marriage researchers saw themselves as playing a direct and immediate role in these processes. Thus, advice to women revolved around marriageability, while advice to men revolved around not marrying the wrong woman. Men enhanced their "marital risk" when they paid too little attention to their mates' intelligence and too much attention to their immediate sexual impulses and to physical beauty. The danger was entrapment. Women, on the other hand, faced the "marital risk" of remaining single.

One of the main factors affecting a woman's marriageability was her occupation. Calculating marriage rates of women in varying occupations, researchers found that "the chances of finding a mate in certain occupations are much greater than in others."[93] One study ranked fifteen occupations based on how likely the women in those occupations were to marry as follows:

1. secretary
2. bookkeeper
3. stenographer
4. journalist
5. insurance saleswoman
6. clerk
7. hotel hostess
8. buyer for a large firm
9. nurse
10. lawyer
11. teacher
12. dietitian
13. librarian
14. social worker
15. physician

Not surprisingly, women in relatively low-paying and low-status jobs were given a greater chance of marrying.

Men, as indicated earlier, did not have to worry about their marriageability, though there were certain characteristics that would ensure them a high happiness reading on the Euphorimeter or other happiness tests. Students of marital happiness emphasized that men who displayed a certain amount of vigor or aggressiveness in attacking problems, particularly economic ones, and men who were able to express tenderness in "unobtrusive" ways were likely to be happily married. Based on information about the qualities that made women good and happy wives and what constituted a bad "marital risk" for men, marriage researchers offered men the following advice: "From the foregoing items, it would seem that if a man who is looking for a wife can fall in love with an underweight, but healthy school teacher in her middle twenties who comes from a happy home and loves her parents dearly, he ought to marry her. . . . The happiness score on the combination ought to be magnificent!"[94]

Through its program of wise mate selection, marriage research promised to guarantee middle-class identity and security. In exchange, marriage researchers called upon the middle class to embrace a new definition of marriage and normality. A normal, middle-class person with a successful marriage was one who understood the fundamental principles of mental health, which included the new goals of psychological and sexual fulfillment, and sought to live his or her life by those principles.

In the therapeutic language of marriage researchers, happiness stemmed from psychological understanding and adjustment. Partners were supposed to find pleasure in identifying their problems and experiencing psychological growth. Satisfaction resulted from knowing oneself and one's partner, dissatisfaction from "failure to grow" and "emotional distortion." The researchers argued that successful and happy marriages were not ones in which there were no problems but rather ones in which couples had developed "techniques of facing their problems." They insisted that only knowledge of their problems and an understanding of "the partner's personality, his needs, his wishes, his unsatisfied longing and his potent attainments" would enable couples to experience marital fulfillment.[95]

Not surprisingly, marriage researchers found that marital failures too often had psychological origins. Some attributed these failures to "emotional immaturity," which they regarded as "the root of a great quantity of dissatisfactions, the antagonisms, and the failures that appear in marriage and family relationships." It is interesting that this quality was itself often defined psychologically. The "emotionally immature" person was one who had marriage problems but "prefers not to see them," or one who did not accept the tenets of the therapeutic gospel.[96] Marriage researchers considered the refusal to engage in introspection and acquire knowledge of psychological processes a cause of marital unhappiness. But they also viewed some level of denial and resulting marital conflict as normal. Domestic trouble, in their view, was not a problem experienced by the troubled few but inherent to the marital relationship. "Some degree of thwarting is inevitable among married people," said one counselor.[97] Another explained that conflict "may be thought of as quite normal . . . a minimum of conflict is consistent with adjustment. Conflict becomes, thus, an inevitable situation and remains normal so long as it does not lead to the disorganization of the personality."[98] Indeed, marriage researchers considered emotional tension within marriage to be normal, but a normal person "was not ashamed to seek counsel." Remaking one's personality became critical to achieving normality. One marriage counselor stated that "normal people can extensively remake their own attitudes and even their own personalities."[99] Having redefined normality to include self-transformation, fulfillment, and sexual expression, marriage researchers promised to help the middle class secure these new goals.

* * *

The establishment of the American Association of Marriage Counselors in 1942 marked the end of an intense phase of professional development for the new field of marriage counseling. Between 1920 and 1940 those interested in the problems of marriage established the first marriage-consultation bureaus, undergraduate courses on marriage, and graduate programs in marriage-counseling.

Marriage counseling's call to arms was largely successful. The profession not only generated a specific body of knowledge and special clinical techniques but managed to institutionalize fundamental aspects of its therapeutic agenda. The profession's areas of influence included secondary and higher education, social-welfare agencies, and private philanthropic organizations. But the therapeutic gospel promoted by marriage counselors did not reach the public at large. College students might take a course on marriage. A small number of mostly middle-class women visited marriage clinics, encountering probably for the first time the therapeutic agenda of happiness, personality integration, and emotional growth. By the late 1930s, marriage counselors estimated that two hundred thousand had sought and received guidance at marriage clinics. But most Americans had no contact with the profession and very likely even remained unaware that there was "a marriage problem." In other words, the "millions" that marriage counselors estimated could use marital guidance (estimated at 70 percent of the population) did not take advantage of such services.[100]

The profession's significance, however, does not lie simply in its immediate influence. Rather marriage counseling's historical and cultural significance lies in its new therapeutic agenda. This agenda turned psychological happiness into a national goal. It transformed seemingly personal issues into matters of public debate. In marriage, counselors saw the potential for public salvation or public disaster. They placed their hope for society in the reform of the personal sphere. Their faith lay in a science of personal relations that would unlock the secret of marriage and discover the techniques for producing happiness. Marriage counselors imagined society reaping vast social rewards from this engineering of individual happiness. They maintained, however, that society would benefit from the solving of personal problems only if it were organized along therapeutic lines. Such a society recognized the importance of the personal sphere and the value of psychological health. It also abandoned a policy of "rugged individualism," embracing instead a policy of guidance and counseling.

Marriage counseling made psychological knowledge and introspection hallmarks of middle-class identity and promised to place its science of personal relations in the service of class maintenance. The profession also promoted a therapeutic agenda that created new areas of gender difference. This new therapeutic regime elaborated the social and personal characteristics of happy wives and of women most likely to marry. It suggested that those women who submitted to their unequal position would be the most happily married and would contribute the most to society. Marriage counseling's therapeutic gospel also ascribed to women a new area of domestic responsibility, the psychological management of their domestic relations. The marriage-counseling profession's investment in the personal and psychological was therefore not merely individualistic, for it represented deep-seated gender and class interests.

4 WAR

The Soldier's Psyche

1941–1945

On 1 September 1939 Hitler invaded Poland. On 5 October he went to Warsaw to survey his victory. A few weeks later Russia invaded Finland. Though brave, Finland's small ski-patrol army of 200,000 ultimately proved no match for Russia's 1.5 million men. Finland surrendered in March, having lost 68,000 men. Even before Russia's victory was conclusive, Hitler ordered the invasion of Norway and Denmark. The Netherlands and Belgium were next, and in June France fell. Less than a year later Hitler invaded Russia with an army of 3.5 million men. This astonishing sequence of events took place with breathtaking speed.

At this time, when Europe was being engulfed by a military machine the likes of which the world had never seen, the U.S. Army was small and ill prepared. In 1940, for example, at the time that France fell, the U.S. Army had only 190,000 men, 10,000 fewer than Finland. America was in no position to engage, let alone defeat, a major military power. And Americans by and large liked it that way. America's present-day involvement all over the globe makes it easy to forget the strength of the nation's isolationist sentiment. Particularly after World War I, many Americans felt disillusioned with war. President Woodrow Wilson had promised in 1917 that the war would "make the world safe for democracy." In the attempt to meet that goal 18 million men worldwide had died, and there was no indication that the goal had been met. Many Americans were reluctant to get involved in Europe's problems again. Moreover, 1940 was a critical election year, and politicians were in no mood to draft their constituents' sons. So although George C. Marshall, President

Roosevelt's chief of staff, wanted desperately to correct the U.S. military's utter lack of preparedness, he was constrained by politics.

Marshall therefore had to proceed cautiously, but proceed he did, not just to expand the Army but to plan for total war. For this planning project Marshall chose Major Albert C. Wedemeyer as his point man. Wedemeyer had recently studied at the Kriegsakademie in Berlin and witnessed firsthand the Germans' burgeoning military machine, putting him in an excellent position to estimate what it would take for the Allies to defeat Germany. His starting assumption was that Hitler and his allies could field 400 divisions (divisions usually had about 15,000 men) by the end of 1943. Victory, he believed, would require a 2-to-1 margin. The British could provide 100 divisions, which meant that another 700 were needed. For every division of 15,000 put into the field, another 25,000 men were needed to supply it. Therefore, the military needed 700 × 40,000 (15,000 + 25,000), or 28 million men. Fighting strength was not the only concern, however. If too great a proportion of the population were taken, the economy might be severely damaged. Faculty members at the Industrial War College warned that at most 10 percent of the population could be diverted to fight.[1] At the time the United States had a population of approximately 135 million. Wedemeyer reasoned, therefore, that the country would have to settle for 13.5 million men and figure out how to win the war with fewer personnel than ideal. Marshall signed on to Wedemeyer's rough estimates, and military planners rushed to work out the details for obtaining everything from soldiers to blankets, binoculars, trucks, and tanks.

But top military planners were not the only ones on the march. Psychiatrists and psychologists too were organizing for total war. And like their military counterparts, they found the nation's soldiers unprepared. Indeed, the psychiatric staff for the entire military consisted of twenty-five psychiatrists. Creating their own kind of war cabinet, they began planning for the "psychological front." In the summer of 1940 the American Psychological Association sponsored a conference on government service, thinly veiling the anticipated military service. Members from the six national psychological organizations, representing three thousand professionals, were invited. Out of this conference came the emergency committee to plan and organize the psychological profession's response to U.S. entry into World War II. Four subcommittees were formed, on perceptual problems, military psychology, bibliography, and neurosis. The psychological profession also reoriented its journals to prepare for war. The prestigious *Psychological Bulletin,* for example, began a new section on military psychology. Most concretely, the majority of the profession registered with the hastily put together employment agency. More than three thousand psychological professionals registered with the National Roster of Scientific and Specialized Personnel, the agency designed to quickly and efficiently obtain key personnel for wartime jobs.

The psychological front created in World War II was unprecedented. Psychiatrists and psychologists served in seven theaters, nine service commands, and ten armies. They also served in 217 general hospitals, 196 station hospitals, and 91 evacuation hospitals. Indeed, 8 overseas general hospitals were devoted entirely to neuropsychiatry, and about the same number of station hospitals were devoted exclusively to combat exhaustion. Ninety-one psychiatrists were assigned directly to combat divisions. Finally, some of the fifty thousand medical officers who had received special psychological training also worked with psychiatric combat casualties.

The number of psychiatric casualties was similarly unprecedented. World War II brought 1 million psychiatric admissions to Army hospitals, compared with the approximately 100,000 cases of shell shock treated in World War I. Many more were treated outside of the hospital context. The working assumption was that for every four men wounded, one man would become a psychiatric casualty. In some instances the rate was much higher. During the first two months of the D-day campaign, for example, there was one psychiatric casualty for every two medical casualties.[2]

But the psychological work was unique in not only scale but also scope. Total war as it had never been conducted before radically expanded the reach of the therapeutic gospel, bringing it directly to millions of men and women who served their country during World War II. The extraordinary circumstance of the war allowed psychological professionals to put into practice what they had been envisioning for their discipline and clinical practice. What marriage researchers and counselors, for example, had only been able to hope for—that normal men and women would be required to learn the psychological processes of adjustment—psychological professionals implemented, indeed commanded. For a short period of time, 1941–45, the U.S. military made the therapeutic gospel an important element of its strategy, ensuring that millions of Americans, many for the first time, were exposed to its tenets.

New Thought advertisements for psychotherapeutic services in *Nautilus* magazine, 1898–1912.

Courtesy of the Burke Library, Union Theological Seminary.

GOD
IS
HERE.

I
AM
SOUL.

SPIRIT
IS THE ONLY
SUBSTANCE.

"ALL THINGS
ARE YOURS."

I RULE
THE BODY.

HEALTH
IS NATURAL.

MENTAL HEALING
IS SCIENTIFIC.

I AM
HEALED

Mental Suggestions from Henry Wood's popular self-help book, *Ideal Suggestions Through Mental Photography* (1893). Courtesy of the New York Public Library, New York.

Cover for November 1909 issue of *Nautilus,* a popular New Thought magazine.

Courtesy of the Burke Library, Union Theological Seminary.

Basket weaving as a therapeutic activity at the Bedford Reformitory for Women.

Photo from *An Experimental Study of Psychopathic Delinquent Women,* by Edith R. Spaulding (New York: Rand McNally, 1923)

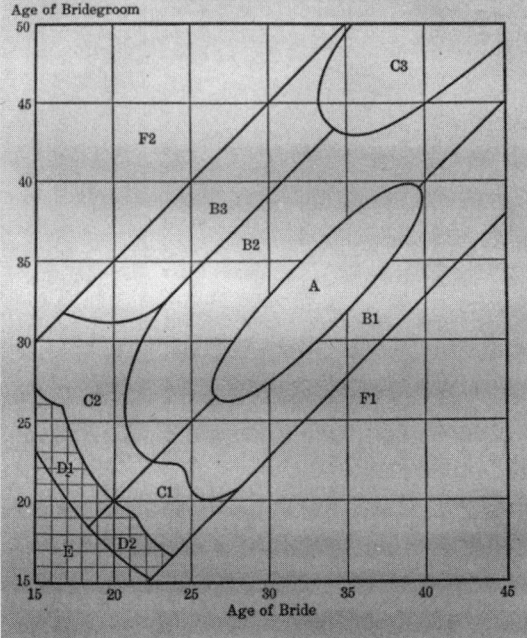

Correlation between the age of the bride and happiness.

Graph reprinted from Hornell Hart, *Chart for Happiness* (New York: Macmillan, 1940).

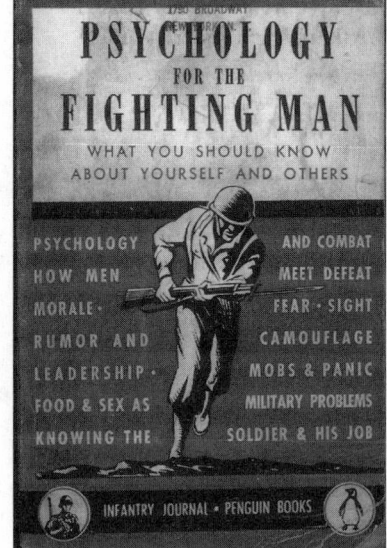

Cover for *Psychology for the Fighting Man* (1943).

Courtesy of the Oskar Deitholm Library.

ER SIGNAL: *When daily demands make you want to scream, "How much more can I take?"*

From "Have Your Reached Your Emotional Breaking Point?" *Cosmopolitan*, January 1957.

From "It's Good to Blow Your Top," *McCall's*, January 1950.

American housewife, *Reader's Digest*, January 1961.

Ask Yourself: Is Your Life Satisfying?

Health and temperament, job, friends and marriage all play a part in a full life. These questions will help you assess your achievement this past year. Omit the last five questions if you are single.

1. Are you usually happy and contented?
2. Does the future have real purpose (meaning) for you?
3. Is your life free from any serious frustration?
4. Do you look forward to each new day?
5. Are you in good physical health?

1. Do you plan ahead for greater work efficiency?
2. Are you more skilled at your job than last year?
3. Do you find increasing pleasure in your work?
4. Are you proud of your job?
5. Does its income cover your essential needs?

1. Are your social activities satisfying and rewarding?
2. Do you have more friends today than a year ago?
3. Have you improved at least one social skill?
4. Do you have someone in whom to confide?
5. Is your program of recreation balanced and complete?

1. Do you and your husband love each other?
2. Are you two free from financial strains?
3. Has your husband been a good companion?
4. Do you and he talk things over freely?
5. Is your marriage free from any serious disappointment?

Ideally all questions should be answered "Yes." A score of less than 4 in any group suggests a real handicap in that area. Your "No" answers can show you where to seek improvement in 1950.

Are You a Restless Wife?

After the first few years of marriage, some wives feel frustrated by restrictions and a lack of challenge. Is this your attitude? Be absolutely honest in answering these questions yes or no.

Are You:

1. Restless, and dissatisfied with life?
2. Bored by your household routine?
3. Envious of the freedom men have?
4. Very fond of lively, exciting parties?
5. Uncertain of your love for your husband?
6. Thinking more about tomorrow than today?
7. Reluctant or hesitant about making decisions?

Do you often feel that:

8. You are lonely and misunderstood?
9. Your husband is too settled?
10. You have more men than women friends?
11. Most marriages are not very happy?
12. You may have married too soon?
13. Life is passing you by?
14. You may have married the wrong man?

With four or fewer "yes" answers, you seem no more restless than the average wife. The higher your "yes" score, the more serious your maladjustment. If your score is five or more, you are neither very happy in your marriage nor in most of your close relationships. Though your husband may be partly responsible, your trouble is probably within yourself. Unless you can take a greater interest in your marriage and in your husband, you should seek professional help. To delay action is to court disaster.

Do You Enjoy Life?

Contentment comes from the spirit and attitude with which we face our environment rather than from circumstances alone. Your happiness depends far more on yourself than on others. Answer these questions yes or no in terms of what you think is true most of the time.

Do You:

1. Sometimes fear that people don't like you?
2. Often feel downcast and unwanted?
3. Think that you are unattractive?
4. Feel uneasy with new acquaintances?
5. Dread going to bed—and getting up?
6. Dislike your present living arrangements?
7. Worry excessively over small matters?
8. Usually wonder if your clothes become you?
9. Find your work dull and uninteresting?
10. Let others take advantage of you?
11. Have periods of feeling lonely and neglected?
12. Doubt that the future will be brighter?
13. Get upset and easily discouraged?
14. At times, think that nobody loves you?

If your "No" answers total ten or more, your happiness rating is as good as or better than that of the average woman between 20 and 40. If seven or fewer questions are answered "No," you are not getting the most out of life. Marriage will not solve your problem until you have changed your attitude if you are single, nor will divorce if you are married.

Dr. Mace, known both in this country and in England for his pioneer work in marriage counseling, is Professor of Human Relations at Drew University.

Is it possible to mistake anxiety for passion? In the second of his important series on love and marriage Dr. David R. Mace discusses this delicate problem between a husband and a wife

"He says if I loved him, I'd respond to him when he needs me. I say if he loved me, he'd be more sensitive to my moods and feelings"

Can a husband want too much love?

PUTTING Nancy down while she fumbled for her key, Anne opened the apartment door. A strange smell of burning assailed her nostrils. Fred swung around from the stove and faced her. In one swift glance she became aware of the tension in his body, the anger in his eyes. She saw too the blackened steak in the broiler, the spilled coffee on the floor.

Fred glared at her. His breathing was heavy, labored.

"So you've come at last! Where the hell have you been all this time?"

"I'm sorry, Fred. I took Nancy to see Mother. I figured we'd be back in good time to get your dinner. But Aunt Mildred was there, and you know what it's like trying to get away."

Fred's mouth set in a thin, tight line. "Just what I thought—gabbing at your mother's! Not looking at the clock! No need to hurry back to cook for your husband. Never mind the dope that earns the money to keep you and your kid in comfort—"

"Fred," she pleaded, "don't talk that way! Nancy is yours as much as mine!"

"That's what you tell them, is it?" He seized her shoulders and stared darkly into her eyes as if searching for something. "Well," he cried, (Continued on page 83)

From "Marriage Is a Private Affair," *McCall's*, June 1959.

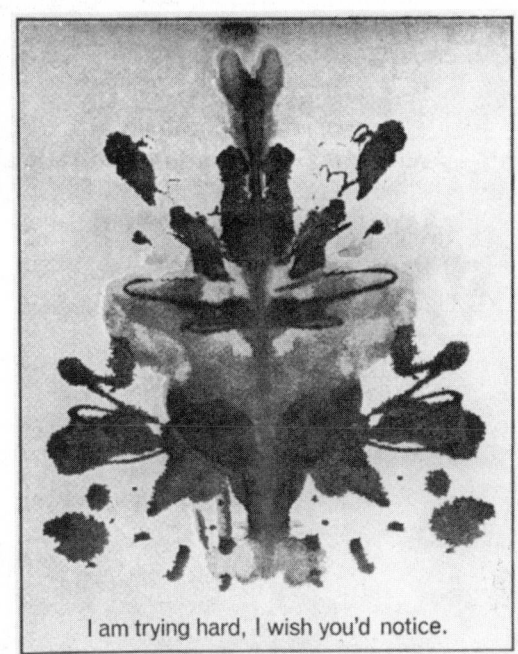

I am trying hard, I wish you'd notice.

The hang-up Rorschach greeting card by Sensitivity Inc.
From *Newsweek*, 7 September 1970.

Family members expressing their feelings through drawing. From *Psychology Today*, December 1967.

Drawing from a family
group-therapy session.
From *Psychology Today,*
December 1967.

Underwater session of twenty-four-hour nude encounter group.
From *Psychology Today,* June 1969.

Mood Mender, an antidepressent tea
made by Celestial Seasonings, Inc.

Psychological Professionals Make Their Case

Psychological professionals wanted to be responsible for all aspects of the psychological front. Military personnel, however, were not likely to simply hand over jurisdiction to those whose "science" they barely understood. Psychiatrists and psychologists would have to make their case. They began at the beginning, which was with induction. This was something of a tried-and-true argument because psychological professionals had been successful before in obtaining resources for induction. Nonetheless this was a new war and the case had to be made afresh. In any case, psychological professionals had something grander in mind this time. They were not simply interested in selection or rejection of the mentally unfit: they wanted to be in charge of the inductee's entire psyche.

To persuade top military leaders of the value of their services, psychiatrists and psychologists did not rely on one of their own. Instead, they turned to General John Pershing, leader of the American Expeditionary Force during World War I. His terse cablegram of July 1918 had said it all: "Prevalence of mental disorders in replacement troops recently received suggests urgent importance of intensive efforts in eliminating mentally unfit from organization of the new draft prior to departure from U.S."[3] If Pershing was dissatisfied with selection in World War I, a war in which about 4.5 million men served for less than two years in a limited region, then a war that would call upon 13.5 million men to fight for an extended period all over the world would require more and better psychological supervision.

By September 1940, when Congress, after long delays and near defeat, finally passed the Selective Service Act, mandating the first peacetime draft in U.S. history, psychiatrists had secured a firm but limited role in the selection process. Henry Stack Sullivan, a psychiatrist well known for his work on frustration and aggression, was appointed the psychiatric consultant to the Selective Service System. His first task was to deal with the manpower shortage. There were 6,403 local draft boards. Even if every available psychiatrist were put to work, there would be too few to directly supervise psychiatric screening. Instead, one psychiatrist was appointed to each of the 660 specially created medical advisory boards, which were to alert local draft boards to the "significance of mental and personality factors" in selection.[4] To ensure that this would be done well and uniformly, special two-day seminars were held in nine major cities around the country to train psychiatrists and psychologists in their duties.

Shortly after the bombing of Pearl Harbor, however, the Army abandoned the system of civilian local draft boards and created regional induction centers directly under Army control. Psychological professionals welcomed this change, for they wanted to do more than advise; they wanted to be directly involved in selection. They got that opportunity at the 108 induction centers. There they faced the problem of how a relatively small number of psychological professionals could determine in a short period of time who should be inducted and who rejected. World War I provided only a limited model, for then their task had been limited to identifying the "mentally defective" and those suffering from psychosis. The now infamous Army intelligence tests had been widely used to determine "mental capacity" during World War I, leading the Army to reject about 700,000 men as "defective" and 70,000 as psychotic or psychopathic.[5]

In World War II, however, psychiatrists and psychologists approached the problem of the inductee's psyche with a much broader mission. They sought not only to reject those with psychological disorders but to induct psychologically healthy men. This new, higher standard led to a expansion of diagnostic categories; thus began the diagnostic mushrooming that would characterize the postwar period. For example, they added "psychoneurosis" to the list of illnesses to be screened for. This was a remarkable expansion. It meant that the relatively ordinary disorder "neurosis" was to be included in Army screening. Exactly how psychoneurosis became an officially recognized illness is not known, but it involved a lot of explaining à la Freud. Apparently, psychiatrists dazzled or confused top military brass with such phrases as "the unconscious," "the ego," and "neurotic reaction."

Having psychoneurosis officially recognized as an illness by the Army created a number of unanticipated problems, the biggest problem being that too many men were rejected as a result. Another problem was that the draft itself apparently tended to bring out psychoneurosis. Simply commanding people to give up their civilian lives and join the military caused an intense emotional pressure that brought men's neurotic tendencies to the surface. Such false positives contributed to the high rejection rates.

Pressure from the military to find some way of reigning in the category "psychoneuroses" happened to mesh well with psychological professionals' own sense of the current policy's limitations. They complained, for example, that Army regulations "totally ignored any potential restorability or prompt recovery";[6] the Army assumed that men who suffered from neuroses could not become good soldiers. This, they believed, was not only bad policy, because it resulted in high rejection rates, but also clinically inaccurate, because "men who exhibit isolated neurotic traits are not necessarily neurotic to the extent that they cannot become effective soldiers."[7] This analysis, of course, opened the door for the Army's involvement in psychological treatment. Finally, psychiatrists and psychologists complained that current Army induction regulations were unsatisfactory because they did not take into account the psychological effects of labeling. A diagnosis of "psychoneurosis" often had a "traumatic" effect on the rejectee. Changes in Army regulations eventually reflected all of these concerns. A War Department Technical Bulletin, for example, avoided the psychological effects of labeling by eliminating the requirement that each neuropsychiatric rejectee be given a specific diagnosis, permitting psychiatrists to simply record, "Not suited for military service." It also rescinded Army regulations urging that caution be exercised to prevent "all individuals predisposed . . . to psychoneurosis from entering the service."[8] Neurotics too would now be called to serve their country. They suffered from an illness, but one that was too normal and common to eliminate them from the induction pool.

Ultimately, 15 million draftees passed through the induction process, most of them encountering psychological logic for the first time.[9] Draftees encountered this logic in the form of psychological tests and the psychiatric examination. At induction centers, for example, draftees in large groups took the Neuropsychiatric Screening Adjunct, a psychological test designed "to provide a means of rapidly selecting those registrants with indications of psychoneurotic tendencies" or those "who indicate personality conflicts."[10] This test increased efficiency because it identified those recruits who needed to take an additional psychiatric examination. The PULHES rating system—for Physical capacity or stamina, Upper extremity, Lower extremity, Hearing defects, Eyes, and emotional Stability—used at Army induction centers, was also designed to increase efficiency. This rating system evaluated and recorded pertinent information about the recruit, including his psyche. Each recruit was given a PULHES score, and every job had a minimum PULHES. Psychiatrists were in charge of S, or emotional stability.

To determine each inductee's S level, an examining psychiatrist asked a number of standard questions, including "How are you?" "Have you any complaints?" "Do you have any worries?" "Have you ever had a nervous breakdown?" "How do you feel about the war?" and "How do you feel about coming into the Army?" The examiner was looking for "the total assets and liabilities of the inductee as a prospective soldier."[11] Each exam was supposed to last fifteen minutes. Army psychiatrists reported, however, that they generally determined a soldier's S level in five to ten minutes. Psychiatrists rated inductees on a scale from 1 to 4: 1 meaning that the recruit had no psychological disorders; 2, mild, transient psychoneurotic reactions; 3, mild but chronic psychoneuroses; and 4, psychosis.[12] Using various sorting devices as well as the psychiatric examination, the Army rejected close to 2 million men for psychiatric reasons. Those who were accepted were sent on to basic training.

Basic training was a World War II invention. All inductees, whether they eventually became gunners, tankers, bakers, mechanics, or clerks, underwent the same fundamental training. The philosophy behind standardized universal training was that total war required that soldiers be interchangeable and therefore each soldier had to learn the Army's basic mission. Lesley J. McNair, who was in charge of basic training, explained this mission to all future soldiers on a national radio broadcast: "It is the avowed aim of the army to make killers of you all."[13]

Accomplishing this most fundamental of aims required time, money, and suitable facilities. The tents and fairgrounds used to teach World War I trainees close-order drill for a few weeks before they were sent to the front would not do. Permanent modern housing was needed for millions of inductees, who were to be thoroughly trained for fast and mobile fighting. McNair arranged for the purchase of hundreds of thousands of acres of land so that trainees would have ample room to hone their skills. The Army also hired builders, such as Arthur Levitt, later famous for his creation of Levittowns, the first planned communities using interchangeable materials and design, to build suitable facilities.

Marshall demanded that in addition to a rigorous basic-training program, men gain fighting experience by training with their units and divisions. He had pioneered this new practical vision of training in the 1930s, when he headed the Infantry School at Camp Benning, Georgia. His method of training seemed to rely heavily on the ideas of the famous educator John Dewey, for Marshall wanted infantry officers to learn experientially and cope with the difficulties of real warfare. To simulate battle conditions, he purposely sowed confusion. Marshall was notorious for sending men out on assignments with ambiguous instructions and poor or even inaccurate maps. As Chief of Staff, he institutionalized this approach to training on an even more ambitious scale, ordering that mock battles involving entire divisions be fought. At Monterey Bay in California, for example, the military practiced its first amphibious assault, landing 10,000 men and their equipment and supplies with the goal of capturing San Francisco. The Army also turned the entire state of Louisiana into a major mock war zone, pitting two divisions with a total of 400,000 men against each other for possession of the state.[14]

Army psychiatrists and psychologists, however, found this program inadequate in a crucial respect. To be sure, Marshall's basic training and mock battles developed soldiers' fighting skills and tested equipment, communication, and logistical systems of supply. However, they did nothing to train the new recruit's psyche. Without emotional preparation, psychiatrists and psychologists maintained, the soldier would not be able to carry out his military assignment and the Army's training efforts would be wasted. They suggested that they would be able to fill the void. Doing so, however, presented them with an unusual mission, one at complete odds with their peacetime role. Modern civilian society tended to require individuals to repress their aggressive instincts and channel their energies into nondestructive projects. Psychiatrists and psychologists themselves were handmaidens to this process. But war had different requirements. The mind-set of the ideal citizen in peacetime was not that of a soldier. The soldier's mission was to kill, and the psychologist's mission would therefore be to help the soldier to kill, to release the violent instincts that society had formerly sought to repress. As psychiatrists and psychologists themselves described it, their new task would be to facilitate "emotional regression."

In practice, however, the aims of psychological professionals and those in charge of training were not always so harmonious. Sometimes, in fact, they were in direct opposition. What made for good military training was not always good for the trainee's psyche. The Army turned out to be a breeding ground for emotional turmoil and insecurity. Its impersonality and regimentation entailed "the loss of personal identity and awareness of Self as a unique person" and could be "devastating" for the new recruit.[15] Strict discipline and hierarchy also took their psychological toll. Constantly taking orders, for example, led some men "to be overwhelmed by feelings of humiliation" and "to feel that their personal integrity is threatened."[16] As a result, many trainees came to view their superiors as "dangerous persons" and felt tremendous anxiety around them. The authoritarian atmosphere of the Army could turn a "normal" trainee into an emotional basket case, suffering from depression, worry, and low self-esteem.

Army psychiatrists and psychologists agreed that the transition from civilian to military life was "traumatic." As one psychiatrist explained, "Nowhere so much as in the Army is the individual required to make so many major readjustments in his whole living." Hence, "dynamic alterations in the personality of the soldier were necessary in order to effect the adjustment from civilian to military life."[17] So intense and difficult was Army adjustment that it was compared to the crisis of adolescence.[18] And like the adolescent, the new recruit needed special support.

During the first year of the Army's new basic-training program little was done to help the soldier deal with the adjustment to life in the Army or his feelings of anxiety and fear. The psychic costs of Army life went unrecognized, and no "psychological aid" was offered. Sometimes, in fact, basic-training instructors exacerbated the situation with what Army psychiatrists and psychologists derisively referred to as the "dead ducks" training method. This was a method of training that used fear as a motivator. It was first noticed in military classes dealing with self-protection. In these classes, barking instructors regularly informed trainees that if they failed to protect themselves, they would be "dead ducks."[19] This untherapeutic approach not only did not help but according to psychological professionals made things worse.

Criticizing Army methods, however, was a dangerous way to lobby for more therapeutic policies. Psychiatrists and psychologists had to show that their main interest was in contributing to the Army's success rather than in assuaging the soldier's psyche. They did so by suggesting that psychological expertise could shed light on familiar and yet intractable Army problems. It seemed that Army psychiatrists and psychologists had a new explanation for every problem. Homesickness became "separation neurosis," drunkenness afflicted those "in whom the alcoholism symbolically represents a craving for the original nursing bottle,"[20] and goldbricking, the Army's term for looking busy without doing any work, was not simply laziness but "a psychological mechanism which enables a man to avoid loss of self-esteem" by "disassociating" himself from the job.[21]

Army psychiatrists and psychologists also maintained that they could explain the Army's sick-call problem. The reason that so many men reported to sick call was that some men expressed their anxiety physically, as aches and pains. This was a particularly difficult type of adjustment problem since most medical officers remained "entirely ignorant of the mechanism by which chronic emotional tension at an unconscious level may produce major physiologic changes which interfere with the normal function of body processes."[22] Ignorance, however, was not the only explanation offered for doctors' unsympathetic treatment of such trainees. There were also "unconscious" motivations. Psychological professionals predicted that if physicians verbalized these motivations, they would go something like, "If I can't get away with it, I certainly won't let him do so," and at a deeper level, "The lucky devil! I wish I could."[23] If the Army was to avoid the significant manpower shortages caused by this problem, it would have to sensitize medical personnel not only to the existence of this form of anxiety in soldiers but perhaps also to their own unconscious refusal to acknowledge it.

In addition to explaining familiar problems, Army psychiatrists and psychologists also discovered a host of new problems that only they, with their special expertise, could explain and solve. Their psychological theories allowed them to explain such diverse phenomenon as griping, homosexual buffoonery, "reversion to adolescent erotic attitudes," "use of taboo words" or cursing, homesickness, and accident-proneness. They even offered interpretations of mimicry of superiors, which instructors might interpret as simple insubordination, when actually the trainee who imitated his superior was wracked by "doubt about his own personal worth" and plagued by the question whether he was really an inferior person. He suffered from "status deprivation," and mimicking his superiors provided an indirect outlet for the trainee's feelings of inferiority.[24]

Psychiatrists and psychologists believed that soldiers' various problems in adjusting to the Army stemmed from emotional immaturity. The soldier who was extremely sensitive to "devaluation" had a strong need to be recognized. This "infantile desire" for affection and attention explained many of the Army's "behavior problems." As one psychiatrist put it, "Scratch an adult and one finds a child."[25] Promoting an inner-child theory of the problems of military life, psychological professionals found that a sea of emotional immaturity surrounded them.

Interestingly, these perceptions of arrested emotional development were heavily filtered through the lens of gender. Women's "infantile desires" and "inner needs" were deemed to be quite different from men's, and Army life traumatized them in different ways. Women served in a large range of capacities during World War II. They did many of the same jobs that men did, as well as jobs almost exclusively reserved for women. The Army determined that half of its jobs could be done by women, though it paid them less to do these jobs.

Most prominently, 140,000 women, 4,000 of whom were black, served in the Women's Auxiliary Army Corps, or WAAC, which later became the Women's Army Corps, or WAC. Women also served in the Women's Air Force Service Pilots (WASP), flying noncombat missions; with the Navy in Women Accepted for Volunteer Emergency Service (WAVES), in the Coast Guard; and in the Marine Corps's Women's Reserve. Like men, women underwent basic training and also received special training, ultimately working as decontamination experts in the Ordinance Corps, medical technicians in the Medical Corps, photographers and cryptanalysts in the Signal Corps, supply officers in the Quartermaster Corps, and in various other capacities. Women also served in the Nurse Corps, whose more than 70,000 women provided medical care to troops all over the world. Though not to the same degree, women overseas, like men, worked under difficult and dangerous circumstances and faced the horrors of war.

One might expect psychiatrists and psychologists to have viewed the dangers, stresses, and violence of war as the primary threat to the psychological health of women just as they considered it to be to the psychological health of men. Instead, however, they viewed women's psychological difficulties as stemming from the fact that Army life deprived women "of various means of expressing their femininity."[26] The organization, strictures, and culture of Army life threatened women's sense of themselves as women. Army food, for example, affected women's psyches. Women's eating habits reflected "a feminine attitude," and therefore it was psychologically difficult for them to eat meals presented in an unattractive way.[27] Housing too created a problem for the sensitive female. Army barracks and their lack of privacy were found to be "distressing" for many women. Added to the problem of food and housing was that of dress. Army uniforms not only did little to reduce women's frustration and unhappiness but actually increased it. This, again, was explained by gender difference: "Whereas men are uncomfortable if they dress differently from other men, women are unhappy if they dress like other women." Women felt the effects of uniformity "more acutely when they could not even wear skirts."

Nurses suffered from similar types of problems. Like WACs, they often found themselves in outposts with few amenities. Many nurses experienced "handicaps in attending to their personal wants." They had difficulty laundering, lacked beauty parlor equipment, and could not wear evening clothes. Fortunately, however, they took these hardships with "good graces," and "psychiatric breakdowns among nurses, at least those labeled diagnostically, were low." Unfortunately, escaping from entanglements with men psychologically unscathed was far less common.

Apparently, romance had special implications for women since their passion disturbed their psychological equanimity in unique ways. So serious were women's distinct emotional conflicts in the India-Burma theater that Lieutenant Colonel Margaret Craighill was dispatched there to report on them. Craighill described women as suffering from special "inner conflicts" regarding their attraction to men. "Men are apparently better able to partition off their lives adequately so that they do not as readily become deeply or permanently involved emotionally," wrote Craighill. "They are therefore less liable to lasting psychological trauma from transient attachments."[28]

Women's special psychological burdens and their feminine nature should have led the Army to be particularly careful in selecting women. Unfortunately, the opposite apparently was true. The selection of women was handled poorly. Why this was the case is not clear. Perhaps it was because women were a kind of afterthought militarily. When leaders like Marshall and Wedemeyer sat down to plan for total war, their first preoccupation was to find men to fight and command. Furthermore, women were not inducted; and since their numbers were so much smaller, psychological professionals were not involved in the screening process. Psychologists and psychiatrists would ascribe women's high rate of maladjustment in WAC, for example, to their being accepted "without even a semblance of a psychiatric examination."[29] They found this practice particularly troubling because WACs, they believed, needed even more psychological scrutiny than male inductees.

Psychological professionals saw women as less predictable than men and therefore believed that screening was even more important in their case. They also believed that better selection was needed for WACs because of the high age limit and women's special motivations for joining the Army. Initially, women up to the age of fifty were eligible for WAC. Army psychiatrists and psychologists thought that the onset of menopause, which they believed caused emotional instability and "rigidity of personality," increased women's likelihood of becoming psychiatric casualties. Women also needed more screening because of the particular pool from which WAC drew. WAC was believed to attract women with an "unconscious masculine identification." Given the psychological profession's focus on the difficulties Army life posed for women because of their feminine nature, one might expect women with an "unconscious masculine identification" to have been viewed as particularly well suited to Army life. In fact, however, such women were thought to be prime candidates for psychological breakdowns. It seems that women, whether feminine or masculine, were not meant for Army life.

Moreover, psychiatrists and psychologists found that the presence of women created added problems of adjustment for men. They noted that even though women contributed substantially to the war effort, soldiers had difficulty recognizing their contribution. Even when trainees did so consciously, they often "denied its value emotionally." Many soldiers believed that women were in the Army to serve men and were grateful to the Army for "providing a female contingent." This, psychiatrists and psychologists explained, was a narcissistic response stemming in part from the "need for an antidote to the unconscious, vague fears of impotency that exist in a strictly one-sex group."[30] Whatever its roots, men's narcissism created certain tensions between the sexes and additional adjustment problems.

These difficulties created by men's narcissism, which psychological professionals delicately refer to as "unpleasant pressures," placed psychiatrists and psychologists in the role of chaperone. Men's narcissism often turned into what today would be called sexual harassment. Women were often required to attend social functions, and sometimes the requirement involved more than simply their attendance. Such pressure could be emotionally painful. To address the special dilemmas women faced, orientation courses were established that taught women "how much legitimate authority a 'superior' officer had" and "with whom they could demand counsel when official demands were excessive."[31] Relations between the sexes therefore became yet another area of maladjustment.

Whatever form adjustment problems took and whether they were experienced by men or women, it was clear that they had to be reckoned with. Indeed, many psychological professionals went so far as to conclude that only "the strong, unusually well-adjusted personalities are capable of effecting the transition between civilian and military life without confusion and maladjustment at some point."[32] It was the pervasiveness of psychological problems that provided ammunition for psychological professionals' argument for fundamental changes in the training program.

Yet in 1940–41 convincing top military commanders to put basic training on a psychologically sound basis was not easy. Germany's blitzkrieg through Europe and its devastating invasion of Russia had left American military commanders contemplating the awesome size, speed, and sophistication of Germany's military strength, not the American trainee's psyche. American psychiatrists and psychologists responded to this indifference by calling attention to a "therapeutic gap." Germany, they pointed out, understood the importance of the soldier's psyche. In its army, regiment colonels personally congratulated each soldier on his birthday. The German officer was also expected "to look into the eyes of his men to detect personal problems."[33] Americans, Army psychologists and psychiatrists insisted, deserved no less personal attention. In fact, they would receive much, much more.

One of the first places the new inductee learned about the attention he was to receive was on his barracks bulletin board at basic training, where he read the following announcement:

> There are many men who have personal problems and grievances. . . . Should any man have a personal problem or difficulty or grievance, on which he needs advice or assistance, he is encouraged to obtain permission from the first sergeant to see the company commander. Some men will frequently prefer to talk to an experienced enlisted man before or instead of presenting their troubles to the company commander. To make this possible, an experienced man has been carefully selected in this barracks as an advisor. He has been selected because of his knowledge of soldiers' problems and his ability to give sound advice; he will be glad to talk to you. . . . His name is ————.[34]

The Army's Adviser Program attempted to provide millions of trainees with an outlet for their psychological stresses and anxieties. It was a mass system to deal with the problems of individual soldiers. The tradition of the personal adviser begun by men like Phineas P. Quimby and institutionalized in the schools by figures like the visiting teacher was fundamentally broadened to include all servicemen during World War II.

To ensure that this assembly-line psychological aid was provided swiftly and efficiently, advisers underwent uniform training. They learned about typical psychological problems and special therapeutic techniques for handling them, such as "sympathetic listening." The Army provided standard forms for reporting on trainees' personal problems. These forms emphasized brevity. In space allowing two-sentence responses advisers were expected to answer such questions about the advisee as "How does he get along with others?" "What does he do with his free time?" and "Does he mix easily?" Finally, advisers learned about confidentiality and the "necessity of holding inviolate any confidential information that is given them." This directive appears to have been only a prohibition against sharing information with advisees, for advisers were required to bring trainees' psychological problems to the attention of the psychiatric director of the Adviser Program. In fact the Army expected psychiatrists to meet regularly with advisers to discuss not only trainees' problems but also advisers' handling of those problems. Supervision too was standardized.

The Adviser Program was designed to help the soldier deal with the many difficult feelings and personal problems that might affect him or her during the first seventeen weeks in the Army. The impetus for the program was the general sense that without concern for "the ultimate worth of the human personality" military victory could not be counted on. More specifically, however, psychological professionals believed that there was an ingrained indifference on the part of noncommissioned officers toward the personal problems of their men. Too often officers dismissed "as trivia the problems that to the raw recruit are of paramount importance." Since providing every soldier with a psychiatrist was not feasible, an adviser was provided instead.

Many commanding officers objected to the Adviser Program. Psychological professionals, however, viewed those who objected as unable to appreciate the benefits of a therapeutically organized approach to basic training. One officer whom psychiatrists and psychologists described as "notorious" for his "indifference to the personal problems of men in his control" reportedly said, "We do not need advisers here. We've got He men in our company. It's a Girl-Scout idea and anyhow I never heard of it before." To designers of the Adviser Program this officer's statement indicated not only that he did not understand the program but also that he did not understand that men "can be better soldiers to the degree that they are whole and adjusted human beings."[35]

Such failings on the part of commanding officers were all too common, and Army psychiatrists and psychologists resolved to raise officers' consciousness about the importance of personal problems and soldiers' psychological well-being. In this they had the support of the Army, which required all officers to take a mini-course on personal adjustment problems. The six-hour lecture course covered six topics: the personality structure of the normal soldier, specific factors of stress in the Army affecting adjustment, sources of soldier motivation, the causes of nervous breakdowns, signs and symptoms of poor mental health, and measures to maintain mental health in command. Officers were taught that logistics, strategy, and weapons were insufficient to win the war; officers also needed a thorough understanding of "the psychology of the fighting man." Lecturers presented officers with examples of the types of psychological problems they might have to face: Private Hank White, who has gone AWOL; Pfc. Jim Jones, who has "suddenly become seclusive and won't talk"; Sergeant Rod Smith, who "is so hardboiled that other men dislike him"; and Private Joe Danks, who "constantly reports to sick call."[36]

Another way the Army sought to raise officers' consciousness was by providing instruction in the psychology of leadership. The officer needed to understand that he "became the symbolical father of his group." The enlisted men would look to him for help with their emotional problems in the way "every child seeks satisfaction from his father." It was therefore imperative that the officer met his men's needs so that he would be "supported against personality disturbances." He had to get to know each of his men personally, particularly "something about their home situations and problems."[37] The flip side of this highly therapeutic approach to leadership was its disciplinary goals. In return for meeting men's emotional needs, officers would get obedience. To achieve this kind of patriarchal authority, however, was not so easy; both rebellious sons and inadequate father figures upset the ideal psychodynamic.

Army psychiatrists and psychologists were so concerned about the problem of inadequate father figures that they insisted on changing the procedures of officer selection. The Army, they claimed, was old-fashioned if not downright "unscientific" in the way officers were selected. Indeed, psychological professionals ridiculed the Army for relying on such qualities as dash, endurance, and courage. Not only were these qualities abstract and therefore meaningless but they failed to take psychodynamics into account. In the view of psychological professionals, "the officer candidate should have a strong ego, one that can hold the superego within bounds and direct the subliminary energies of the id along constructive lines." For the candidate to be able to do this, that is, he had to have resolved the oedipal conflict! Of course, which candidates had achieved such resolution could only be determined by those "who have a daily traffic with the unconscious." Those who had such experience did indeed play an important role in officer selection. Army psychiatrists and psychologists, for example, screened applicants for Officer Candidate School. They also evaluated candidates in training. At the U.S. Coast Guard Academy, for example, more than four thousand candidates were evaluated psychologically for their leadership abilities. Whether their evaluations, which included psychological tests and usually one or two interviews lasting ten to twenty minutes, determined which men had resolved the oedipal conflict cannot be known, but it was these kinds of improvements in selection and officer training that closed the "therapeutic gap."[38]

The gap was also diminished by the Army's effort to raise the inductee's consciousness about mental health and the problems of adjustment. The Army embarked on a massive educational campaign that took several forms. First, it commissioned the writing of a pop psychology book, *Psychology for the Fighting Man*. This book, which was distributed to more than 9 million men, sought to explain to the average soldier what feelings and emotions he was likely to encounter in the Army and how to handle them. The Army also created the *Mack and Mike* booklet about two cartoon characters, Mack, who adjusts poorly to Army life, and Mike, who adjusts well. Lieutenant Colonel R. Robert Cohen, who created the booklet, explained that he came up with the idea because he realized that the ordinary soldier had difficulty pronouncing, let alone spelling, words like *resentment, emotion, brooding, fear,* and *rage*.

To explain such concepts the Army also relied on the more traditional method of lectures, which were to "be illustrated by thumbnail case histories or examples of specific instances."[39] All trainees were required to take the Army's mini-course on personal adjustment. The purpose of this course, according to War Department Circular 48, was "to give all enlisted men an understanding of personal adjustment problems in the Army and a healthy viewpoint in the handling of emotions and feelings by the soldier."[40] The first lecture, "Personal Adjustment Problems in the Army," informed the new trainee that there were substantial differences between civilian and military life and that making the transition could be psychologically trying. The lecturer advised that the trainee be patient, make friends, and "realize that many other men are having just as difficult a time getting used to things as you are." The trainee was also told about the problems of homesickness and loneliness. Sublimation was explained. The trainee had to wait until the second lecture, however, to find out "how a man reacts when he runs into one of these difficulties" and how they "affect his feelings and thoughts."

Lecture 2, "Emotions and Feelings and How to Handle Them," informed the trainee that worry, anxiety, feelings of resentment and irritability, loss of self-confidence, depression, self-consciousness, feeling lonely, or wanting to get away from people were all natural. He was also told, however, that certain reactions to such feelings would be inappropriate. No trainee was to lie down on the job, malinger, or go AWOL. Understanding his emotional reactions would, he was informed, help him avoid such behaviors. The trainee therefore was taught about the relationship between bodily functions and emotions and about such key emotions as fear and resentment. About fear, for example, trainees learned that it was an emotion and had many causes. On the one hand, there was the fear of bodily injury and death. On the other hand, there was the fear of being helpless or alone, the fear of the unknown, the fear of being laughed at or disliked, the fear of being a coward, or the fear of doing something wrong. Trainees were not to fight their fear but to admit it because such an admission was the first step toward overcoming it. They were urged to talk about their fear—to a friend, an adviser, a doctor at the dispensary, or their company commander.

The final lecture, "Healthy Viewpoint toward Being in the Service," combined propaganda, both American and enemy, with principles of mental health. Trainees received handouts of exemplary German and Japanese propaganda for the purpose of convincing them that America's enemies were worth fighting against. This perspective was considered "healthy." Conversely, it was considered unhealthy to leave the war unexplained. Therefore, in lecture 3 trainees were told the war had to be fought. Army psychiatrists and psychologists commented that this was done "not to be 'intellectual,' but because it is a fundamental necessity in being able to handle the stresses and strains a soldier is bound to encounter." It was considered important for men to be forewarned about the feelings they would have toward the Army. To prepare their psyches, trainees learned that their job was a "tough" one, involving much "unpleasantness." They conceded that "the average man who is used to civilian life cannot be expected to enjoy it." And though by participating in the fight he could avoid feeling "unhappy and guilty about not being in [it]", much of the time he "must expect to feel tired, bored, worried, and fed up." Informing trainees of the "realities" of war and preparing them emotionally was believed to be necessary for the development of emotional commitment to the war effort.[41]

That at times there might be a conflict between these two goals seems not to have occurred to psychological professionals. Apparently, they did not notice that misinformation was being used at least as often as information to emotionally prepare trainees. For example, men were told that "combat is not nearly as dangerous or frightening as most men think" and that the "worst part is not the danger and bloodshed; it is the mud, the fatigue, the cold, the food, the loneliness, the waste, and the petty annoyances." For men to cathect to the war, the nature of their sacrifice had to be somewhat obscured and they had to "think positively" about their participation in it. To help them accomplish this aim, as lecture 3 explained, the Army had devised a special "orientation hour." Once a week one hour of basic training was reserved for the discussion of the war and soldiers' feelings about it. Trainees who needed more than an hour were encouraged to make use of the Adviser Program. There were also the mental-hygiene consultation services, later known as mental-hygiene units (MHUs).

MHUs, located at Army training camps, provided psychological outpatient care to trainees, significantly extending the war's psychological front. In World War I treatment was limited to psychiatric battle casualties. By contrast, in World War II MHUs extended treatment to the casualties of training, who suffered not from war wounds but from the psychological pressures of Army life. In addition, they treated those who came to the Army in less than full psychological health or those with personal problems that erupted once they were in the Army. As one psychiatrist explained, "Comparatively few men came into the Army or remained any length of time without being troubled by personal problems."[42] To help trainees with these problems, MHUs provided psychotherapy.

The Army embarked on this unusual experiment because psychological professionals convinced military leaders that it was the solution to the manpower shortage. Hospitals had become repositories for those men unwanted by company commanders or dispensary doctors. The easiest way to rid oneself of a difficult or inefficient soldier was to send the man to the hospital, where at the very least a man might be warehoused for the length of time it would take the medical and psychiatric staff to make a diagnosis and recommendation for disposition. Overflowing hospitals as well as the Army's desperate need to conserve manpower led to calls for a new approach. Army psychiatrists and psychologists suggested outpatient psychological care. Psychological treatment would not only save hospital beds but also increase soldier retention rates. In this unprecedented experiment soldiers received both individual and group therapy. To be sure, their therapy was brief by today's standards: a soldier might have only one session or at most be seen for a few weeks.

In addition to limiting time, the Army set definite limits on the goals of treatment. The Army prohibited treatment that did not benefit the Army. Thus, for example, only those patients with a "correctable maladjustment" could be seen at MHUs. Once again, the goal had to be to help men return as quickly as possible to their training so that they could be sent off to war. Of course, Army psychiatrists and psychologists continuously pointed out that there was a direct relationship between solving the soldier's psychological problem and the Army's problems. Individual mental health meant national strength. They also pointed out that the Army could not afford to let minor maladjustments become major psychological crises. Psychotherapy was the way to avert such a disaster.

While Army psychiatrists and psychologists hoped that those who needed psychological help would come to them voluntarily, more often than not they came because they were ordered to do so by their company commander, the dispensary, the provost marshal, the judge advocate, or the chaplain. Trainees sent to MHUs suffered from problems that "prevented them from doing their utmost toward the war effort."[43] Before they received treatment, they were examined extensively to determine why they were unable to fulfill their responsibilities. The MHU's entire "clinical team"—psychiatrists, clinical psychologists, and military social workers—set to work to uncover the psychological sources of trainees' problems. At Drew Field, in Tampa, Florida, for example, the MHU had a staff of fourteen; the director, who was a psychiatrist, ten military social workers, and three clinical psychologists. A trainee was first seen by the psychiatric social worker, who took the trainee's case history. The social worker asked about the trainee's childhood development as well as about his or her medical, scholastic, occupational, and legal history; the trainee was also questioned about his or her sociosexual development. Finally, the social worker made general observations about the trainee's attitude, manner, emotions, interpersonal relationships, and in the case of women, appearance.

The case history was then forwarded to the unit's clinical psychologist. Although clinical psychologists sometimes did counseling, their work more often centered around diagnosis. They conducted psychological interviews and interpreted psychological tests. Among the most common tests they administered were the Rorschach test, the Thematic Apperception Test, the Minnesota Personality Test, and Gestalt drawing tests. The Rorschach test was often used to determine "areas which may be positively affected by psychotherapy."[44] The Thematic Apperception Test diagnosed underlying emotional conflicts as well as "the kinds of attitudes and relationships which the patient has to various persons, towards being in the Army and occasionally toward his own problem." Finally, the tests helped psychologists determine who would most likely benefit from psychotherapy.[45]

What makes the psychological tests of World War II so remarkable is their broad diagnostic aim. Unlike in World War I, when psychological tests were used to measure mental capacity and identify "defects," in World War II the goal was to uncover the "total personality" and each individual's underlying emotional conflicts. The tests themselves reflect this open-ended goal. For example, the Tender Emotional Inquiry, a projective sentence-completion test, sought to ascertain the soldier's fears, worries, associations, and even sexual fantasies. These were elicited by "free association." Psychologists instructed soldiers to complete certain sentences with the first thought that came to mind and to let their responses "be an expression of your real feelings":

> I wanted to know ———; I feel ———; At bedtime ———; Army food ———; My worst ———; Back home ———; I regret ———; The best ———; Other people usually———; If my mother ———; What puzzles me ———; If I had my way ———; Most sergeants ———; Other men ———; My nerves ———; My childhood ———; My greatest fear ———; My best friends ———; The most dangerous ———; I suffer ———; My father used to ———; My hardest job ———; The men in my company ———; My strongest ———; A wife ———; The happiest time ———; My great hope ———; The only trouble ———; I am very ———; This war ———; I secretly ———; Most girls ———; Today, I ———.

Clinical psychologists considered such tests critical diagnostic tools. In one case, for example, a soldier's answers on the Tender Emotional Inquiry helped the psychologist to determine that the soldier suffered from sexual psychopathy. His most incriminating answers included the following: "I feel ——— lousy"; "In bed ——— a young man's fancy"; "A woman——— is only good for one thing"; "If only ——— I were out of the Army"; "This war ——— is pointless." According to the clinical psychologist, the responses "show impulsivity, an anti-social attitude, indifference to social values, and abnormality in respect to sex concepts."[46] This apparently open-and-shut case did not require further testing.

Clinical psychologists were as quick to make judgments based on other types of personality tests. Rorschach tests used on suspected malingerers, for example, produced equally conclusive results. Patterned responses, including misunderstanding test instructions, few distinct responses, qualification of responses, refusal to elaborate on responses, long reaction time, and desire to know why the test was being given, separated malingerers from nonmalingerers. For example, when questioned about inkblots, malingerers typically and repeatedly gave such answers as "I don't know," "It's an Inkblot," or "Doesn't look like anything to me." Other signs of malingering included the tendency to respond with the same answer to different cards or to partially reject a statement by "loading it with qualifications." Thus, a malingerer would always begin with such qualifying words as "It might be" or "It looks to me like, perhaps." Or he or she might respond in the form of a question, such as "A ———?" or "Could it be a ———?" Test givers found this to be an indication of a "tendency to hedge or refusal to commit oneself." This refusal was particularly noticeable when test takers were asked whether an animal they saw in an inkblot was dead or alive. A malingerer frequently responded by saying, "Well, these are pictures and so, of course, they can't be alive." When the question was repeated as "Does this represent a ——— dead or alive?" the malingerer would reluctantly and perhaps even hostilely respond, "Dead."

The tests themselves seem to reflect not soldiers' malingering but their incredulity. To soldiers during World War II, who had never seen or heard of a Rorschach test, it must have seemed awfully strange to be asked to look at a bunch of cards with ink on them and to report what they saw in the splotches of ink. The following excerpt of a Rorschach test transcript reflects a certain confusion and perhaps frustration that seemingly pointless questions are being asked:

soldier: "No I don't quite understand."
test giver: repeats instructions
soldier: "If I can tell you what they look like I'm sure I'd understand."
few minutes elapse
soldier: "I don't know. Looks like a louse or something."

After showing the soldier ten cards and receiving only six responses, the psychologist concluded that his nineteen-year-old charge was a hardcore malingerer.

In another case, which clearly annoyed the psychologist, a twenty-three-year-old soldier frequently interrupted the test and demanded to know why he had to take it. A brief excerpt from his Rorschach test transcript follows:

> Soldier shown Card 1
> soldier: What this looks like? Looks like a bat here. Looks like a bat on this one.
>
> Soldier shown Card 2
> soldier: Looks like the same thing.
> Soldier shown Card 3
> soldier: Looks like some part of the body or something. It's based on the same thing. I have to look at all these cards? What you got me looking at all these cards like this for? I would like to know why I'm looking at all these cards?[47]

In this case the malingering signs are inconsistencies, no additional responses, and an intense desire to know why the test is being given. Indeed, Rorschach tests were used so frequently during World War II that there were not enough clinical psychologists to administer them. The Army had to specially train Rorschach workers for the task.

At MHUs Rorschach workers were needed to identify and categorize patients' "personality disturbances." Once these were determined, a judgment was made about treatability. If a trainee's problem was treatable, he received psychotherapy. At MHUs psychotherapy was conducted by all member of the clinical staff. Those who came, or more likely sent, suffered from a variety of problems. Twenty-two-year-old Private J, for example, developed a fear of pole climbing midway through his training. At pole-climbing exercises he refused to climb, so he was sent to the MHU. The military psychiatric social worker who took his case history reported that he "was a somewhat timid, immature man, who had been dependent on his parents for help in making decisions and in facing unpleasant situations." The psychiatrist determined that the trainee feared maladjustment, which caused him great anxiety. This was "ultimately expressed in a fear of pole climbing."[48] After several counseling sessions in which his Army adjustment problem was discussed the soldier gained insight into his fear and successfully climbed the pole. Because the psychological staff were ever striving to convince the military that their efforts would lead to practical results, the prototypical successful case involved a rather practical outcome. Men completed exercises like pole climbing, did not go AWOL, and became good soldiers directly as a result of therapy.

Sometimes a little extra something was needed. Take the case, for example, of Private L. Unable to absorb his training, he came to the MHU "emotionally distressed." This eighteen-year-old soldier was "excessively attached to his mother" and felt badly because she wrote him frequently complaining of his absence. The Army psychiatrists reports that "in psychotherapy Private L was given insight into the neurotic nature of his relationship to his mother," and therapeutic techniques were suggested for his adjustment. This apparently did wonders, and Private L became a "good soldier." To ensure this outcome, however, a letter was also sent to the mother insisting that she cease her complaining. In Army psychotherapy, boundaries were not respected.[49]

Many of the cases seen at MHUs had to do with job assignment. Waiting for assignments for weeks on end and then being disappointed by the results was a major source of psychiatric casualties.[50] A nineteen-year-old enlisted man who had been assigned to the Wire Line Section of the Signal Communications Division was sent to the MHU because he was unhappy and "not making satisfactory progress." He arrived "sullen" and "angry." During his first psychological interview it was discovered that his "emotional reaction" was directly related to his feelings about his job. A truck driver in peacetime, he had hoped to be sent to chauffeur school in the Army. After several psychological interviews during which his problem was explored, arrangements were made for him to attend chauffeur school.[51]

WAC MHUs also dealt with job-dissatisfaction cases, many of which involved women who were dissatisfied with traditionally feminine jobs. Women assigned to cooks' school, for example, often came to the MHU "frustrated" and "disgruntled." MHU clinical staffs reported that to their great surprise, "although this is a typical feminine occupation, it does not satisfy the women's psychological need." Somewhat to their dismay, they further observed that "the fewest patients referred to the consultation service come from the motorvehicle operators' course." This "masculine type of occupation" appeared to go "furthest in fulfilling the needs" of many women.[52]

Though the clinical staff at MHUs insisted that each case be treated individually and that generalization was impossible, there was a conspicuous regularity to their diagnosis and even their treatment. Overbearing mothers, for example, explained a great many of the MHU cases. Depressed, anxious, immature, and dependent men were found to come from homes where the mother had destroyed the young man's "sense of self." Female trainees' problems also conformed to certain patterns, one of the main ones being "over masculine identification." Equally common was the diagnosis of menstruation as a source of women's maladjustment. "A composite picture of the maladjusted Wac" would have to include the woman "unprepared by her family for menstruation," the director of one MHU stated. The woman's profound embarrassment, which in turn made her interpersonal relationships poor, was a fundamental cause of her adjustment difficulty.

Accompanying these standard analyses were common treatment responses. Whether a man came in worried about the unfaithfulness of his girlfriend, feeling depressed and anxious, or resentful because his request for a furlough had been denied, the counselor got the trainee to explore his feelings. The goal was to help the patient move from a "destructive attitude to one more conducive to adequate adjustment in the army" by giving the soldier insight into his emotional condition. The problem of Private H, for example, who had gone AWOL, was discovered to be one of "separation neurosis." His treatment consisted in explaining the problem of separation and exploring the trainee's feelings toward his mother.

Equally quick was the solution for a trainee who suffered from feelings of failure. The trainee, who was doing poorly in his training program, was afraid that he would be unable to live up to his father's accomplishments. The treatment was simple: the psychiatrist explained to the man the source of his psychological disturbance and helped him "to realize his true worth." The psychiatrist reported that subsequently the soldier "appeared to be making an excellent adjustment, both in his school and in his general army living."[53]

The success of the clinical staff at MHUs emboldened them. They sought to do more than simply treat trainees; increasingly, prevention became their goal. Prevention required that they move beyond the confines of their clinical offices. They were granted the authority to do so by War Department Circular 81, which expanded the responsibilities of MHUs. The directing psychiatrist was now expected to be in charge of "indoctrination of the dispensary surgeons with the knowledge of the psychological factors of illness."[54] He was also "to be alert to the situational factors which are precipitating psychological disorders and to recommend measures necessary to alleviate or remove these factors. He should survey the training program from a psychiatric point of view."[55] This point of view was that of mental health. As mental-health advisers, Army psychiatrists and psychologists were now to be on the lookout for psychologically damaging Army practices as well as improvements that could positively affect the soldiers' morale.

The Morale Problem

World War II is remembered as the "good" war, a war for which Americans were willing to sacrifice their lives without question. At the time, however, it was not always viewed in this way. Commanders, who day in and day out faced the realities of war, considered morale a major problem. They viewed the average American as unmotivated to fight, and they feared that the problem would worsen with time. Indeed, after the first year of fighting, psychological professionals reported "a disconcertingly large number of men who wanted to pick up their marbles and leave the game."[56] Too many soldiers lacked "an emotional urge toward the real purpose of American participation in World War II," and some even resented being in the Army.[57]

At its most basic level, the problem of morale was the problem of getting people to be willing to kill and to die. As psychological professionals explained, "This does not just happen merely because a man is drafted in the Army, given a gun, and told to use it." It depended on personality, environment, attitude toward the enemy, and such nonspecific factors as equipment, training, and food. A soldier's personality and level of maturity were believed to affect his ability to sustain a positive commitment to the war effort. Immature personalities, or those who lacked "ego-strength," suffered morale breakdowns. Difficult environmental circumstances, including living at isolated posts, also tended to weaken morale. Army psychiatrists and psychologists explained, for example, that "an 'average' soldier who was gregarious, friendly, and talkative, might lose his will to fight if he were put on duty at a lonely observation post; whereas if he were placed among other people to talk to, even if the duty were otherwise unpleasant, he might remain in the best of mental health." It was not suggested, however, how the gregarious soldier was to be matched with the fun-loving observation post. It was simply pointed out that the soldier's individual happiness had a direct bearing on his ability to cope with adverse circumstances.[58]

This was also true of the soldier's adjustment to living conditions. Food, symbolic of home and pleasure, was considered critical to morale since soldiers invested it with enormous value. To deal with this problem, civilian chefs were sometimes consulted. In one case, for example, the Army commissioned a nationally known chef from San Francisco, George Mardikan. This famed chef and restaurateur was sent to Europe, where he advised Army mess sergeants. Surprisingly, he did not offer culinary advice. Instead, in pep-rally style he sought to raise the morale of mess sergeants, "telling them that soldiers liked mother's cooking so they have to be more like mothers."[59]

In addition to good living conditions, the soldier needed to have a good attitude toward the war. Positive thinking about the war required that he raise "his attention from the petty rivalries, discontents, and personal problems to the single aim of defeating the enemy."[60] Psychological professionals promised to help in this consciousness-raising mission, even though much of their consciousness-raising energy had gone into promoting attention to personal problems. They could make good on their promise because they possessed a special knowledge of the soldier's psyche and how to influence it. Psychological professionals applied their expertise in a variety of settings, including the Mental Hygiene Branch of the Neuropsychiatric Division and the Morale Branch of the Morale Services Division, later called the Information and Education Division.

Marshall created the Morale Branch even before the bombing of Pearl Harbor, anticipating the need to enhance men's motivation and cultivate positive feelings about the war. Like everything else the Army did, the boosting of morale was undertaken on a massive scale. To set policy, the Morale Division wanted large amounts of information, and so it created a subagency, the Research Branch, to provide it. The Research Branch conducted large-scale surveys to determine the state of soldiers' morale and the factors influencing it. As one member of the Research Branch's staff recalled, "Army commanders wanted information about a great many matters. . . . The top command needed to know as much as possible about what motivated their enlisted men. . . . They needed to know how to improve training programs. They needed to know something about sources of disaffection and misapprehension as well as sources of esprit de corps."[61] In short, the Research Branch was authorized to obtain a composite picture of the soldier's state of mind. Initially, however, the Research Branch found itself unable to carry out this directive fully.

Secretary of War Henry Stimson had proscribed polling. He believed that "anonymous opinion or criticism, good or bad, is destructive in its effects on a military organization where accepted responsibility on the part of every individual is fundamental."[62] Such a restriction constituted a significant obstacle for the Research Branch. At first the Research Branch evaded the limitation on polling simply by saying that what it was doing was "not polling."[63] While this tactic worked for the first survey project, the secretary of war denied the Research Branch permission for its second survey on the grounds that the proposal fell outside the Army guidelines. How the Research Branch gained a freer hand in the area of surveying seems to have turned on the question of alcohol.

Secretary of War Stimson had been battling Congress over the sale of beer at Army posts. Congress obstinately refused Stimson's request to allow the Army to sell beer to soldiers, which was considered critical to morale. It happened that one of the areas in which the Research Branch had "not polled" soldiers concerned their alcohol consumption and adjustment to Army life. The survey showed that beer drinkers adjusted a little better than those who did not drink beer. Stimson relied heavily on the Research Branch's "hard scientific facts" in his battle with Congress. After he won, Stimson dropped the ban and the Research Branch began a period of intensive information gathering.

Its first survey dealt with the psychological effects of adjustment. The surveyors began with the assumption that the "trainee, at the bottom of the Army status hierarchy . . . was subjected to continual demands from his superiors, regulating the most minute details of his daily life. Not only was the new recruit confronted by the stresses of adjustment to a new way of life, but he was also subject to highly impersonal treatment. . . . More than any other time in the soldier's Army career, the initial period was characterized by exposure to explicit coercive threats, frequent overt punishment, and almost complete disregard of his personal feelings."[64] The Research Branch set out to identify what the soldier found most difficult about this experience and where his bad feelings lay.

Ultimately, the Research Branch distributed over two hundred different self-administered questionnaires to more than a half-million soldiers.[65] These surveys sought information about the soldier's attitude toward his own role in the Army, the branches of service, combat duty, training, provisions and equipment, recreation, and the Allies, as well as his or her postwar plans. Soldiers were also questioned about their level of job satisfaction and their worries. To determine his worries, for example, a sample group was given a list of worries and asked to rank them. The worries the soldier could choose from included "physical danger I might be faced with before the war is over," "the progress of the war," "financial matters," "matters concerning my family or friends back home," "the way I am getting along in the Army," "whether we will get what we are fighting for," and "being a long way from home."[66] Not surprisingly, most men worried about their physical danger.

Soldiers were also given questionnaires about their level of contentedness. They were asked to check the appropriate response for such questions as "In general how would you say you feel most of the time?" The choices included "I am usually in good spirits," "I am in good spirits some of the time and in low spirits some of the time," and "I am usually in low spirits."[67] Based on soldiers' responses to such questions, the Research Branch concluded that discontent was a serious problem. Indeed, its conclusions were considered so important that they were distributed monthly in *What the Soldier Thinks*, a newsletter for officers.

To confront the problems reported on in *What the Soldier Thinks*, the Morale Division turned to its Information and Education Service as well as its Special Services. These agencies hoped to raise morale by keeping men busy with entertainment, reading, and education. For example, a massive system of correspondence courses was established, educating close to a million men. Grade-school, high-school, junior-college, and even postgraduate courses were offered. The Army also made available 364 self-teaching education manuals covering a wide variety of subjects, including twenty-nine foreign languages, carpentry, auto mechanics, welding, and plumbing. Reading for pleasure was also promoted as a morale booster. Books and magazines were viewed as "supports against stress" as well as diversions from boredom and loneliness. By the end of the war the Army had provided soldiers with 62 million books and 120 million copies of popular magazines. The Army also published two newspapers, *Stars and Stripes* and *Yank*, a newspaper specifically for servicemen, which contained, among other things, columns by Army psychiatrists and psychologists dealing with the serviceman's problems of adjustment and issues of mental hygiene.

The Army also sponsored films, shows, and radio programs. The Armed Forces Radio Service, for example, broadcast on 177 Army radio stations worldwide. The Army Motion Picture Service sent an average of three films per week to all theaters. In addition to showing films to boost morale, the Army made them. Marshall strongly believed that "to win this war, we must win the battle for men's minds." He therefore took the unusual step of asking movie director Frank Capra, instead of the Signal Corps, which was usually in charge of producing the Army's audio-visual material, to make films that explained to the ordinary soldier why he had to be taken away from his home, family, and friends to fight a war in faraway places. He produced the now famous "Why We Fight" series, shown to more than 45 million viewers in the United States alone. This series included such films as *Prelude to War, The Negro Soldier, Our Ally Britain, Enemy Japan,* and *Your Job in Germany.*

While some Army psychiatrists and psychologists worked directly for the Morale Division on its massive projects to address the problem of soldier motivation, others worked for the Mental Hygiene Branch of the Neuropsychiatric Division, and still others worked as consultants who made their recommendations directly to military commanders in the field. Colonel Fred Hanson, a neuropsychiatric consultant to the Mediterranean theater, for example, traveled the globe offering advice on morale and mental hygiene. His unexpected appearances at distant Army posts earned him the nickname Phantom. Once, for example, on a surprise visit to troops in a remote corner of the world he noticed that soldiers were forced to stand in mud and water up to their ankles and that their socks were always wet. Thanks to Hanson, an order was given that a change of socks be provided at definite intervals. Psychiatrists and psychologists repeated this story, for they liked to point out that improving the soldier's morale and therefore fighting efficiency could sometimes be as simple as ensuring that each soldier had an additional pair of socks.[68]

Indeed, psychological professionals catalogued a whole set of small, cheap, and easy "ego-builders" that significantly increased morale. They found that "decorations" and "insignia" were ego-builders for men. And beautifying amenities did wonders for women's morale and self-esteem. Army psychiatrists and psychologists reported with much admiration that women stationed in Burma had taken morale into their own hands. With the help of an engineer, they had set up a beauty parlor that even Charles of the Ritz would have been proud of. This morale booster had an added advantage: it also boosted the morale of the men who got to look at the women and their beautiful hair![69]

Other aspects of morale that preoccupied Army psychiatrists and psychologists were mail and the weather, both considered to be potential morale killers. They believed that soldiers feared extremes of climate and were apprehensive about how they would function. To reduce such fears, the Army created pamphlets such as *How to Keep Alive in Persia!* which sought to lessen soldiers' anxieties about the heat.[70] While there is no indication that soldiers read this pop psychological pamphlet, we do know that soldiers used the heat as a form of entertainment. In the Persian Gulf command soldiers and officers held a "Perspiration Handicap" every week. Three towns in southern Iran where temperatures reached to more than 150 degrees competed for the dubious honor of being the hottest place on earth. The competition required that a C ration can be placed below a bended arm. Sweat dripped, or perhaps more accurately, flowed, from the arm into the can. Whoever filled the can first won. The all-time record was achieved in 8 minutes, 41.4 seconds by a "fat but fading major." Ennui appears to have been more of a factor here than fear.[71]

Boredom could lower morale as much as fear did. Mail was considered critical to men's stimulation. In foxholes men would read their letters over and over again. Getting letters to soldiers, however, was not easy. Unlike in civilian life, soldiers were constantly on the move and so their addresses were constantly changing. During the Normandy campaign, for example, a special postal-directory battalion commanded by Major Charity Adams had to deliver letters to men whose locations changed three to four times per week. Nonetheless, this battalion of Black women kept track of every man with an unprecedentedly low number of mail mistakes.[72] The Army's system of delivery was made somewhat easier by the use of V-mail, a form of microfilm. By April 1944 soldiers around the world were receiving 63 million V-mail letters a month. While this fast and efficient system of mail delivery had the potential to boost morale, letters could either raise or lower men's spirits. Upbeat news from home reenergized men to go out and defeat the enemy. Bad news, as Army psychiatrists and psychologists often repeated, could be more dangerous than a German howitzer. The speedy mail system did nothing to stem this problem. Army psychiatrists and psychologists regretted that a nationwide course on writing letters to soldiers that taught those back home about the psychology of mail was never implemented.[73]

Maintaining high morale is difficult in any war, but the nature of World War II made this especially true. World War II was by far the most violent episode in human history, claiming the lives of 50 million persons in six years. Though U.S. losses were comparatively low, with 240,000 killed and 600,000 wounded, those who saw combat experienced a war whose speed, intensity, and brutality were without precedent. New weapons, including rockets, bombs, and flame throwers, dramatically increased the lethality of war. So too did the deadly concrete bunkers surrounded by a web of barbed wire and mines for which the Germans were renowned. In addition to these man-made trials, soldiers faced temperatures that ranged from -70 degrees in the Aleutian Islands of Alaska to 150 degrees in the Middle East.

The soldier's daily confrontation with death is captured in the Army's *Handbook for Emergency Battlefield Burials and Grave Registration*. This document provided that before battle even began, grave-registration teams were to survey the fighting area for suitable burial locations and mark these graves with stones. Advancing soldiers would therefore often pass by the locations that had already been identified for their burial. After battle, grave-registration teams combed the area for the dead, who were temporarily buried if another attack was imminent or time was short. Teams emptied men's pockets, removed dog tags, pinning one to the body, and dug shallow graves. When the situation stabilized, the teams returned to take bodies to a division cemetery, where fingerprints were taken and the bodies were blessed. This burial too was only temporary, however. Final burial occurred only after the war, when bodies were sent home.[74] The reality and threat of death powerfully contributed to mental destabilization. While in World War I the thinking had been that combat would break particularly susceptible soldiers, World War II psychologists came to believe that even "the most stable individual could not face death for days and weeks on end and remain 'normal.'" They found that half of all soldiers in combat suffered from "nervousness" and intense headaches and close to one third had nightmares. The issue was not *if* a soldier would breakdown but rather *when*.[75]

The Psychological Front

Having successfully inserted themselves into the selection process and basic training, psychological professionals were determined to service the massive number of emotional casualties expected from actual battle. The psychological front at the beginning of the war was deemed wholly inadequate. In North Africa, for example, psychiatric casualties had to be transported 300-500 miles from the fighting area, and even then the procedures for diagnosing and disposing of psychiatric cases were hardly up-to-date. At one facility, psychiatric patients were lined up in a field in front of their tents and called to attention by the supervising medical officer. On his signal, nearby trucks backfired. All those who did not duck for cover, cower, scream, or yell were determined to be sufficiently recovered to return to duty.[76]

Though a more extensive and professional system for treating psychiatric casualties was desperately needed, many obstacles stood in the way. First, there was simply a shortage of manpower. At the time, trained clinical psychologists and psychiatrists simply did not exist in large numbers in the civilian population from which the Army drew. More fundamentally, however, was the problem of convincing the military commanders that a more therapeutic approach was a good idea. These commanders tended to suspect that psychiatric casualties were malingerers rather than truly sick. They feared that giving further legitimacy to the concept of the psychiatric casualty would merely provide a great opportunity for soldiers to avoid combat. Moreover, they believed that if a soldier was truly psychologically troubled, the solution was expulsion rather than therapy. In fact, Army regulations prohibited treatment of psychiatric casualties.

The psychologists eventually succeeded in convincing military commanders that a more therapeutic approach was needed. Their success may have stemmed in part from the Army's discovery that a substantial number of psychiatric casualties were inevitable and that its existing system was not succeeding in staunching this hemorrhaging of men. In the North African campaign only 10 percent of the men who suffered psychiatric casualties ever returned to duty. Army psychiatrists and psychologists promised that with adequate facilities and treatment plans they could return 60–80 percent of psychiatric casualties to combat.

Once commanders were convinced of the need for psychological treatment, the next step was to address the shortage of psychological personnel, which was accomplished by setting up courses and even schools for this purpose. Army nurses were given the opportunity to take postgraduate courses on psychiatric nursing. Similarly, Navy WAVES who had majored in psychology were encouraged to do postgraduate work. A thousand doctors were trained and reclassified as psychiatrists at the School of Military Neuropsychiatry and the Army's Medical Field Service School. Arrangements were also made with private universities, including Columbia and New York University, both of which offered three-month courses for Army doctors. Overseas, the Army established training programs in psychiatric treatment in the European and South Pacific theaters. In addition, the Army created manuals and pamphlets to supplement these educational efforts.[77]

The striking shift in the Army's attitude toward psychiatric casualties and their treatment is well illustrated by an episode involving General George S.

Patton. On a visit to a field hospital during the battle of Tronia, in Italy, General Patton came upon a psychiatric casualty. Rather than giving him the words of encouragement he had given to other men, Patton slapped him on the back and called him a coward. At the beginning of the war such an act would probably have been ignored. In this case, however, it was brought to General Eisenhower's attention, whereupon Eisenhower had Patton reprimanded and ordered him to apologize to the man.[78] That even Patton could be brought to acknowledge this new vision of psychiatric diagnosis and treatment suggests the greater influence and status psychologists had achieved through their promise to return a significant number of men to duty.

Making good upon this promise proved no small task. Even with the military's efforts to address the manpower shortage, the personnel available were woefully inadequate for the task if any traditional concept of therapeutic treatment was to be applied. The civilian model, after all, involved extensive one-on-one investigation of the patient's psyche by trained psychotherapists. The manpower for such a careful investigation did not exist in the Army, and even if it had, such long-term cures were of little interest to the Army.

The system of psychiatric treatment that was put in place reflected the Army's overall organization: a complex system of therapeutic triage in which soldiers' injured psyches, much like their wounds, were examined for treatability and, if they were found to be treatable, patched up as quickly and as close to the front lines as possible. As with the physically injured, the first stop for psychiatric casualties was generally the battalion aid station, though the mode of arrival was not usually the same. The physically injured were generally carried back under fire by a medic after he had attempted to stop the bleeding by sprinkling sulfanilamide on the wound and applying a tourniquet. Most psychiatric casualties walked to the station. Some of these soldiers were sent by their company commanders. More commonly, they came voluntarily because they felt jittery, "couldn't take it any more," or found themselves weeping uncontrollably. Often these men had been separated from their units during fast, mobile fighting or as a result of deaths in their units.

From this point on, the treatment men would receive reflected the Faustian bargain that the psychologists had made. The role they had agreed to play was very different from that played by psychologists in private civilian practice. They had promised, not to cure the men, to make them happy, or to assist in their self-actualization, but to return as many men as possible to combat, and so they did.

The person initially responsible for assessing psychiatric casualties who reported to the battalion aid station was the battalion surgeon, who had been given a crash course called "First-Aid Psychiatry." One battalion surgeon observed that "if the soldier was uncommunicative, withdrawn and seclusive, the chances of returning him to effective duty were unfavorable. The more accessible he was, the better was his response to reassurance and suggestion." Since battalion aid stations were so close to the front line, however, the battalion surgeons received considerable pressure to return as many men as possible to the line, so treatment was provided on site where at all possible.

This treatment was generally extremely brief. Almost 50 percent of men who complained of anxiety, for example, were returned to duty within one to six hours; others remained for twenty-four hours. Much of their time at the aid station was spent sleeping. Sedation was an important part of treatment. "A quick-acting barbiturate is imperative. . . . ," one surgeon stated. "All patients should be given .2 grams of sodium amytal immediately on arrival at the aid station to lower irritability and distractibility." This also undoubtedly freed the battalion surgeon to care for maimed soldiers requiring his immediate medical attention. When he had a free moment and the patient had slept for a few hours, he could return to the care of psychiatric casualties.

After sedation, a brief inquiry was made into the soldier's problem. He was then offered a standard four-step treatment: explanation, reassurance, suggestion, and exhortation. The first step was a "short talk" in which the battalion surgeon explained the nature of the soldier's psychological problem and suggested ways of coping with it. The soldier was then assured that he had "a common type of transient emotional reaction." The third step, suggestion, was unabashedly straightforward: the surgeon simply suggested to the soldier that his health had returned, that in fact he was stronger than ever, and therefore ready to return to combat. Finally the soldier was exhorted to return to the line and do his duty. As in all of the Army's therapeutic programs, coercion was never far from the surface of treatment.

If the battalion aid station's four-step treatment was inadequate for putting the soldier back in fighting trim, his next stop would be the division clearing station. The division clearing station reflected a particularly strange melding of the psychologists' somewhat contradictory impulses, to cure and to coerce men to return to the business of war. Division clearing stations were located two to five miles from the front line; and not surprisingly, moving the soldier "back an anxiety zone" was thought to benefit the soldier's psyche.[79] However, psychologists thought moving the soldier a greater distance from the front line would be too much of a good thing. Some "artillery rumbling in the distance and occasionally nearby" was "helpful in reminding the soldier that he is still in the war," though "acute anxiety patients should . . . be relatively free from actual danger."[80]

Soldiers for whom forty-eight hours of rest, a short psychological interview, and a dose of explosion therapy did not do the trick were sent to the exhaustion centers, about ten miles behind the division clearing stations. These centers treated 200-500 patients at a time for 5-10 days. The centers took their name from the presumed diagnosis for the soldiers who arrived there, combat exhaustion. The term *combat exhaustion* was meant to cover nonorganic symptoms and was created as "a precaution against suggesting disease or neurotic taint and to emphasize the occupational and transient factors" in the soldier's condition.[81] The care in choosing this term suggests how fine a line psychologists sought to walk. On the one hand, they wished to establish that the condition was not merely imaginary or a disguised form of malingering but a real condition whose amelioration required their expert services. Yet they also sought to convey the view to both Army command and the individual soldier himself that psychiatric casualties, unlike many wounded in battle, suffered from something temporary and fixable. Thus, Army psychiatrists and psychologists sought to avoid endorsing invalidism while legitimizing the treatment of a broad range of psychological symptoms.

The men who arrived at the exhaustion centers were "dejected, dirty, weary," with "trembling or jerking" hands and expressions "of depression, sometimes of tearfulness."[82] Their first stop was reception, generally an open tent, which became "a noisy, smoke-filled room [where] occasional aerial activity helped to foster a mood of intimacy and uninhibited talk." The open environment of the tent was often exploited by the psychologists to begin the process of pointing the men back toward combat even before they had been individually interviewed. Comments made to one patient were intended for all patients to hear. A psychologist interviewing a soldier might suddenly pound his fist on the table, attracting the attention of the other soldiers, and say to a nearby psychiatrist in loud and enthusiastic tones: "Hey, Major, here's a real soldier for you. Forty days on the line, knocked on his can by an '88' and he wants to go back and give those bastards some more!" Other psychiatrists in the tent were expected at this point to "beam and shout approval." The problem with this morale-boosting approach, as many psychological professionals admitted, was that many men at exhaustion centers had no desire to "give those bastards some more." For men who were weeping uncontrollably or "mute or staring into space" much more than a morale booster was needed.[83]

At the soldier's reception interview the psychologist appraised his condition, devised a treatment plan, and helped the soldier to understand "the objectives of his hospital stay." Men with combat exhaustion were viewed as having lost their psychological equilibrium and suffering from various stages of "personality disorganization." This was not surprising, particularly for those men who had seen their whole platoon wiped out. Nonetheless, it was hoped that treatment would render the soldier "refreshed, reequipped, and psychologically ready for combat, with some insight and ability to detach himself from future disconcerting anxiety." It is unclear precisely what insight the psychologists hoped to provide to soldiers who might have seen their whole platoon killed and the source of whose troubles were therefore not particularly mysterious.[84]

Soldiers who could not be refreshed and reequipped for combat at the exhaustion centers would be sent on the last leg of their therapeutic odyssey, to station and general hospitals. These represented the military's last effort; if the soldier was not rendered serviceable for combat or for some other military function, he returned to the United States.

The functioning of this complex system for treating psychiatric casualties often posed great organizational challenges. Troop movements required that facilities for treatment be set up quickly. Moreover, predicting the number of psychiatric casualties a given military operation might produce was something of an art, depending, as it did, on not only the number of soldiers involved in the operation but also how the expected combat conditions would impact upon the soldiers' psyches. The Normandy offensive illustrates these challenges. It began with D-day, a military operation of unprecedented complexity, combining the largest amphibious assault in history (some 200,000 Allied troops crossing the English Channel under the command of General Dwight D. Eisenhower) with an air drop of 17,000 parachutists, who landed behind the Germans poised to attack the Allies arriving by water.

The casualties, particularly psychiatric ones, during the two months of the offensive far exceeded expectations. From the First Army, for example, there were 60,000 battle casualties and 11,000 psychiatric casualty admissions.[85] The figure for psychiatric admissions does not include those who were treated at exhaustion centers, which were quickly overwhelmed. Within forty-eight hours of its establishment an exhaustion center at Bernesq, twelve miles inland from Omaha Beach, one of the D-day beachheads, had received 275 psychiatric casualties. Moreover, most of these casualties had been held at the division clearing station awaiting the establishment of the evacuation center. The center was soon receiving 300–400 new patients per day. At times it cared for as many as 800 patients at once, twice the number planned for.

The shortage of psychologists, the unrelenting flow of psychiatric casualties, and the need to return men to combat as soon as possible led the military psychologists to develop time-saving methods of treatment. One of the most popular, and one recommended by Army Technical Bulletin, Medicine, 84, was narcosynthesis, or psychotherapy under sedation, described by a psychiatrist as "a method which enables the psychiatrist in a short period of time to expire and aerate in some degree, the man's unconscious mind." The soldier was given sodium pentathol, sodium amytal, ether, or nitrous oxide; once the drug had taken effect, he was helped to recall the incident of his trauma: "[The patient] was told that he was again on the battlefield and the statement was reinforced by loud warnings, such as 'Look out,' of 'Watch those shells,, or 'Duck'. . . . Usually, the patient responded with a dramatic startle pattern, cowered on the couch, sought cover, and at times jumped to the floor to dig in or to take flight."[86] With this provocation, the patient let loose a torrent of emotions, relayed fears, anger, and resentment to the therapist as if he were a fellow soldier at the scene of the traumatic experience. This cower-on-the-couch approach apparently had the therapeutic value of enabling the psychiatric casualty to assimilate painful material and to establish "orientation."

Time pressures also led to the use of hypnosis. This method of treatment saved time and bypassed the difficulties of preparing drugs, maintaining sterile conditions, and injection itself, which "in near combat conditions . . . was a distinct advantage."[87] Hypnosis also made abreaction, the reexperiencing of fears and conflicts, easier to control. Sigmund Freud had experimented with hypnosis as a method of treatment before his development of psychoanalysis but had abandoned it after discovering that although it was effective and quick, the resulting cure was temporary. For Army psychologists working in the war context, however, the speed of treatment was a greater concern, and the permanence of the cure a lesser one, than for Freud.

Hypnosis was used primarily with patients who did not respond initially to narcosynthesis or regular psychotherapy. For example, at a forward island hospital set up to treat psychiatric casualties from the Okinawa campaign a twenty-four-year-old patient suffering from unbearable headaches, insomnia resulting from recurring nightmares, and "a feeling of impending death" would not participate in group psychotherapy. When asked about his combat experiences, he remembered only that the ammunition dump at which he had been stationed was hit. Extensive physical examinations revealed that there were no organic causes for his complaint. Exhausted, he finally agreed to undergo hypnosis at the urging of other patients who had done so. In a hypnotic trance the soldier reexperienced the attack upon his ammunition dump:

> On that evening he and his buddies were discussing the future of the war. They heard the enemy plane approaching and started running for their foxholes. The patient cried out "I'll never make it! It's coming right at me!" He threw himself to the ground and the bomb landed approximately 75 yards in front of him, the concussion throwing him several feet in the air. (At this point in the hypnotic trance he became limp and unresponsive for a matter of seconds and then stated "I don't remember, I don't remember." He had apparently been knocked unconscious for a few seconds. He then began to shake vigorously and an expression of terror formed upon his face and he cried out, "I'll be killed, I'll be killed! I'm scared to death and can't move!"

In another case a twenty-five-year-old infantry rifleman suffering from insomnia, anorexia, and mild episodes of tremor complained of a mysterious lump in his throat. Physical exams were negative. He participated in group therapy, but this did not lessen his complaint about his throat. Under hypnosis he revealed a combat experience that he had not previously related. For about a week he had held the duty of carrying ammunition and supplies to a forward area. Unfortunately, an enemy corpse lay along the path to the forward area, and he therefore passed it daily. The odor and sight of the body nauseated him, though he did not vomit. Then one day, moving in the dark, he accidentally stepped into a pile of corpses. The psychiatrist recounted that "at this time a sudden 'horrible' convulsive motion of the stomach occurred and his throat tightened in an unsuccessful effort to prevent regurgitation." Under hypnosis, he felt the same "mass like" feeling in his throat. After reliving this experience under hypnosis and after several more group psychotherapy sessions to better understand it, the soldier was able to return to duty.[88]

Much more common than hypnosis or psychotherapy under sedation were regular individual and group psychotherapy sessions. Group therapy was first used in one combat area somewhat accidentally. Because there was little space, acute psychiatric casualties from the North African campaign were treated in an open tent. An individual patient was treated in full view of others. The treating psychiatrist found that surrounding patients began to discuss among themselves the patient's problems and experiences and its relation to their own. He saw the therapeutic value of these discussions and formalized this approach to treatment. Plainly, the efficiencies of group therapy also attracted military psychologists.

Whether they practiced group or individual therapy, Army psychiatrists and psychologists found that the challenges of the military context were quite different from those of the civilian context. For example, many soldiers simply did not want to get well. Physically wounded men who received psychological treatment often said their wound was "worth a million dollars." Others simply declared, "I have done my share." Psychologists found this "negativity" toward therapy quite frustrating. The difficulty, of course, was that psychologists' role included not only healing but also detecting cases of malingering and invalidism, a dual role famously captured in Joseph Heller's novel *Catch-22*. To be sure, it would be psychologically healthier not to return to battle, but a soldier's feeling that way simply proved that he was not crazy.

If Army psychiatrists and psychologists noted the differences between the combat and civilian therapeutic contexts, they often had difficulty setting aside their civilian therapeutic training even though it was often curiously irrelevant in the military context. Their civilian training had focused on the necessity of uncovering the underlying and often obscure causes of mental afflictions, generally by dredging up childhood memories. In war, however, these causes were often all too obvious. When an infantryman showed up with shaking hands or facial twitches or compulsively biting his nails, a harrowing story would all too quickly emerge. He might have been subject to heavy fire for four days and carried two wounded men to an aid station, or been "caught in an exposed position during a strafing raid," or seen his buddy loose his legs.[89]

Perhaps the most dramatic illustration of how combat horrors could prey upon psychological health was presented by the battle over Guadalcanal in 1942. The U.S. Navy, determined to prevent the Japanese from building an airfield on this South Pacific island, sent the First Marine Division, with a fighting strength of 19,000 men. Though the marines landed against weak opposition, the Japanese soon launched counterattacks. Unfortunately for the marines, the Japanese had cunningly ringed Mount Austen, 1,500 feet high, with a series of concrete pillboxes housing a machine gun or two plus a few riflemen. When the Americans tried to take the mountain, the number of casualties was enormous.[90] But the misery caused by fighting may have been less than the misery caused by the unbearable heat, thick mud, malaria, dengue fever (which could lead a physically fit twenty-two-year-old to have a heart attack after any activity, such as digging a foxhole), catastrophic supply problems resulting in starvation rations, and lack of clothing. Of the 60,000 troops eventually sent to Guadalcanal, 6,000 became combat casualties and another 9,000 became seriously ill. Thus, it should not be surprising that the death and maiming on Guadalcanal caused psychological difficulties. One psychiatrist noted that "on Guadalcanal the life held little in common with any mode of existence previously known to the patient or physician, or even imagined in training."

The horrors of combat on Guadalcanal and the plethora of psychological troubles it caused gave psychologists plenty to do. But while the number of combat neuroses was unending, they were a poor medium for psychological practice because their causes were too obvious to be the subject of sustained psychological inquiry. Moreover, the very nature of these neuroses threatened the efficacy of psychological treatment: if, after all, combat was simply too horrible for psychologically healthy and ordinary soldiers to handle, then what did psychologists have to offer?

Perhaps for these reasons, psychologists tended to deemphasize the importance of the immediate and obvious causes of combat neuroses and to instead find more obscure explanations in the soldier's psychodynamic past. Thus, when a twenty-year-old marine on Guadalcanal reported that in addition to the routine horror of combat, he had witnessed the death of his best friend from high school in heavy bombing, the psychiatrist who heard this story suggested that "the bomb might have meant little had the patient been capable of an independent existence."[91] Psychologists had a similar attitude toward nightmares. Nightmares reached epidemic proportions on Guadalcanal, preventing many of the men from getting the sleep they needed. Yet psychologists viewed the nightmares as reflections of "problems which are relatively extraneous to the fighting." Looking to the soldiers' childhood, they found that in men with nightmares an "absence of affection had left a lasting scar." The psychologists also speculated that the danger in these nightmares was the product, not of the actual violence and destruction surrounding soldiers on a daily basis, but of suicidal impulses: "The suicidal thoughts are repressed and the danger from within the self is projected in the nightmares as an external threat."

Perhaps because they tended to discount the immediate conditions' role in creating psychiatric casualties, psychologists were sometimes surprised by the effect simply removing soldiers to a safe location had upon their psyches. A psychiatrist who treated Guadalcanal casualties in a ship anchored off the island and sought to restore to these men the sense "that a happy life is possible" observed how surprisingly soon after being withdrawn to safety the soldier became free of obsessive concerns with death and his desire to live returned.

Later, when psychologists looked back on the war, it had much the same meaning for them as it did for the soldiers they had treated. If they had not directly experienced combat, they had nonetheless shared with other veterans a sense of adventure and pride. Combat psychiatry, they believed, like combat itself, had required courage, dedication, and ingenuity. Their war stories were not about combat but about heroic feats of treatment under adverse conditions, intense time pressures, and what they perceived as meager resources. They had treated men who had seen it all and whose psychic misery had left an indelible impression on them: "The sight of them remains unforgettable. They were bedraggled and emaciated youths with frozen expressions on their aged faces and a far off stare in their eyes. The stories they told were harrowing beyond all anticipation."[92] Indeed, the intensity of their job had been so great that psychological professionals believed that they had been in danger themselves of becoming casualties. Thus, combat psychiatry had been "far removed from psychiatry as practiced in a comfortable room, where the psychiatrist quietly sits in a leather swivel chair, patiently listening to the mental meanderings of a fair, fat, and forty matron who frettably tosses on the analytic couch."[93] The psychologists were proud of their military role of salvaging depressed, terrified, and listless men.

If psychologists may have overdramatized their role, their pride may not have been entirely unjustified. To be sure, they had not fulfilled the ideals of their profession in their treatment of soldiers. As they recognized, often they had merely bandaged deeper psychic wounds, for their mission had been not to render soldiers psychologically healthy but to make them fit for battle.

Their professional ideals had given way to the goal of winning the war, which had required that soldiers put not only their bodies but also their psyches in danger.

Nonetheless, however justified, the incongruity of combat psychiatry cannot be erased. It is particularly surprising that psychologists were able to convince military commanders that the waging of total war was compatible with the excavation of soldiers' "repressed memories" and the discussion of their "emotionally painful experiences." The psychologists' success stemmed perhaps from their strange and deep faith in the power of psychological therapy, a faith that permitted them to declare in the midst of total war that "group psychotherapy is our greatest hope."[94]

The psychological front during World War II extended beyond the Army's ground forces. Fighter pilots, merchant marines, and even secret agents found themselves under the scrutiny and care of psychiatrists and psychologists. Psychological professionals worked in every conceivable setting, offering to improve the mental health of all those who contributed to the war effort. The United Service Organization, or USO, for example, which sponsored entertainment and other services for soldiers and war-production workers, provided psychotherapy "to preserve the personality, the personal integrity of the men and women who come within the scope of our operations."[95] Even scientists working on the Manhattan Project, the government-sponsored program to build the first atomic bomb, received psychological treatment. At Oak Ridge, Tennessee, for example, where uranium 238 was converted to uranium 235 for Los Alamos, New Mexico, psychiatrists and psychologists treated scientists and engineers in "closed treatment units" so that patients with different kinds of top-secret information would not mix.

Psychological professionals adapted to both the particular circumstances of their patients and the distinct psychological problems they faced. The treatment of parachutists, for example, focused on jumping. In the case of a parachutist who refused to jump after a certain point in training because he feared paralysis, the treating psychiatrist searched for the origins of his concern with immobility. With the help of hypnosis he found them. When the patient was five years old his uncle had seriously injured his back, and the patient recalled that his "face looked sad." At age eight the patient had been disturbed by seeing paralyzed children in a hospital. Finally, the patient's brother had been paralyzed in a train accident and then died. The psychiatrist found that "the dominant note in all these memories is helplessness, pain, loss of mobility." He also acquires helpful pieces of miscellaneous information, including that the parachutist's first experience of sexual intercourse had occurred while he was in the Army and that his earliest nonhypnotic memory was a happy one, receiving presents at Christmas. Finally, the psychiatrist administered a few psychological tests. He reports that fantasies elicited by the Murray Test pictures indicated "marked repression and the holding in of aggressive feelings." What exactly all this had to do with the patient's fear of jumping or paralysis is not made clear. The Army, however, was not concerned with the merits of such a psychological investigation. If hypnosis or psychotherapy could get more men to jump when they were told to do so or help those who feared jumping overcome their fears, then this attention to the parachutist's psyche was worth it.

If parachutists had to be free of neuroses in order to jump, secret agents had to be free of them in order to keep secrets. At the Office of Strategic Services (OSS), the precursor to the Central Intelligence Agency, the secret agent's psyche became a critical factor in both selection and training. The agency sought to weed out persons who were ill suited for the clandestine work of the agency. It did not want candidates who might cause "friction," impair the "efficiency and the morale" of other OSS men, or injure "the reputation of the organization." OSS psychological professionals attempted to eliminate those who possessed a tendency to be "apathetic," "sullen," or "resentful." They also tried to save the OSS from the "irreparable damage" that could be caused by "the one who blabs."

To find secret agents who could keep secrets, the OSS adopted a system of psychological assessment in 1943. By the end of the war it had screened 5,900 recruits, some from as far away as Yunnan, China. Initially, however, the OSS selected employees for its five major branches—Secret Intelligence, Research and Analysis, Special Operations, Morale Operations, and Counter-Intelligence—without the aid of psychologists. As OSS psychologists later explained, "lacking the benefit of professional help" and not knowing "who would make a good spy or an effective guerilla," the OSS, like other wartime agencies, worked through existing Army and civilian personnel agencies to acquire its staff. But the inability to develop more exacting standards created problems.

According to Donald MacKinnon, director of an OSS evaluation center, this situation "might have continued had it not been for several disastrous operations." During the first few months of operation, someone discovered that in Italy, "on the assumption that it takes dirty men to do dirty works," the OSS had been recruiting foreign agents from an organization called Murder Inc. The agency had also done some recruiting from an organization known as the Philadelphia Purple Gang. The discovery of these operations, according to OSS psychologists, finally convinced those at the head of the agency to incorporate psychological assessment into the recruitment and screening process.[96]

Psychologists first implemented their policy of psychological assessment at Station S (S for Secret), formerly a country estate in Fairfax, Virginia. In order to keep the work being done there secret, psychologists at OSS misrepresented their activities to the surrounding community. Recruits were informed when they arrived at Station S that "to hide the nature of our work here" they had given out a "cover story" for local consumption. The story was that Station S was an Army rehabilitation and reallocation center for men returned from overseas, which in plain language meant that the residents of the nearby town "are firmly convinced that you are all serious mental cases."

In reality, however, Station S was "an ideal space for setting up all sorts of stressful situations, indoors and outdoors," to assess candidates' personalities. All candidates for OSS work arrived at assessment centers in Army fatigues. The staff immediately instructed all recruits to adopt fictitious names and invent plausible life stories. Recruits were allowed to reveal their true identity at a specifically designated time toward the end of the evaluation. This procedure allowed psychological professionals to assess candidates' ability to maintain a cover story. Along with this new vision of what they were testing for came a new conception of the testing circumstances. OSS psychologists sought to assess men in ordinary situations, so they trained, ate, and slept with the new recruits. As one OSS psychologist explained the rationale of this new approach to psychological testing, "Our experience shows that the staff can acquire invaluable impressions of the candidates during the hours of relaxation; from a wisecrack overheard in the hall, from a heated dinner conversation, from a way a clique forms in the living room, from the gesture with which a man reacts to defeat in a game of bridge." In observing men's reactions to the outcome of a bridge game and using this information to determine whether a given person would make a good secret agent, the OSS had moved psychological testing a long way from its origins. No longer limited to measuring intelligence with paper-and-pencil tests, the OSS examined the secret agent's total personality in the context of a specially created living-room laboratory.[97]

The procedures the OSS developed to select secret agents and the practice of treating patients such as parachutists, military prisoners, and aviators fundamentally expanded the boundaries of clinical practice, but they did so within the confines of the goal of military victory. It was not until the end of the war that a civilian rationale emerged for mass therapeutic intervention. According to this logic, returning to civilian life could be traumatic and the Army had an obligation to help men through it. This argument conflicted with psychological professionals' earlier argument that war and Army life were abnormal conditions that called for an unprecedented therapeutic response. It turned out that peacetime no less than war entailed emotional turmoil and therefore psychological aid.

To deal with these anticipated emotional problems of returning to civilian life, the Army set up therapeutic services at its separation centers, where men were processed before being released from the armed services. Men stayed at these centers for forty-eight hours, during which time they received a physical exam, a clothing check, payment, and counseling. Counselors received four weeks of training at a special Separation-Classification-and-Counseling School. There they took courses, practiced "good listening" skills, and were issued a "counselor's kit" that included information about Army discharge regulations and the mental hygiene of separation. At separation centers the Army expected counselors to explain the GI Bill, life insurance, and the soldier's legal obligation to report to a draft board. The Army also expected the counselor to encourage the soldier to talk about his feelings—his worries, anxieties, and even anger. As one separation counselor explained, soldiers had "a chance to blow off steam in a counselor's booth" and "get it off his chest.[98]

The Army supplemented separation counselors' work with its own *Psychology for the Returning Serviceman*. This pop psychology book aimed to provide psychological facts that might "help the serviceman in fitting back into civilian life." Its central premise was that returning home involved substantial psychic stress. Though the soldier had dreamed of his return for months, perhaps even years, the rosy picture he had formed in his head probably bore little resemblance to the situation he would face upon return. "You may have heard a lot in the army or navy about the importance of morale. Well morale, you will find, is something you need just about as much after you get home." Readers were also warned that as veterans they must "learn how to fit into civilian life again" just as you had to learn how to fit into the Service when you left home." The problems encountered by the returning serviceman required that he and his family familiarize themselves with their own psychologies. Veterans were advised to take the time to understand their needs and desires. Successful adjustment to civilian life depended on the returning serviceman's ability to "understand what [his] needs are—not only the things he knows he wants, but the deeper needs he may not think much about but for which he must obtain some satisfaction, if he is to be truly content with life in general." Once he understood himself and knew what his needs and desires were, he could begin to address his problems. Following these procedures of self-knowledge, however, might prove difficult for several reasons. First, the returning serviceman might experience a feeling of resentment that prevented him from recognizing his psychology. Having experienced hardship during the war, the returning serviceman often "has built up a state of discontent." He carried home "an accumulation of anger" that he was "ready to let out against anything." *Psychology for the Returning Serviceman* warned readers not to become alarmed by this, for it was a feeling experienced by "hundreds of thousands of other men all over the country." Anger, returning veterans learned, was an emotion that must be released: "If there is no way for you to let off steam, your feelings of anger and aggression will accumulate until you are under great pressure and you reach a point where you may do something rash."

In addition to anger and resentment that camouflaged the returning serviceman's true needs and desires, worry also plagued him. Readers learned that "getting rid of the continual feelings of worry that come from such opposing desires is one of the hardest things you ever have to do." The book advised that when a returning serviceman found himself in this situation, he should attempt to satisfy himself without acting against his other desire: "Maybe you can't boss your family in every detail and still keep their affection, but you can partly fill your need for power by breaking horses or controlling a powerful machine."

Whereas the problem of worry could be diffused if it was properly understood, the returning serviceman's most troublesome problem occurred when he could not figure out what was bothering him. Men, *Psychology for the Returning Serviceman* explained, frequently came home feeling a vague sense of dissatisfaction. They were worried, angry, and frustrated. Unable to locate or describe this sense of discontent proved disquieting, sometimes downright maddening. "You may also have a feeling of discontent without knowing just what is wrong. This is a sign that you need something deeply, even though you don't know what it is." Returning servicemen were reminded that they were not alone in feeling a vague sense of discontent: "Your feelings are shared by hundreds and thousands of other men coming back home."

Plagued by anger, worry, and vague feelings of dissatisfaction, returning soldiers would find that home was not a haven but an emotional battlefield. The returning serviceman could not expect automatic happiness and peace of mind; obtaining these would be a struggle. Like war and the Army, civilian life tested the serviceman's ability to adjust and deal with psychic stress. The intervention of psychologists, the book explained, might be necessary to help the veteran and his family address the new tensions in the home. It might be necessary to talk these problems over "with someone who understands the causes and remedies of such problems—a psychiatrist, a clinical psychologist, psychoanalyst, social worker or trained advisor."[99]

To help returning servicemen who needed professional help, the Army made special provisions. The directive for this kind of help came straight from the top: the Commander in Chief, Franklin D. Roosevelt, requested that his secretary of war, Henry Stimson, make adequate provisions not only "for the soldier who is emotionally sick as a result of combat" but also for the man with a "service maladjustment." He wrote Stimson, "I feel, as you know, that the ultimate ought to be done for them to return them as useful citizens."[100]

For this therapeutic task, veteran rehabilitation centers, in conjunction with private hospitals, were established around the country. These centers were initially created to deal with rejected inductees, who often "felt guilty and rejected" and "ashamed to return to their communities" as well as the psychological problems of war wives. But toward the end of the war it became clear that the overwhelming need was for a center that would help rehabilitate veterans with psychological difficulties. This need was officially sanctioned after the war by the Veterans Administration. As Vice Admiral J. T. Boone, chief medical director of the Veterans Administration, explained, "The medical job is not really complete until the veteran has been restored to a life as socially productive and personally satisfying as possible."[101]

Restoration and satisfaction would be achieved by psychological exploration. Veteran rehabilitation centers aimed to help veterans in a short period of time to uncover the roots of their psychological difficulties and adjust to civilian life. Once again, psychological professionals found soldiers' problems to be internal, more specifically to stem from their infantile needs and desires. It was their hope that they could bring veterans to "a realization of their basic insecurity so that they can recognize the infantile source of their dissatisfaction." On the rare occasions when they found external causes for men's psychological difficulties, they refused to treat the men. For example, helping Black veterans posed insurmountable difficulties because "the problems of racial prejudice are beyond the scope of our Clinic."[102]

* * *

With the end of the war, the returning soldiers turned to the postponed task of starting families and making homes. Psychologists also found their calling in the American home. Since the military no longer needed their services, they turned naturally to the task of helping returning soldiers adjust to peace. Yet, with the stress of combat no longer a factor, they found these men less interested in therapy. Fortunately, however, another occupant of the American home—the American housewife—proved far more interested in their wares. When what had been learned about the American soldier, secret agent, and returning serviceman was applied to the American housewife, the results were startling.

5 HOME

1945–1965

During the era of the cold war (1945–1965) the therapeutic gospel laid claim to a new realm: the American home. Postwar homes, with their station wagons, gleaming appliances, and backyard barbecues, proved to be fertile ground not only for America's growing consumerism but also for its burgeoning faith in the psyche. The public, but especially American housewives, learned an entirely new way of thinking about their lives, and a new language that went with it. Terms such as *ego, inferiority complex,* and *self-esteem,* which had been obscure before the war, became, quite literally, household words.

This domestication of the therapeutic gospel was an important episode in America's journey to the therapeutic altar. Psychological professionals, many of whom had played a key role in World War II, led the way. They sought to translate their wartime investments into peacetime dividends. Having for the first time treated "normal" men on a mass scale in the abnormal circumstance of war, they wanted to expand the boundaries of therapeutic intervention to the "normal" but psychologically troubled person in the ordinary course of his life. With such new ambitions, the professions of psychology and psychiatry undertook a massive lobbying effort directed at both the public at large and elected officials.

The consumption engine of the 1950s also played an important role in the spread of the therapeutic gospel. America emerged from World War II as a superpower with unprecedented economic and organizational strength. The development of brand-new methods of marketing, including the application of psychodynamic theory to selling, sustained this strength. With the advent of "motivation research," advertisers sold products by appealing to customers' unconscious motives, fears, and desires. Finally, women's magazines brought therapeutic principles directly into the American home. These magazines, at the height of their cultural power during the cold war, preached the virtue of domesticity and the gospel of fulfillment.

Psychological Professionals and Mental-Health Policy

The GI Bill (1944), one of the most popular laws in American history, provided a living allowance and tuition payments for college-bound veterans. The law's actual name was the Readjustment Act, an indication of the extent to which the concept of adjustment had become institutionalized. As World War II came to a close there was a general consensus that the government was responsible not only for the returning serviceman's material needs but also for his "readjustment," or psychological, needs. It had to help him by providing resources and social services.

For many soldiers the main difficulty in returning to civilian life was that they were afflicted with psychological problems. After the war, approximately 50 percent of disability pensions were paid to veterans suffering from psychological problems. In 1946 psychiatric patients made up 60 percent of the Veterans Administration's (VA) total hospital population. The VA's outpatient clinics served an additional 100,000 veterans and their families. The military system was ill prepared to deal with this large postwar problem. Both space and personnel were in short supply. When the war ended, there were more openings at the VA for clinical psychologists than there were trained clinical psychologists in the entire country.

This situation led the federal government to its first large-scale underwriting of therapeutic services during peacetime. To deal with personnel shortages, the VA initiated an ambitious four-year training program that offered students of clinical psychology free tuition and prorated salaries if they worked half-time for the VA while completing their studies. After only three years more than seven hundred students and forty-one universities had benefited from this federal largesse. The VA became the single largest employer of clinical psychologists in the country. It also actively recruited psychiatrists. By the mid-1950s the VA employed roughly 10 percent of all psychiatrists and hired an additional 10 percent as consultants.

While the government was increasing its ability to handle the volume of psychological problems experienced by veterans, psychological professionals were themselves on the march, advocating further governmental expansion of therapeutic services. Indeed, wartime psychiatry led the way. William Menninger, chief of the Army's Neuropsychiatric Division; Roy Grinker, who studied the psychological functioning of soldiers in the Tunisian campaign; Robert Felix, director of the Mental Hygiene Division of the Public Health Service; and Daniel Blain, head of psychiatry for the VA, all played key roles in the reconceptualization of psychology and psychiatry's purview.

As a vehicle for such pressure psychiatrists founded the Group for the Advancement of Psychiatry (GAP). In its mission statement GAP declared, "We favor the application of psychiatric principles to all those problems which have to do with family welfare, child rearing, child and adult education, social and economic factors which influence the community status of individuals and families, inter-group tensions, civil rights and personal liberty." Emboldened by their wartime experience, in which a premium had been placed on usefulness, psychological professionals began to argue that they had a duty to serve the entire community. "We would surely be guilty of dereliction of duty did we not make a conscientious effort to apply whatever partial knowledge we now possess in the interests of counteracting of social danger and promoting of healthier being. . . . This, in a true sense, carries psychiatry out of the hospitals and clinics and into the community."[1] Having gained a small foothold during the Progressive era in the hospitals, schools, and courts, the helping profession sought now to serve every facet of the community.

It was not simply that psychological professionals wanted to serve in new venues, for they also envisioned dramatically reorienting the constituency they served. Alan Gregg, an influential figure in the American Psychiatric Association as well as at the Rockefeller Foundation, characterized the new vision this way: to apply their findings to the "human relations of normal people—in politics, national and international, between races, between capital and labor, in government, in family life, in education, in every form of human relationship, whether between individuals or groups." He added that the specialty had to concern itself with psychological "optimum performance." No longer satisfied or even primarily concerned with treating the mentally ill, a leading group of psychiatrists began to define their mission in the grandiose terms of solving problems of international affairs and ensuring maximum psychological functioning for ordinary Americans.[2]

The story of how the nation came to embrace such expansive therapeutic goals begins with the popular press in the late 1940s and early 1950s. During this time there was a series of exposés on the treatment of the mentally ill. Such magazines as *Life*, the *Saturday Evening Post*, and *Reader's Digest* published scathing reports on the inhuman treatment of the mentally ill. In "Bedlam, 1946," for example, published in *Life*, with its dramatic oversized photography, Albert Maisel shocked the nation with his stories of deprivation and abuse. "Through public neglect and legislative penny pinching," he wrote, "state after state has allowed its institutions for the care of the mentally sick to degenerate into little more than concentration camps on the Belsen pattern."[3] His article was filled with descriptions and arresting photographs of neglected and abused mental patients. Two years later Albert Deutsch published his *Shame of the States* (1948), whose title refers to Lincoln Steffans's *Shame of the Cities* (1904), a Progressive-era exposé of political corruption), which exposed the conditions in state mental hospitals.[4]

Radio, film, and television also got into the act. In 1949, CBS aired an hour-long radio program on the conditions in mental hospitals. The show, "Mind in the Shadow," with none other than William Menninger as the commentator, received wide acclaim. Perhaps the largest audience was reached by film. The extremely popular film *The Snake Pit* (1948) not only exposed the poor treatment but also showed viewers a therapeutic alternative to the treatment of the mentally ill. The main character, a middle-class woman who suffers a mental breakdown, must be hospitalized. At the hospital she is abused by the staff and subjected to awful conditions. The film embraces the therapeutic gospel as the alternative. Only when the woman encounters an understanding and wise psychoanalyst who takes her off electric-shock therapy and provides her with psychotherapy does she begin to recover. The psychotherapy sessions take place in a room with a couch and a portrait of Freud. Through all her sessions Freud remains in the frame. By going back into her childhood, the psychiatrist and the patient together discover the sources of her illness, and she is rather magically cured. The psychotherapeutic methods of the psychiatrist are contrasted directly with the abusive and neglectful methods of custodial care, hearkening back to a major theme of the therapeutic reformers of the early twentieth century.

Such dramatic exposés and the increasingly influential mental-health lobby made a powerful combination. Elected officials felt increasing pressure to do something. The spotlight on institutional care came at a time when federal legislators were already demonstrating increasing enthusiasm for addressing Americans' health-care needs and the role advanced science might play. For example, immediately following World War II Congress passed the Hill-Burton Act, which provided for federal subsidies for the construction of hospitals. This legislation added tens of thousands of new beds to the nation's supply. Following the recommendations of President Truman's Scientific Research Board, the federal government increasingly subsidized biomedical research. It was in this context that the mental-health lobby succeeded in getting its first piece of national legislation passed.

Congressman J. Percy Priest, of Tennessee, in the House and Senator Claude Pepper, of Florida, in the Senate were perhaps most responsible for passage of the National Mental Health Act (1946).[5] Both held extensive hearings and were responsible for shepherding the legislation through, though committee members expressed very few reservations. Those who testified tended to focus on the inadequacies of the mental-hospital system. They criticized not only the shortages of personnel but also, implicitly, the mission of custodial care. On therapeutic grounds, they objected to treating people only after they fell ill. Ironically, while it was the poor treatment of the mentally ill that initiated the urge to reform, the legislation staked out the much more ambitious goal of prevention, ultimately neglecting those who were most in need of care. The mentally ill themselves tended to get lost in the grandiose plans established by the federal government.

Passage of the National Mental Health Act was a dramatic moment in the history of the therapeutic gospel. The federal government during peacetime had taken on a major new responsibility, a therapeutic responsibility. The law's broad purpose was "the improvement of the mental health of the people of the United States through the conducting of researches, investigations, experiments, and demonstrations relating to the cause, diagnosis, and treatment of psychiatric disorders; assisting and fostering such researches and activities and the useful application of their results; training personnel in matters relating to mental health; and developing and assisting the States in the use of, the most effective methods of prevention, diagnosis, and treatment of psychiatric disorders."[6] For these purposes Congress authorized $30 million. What marriage counselors of the 1920s and 1930s had only dreamed of, the adoption of a national policy of mental hygiene, was becoming a reality.

On a practical level the infusion of federal funds allowed universities and colleges across the nation to start or expand their training programs for mental-health professionals. For example, with federal financial support the number of residency programs in psychiatry expanded from 155 in 1946 to 294 in 1956, and the number of medical residents in psychiatry taking advantage of such programs leapt from 758 to 2,983 during the same years. The increase in psychology was equally dramatic. Between 1945 and 1960 membership in the American Psychological Association increased from 4,173 to 18,215.

Leading American psychiatrists and psychologists, with an expansive view of their profession, took the opportunity of flush funding to reorient the curriculum. In medicine this effort was not limited to students of psychiatry. Leading figures in medical education recommended that all medical students be exposed to "theories of personality growth, development, structure, and integration; adaptive needs; social and cultural forces affecting personality and behavior; the role of language and mentation; the part played by emotions in physiological functioning; and psychopathology." Clinical psychologists with equal fervor prescribed psychodynamic education. Indeed, the Committee on Training in Clinical Psychology in its guidelines for graduate programs insisted that no clinical psychologist "can be considered adequately trained unless he has had sound training in psychotherapy." This requirement helped to move psychotherapy from the margins to the center of American culture in the postwar era.[7]

In addition to funding training programs for mental-health professionals, the National Mental Health Act also provided funds for the construction of a facility for the National Institute for Mental Health (NIMH). After authorizing $7.5 million for its construction, Congress created this federal agency in 1949. The first director, Robert Felix, explained its purpose as follows: "to help the individual, by helping the community; to make mental health a part of the community's total health program, to the end that all individuals will have greater assurance of an emotionally and physically healthy and satisfying life for themselves and their families."[8] To accomplish these goals, NIMH was given an initial budget of $8.7 million. By 1960 its budget was more than $100 million.

This skyrocketing budget was used to institutionalize the therapeutic gospel in American life. The NIMH had several branches, including Research, Biometrics, and Publications and Reports. The Publications and Reports Branch was charged with educating the public about mental illness and mental health. It produced films, exhibits, study kits, and catalogs for the general public. The Biometrics Branch collected data and conducted surveys as well as statistical and epidemiological analyses of the mental-health field. The Research Branch supervised a range of federal research projects, including the Drug Addiction Research Center and the Cellular Pharmacology Laboratory. Most of the NIMH funding, however, went to extramural branches responsible for implementing federal grant programs in the mental-health field.

A significant portion of NIMH funding went to help states extend or create mental-health authorities. NIMH asked each state to create a mental-health agency and to have that agency submit a plan for how it would use the newly available federal funds. By 1950 every state in the nation had done so. States were specifically forbidden, however, from using federal funds for state mental hospitals. Plans had to be geared toward outpatient services, reflecting once again the emphasis on prevention and the new therapeutic ideal of mental health. NIMH regulations specified that for every dollar it gave to the state agency, the state had to give fifty cents. By 1951 the NIMH had assisted in the establishment of 342 clinics nationwide.

While the federal government took an activist stance toward the whole issue of mental health, the states were far from unwilling partners. Indeed, the states played a leading role in institutionalizing the therapeutic gospel. In 1949, at the annual governors' conference, the state governors took what at the time seemed like an unusual step: they asked their council on state governments to prepare a comprehensive report on the care and treatment of the mentally ill. The goal of the research was to inform policy discussions. The resulting report, *The Mental Health Programs of the Forty-eight States,* was published a year later.[9] The report documented severe overcrowding in state mental hospitals, a lack of trained personnel, and the inadequacy of treatment programs. In 1950 the governors' conference gave the report strong backing and called for a comprehensive survey of training and research in all states. Several years later the conference adopted a ten-point program. On both the federal and the local level the therapeutic gospel's core concepts were being institutionalized through the creation of new bureaucracies whose main mission was feeling management.

The implementation of this new vision varied from state to state of course. But even in the South, perhaps the region least sympathetic to the therapeutic gospel, some form of action was taken. In 1953 southern states joined forces to create the Mental Health Training and Research Project, which sought to help southern states deal with the shortage of personnel and to evaluate demonstration projects. Not surprisingly, New York and California took the lead in the mental-health field. In 1949, for example, New York State had already created a State Mental Health Commission. Its function included mental-health planning and administration of federal funds. In 1954 New York passed the Community Mental Health Services Act, which provided state aid to localities for the provision of mental-health services. In the first eight months state subsidies amounted to $4 million. Four years later the figure was almost $11 million.

Despite these significant state investments and the flurry of organizational activity that characterized state mental-health agencies, the mental-health lobby continued to demand federal leadership. One response to these demands was the creation of the Joint Commission on Mental Illness and Health in 1955. This commission was to conduct a nationwide study of Americans' mental-health needs and make policy recommendations. The commission's final report, *Action for Mental Health*, sketched out a brave new world of therapists involved in every aspect of public policy.[10]

Between 1946 and 1955 the federal government, with a series of legislative initiatives, including the National Mental Health Act (1946), the creation of the National Institute of Mental Health (1949), the National Mental Health Study Act (1955), and the creation of the Joint Commission on Mental Illness and Health (1955), for the first time took responsibility for promoting Americans' mental health.

The incorporation of the therapeutic gospel into federal social policy had a lasting effect on American society. It dramatically transformed the country's institutional landscape with the creation of new mental-health centers, training programs for mental-health professionals, and venues for the dissemination of mental-health principles. The new federal legislation also contributed to a shift in perspective: it endowed prevention with scientific and federal legitimacy. The new legislation embodied the idea that early intervention could prevent and ultimately eliminate mental illness. It also shifted the goal of therapeutic intervention. No longer was it mere prevention of illness; the federal government could play a role in actually producing mental health. This goal came increasingly to be defined in terms of happiness and personality growth. The legislation's ultimate aim was to prevent "unnecessary unhappiness" and to promote "the growth of creatively healthy American personalities." The American federal government had come a long way since its early beginnings in the swampy cluster of buildings known as Washington, D.C.[11]

Advertising and the Therapeutic Gospel

The cold-war era was unique in the history of American marketing. Never before had there been such intensive and widespread selling campaigns. By 1955 the United States was spending $9 billion to sell its wares. The unique scale of the marketing effort was partly a product of high production levels. A 1955 article in *Advertising Age* explained the pressure to sell as follows: "As a nation we are already so rich that consumers are under no pressure of immediate necessity to buy a very large share—perhaps as much as 40%—of what is produced, and the pressure will get progressively less in the years ahead. But if consumers exercise their option not to buy a large share of what is produced, a great depression is not far behind." The good news was that by the mid-1950s the average American had five times as many discretionary dollars as he had had in 1940. The bad news was that customers might chose to save or to defer expenditures.

The trick was to get the customer to spend this money on products he did not know existed and did not know he needed. Increasing standardization only made this task more difficult. Products like detergent, milk, cigarettes, and gasoline were so similar that it was hard for companies to establish sufficient brand loyalty to control the market. How was a customer supposed to decide whether to buy Tide or All when the products were essentially the same? Selling became a high-stakes game, resulting in major marketing innovations. One car salesman who was frustrated by the drop in consumer spending inadvertently hinted at the solution when he explained, "If buyer shopping gets any worse, we'll have to hit the customer over the head and get him to sign while he's unconscious."[12]

Indeed, targeting the unconscious became a key selling strategy in the 1950s. *Advertising Age, Printer's Ink, Tide, Business Week,* and *Fortune* alerted their readers to a new marketing approach that increasingly dominated Madison Avenue. In 1954 the *Wall Street Journal* told readers that "more and more advertising and marketing strategists are adapting their sales campaigns to the psychologists' finding and advice." In February 1955 *Sales Management,* a sales trade magazine, estimated that $12 million was being spent on this new kind of marketing annually.[13] As the foremost reporter of this new marketing trend, Vance Packard, in his well-known book *The Hidden Persuaders,* estimated that two-thirds of the nation's hundred largest advertising firms were using the new method, which he called "mass psychoanalysis."

This new approach to marketing was called the "depth approach" or "motivation research." Motivation research was an approach to marketing that relied on several key tenets of the therapeutic gospel. The "analysts" who practiced it assumed that consumers were motivated by thoughts and feelings that they were not even always conscious of. They saw consumers as full of hidden desires, guilt complexes, and irrational feelings. Selling products to them was ultimately a matter of understanding these underlying psychological realities.[14]

To uncover them, ad agencies hired psychologists and psychiatrists as well as psychological-research firms. The need for experts in this new area became so acute that the Advertising Research Foundation published several directories, including *A Directory of Organizations Which Conduct Motivation Research* and *A Directory of Social Scientists Interested in Motivation Research* (both 1954). It also published *A Bibliography of Theory and Research Technique in the Field of Human Motivation* (1956), listing close to five hundred books and articles on the subject. By the mid-1950s more than seven thousand accredited psychologists and psychiatrists were offering their services to companies.[15]

A key weapon in motivation analyst's psychological arsenal was the "depth-interview." These interviews were like those conducted by psychiatrists, "except there is no couch since a couch might make the chosen consumer–guinea pig wary."[16] As Dr. George Smith, one of the leading experts on motivation research, explained in his book *Motivation Research in Advertising and Marketing,* in the typical depth-interview the goal was "to get the consumer into a reverie of talking, to get him or her musing absent-mindedly about all the pleasures, joys, enthusiasms, agonies, nightmares, deceptions, apprehensions the product recalls."[17] By 1956 the depth-interview was considered such an important technique that when the American Management Association met in New York City its eleven hundred members received a closed-circuit TV demonstration of the method.

When Maidenform, the bra company, sought to give a dramatic lift to its sales, it hired "depth-probers" skilled at the depth-interview to help. Dream analysts set to work to discover whether women's secret sexual desires or hidden fantasies might help sell lingerie. They discovered that "the wish to appear naked or scantily clad is 'present in most of us'" and that such a wish "represents a beautiful example of wish fulfillment." Out of these psychological investigations of dreams came the "I Dreamed I Stopped Traffic in My Maidenform Bra" ad campaign, featuring an attractive young woman with an arresting figure who, wearing only a bra above the waist, stops traffic. The ad campaign was so successful that Maidenform decided to conduct a contest in which participants could win up to ten thousand dollars for ideas about dream situations that could be depicted in lingerie ads.[18]

Whether selling bras or milk, companies became increasingly convinced that consumers' fantasies and desires as well as their feelings about themselves were critical to marketing. Indeed, psychological-research companies gathered "personality profiles" on consumers to ascertain which constellations of characteristics defined key groups of buyers. Gasoline purchasers, for example, could be classified because buying gas reflected a consumer's identity. As one psychological researcher explained, "In buying a gasoline you get played back to you who you are. Each gasoline has built up an image or personality. Each helps a buyer answer the question Who am I?" Motivational analysts claimed to be able to predict which personalities would be likely to buy which brands of gasoline. If companies wanted to expand their market share, they would have to take these "personality profiles" into consideration and gear their ad campaigns accordingly.[19]

Though hundreds, if not thousands, of "motivational analysts" were practicing their trade in the 1950s, there were several key industry leaders. Louis Cheskin, director of what was known as the Color Research Institute of America, was one of the earliest advocates of applying psychodynamic principles to marketing. In 1948 Cheskin published in the *Harvard Business Review* one of the seminal articles on motivation research, "Indirect Approach to Market Reactions." Cheskin's Color Institute specialized in, among other things, advising clients on package design. "We use the psychoanalytical approach," he explained.[20] In the 1950s all his field investigators had majored in psychology and some had done work in psychoanalysis. Among his clients he claimed Philip Morris, Procter and Gamble, General Foods, and General Mills.

James Vicary, of James M. Vicary Company, was also well known at the time for his "depth-probing." His specialty was testing the connotations of words in ads. Trained in psychology, Vicary wrote another of the seminal articles in the new field, "How Psychiatric Methods Can Be Applied to Market Research."[21] He employed these methods with great success when he "diagnosed" why housewives, particularly young ones, were disinclined to use the butcher section of large supermarkets. Apparently, these young married shoppers felt a sense of inferiority when it came to their knowledge of cuts of meat. Vicary recommended that butchers receive special training to avoid intimidating language and to learn how to build women shoppers' confidence when it came to meat. Apparently, the strategy paid off.

Perhaps the most influential leader in the industry, however, was Dr. Ernest Dichter, also known as "Mr. Mass Motivations." Born in Vienna to a psychoanalyst mother, Dichter is thought to have undergone analysis himself. He also worked as a lay analyst for some time before founding the Institute for Motivational Research in Peekskill, New York, in 1946. His research institute conducted hundreds upon hundreds of studies for major corporations around the country and also published the monthly magazine *Motivations*.

When Jell-O found itself with an advertising disaster on its hands, the company called in Dr. Dichter. During the 1940s Jell-O had been a popular dessert. It had been established in the public mind as simple, good, and easy to make. In the 1950s Jell-O began a new ad campaign in women's magazines, with their new oversized formats and glossy color photographs, showing an elaborate multicolored and multilayered Jell-O design. These spectacular, expensive ads produced no results. The company wanted to know why its costly investment had not been paying off. To analyze the situation, it turned to Dichter. Dichter discovered after lengthy conversations with housewives that women did not feel capable of making such complicated desserts. The prospect of duplicating them brought up vague feelings of inadequacy. Jell-O went back to advertising its simple, one-color mound, and sales steadily improved. It apparently never occurred to Dichter's researchers—and of course such analysis was not what they were getting paid for—that women's feelings of inferiority may have stemmed from their circumscribed roles rather than the complexities of making multilayered desserts.

When banks irked by what they considered the "illegitimate" competition of loan sharks had had enough, they called in Dichter. The problem was that even though banks offered lower interest rates and did not use strong-arm tactics, many people in need of loans still went to loan sharks rather than respectable financial institutions. The problem? Customers tended to see banks as "father figures" whose moral disapproval intimidated them. When going to a bank for a loan, many felt like "an unreliable adolescent." Banks brought up a host of fears, including the fear of rejection and the fear of being scorned for having allowed one's finances to get into such a state.

New companies launching new products also called upon Dichter. He proved enormously helpful to a company that thought it had an ingenious idea of saving the housewife time and energy by providing her with a cake mix so that she did not have to bake the cake from scratch. But the pitch was not working. Dichter discovered that ready mixes generated guilt and other negative feelings among housewives. He also discovered, to the company's surprise, that women were unhappy with the product. Cake mixes were initially designed so that housewives simply had to add water. In fact, the instructions specifically stated not to add milk, "simply water"; they also stated not to add eggs. But many wives ignored the instructions, believing that eggs or baking soda were their "creative touch" and that their substitution of milk for water would make the cakes more like homemade cakes. As a result, the cakes often fell or turned out poorly. Dichter concluded that the housewife wanted to feel useful and creative and that cake mixes would only succeed if women were left with something to do. Not only did the company change the mixes so that women had to add more substantive ingredients but the ad campaigns emphasized the housewife as an active participant in cake baking.[22]

When the prune industry faced steadily decreasing sales, the California Prune Advisory Board went to Dichter. Dichter suspected that unconscious factors were leading Americans to shy away from prunes. But even Dichter's caseworkers at the Institute of Motivation Research were surprised by the things people associated with prunes. Word-association tests revealed that prunes were associated with words and phrases like *shriveled, dried up,* and *old maid.* "Prunes were associated with boardinghouses, where they were served by parsimonious landladies, with stingy, ungiving people, with joyless puritans," said Dichter. "The black murky color of prunes as commonly served was considered somehow symbolically sinister, and in at least one case the poor prune was associated with witches." Adding insult to injury was the laxative association. While this had not always hurt the prune companies, the number of drug laxatives on the market made it difficult to compete.[23]

In any case, Dichter recommended a wholesale revision of the prune image based on his in-depth interviews. The prune, he argued, had to be sold as the new "wonder-fruit." The idea was to assure housewives that it was just as acceptable to serve people prunes as it was to serve them peaches, apples, or cherries. The new ads used bright colors (prunes were depicted as having the color of purple grapes) and stayed as far away as possible from the old image of four black prunes floating in their dark juices. A few years after Dichter's "couch treatment," the prune's success was hailed in the advertising press as a miracle.[24]

Today psychological interpretations and advertising are so linked in our minds that it is hard for us to imagine the novelty of applying psychodynamic insights to the marketing of goods. But when the president of the Public Relations Society of America announced at the society's annual conference in the late 1950s that "the stuff with which we work is the fabric of men's minds," he was perceived to have hit on a recently discovered but nonetheless fundamental truth.[25] During the cold war, understanding the consumer's psyche became critical to selling him goods and services. Motivation research grafted therapeutic principles onto marketing, an increasingly influential sphere of American life.

Women's Magazines and the Therapeutic Gospel

Although the champions of the therapeutic gospel during the 1940s and 1950s were many, none were more devoted or more influential than women's magazines. In the 1950s and early 1960s women's magazines were at the height of their cultural power. Never before or since have they been such important disseminators of mass culture. During the cold-war years circulation rates skyrocketed. By the early 1960s the *Ladies' Home Journal* had 8 million readers, while *McCall's* and *Cosmopolitan* each boasted 6 million. In comparison, today women's magazines such as *Vogue, New Woman,* and *Working Mother* have circulations of fewer than 2 million, and even *People* has only 3.5 million.

The success of women's magazines was partially a result of the strict division of sex roles that reigned in America during the cold-war period. The 1940s and 1950s produced a now infamous domestic ideology that confined women to the home. While the reality of women's lives was far more complex, there was a substantial homogeneity among white middle-class women, particularly compared with the periods before and after the cold war. This homogeneity created enormous marketing opportunities and efficiencies. There was no need to waste resources pitching a publication to a narrowly defined niche market. Only one market really mattered: housewives.

The robust growth of women's magazines was also a product of America's expanding prosperity. Tied to the home but unprecedentedly well educated and affluent, women had both time and money—just what advertisers were looking for. As a result, advertising poured into the women's magazines, causing them to swell to more than 250 pages in length and having a similar effect upon their bank accounts.

This wealth in turned attracted top-notch staffs. Though it may be difficult to imagine today, during the cold war women's magazines, with their abundant resources and accompanying prestige, were meccas for talented and well-educated people. A staff position on a women's magazine was considered a ripe plum for an ambitious young person. The efforts of these talented persons further boosted readership by improving the quality of the magazines. The editors developed new kinds of articles and feature stories and a colorful oversized format that was innovative and influential.

Although the special cultural power of women's magazines during the cold-war era is today widely accepted, their impact has been greatly misunderstood.[26] Women's magazines have been blamed for ignoring women's psychological condition, particularly their unhappiness, and for teaching women to do the same. Betty Friedan, considered the mother of recent feminism, made this the premise of her famous critique of the period, *The Feminine Mystique*. She accused cold-war American culture, in particular women's magazines, of falsely portraying women as "gaily content in a world of bedroom, kitchen, sex, babies, and home," while the truth was that women suffered from depression and loneliness.[27] Maintaining that women did not even have a language for understanding their dissatisfaction, she called their unhappiness "the problem that has no name."

Friedan's critique was instantly influential and has proved remarkably enduring. There seems to be a general consensus that the unhappiness of women in the 1950s was either neglected or censored. In particular, women's magazines have been accused of "depict[ing] happiness where there was frustration," portraying the "home" as a "haven," and "promulgating a happy-housewife syndrome."[28] Just how durable Friedan's critique has been is illustrated by David Halberstam's book *The Fifties*. Though published three decades after Friedan's, his account of women's magazines is hardly distinguishable from hers. In the 1950s, according to Halberstam, "no one was paying close attention to what the new home-oriented, seemingly drudgery-free life was doing to the psyche and outlook of American women"; women's magazines instead promulgated "relentlessly happy" images of women.[29]

It is important to discover whether this view of the cold-war era and women's magazines is right. We need to know whether it is true that there was some sort of cultural cover-up surrounding the "psyche and outlook of American women" and whether women's magazines played a major role in it. If this was the case, then the 1950s were not a good time for the therapeutic gospel. Clearly, a culture bent on telling women to ignore their feelings could hardly have nurtured America's faith in the psyche. But did this era in fact discourage emotional inquiry? Was it silent on the question of unhappiness, particularly the unhappiness of women? In short, did the therapeutic gospel suffer a decided setback during this period?

My answer to all these questions is a resounding no! Rather than hiding women's psychological condition, these magazines placed it in full display for millions of women. Rather than presenting relentlessly upbeat images of women, the magazines often portrayed women as profoundly unhappy. Rather than dissuading women from considering their psychological condition, the magazines actively encouraged it.

One can easily get to the bottom of this by making a visit to the library and leafing through issues from the 1950s of *Ladies' Home Journal, McCall's, Cosmopolitan*, the *Women's Home Companion, Better Homes and Garden, Colliers*, and *Good Housekeeping*. Instead of ignoring the housewife's discontent, they devoted a great deal of attention to it. In fact, women's magazines were in the forefront of a new campaign to raise women's consciousness about their psyches.

Take the *Cosmopolitan* article "How Emotions Cause Unnecessary Surgery," which tells the gruesome story of a middle-aged woman from "New York's fashionable Westchester County" who had twenty-nine needless operations. Why so many? The woman was reported to be a "surgical neurotic." Profoundly unhappy and experiencing severe "inner turmoil," she insisted that her doctor operate. Surprisingly, this woman was presented not as a bizarre case study but rather as representative of women "whose husbands are too busy to notice them" and who "may, in desperation, use the operating table to regain their love."[30] Women were advised not to rush to the doctor but instead to scrutinize their emotions and uncover the true source of their pain.

Far from neglecting women's unhappiness, the magazines featured a steady stream of articles about overwrought and depressed women. A sampling of article titles indicates that the magazines were not bashful about discussing the unhappy housewife:

"How Do You Beat the Blues?"
"What Do You Do When Worries Get You Down?"
"I Can't Stand It Anymore"
"Why Do Women Cry?"

"How to Recognize Suicidal Depression"

"Blues and How to Chase Them"

"How to Get Over Feeling Low"

"Crying as Catharsis"

"Lonely Wife"

"Where to Take Your Troubles"

"Are You Afraid You're Going Crazy?"

"What's Your Emotional Breaking Point?"

Often women's magazines tried to quantify women's unhappiness. In addition to reporting on it, they even directly commissioned studies on the topic. Sometimes the results were what one would expect to find in an antimarriage tract rather than in a women's magazine. For example, in 1948 the *Ladies' Home Journal* published "a scientific study" to discover "the hard, cold facts of what causes happiness and unhappiness."[31] This study revealed that only one in twenty women considered themselves happily married and that women were twice as likely as men to be unhappy. Another article reported that more than 30 percent of women were so dissatisfied with their marriages that if they could go back, they would not marry their husbands again.[32] Why were women so unhappy? The *Ladies' Home Journal* gave the following rather pessimistic assessment: "Women are inclined to think an undue share of [household] responsibilities falls on the wives; the majority of women think they lead a harder life than men; and they think their happiest years end sooner. Perhaps too, they think a housewife's life is duller; an earlier *Journal* survey found that the group of workers least likely to enjoy their jobs was—housewives!"[33]

Surprisingly, even those authors who argued in no uncertain terms that a woman's place was the home acknowledged that she often was not very happy there. Even the archconservative Marynia Farnham, author of *The Modern Woman: The Lost Sex* (a book on every feminist's list of the ten most hated books), who made a career out of arguing that women should stay at home, did not try to hide their unhappiness. For example, in the article "Women and Wives" she noted that many women felt envious of their husbands' "supposedly exciting and stimulating life" and resented the "drudgery and the monotony of dirty dishes, difficult children, and household routines."[34] Farnham's point was not that women *were* always happy in the home, but that they *should be*.

Nor do the articles of Dorothy Thompson, a well-known writer for women's magazines who was a strident antifeminist (before that term was in use), portray blissfully happy housewives or contented mothers. In "Occupation: Housewife" Thompson noted that many women find themselves thinking, "Here I am, a middle-aged woman with a university education and I've never made anything out of my life. I'm just a housewife." These women, she said, suffered from "an inferiority complex": instead of appreciating their important contribution to their families and society, they tended to feel bad about their domestic roles and responsibilities.[35] Like Farnham's, Thompson's point was that women should be happy, but she acknowledged that they often were not.

Clearly, there was more acknowledgment of unhappiness in the women's magazines than Betty Friedan and others have admitted. In fact, the myth of domestic bliss—the myth Friedan accused women's magazines of promoting—was one the magazines actually often warned *against*. One article, for example, stated that "we've all been sadly misled by fairy tales that ended 'and so they were married and lived happily ever after.' It simply is not true."[36] Rather than building them up, the magazines often tried to deflate women's expectations of marriage and home life.

Given that women's magazines clearly supported the idea of domesticity, why did they spend so much time focusing on women's unhappiness? After all, the argument of Betty Friedan and other 1960s feminists that the magazines' zealous commitment to domesticity led them to ignore and even censor the topic of how women felt about their lives is logical. If the magazines' goal was to keep women in the home, it follows that they would portray women as always happy there. Why, then, did they often expose women's unhappiness?

The answer is that a magazine is a business: the magazines published these articles because they boosted sales. The phenomenal success of women's magazines following World War II was due in large measure to their incredible creativity in responding to women's needs and desires in the new consumer age. As a result, both the look and the content of the magazines changed dramatically. Many adopted an oversized format and used full-spread technicolor ads. Brighter and glitzier, the magazines were also longer. Finally, the widespread use of life-sized photographs contributed to the bold look of the magazines. This new look paralleled their new content: "close-up" stories of women's lives that turned a public spotlight on what had previously been women's private dilemmas and struggles. Publishers found that these intimate portrayals of women and their home life sold magazines. Women apparently liked to read stories about other women's unhappiness.

In large measure, women liked these articles because they themselves were unhappy and they took comfort from evidence that they were not alone. Sensing this, the women's magazines began to make the idea that women should not feel abnormal because they were unhappy an explicit theme. In "Crying as Catharsis," for example, readers were told not to worry if they wept when they felt sad or lonely because "tears are a natural and universal release for many minor emotions" and can help "siphon off the small frustrations that confront all of us every hour of every day."[37] Such articles sought to convince women that expressing their feelings was not only normal but a positive good because it was a healthy way of dealing with emotions.

Another feature that reassured women that unhappiness was quite normal was the enormously popular marriage-advice columns, such as "Can This Marriage Be Saved?" "Why Marriages Fail," and "Making Marriage Work." The content of these articles was reflected in the photos that accompanied them, which invariably showed an anguished woman alone or with her husband. A typical example is the *Ladies' Home Journal* column "Making Marriage Work" for January 1948, devoted to the travails of Alice Rand. In typical no-punches-pulled style the author of this column pronounced that Mrs. Rand "is an unhappy woman and she and her husband have a thoroughly unhappy marriage." And, of course, the author reassured the reader to whom this might sound uncomfortably familiar that "Alice is not unique."[38] The column "Marriage Is a Private Affair" in the October 1960 *McCall's* quotes a series of rather painful exchanges between a husband and wife and assures readers that "similar conversations go on day after day in thousands of homes."[39] Such columns insisted that marital difficulties were the "daily dilemma of millions of married couples in the modern world."[40]

Another popular innovation in women's magazines was psychological self-help articles. These articles were much like the cooking recipes and cleaning tips that could be found elsewhere in the magazines: simple, straightforward instructions that could be followed in the home. Instead of recipes for cakes, however, these were recipes for curing unhappiness. Take the lead article in the January 1950 issue of *McCall's*, "It's Good to Blow Your Top." It describes American women as frustrated and angry, comparing their plight to that of a pressure cooker: "When things are going smoothly, the steam is under control—and the meat gets done to a turn. But when problems begin to pick up, the pressure rises to a dangerous level. Unless it is released in some unusual manner, the cooker may explode." The article advises women that rather than "suffer in silence," they should throw old plates against the wall to express their anger: "When you are on the verge of a blow up, *let fly*." Or instead they could put it in writing: "Write it down—all of it. Go into detail. Use unmaidenly language. Say every horrible thing you've ever wanted to say." Sports or cleaning might also help release pent-up feelings of dissatisfaction or anger: "You can even beat the daylights out of your rugs or superpolish every table in your house."[41]

Simple voyeurism was another reason why women liked articles about other women's unhappiness. This was particularly true in the case of the marriage-advice columns. Today one learns about other people's personal lives via talk shows, celebrity magazines, and revealing biographies. In the 1950s, however, matters were far more private. On the *I Love Lucy Show* Lucy and Ricky's bedroom had two single beds rather than a double bed, avoiding even the implication of sexual relations. Against this background, reading the marriage-advice columns was like peering into the neighbor's bedroom window. Embracing a tell-all style, the columns brought the personal conflicts between husbands and wives into the public spotlight. They provided intimate details about couples' inner lives and marital circumstances. Readers could learn about real women's disappointments and emotional suffering and their narrow escapes from marital dissolution.

Though the titles of these columns were melodramatic, they actually showed real couples in great pain. One of the more common sources of this misery was the strict division of sex roles: marital conflict arose because wives found their domestic responsibilities unfulfilling and began devoting more attention to themselves, further alienating their husbands. For example, an October 1957 column titled "Is My Marriage a Mistake?" describes a woman named Thelma who is overwhelmed by sadness and a feeling of resentment toward her husband, Joe. After quitting college to marry, she devotes her life to her husband, leaving behind her interests in literature and music. On the surface her marriage seems perfect, but underneath there is deep unhappiness that no one seems to understand: "As the world sees [my husband], he's a steady, hard-working, up-and-coming young executive in a safe job with good prospects," says Thelma, but to her "he's just a big disappointment. I feel thwarted. I get mad at Joe. Not a fighting mad—just a dull, growing anger. Yet its hard to justify this. As I said, he doesn't beat me up or run around or come home drunk." Even Thelma's friends cannot understand her feelings of desperation: "My girl friends say I should feel fortunate to have such a husband—so steady and dependable, so hard-working. When they say that, I get even madder still. I say to myself, 'If only you could know how I feel inside!'" Thelma goes on to explain that "it's a shut-in kind of feeling. . . . I feel trapped, and somehow Joe is to blame." Articles like this dealt with the conflict that many women experienced: according to the prevailing values of the cold war, they had it all, but they were still unhappy. These articles did not reject these values, but they did show women that they were not alone in their unhappiness and alienation.[42]

The women's magazines also provided women with an entirely new language for expressing their feelings of dissatisfaction, terms such as *unconscious, ego, inferiority complex, psychosomatic, defensive reaction,* and *self-esteem.* The use of these terms legitimatized women's psychological inquiries and complaints. How this therapeutic vocabulary came to be embraced by women's magazines has much to do with World War II and its aftermath.

World War II was a transforming event for the mental-health professions. Legions of psychiatrists, psychologists, and social workers were drafted into the armed services and asked to ply their trade for the cause of the war. Their task—to maintain the mental health of the fighting man—was a monumental one both because of the number of soldiers, more than 10 million, and because of the unprecedented brutality of the war. Never before had mental-health professionals been showered with such resources or asked to play so vital a role in world affairs. It was a shot in the arm for the young profession, reaffirming its social importance and broadening its members' ambitions.

With the end of the war mental-health professionals began to wonder where they could apply the skills and knowledge they had acquired in the war. Like the returning soldiers, psychiatrists and psychologists found their new mission in the American home. These professionals would no longer confine their treatment to the mentally ill and others at the margins of society; but would help ordinary persons use therapeutic thinking to strengthen the American home.

In another stroke of luck, just as they turned their attention to this task, the home came to be viewed as a bulwark against Communism. Strong "family values" were seen as critically important to freedom, democracy, and capitalism. This connection between the home and the containment of Communism could be seen in such films as *The Commies Are Coming* and *Kiss*

Me Deadly, in which inattentive fathers and overly doting mothers or overly sexual women lead to Communist infiltration or takeovers. The strategic importance of the home was also reflected in the political rhetoric of the era. Then Vice President Richard Nixon, in his famous "kitchen debate" with Premier Nikita Khrushchev, pointed to a model American kitchen with its gleaming new appliances as proof of America's superiority. This emphasis on the home provided the expanding and increasingly well-organized mental-health professions with a golden opportunity to take their therapeutic case to the public.

But how could they reach into the home? How could they convince ordinary Americans that family life could be improved and solidified by applying psychological principles? The answer was women's magazines, which were read by the very people the mental-health establishment most wanted to reach: housewives. The content of these magazines also dovetailed perfectly with mental-health professionals' message. Family values were easily expanded to include therapeutic goals; home improvement easily expanded to include psychological maintenance. Psychological professionals could not have created a better vehicle for disseminating the therapeutic gospel.

When these professionals turned to their task, the legacy of World War II helped them in yet another way. Historically, professional psychological treatment had been connected with psychological illness. While first mind cure and New Thought, then therapeutic reformers, followed by marriage counselors, had tried valiantly to change this, the vast majority of Americans who received treatment suffered from severe psychological troubles. But whatever the reality, until World War II the perception was that those who received treatment were sick or abnormal. The average American thought of it as something for "weirdos" or "wackos"; he did not want professional help, nor did he want to see his difficulties in psychological terms. The war helped to break down this stigma. Millions of servicemen were told during the war that their insecurities, frustrations, and feelings of depression were a normal reaction to the circumstances of war. They no longer necessarily equated psychological problems with psychological illness.

But while psychological problems during wartime might be considered normal, this tolerance did not necessarily extend to psychological problems in civilian life. However, a crack had been made in the edifice of stigmatization, and psychologists realized that they could exploit it: if the stresses of ordinary life could be compared to those of combat, then it could be reasoned that psychological problems were just as normal for civilians as for soldiers. This was exactly the tack that was taken, and the kitchen was transformed into a battlefield. As the famous World War II psychiatrist William Menninger explained in an interview published in *Cosmopolitan,* "A kind of operational fatigue occurs in civilian life just as it did in the Army."[43] Indeed, the symptoms were similar: domestic breakdown, like combat fatigue, produced the blues, frustration, anger, vague fears, and sometimes tears at the slightest provocation. This same analogy was used to demonstrate that "yes, everybody has an emotional breaking point," in a 1955 article in *Cosmopolitan:* "In the last war, for example, fighting men exhibited neurotic behavior extreme enough to have sent a civilian to a sanitarium yet such reactions were recognized as perfectly normal responses to great stress. The vast majority of these men reverted to normal behavior when removed for a while from the strain of combat." *Cosmopolitan* suggested that the strains of home life, just like the horror of the battlefield, could make even a normal person suffer from neuroses.

This new view of psychological problems is illustrated by the very title of one article: "Are You an Everyday Neurotic?" The radical suggestion implicit in this title was that even a condition serious enough to merit a scientific name could be considered an "everyday" condition. A 1956 *Cosmopolitan* article informed readers that experts estimated that one in ten people would suffer a breakdown at some point in their life. This did not even include the many who "do not collapse, but drag joylessly through dismal days." Readers, who were "churning with tension, wondering how much more their nerves can take before they cave in," were told not to worry: "This doesn't mean that you are 'abnormal,' but simply human."[44]

The women's magazines suggested that the real danger was not *having* problems but *ignoring* them. For the first time, millions of women were told that they needed to understand psychology in order to understand their feelings and behavior. For example, they were supposed to know that neuroses developed if fundamental human needs were left unfulfilled, a novel concept at the time. In addition, women had to become intimate with their "selves," their needs, desires, and dissatisfactions, in order to find happiness. Women's magazines urged readers to "search yourself thoroughly" and "study your reactions to the pleasures and frustrations of daily life."[45]

The first step along the road toward psychological self-discovery was disarmingly simple: taking a psychological mini-test. These tests were so popular that they appeared regularly and generated a whole new genre of articles. The tests typically asked questions such as "What are your grievances?" "Is your marriage happy?" "What are your personal needs?" "Are you a restless wife?" and "Do you enjoy yourself?" In "Ask Yourself: Is Your Life Satisfying?" for example, women were given a few simple questions, such as "Are you usually happy and contented?" "Does the future have real purpose (meaning) for you?" and "Do you look forward to each new day?"[46] Women were told that "ideally all questions should be answered 'Yes'" and reminded that "a score of less than 4 in any group suggested a real handicap in that area."

The brilliance of these tests was their accessibility and simplicity. A reader could enter the realm of the psychological while sitting at the kitchen table. Inner knowledge was achievable by using the "emotional temperature chart" or the "mood-meter scale." All that was needed was a pencil. But like a Trojan Horse, happiness tests gained entry by their seeming innocuousness and then sprung a surprise: if you scored poorly, they advised, you should seek treatment. In this way magazines introduced the reader to the cardinal principle of the therapeutic gospel: that unhappiness was a condition that could be— and *should* be—treated.

Treatment did not necessarily involve consulting a counselor. Instead, the magazines showed a somewhat naive faith in easy cures. Readers were offered a variety of do-it-yourself psychological cures, including "managing emotions steps" and techniques like "autoconditioning." An article optimistically titled "Autoconditioning Can Make You a Happy Person," for example, recommended this technique "if, like most people you are searching for a way to live your daily life free from worry and depression."[47] Fundamentally, autoconditioning appears to have been nothing more than thinking positively about one's life and "banishing" thoughts of loneliness, sadness, and anger. Nonetheless, the article claimed that autoconditioning had helped the depressed—even the suicidal—score "high marks on the mood-meter," some achieving moods ranging from "purposeful" to "joyful."

For those who repeatedly failed their "happiness tests" and had no success with therapeutic techniques like autoconditioning, professional help was advised. An important component of the articles was quite practical information about to whom women should go when they felt lonely, depressed, or angry. Readers learned about the various kinds of therapeutic services available to them in such articles as "Where to Take Your Troubles," "Where to

Get a Marriage Counselor When You Need One," "What You Should Know About Psychiatry," and "How to Choose a Psychiatrist."

Women's magazines also sought to demystify the therapeutic process, which, unlike today, seems to have been shrouded in secrecy. The magazines sought to reduce women's anxiety about seeking professional help by providing interviews with marriage counselors and psychiatrists that explained what to expect in a therapeutic session. The magazines took nothing for granted: one article explained, for example, that the counselor would ask many questions about the patient's upbringing and feelings before the patient explained her problem.[48]

The main message was quite simple: *women had the right to be happy.* Never before had this proposition been spelled out so clearly. This message was particularly evident in the marriage-advice columns, which emphasized that a woman, like a man, was entitled to judge the adequacy of her marriage based on whether it made her happy. As one counselor explained, "Any woman has a right to feel unsatisfied if she isn't getting what she really needs from her marriage." Another insisted that the "first step toward a well-adjusted personality [and therefore marriage] is to face [one's] needs, then make an *honest* effort to satisfy them."[49] Marriage counselors claimed that "an essential ingredient of every truly satisfying human relationship" was "the development and realization of the individual's potentialities for growth, achievement, and well-being."[50]

While the explicit message of the magazines was that women had a right to happiness, lurking beneath this psychological nirvana was an unstated loyalty to more traditional cold-war values that gave the magazines a strange, schizophrenic air. On the one hand, women were assured that they were entitled to happiness and could achieve it with the help of marriage counselors and "constant attention to the quality of your marriage."[51] On the other, the solutions actually proposed by the marriage counselors seem woefully inadequate, geared more to cold-war values than to women's needs.

Two articles about couples illustrate this point. Each begins with a lengthy description of the couple's painfully dysfunctional marriage. In one—about Marcia and Phil—Marcia is lonely and overcome by feelings of uselessness. She does nothing but cook, clean, and take care of the children. The counselor notes that she more often than not "feels inadequate" and is possessed by a "deep sense of inferiority." To prove her "self-worth," she "seeks to excel at the things Phil does." She competes with him intellectually and corrects him when he has made a mistake. This competition brings their marriage to the brink of disaster.

In the second article—about Alice and Ralph—Alice begins her counseling session by announcing that "everything is dead between Ralph and me" and sobs uncontrollably. With coaxing, she explains that for five days Ralph has not spoken a word to her: "Not one. I ask and ask if he loves me and he just turns his head. He won't even look at me. He eats his meals without speaking, without noticing that I've specially cooked chops or steak, his favorite foods. After he finishes eating, he picks up a book or magazine and reads or just sits in a chair staring into space and shutting me out." As these examples attest, though the "marriage" is a problem, it is typically the woman who does most of the suffering. She feels the unhappiness most keenly because the family is her whole world, whereas her husband escapes it by going to work.

These marriages do not function on the most basic level, making the wife's reliance on her husband and family for fulfillment even more disturbing. By the end of these descriptions one is often inclined to answer the question "Can this marriage be saved?" with a rather decided no. At the very least it seems that somewhat radical changes, especially in the man's behavior, would have to be made to keep the marriages afloat.

But radical changes are rarely in order. Though the marriage counselor lays the problems out in considerable detail and often with a surprising dose of psychological insight, the solutions proposed often seem like careless and unconvincing afterthoughts that provide little solace for the woman. For example, Alice is told that she must accept the fact that her husband is "reticent," and the counselor offers the following insight: "In cooking him expensive steaks and smothering him with excessive protestations of love, she was offering him not the kind of attention he wanted and needed but the kind she wanted herself. . . . When Alice recognized this fact and acknowledged that the language of courtship and juvenile dreams is seldom the language of marriage, she started keeping household accounts and *padlocking* her tongue." The marriage counselor recognizes Alice's desperate need for love and attention but then blames her for failing to make this psychological insight herself and for not keeping her mouth shut. Marcia fares little better; she is advised to "cultivate self-respect, not by competing with Phil but by pursuing her own talents and skills independently. Perfecting her needlework, becoming an expert gardener—these are just a few of her opportunities to demonstrate her worth."[52] It is difficult to believe that these solutions, which bear no relationship to the insights into the couple's problems, were entirely convincing to either their authors or their readers. The solutions were dictated not by what would be most efficacious or successful in helping the marriage but instead by the values of the day: marriages were inviolate, a woman's place was the home, and wives had to submit to their husbands.

The schizophrenia in the magazines resulted from a fundamental conflict of values. A central tenet of the therapeutic gospel espoused in the magazines was that women should seek self-fulfillment. But the magazines also subscribed to the ideal that a woman's place was in the home. When women were left unfulfilled by the domestic life, the obvious solutions—that a woman divorce or seek a career—were never stated because these solutions were contrary to the dominant values of the day.

Another sign of this conflict between the domestic ideal and the therapeutic gospel was that the magazines encouraged women to explore their unhappiness but then sought to confine this exploration within the limits of domesticity. This is clear in so many cases where a women was supposed "to take stock of [her] marriage" to determine whether it still made her happy or whether it "had stopped growing." She was never given any meaningful alternative in the case that the results turned out negative.

Cold-war values and the therapeutic gospel were a highly combustible combination. Every issue of the women's magazines added fuel to the fire of women's discontent while providing ridiculously inadequate balms for their unhappiness. And though the magazines never acknowledged the inherent contradictions between the therapeutic gospel and cold-war values, this did not mean that the women were unaware of them. It was precisely because women did come to see these contradictions that one of the first controversies over women's role in the home occurred in the pages of women's magazines.

The immediate cause of this controversy was the publication in *McCall's* of Betty Friedan's "The Fraud of Femininity" in 1963. In this article Friedan first put forth the argument, made at more length in *The Feminine Mystique,* that women's happiness was a lie and women should reject the myth of domestic bliss. The response to her piece was overwhelming. *McCall's* received an avalanche of letters from its readers, many expressing views very different from what one might expect.

The conventional wisdom is that Betty Friedan's message was the exact opposite of that found in women's magazines. We remember her as the one who, in the words of one commentator, "broke the silence about women's lives of quiet desperation." But this is not how the readers of Friedan's article saw it. They saw her article as part and parcel of the magazines' "negativistic attitude" toward the housewife.[53] Not only did these readers reject Friedan's message about the myth of domestic bliss, insisting that their own perfectly happy and contented lives were proof that the "myth" was real, but they claimed that they had heard it all before in the magazines, that the magazines were actually supersaturated with portraits of women as unhappy, lonely, and frustrated. As one devoted women's magazine reader proclaimed: "I am a proud and fulfilled wife, mother, daughter, sister, daughter-in-law, and friend; trying to live up to my purpose of being here on this earth; no small nor ignominious task, I can assure you. And I am sick, sick, sick of reading just this type of article, as I am sure many other happily married women are." Another reader objected to the magazines' image of women as "empty, wasted, or filled with frustration," and yet another considered Friedan's article "only one of many similar articles that are making me more and more disgusted." Women wrote that they had "been reading articles similar to Mrs. Friedan's for years and boil with rage" every time another appeared. They insisted that they were "tired of hearing about the poor little housewife who is trapped, frustrated, guilty, wasting her life, unappreciated, dependent, passive and whatever else she is called," and they railed against the "public barrage of vapid articles" that were "designed to trigger a few insecurities in neurotic women and cause the rest of us to doubt our own eyes." They were "fed up with being studied and analyzed, praised and damned" and wished "educated people would quit analyzing and studying us as though we were mcrobes in a test tube." These women wanted Friedan and the magazines to "stop knocking the homemaker." Signing their letters with closures such as "from a very happy, contented, but obviously without knowing it, trapped housewife," some even insisted that they would cancel their subscriptions if the magazines did not stop publishing "Friedan-type articles."

Clearly, these readers overlooked some very real differences between Friedan's feminist message and those typically found in women's magazines. However, they were correct in recognizing that a very important part of Friedan's critique had already been expressed in the women's magazines, namely, that women were entitled to be happy but often were not happy in their roles as wives and mothers. These letters also tell us that the magazines were having an impact on the women who read them. Their volcanic reaction to Friedan's article shows the depth of their feelings about the problem of unhappiness and the way women's magazines had been prodding women to think about their psyches. Of course, many of the readers still defended women's traditional roles. But for every woman who rejected the message that women were unhappy, there were countless others who were becoming aware of their unhappiness.

Ironically, the editors of women's magazines undoubtedly had little idea of the effect that their magazines were having upon women. They certainly lacked feminist intentions and were not making women conscious of their unhappiness out of some sort of political commitment to women. In fact, they probably believed that by addressing women's unhappiness, they were strengthening the traditional home. Precisely the opposite was happening, however. No matter what gloss the magazines tried to put on it, it was an explosive combination that would not be contained for long.

6 SOCIAL PROTEST

Liberating the Psyche

1960–1975

The 1960s and early 1970s were years of social protest. Idealistic and sometimes rash youth made social injustice their rallying cry. With such slogans as "Make Love Not War," "Freedom NOW," "Power to the People," "Hell No, We Won't Go," "Black Power," "Peace NOW," "Sisterhood Is Powerful," and "Stop the War, Feed the Poor" activists hoped to transform not only American politics but also everyday life. They sought a new way of life, one that would foster humane values and eliminate racism, sexism, war, and poverty. They railed against oppression on both the political and the personal level. In fact, they insisted that no such distinction existed: the personal was political and the political was personal. A better world required the adoption of *personal politics,* a term coined by feminists of the era.

On the surface it would seem that these fights for social justice had very little to do with the therapeutic gospel. Those involved in the Freedom Rides, rides made by Black and White students through the Deep South to test federal court orders of desegregation; the free-speech movement, protests by students at the University of California, Berkeley, who objected to restrictions on campus political action; or the Miss America protest, a demonstration against the exploitation of women, appear not to have advocated the therapeutic gospel. The goals of personal happiness, emotional growth, and self-fulfillment seem quite different from those of peace, equality, and social justice.

In fact, radicals prided themselves on their hostility to conventional psychological wisdom. Adopting an anti-expert stance, they emphasized the gulf between their own thinking and that of psychological experts. Indeed, feminists in 1969 went so far as to take over key sessions of the American Psychiatric Association's annual meeting. For many radicals, personal experience rather than experts' knowledge was the only legitimate source of authority. Turning this perspective into a political slogan, 1960s radicals sought to "question the authority" of all others.

Despite these claims, however, the social movements of this turbulent era relied heavily on the authority of psychological experts and the tenets of the therapeutic gospel. In particular, protesters drew upon a brand of humanistic psychology promoted by the well-known psychologists Carl Rogers and Abraham Maslow. More generally, the therapeutic gospel became an important source of ammunition in the fight for civil rights, women's liberation, and a new counterculture. Measuring social evil with a psychological yardstick, radicals judged everything from racially segregated schools to suburban homes. They found the institutions of American life to be dehumanizing, to warp the human personality. To radicals, the whole "system" was designed to eradicate the psychological integrity of man and—increasingly with the birth of the women's movement—woman.

In place of depersonalizing institutions, radicals sought to build institutions that recognized the full humanity of those they served. They worked to create institutions that "cared." At the core of their vision was a society that respected the individual psyche. Sixties radicals saw their demonstrations against segregation, war, and male chauvinism as struggles for the liberation of the self. All forms of tyranny had to come to an end if humans were to realize their full potential. Ultimately, these radicals wanted to organize all human relationships along therapeutic lines. In their hands the therapeutic gospel proved explosive. It transformed the relationship between Whites and Blacks, government and its citizens, and men and women.

The Supreme Stamp of Approval

When the National Association for the Advancement of Colored People (NAACP) set out to establish that segregation in education was unconstitutional, there could be no doubt about the biggest obstacle they faced: *Plessy v. Ferguson,* the Supreme Court's 1896 decision that educating Blacks separately from Whites did not violate the Fourteenth Amendment so long as the education provided was otherwise equal. The problem was that the Supreme Court applied stare decisis—"stand by decided matters"—following rules or principles laid down in previous decisions if the facts were substantially the same. Thus, the NAACP had to convince the Court not only of the merits of its argument but also that it should not apply stare decisis in this case.

Moreover, no matter how much the NAACP despised the *Plessy* decision, it had a certain undeniable logic. If Blacks were truly receiving an equal, albeit separate education, then what right were they being denied under the Fourteenth Amendment? The logic had an internal consistency that made *Plessy* particularly difficult to attack. To be sure, the NAACP could argue that the Fourteenth Amendment guaranteed a right to not only an *equal* education but the *same* education. This, however, would require the Supreme Court to throw out *Plessy* entirely. If equal was what the Fourteenth Amendment required in 1896, how could it require something different now? Such a fundamental shift would leave the Supreme Court open to the charge that it was just reading its own social ideals into the Fourteenth Amendment.

Thus, the NAACP had to convince the Court not merely that the Fourteenth Amendment could be interpreted *differently* than in *Plessy* but that *Plessy* was just plain wrong, that there was a flaw in the seemingly perfect edifice of *Plessy*'s "separate but equal" jurisprudence. A way to show that flaw was discovered by Bob Carter, a young Black NAACP lawyer.

The social sciences, like almost every field of inquiry in the United States, benefited from the talented refugees fleeing German Nazism. Not surprisingly, moreover, the refugee social scientists were interested in understanding the social pathology that they had fled. Theodore Adorno, for example, turned his attention to studying the psychological underpinnings of Fascist political regimes. In 1950 he published *The Authoritarian Personality,* a widely read book funded by the American Jewish Committee, which sought to understand the "willingness of great masses of people to tolerate the mass extermination of their fellow citizens."[1] A key feature of the authoritarian personality, Adorno found, was the "social disease" of racial prejudice. Significantly, although Adorno's inquiry was spurred by Nazism, he did not portray racial prejudice as merely a distant European phenomenon but found it to be a potent force in the United States as well.

Adorno's work was followed by a spate of studies about prejudice in the United States at mid-century. Perhaps the most important of these studies was by the psychiatrists Abram Kardiner and Lionel Ovesey. Whereas Adorno had sought to understand the psychology of the persecutor, Kardiner and Ovesey sought to understand the persecuted, namely, the "negro personality." Kardiner and Ovesey embarked on a comprehensive study, employing a variety of pscyhological tools, including psychodynamic interviews, Rorschach tests, which they described as being the psychological equivalent of an x-ray, and TAT tests, in which the subject was asked to make up a story about an image presented to him or her or about a social situation described.

Kardiner and Ovesey reported their findings in *The Mark of Oppression,* a startling bleak portrait of the Black personality, in their own words "a dismal picture of human misery, one for which it is hard to find a parallel" and which owed its "existence entirely to the arduous emotional conditions under which the Negro in America are obliged to live." Invoking an analogy that had particular meaning at the time, they likened the effects of racism to the "traumatic neuroses of war," in which the soldier "feels himself mangled by the environment." Indeed, in some respects the plight of Blacks was even more dire, for they were "consumed in anticipation of hostile stimuli" but restrained by "the necessity to curb aggressive response." Unable "to give free rein to their assertive aggressive drives and destructive impulses," Blacks were "tense and strained," tortured by "conflict and disability," sitting "uncertainly on the lid of turbulent and explosively simmering cauldron of hostility."

In addition, the Negro's "self-esteem suffers because he is constantly receiving an unpleasant image of himself." Blacks "operate on the assumption that the world is hostile. The self-referential aspect of this is contained in the formula 'I am not a loveable creature.' This together with the same idea drawn from the cast situation leads to a reinforcement of the basic destruction of self-esteem." Permanent damage to the Black personality occurred when he adapted his personality to survive this hostile environment. Kardiner and Ovesey found, for example, that Blacks described scenes containing night, gloom, and fog as "a spring scene with flowers." They observed that "if the subject can do this simply on the provocation of a picture stimulus, he must be actively engaged in doing the same thing a thousand times a day." Similarly, "it is . . . quite natural that the Negro ideal should be white [but] accepting the whole idea is a recipe for perpetual self-hatred, frustration. . . , a slow, but cumulative and fatal psychological poison." These "defects in adaptation," Kardiner and Ovesey concluded, "are truly the mark of oppression."[2]

The work of Kardiner and Ovesey, among others, helped establish what later came to be called the "damage" theory: that racist treatment did permanent damage to Black psyches.[3] Other works concerning the psychological harm of racism included Bruno Bettelheim's *Dynamics of Prejudice* (1950), Gordon Allport's *Nature of Prejudice* (1954), and Kenneth Clark's *Prejudice and Your Child* (1955).[4]

When these numerous studies were coming out, Bob Carter was working for the NAACP. A graduate of Columbia University Law School, Carter, who had grown up in Newark, New Jersey, had graduated from Lincoln University and attended Howard Law school before graduating from Columbia Law School. His formative experience with racial segregation was in the Army, but it was also in the Army that he learned the power of the law. As a trial judge advocate Carter sought to right many of the racial wrongs he saw around him. When a young black private was accused of raping a white woman, Carter was able to show that the charge was false and racially motivated. Some years later, when Carter teamed up with Thurgood Marshall, the Black lawyer who was to argue *Brown v. Board of Education* and ultimately became a Supreme Court justice himself, he lent free reign to his enthusiasm for using the law to achieve racial equality.[5]

Carter thought he could use this social-science evidence to attack the seemingly impervious logic of *Plessy,* in which the Court held that a segregated education was not a constitutional violation so long as the education was equal, which generally meant that the facilities and resources were equal. But Carter saw that psychological studies about the effects of race could be used to challenge the implicit premise that a segregated education *could* be equal by demonstrating that the harmful psychological effects of segregation made such education inherently unequal regardless of equal facilities. To be sure, the Supreme Court had never relied upon social-science evidence in its factual finding. However, the new evidence might be seen as justification for the Court's changing its mind.

But Carter also understood that if the psychological testimony was going to play the role he envisioned for it, he needed experts of stature. The Supreme Court was not going to reverse itself based on the testimony of a junior professor with a controversial thesis. Carter needed psychologists at the top of their profession who could speak *for* the profession.

To find such experts, Carter turned first to Columbia University, where he found the sociologist Otto Kleinberg, perhaps the leading expert in the field of race studies. Kleinberg, who had made a name for himself by using intelligence tests to disprove the supposed intellectual inferiority of Blacks, initially agreed to testify but later backed out. Carter then turned to Teachers College professor William H. Kilpatrick, a native of Georgia, whom no one could have accused of being a psychological carpetbagger. But his advantage was also part and parcel of why he declined: though he approved of the NAACP goals, he believed that court abolishment of desegregation at the primary- and secondary-school level would be too much of a change too fast. Gordon Allport, a leading psychologist at Harvard and former president of the American Psychological Association, also declined. Most troubling of all was the response of Elsa E. Robinson, a well-regarded psychologist at New York University, who wrote that she had "come to the conclusion that there is as yet no scientifically verified material of an empirical nature which bears directly on the issue." If one expert of Robinson's stature testified against the NAACP's position, Carter's consensus on the harmful effects of racism would go up in smoke.

To Carter's great dismay, he was forced to recruit second-stringers: the Vassar psychologist Helen Trager; David Krech, on leave from Berkeley because of his disgust with forced loyalty oaths, an assistant professor at Teachers College, and a dean of a little-known sectarian West Virginian college. Carter also sought out Kenneth Clark, a professor of sociology at City College who had been referred to Carter by Kleinberg, with whom Clark had studied. Like the others, Clark was by no means what Carter had in mind; he was not particularly prominent in his profession, much less the éminence grise Carter was looking for. That he was black probably would not help either since he could be perceived as biased. But Kleinberg had said that he believed certain work Clark had done with dolls might be relevant, so Carter took the time to look at it.

Kenneth Clark had come upon his area of study in an interesting way. As an undergraduate at Howard University, Clark had majored in psychology, studying with Ralphe Bunche and Alaine Locke. But the most prominent influence on his work had been a student of his at Howard, Mamie Phipps, who was studying the effects of racism on Washington, D.C.'s Black schoolchildren. Clark gave her an A in the class and then convinced her to switch her major to psychology and, later, to marry him. Intrigued by his wife's work, Clark offered to work with her, beginning a lifelong intellectual collaboration.

In 1939 the Clarks published their findings in the *Journal of Social Psychology,* and the following year they moved to New York to pursue doctorates, he at Columbia, she at the City University. Their work was interrupted by World

War II, to which they both contributed their skills, Kenneth by studying the morale of Black soldiers for the Office of War Information, Mamie as a psychologist for an armed-forces think tank. When the war was over, however, they returned to the work they had begun. They founded a child-guidance project in Harlem, called the Northside Testing and Consultation Center, and soon published a study in the *Journal of Experimental Education* titled "Segregation as a Factor in Racial Identification of Negro Pre-School Children."

The Clarks were interested in the attitudes of Black children toward race. In one of their experiments, a child would be given a piece of paper with outline drawings of a leaf, an apple, an orange, a mouse, a girl, and a boy and a box of twenty-four crayons that included black, brown, white, yellow, pink, and tan. If the child could color the leaf, the apple, the mouse, and the orange, he or she would then be asked to color in the two children. A boy would be instructed to "color this little boy the color that you are." After he had finished, the tester would then ask the boy to color the girl the color he would like her to be. The Clarks found that most of the children colored the child of the opposite sex white or another color.

In another experiment the Clarks would present Black children three to seven years old with dolls that were identical save for their color. After establishing that the children could correctly identify the dolls by color, the children were asked to identify "the doll you like to play with," "the nice doll," "the doll that looks bad," and "the doll that is a nice color." The Clarks found that Black children as young as three demonstrated "an unmistakable preference for the white doll and a rejection of the brown doll."

Even though the Clarks had largely anticipated their results, they were nonetheless disturbed by them. "What was surprising," Clark later observed, "was the degree to which the children suffered from self-rejection, with its truncating effect on their personalities, and the earliness of the corrosive awareness of color. I don't think we had quite realized the *extent* of the cruelty of racism and how hard it hit." Indeed, even the experience of giving the doll tests could be traumatic: "Some of these children, particularly in the North, were reduced to crying when presented with the dolls and asked to identify with them. They looked at me as if I were the devil for putting them in this predicament. Let me tell you it was a traumatic experience for me as well."

When Bob Carter first met with Clark, Carter was unfamiliar with Clark's work and was not overly enthusiastic about him. Carter candidly told Clark that the NAACP had wanted Clark's mentor Kleinberg. Nonetheless, Carter left toting a copy of Clark's book *Prejudice and Your Child,* which included the doll studies. When he next spoke with Clark, Carter's attitude had changed entirely. "It's just what we're looking for," he exclaimed to Clark, "It's almost as if it were written for us." Clark later confessed that Carter's effusiveness had left him wondering "if I weren't getting a bit of a snow job."

Carter's enthusiasm was sincere, however. Clark's research was perfect for several reasons. First, it was easily comprehensible by judges and even the public more broadly. It did not use Rorschach inkblots or arcane psychoanalytic concepts. Anyone could understand it, emotionally as well as intellectually. It had all the trappings of science—it was an objective experiment—yet it also had obvious pathos: the image of a child rejecting a doll of his own color, rejecting himself in effect, was one that Carter knew would strike a cord. Thus, Clark's work was perfect: it was readily understandable, scientifically objective, and emotionally powerful.

Carter asked Clark to be a witness for the NAACP, to enlist other social scientists, and to help NAACP lawyers with the social-science portion of briefs. It turned out not to be a difficult sell. Clark had met Thurgood Marshall at several social functions and was "envious that they were actually doing something specific to improve things while I was off in the scholarly area, vaguely wishing to be part of what they were doing."

Carter faced opposition in his own camp, however. Some of his fellow civil-rights lawyers were not as enthusiastic about giving psychology such a prominent place in their case. "Jesus Christ, those damned dolls!" commented William Coleman, who had clerked for Felix Frankfurter. "I thought it was a joke." Carter "was way out on the limb, pretty much by himself," Clark later confirmed. "Most of the other lawyers felt this approach was, at best, a luxury and irrelevant."

Fortunately, however, Carter found Marshall to be more receptive. Marshall had thus far been neutral in the debate about the role psychological experts would play in their strategy. But Clark's work met a need that Marshall had perceived. Marshall thought that the secret to setting a radical new precedent was to mold his case into something as conventional as possible. "I told the staff that we had to try this case just like any other one in which you would try to prove damages to your client. If your car ran over my client, you'd have to pay up and my function as an attorney would be to put experts on the stand to testify to how much damage was done. We needed exactly that kind of evidence in the school cases." And Clark could provide such testimony,

Marshall believed. Not only did the doll tests attest to the ill effects of segregation in general but Clark could administer the tests to the particular plaintiffs in question and thus measure the injury to their psyches.

So Marshall gave Carter the green light to use Clark, who was given his first trial run in the case of *Briggs v. Elliot,* in Charleston, South Carolina. When the state learned of the NAACP's plans, it sought to even the odds by obtaining Howard Odum, a prominent sociologist at the University of North Carolina. Fortunately for the NAACP, Odum declined.

The trial would begin on 28 May 1951. Carter and Marshall had been planning to fly to South Carolina but took the train instead when they learned that Clark had a fear of flying. Clark boarded the train with a suitcase and box containing four dolls that he had bought for fifty cents each at 125th Street in Harlem. About twelve inches long and dressed only in diapers, the dolls were identical except, of course, that two were pink and two were brown. When they got off the train in Charleston, they were met by the local counsel, Spottswood Robinson. Just as Marshall and Carter were about to introduce Clark to Robinson, Clark suddenly exclaimed that he had forgotten his dolls and started running back to the train. To Robinson, who had not been briefed on the details of Clark's research, the reference to dolls provoked some consternation: "I know these psychology people are a little strange to begin with, but what kind of fellow is this one exactly?"

At the trial Clark testified about his research and the conclusions he had reached after administering the doll test to the children who were plaintiffs:

> I have reached the conclusion that discrimination, prejudice and segregation have definitely detrimental effects on the personality development of the Negro child. The essence of this detrimental effect is a confusion in the child's concept of his own self-esteem—basic feelings of inferiority, conflict, confusion in self-image, resentment, hostility towards himself, hostility towards whites . . . or a desire to resolve his basic conflict by sometimes escaping or withdrawing.

But the NAACP knew that this was an issue that would ultimately be resolved only in the Supreme Court. The task was to keep pitching cases at the Supreme Court until the Court finally swung at one.

The case that finally caught the Supreme Court's eye was brought by Oliver Brown, father of the now famous Linda Brown, against the Board of Education of Topeka, Kansas. The case began in the trial court in Topeka. As usual, although many of the leading psychologists were from the Northeast, the NAACP wanted to avoid any perception that they were importing a legion of expert carpetbaggers. The NAACP sought to tap the world-famous Menninger Clinic, in Topeka, Kansas. It was believed that several members of the Tenth Circuit Court of Appeals and the daughter of one member, Judge Huxman, had availed themselves of the Menninger Clinic's services. Karl and William Menninger, however, declined to participate, so the NAACP opted for Louisa Holt, who had been trained at the Boston Psychoanalytic Institute and now had a part-time appointment at the Menninger Institute. The case also drew upon testimony from Horace B. English, a professor of psychology at Ohio State University, who had served as a morale analyst for American occupation forces in Japan, and Wilbur Brookover, a social psychologist from Michigan State College. Holt testified:

> A sense of inferiority must always affect one's motivation for learning since it affects the feelings one has of one's self as a person. . . . That sense of ego-identity is built upon the basis of attitudes that are expressed toward a person by others who are important—first the parents and the teachers and other people in the community, whether they are older or one's peers. It is other people's reaction to one's self that basically affects the conception of one's self. . . . If these attitudes that are reflected back and then internalized or projected, are unfavorable ones, then one develops a sense of one's self as an inferior being . . . and apathetic acceptance, fatalistic submission to the feeling others have expressed that one is inferior, and therefore any efforts to prove otherwise would be doomed to failure.

At the end of her testimony Holt reported that she felt "damn good."

Five weeks later the opinion came down. The outcome could be gleaned from the final line: "The prayer for relief will be denied." The Court found that since there was no measurable difference in the quality of the physical facilities offered to Black and White students, the segregation at issue did not violate the constitution under *Plessy*.

But although nominally a defeat, the Tenth Circuit Court's opinion, authored by Judge Huxman, was extremely helpful. "Judge Huxman's opinion," wrote Jack Greenberg, "although ruling against us, puts the Supreme Court on the spot, and it seems to me that it was purposely written with that end in view." Judge Huxman would confirm this years later: "We weren't in sympathy with the decision we rendered. If it weren't for *Plessy v. Ferguson* we surely would have found the law unconstitutional. But there was no way around it—the Supreme Court had to overrule itself."

Indeed the Tenth Circuit Court's decision greatly improved the prospect of obtaining such a reversal. Particularly useful was the following passage:

Segregation of white and colored children in public schools has a detrimental effect upon the colored children. The impact is greater when it has the sanction of law; for the policy of separating the races is usually interpreted as denoting the inferiority of the Negro group. A sense of inferiority affects the motivation of a child to learn. Segregation with the sanction of law, therefore, has a tendency to retard the educational and mental development of Negro children and to deprive them of some of the benefits they would receive in a racially integrated school system.[6]

This conclusion was a tremendous boon to the NAACP. Had the Tenth Circuit Court found that no harm resulted from segregation, then the NAACP would have had the daunting task of convincing the Supreme Court that the lower court had gotten the *facts* wrong, which the Court would be loath to do. But, with the circuit court's decision in hand, the NAACP would go to the Supreme Court with at least a strong hand with respect to the issue whether school segregation had inherently harmful effects on learning.

If the Tenth Circuit Court was pitching *Brown v. Board of Education* to get the Supreme Court to swing, it succeeded. The Court granted certiorari to hear the case in 1953. For the appeal, the NAACP lawyers sought to bolster further their social-science evidence so that it appeared to be the true consensus of the profession. The result was a report entitled "The Effects of Segregation and the Consequences of Desegregation: A Social Science Statement." The report was signed by thirty-two leading behavioral scientists, including Gordon Allport, Hadley Cantril, and Samuel Stouffer—considered the honor roll of World War II experts—and of course the Clarks. It was this report that sought to establish the fact upon which the NAACP's entire argument rested: that separate education was inherently harmful even when otherwise equal. This argument took two forms. First, "segregated schools impair the ability of the child to profit from educational opportunities provided him." Second, "enforced segregation is psychologically detrimental to the members of the segregated group." Segregation, the report's authors claimed, caused "guilt feelings," "a distorted sense of social reality," "mutual suspicion, distrust, and hostility," and feelings of "inferiority and doubts about personal worth."[7]

The oral argument on the social-science testimony was presented to the

Supreme Court by Bob Carter. He described the testimony that had been presented to the Tenth Circuit Court as follows:

> It was testified that racial segregation, as practiced in the City of Topeka, tended to relegate appellants and their group to an inferior caste; that it lowered their level of aspiration; that it instilled feelings of insecurity and inferiority with them, and that it retarded their mental and educational development, and for these reasons the testimony said, it was impossible for the Negro children who were set off in these four schools to secure, in fact, or in law, an education that was equal to that available to white children in the eighteen elementary schools maintained for them.[8]

On 17 May 1954 the Supreme Court issued its decision, one of the most important it had ever handed down. The Court's holding—that educational segregation was unconstitutional—was only one of its precedent-setting features. Another was the evidence upon which it relied. The Court's opinion cited seven studies by leading social scientists—Kenneth Clark, Helen Witmer, Ruth Kotinsky, Max Deutscher, Isidor Chein, Theodore Brameld, E. Franklin Frazier, and Gunnar Myrdal—and made a factual finding about the psychological effects of segregation a key feature of the opinion:

> To separate [Black students] from others of a similar age and qualifications solely because of their race generates a feeling of inferiority as to their status in the community that may affect their hearts and minds in a way unlikely ever to be undone. . . . A sense of inferiority affects the motivation of the child to learn.[9]

Never before had the constitutionality of a government policy turned upon the feelings it engendered.

The role the psychological testimony played was just as crucial as the NAACP had planned it to be. The key question the Court faced was, of course, what to do with *Plessy:* how could the Court justify changing its mind both internally and to the world at large? The Court attributed its change of heart directly to the psychological profession's discovery that segregation led to harmful psychological effects: "Whatever may have been the extent of psychological knowledge at the time of *Plessy v. Ferguson,* this finding is amply supported by modern authority."[10]

Thus, a social-science study of emotions played a crucial role in the Court's decision. Yet, perhaps one of the most curious features of this story was the thinness of the evidence upon which the Court relied, which has largely been overlooked because of the popularity of the result. The Court did not benefit from any empirical studies on the effects of school segregation on children's psyches, studies that actually compared Black students from segregated schools with Black students from integrated schools to determine whether the effects were different. In addition, despite the Court's ruling that separate education was only constitutional if it was equal, the fact was that separate education was almost always unequal. How Black children would in fact fare under separate but truly equal schools therefore remained unknown.[11]

Moreover, the psychological evidence presented in segregation cases was not only inconclusive but often contradictory. Isidor Chein, for example, an expert on self-hate theory, testified that Jews also suffered from feelings of inferiority. However, Chein's testimony suffered from an obvious and profound defect that the defense failed to exploit: unlike Blacks, Jews were not segregated from other White students. Thus, Chein's testimony would, if anything, tend to prove exactly the opposite of what the NAACP purported to demonstrate: that psychological damage could result from prejudice even in an integrated setting.

Yet, although it is clear there could be two reasonable opinions about whether the evidence was adequate, the social scientists all lined up on one side. At oral argument, Marshall was able to proclaim that the NAACP's star-studded roster of social scientists "stand in the record unchallenged as experts in their field."[12] The absence of opposition was crucial. Had the Court been presented with opposing social-science views, it would have had to choose between those views. It would have been awkward for the Court to claim that its decision was guided by expert testimony if it had in fact chosen between differing views.

Thus, the state of Kansas could have poked a large hole in the NAACP's case if it had only had some experts to disagree, even if they had been less prestigious and fewer in number. Why did this not happen? It certainly was not that they failed to try. Nor does it seem likely that all of the psychologists were convinced that the evidence of the harmful psychological effects of segregation was conclusive beyond a doubt. After all, even when Bob Carter was looking for psychologists in support of the damage theory, he stumbled across some that were skeptical of the evidence. Perhaps the psychologists sensed that while they might be on the right side of science, they would end up on the wrong side of history. Who would want to go down in history fighting against one of the most celebrated decisions in civil rights? Even supposing you were right about the science, who would care about that in the years to come?

If that was the judgment that the psychologists on the other side made, it was probably correct, for *Brown v. Board of Education* would do much to promote the reputations both of those involved in the decision and of the psychological profession in general. The Supreme Court's reliance on social science was prominent and crucial. James Reston, of the *New York Times*, wrote that the Court's opinion "read more like an expert paper on sociology than a Supreme Court decision."[13] What greater seal of approval on one's work by one's profession than the Supreme Court's relying upon it?

To be sure, not all commentators praised the social scientists for their role. One observed that "rather than rely on available judicial precedents, the Court invoked two of the flimsiest of all our disciplines—sociology and psychology—as the basis of its decision."[14] An associate justice of South Carolina, James F. Byrnes, stated that "loyal Americans . . . should be outraged that the Supreme Court would reverse the law of the land upon no authority other than some books written by a group of psychologists about whose qualifications we know little and about whose loyalty to the United States there is great doubt." Florida legislators passed a resolution condemning the Court for relying on "the psychological conclusions of Kotinsky, Brameld, and Myrdal and their ilk, rather than the legal conclusions [in *Plessy*] of Taft, Holmes, Van Devanter, Brandeis, and their contemporaries on the bench."[15]

But of course such criticisms could, in the long run, only burnish one's reputation. And while some might carp that sociology and psychology were disciplines too "flimsy" to rely upon, the fact was that the Supreme Court *had* relied upon them in the exercise of its august power. Moreover, it had relied upon them in a manner almost without precedent. To be sure, expert testimony was not novel. Marshall had made this very point at oral argument, noting that "we have arrived at the stage where the courts do give credence to the testimony of people who are experts in their fields." But Frankfurter had challenged Marshall, saying that expert testimony was often used to establish the *facts* of a particular case, such as whether a criminal defendant was insane or whether a plaintiff's injuries were permanent, but that here the NAACP was introducing expert testimony not to establish the facts of a particular case but to advance a broad legal principle. Surely, Frankfurter had said to Marshall at oral argument, what social scientists now thought of segregated education did not determine whether the Constitution permitted it.

But then the Supreme Court had issued its opinion saying exactly that: segregation was unconstitutional because social scientists said so. And even Frankfurter, who had seemed most skeptical, had signed on to the opinion and acknowledged the expertise of social scientists before the eyes of the nation. It was a portentous occasion, a sign of things to come.

The Therapeutic Gospel: A New Frontier

John Fitzgerald Kennedy was sworn into office on a brisk winter day in 1961. Present at the ceremony was the famed Kennedy entourage, including one member of particular interest to the psychological profession, the president's sister Eunice. Eunice was an active board member of the Menninger Foundation, and therefore mental-health advocates saw enormous potential in the Kennedy presidency. The President himself also appeared to be interested in considering new ideas and in expanding the role for government. In addition, he reflected a more liberal attitude in many areas, an attitude that perhaps would extend to mental illness.

On 9 February 1962 William Menninger met with President Kennedy in the Oval Office. It was the first time in American history that a well-known psychiatrist had had the president's ear. The meeting began with small talk about the president's sister, but Menninger quickly turned to the subject at hand. Menninger wanted to obtain not only the president's political support but also his public approval of psychological treatment. As Menninger later recalled, "The whole field of mental illness was woefully neglected—by all odds the most neglected area of all health causes—and what I wanted was his interest and his blessing and, insofar as he could give it, his leadership." Menninger told Kennedy, "We want somebody of your stature who will stand up with us and be counted." But he warned him that "you are probably going to get your leg pulled because you have been talking to a psychiatrist." With typical Kennedy bravado, the president replied, "You are possibly right, but . . . I can take that." In fact, the president suggested that when they finished talking he let photographers in. He explained that this way their historic meeting could be recorded and the public would understand his serious and personal interest in the matter of mental health.[16]

Almost precisely one year later, on 5 February 1963, John F. Kennedy became the first American president to make a national speech on mental health. He called mental illness one of "our most critical health problems," one that in the past has been "unpleasant to mention, easy to postpone, and despairing of solution." Now, Kennedy insisted, the nation must confront it; mental illness was a widespread problem that harmed not only its direct victims but also the victims' families, draining them both emotionally and financially. The president believed that the nation was unduly dependent on sanatoriums and urged "a bold new approach" in which "the cold mercy of custodial isolation" would be replaced by "the open warmth of community concern and capability."[17]

As a result of this initiative, on 31 October 1963 Kennedy signed into law the Community Mental Health Centers Act. This law provided $150 million in funds for the construction of community mental-health centers, with the long-term goal of creating two thousand such centers. The legislation was a milestone, the first federal peacetime initiative to address mental health. Moreover, the emphasis was not on treating the mentally ill in residential facilities, the traditional role of government, but in preventing mental illness. The emphasis on prevention led to a new kind of client. For the first time, those who suffered from mild mental-health problems became the beneficiaries of federal largesse. Indeed, some criticized the legislation because it took resources away from the chronically mentally ill.

The Community Mental Health Centers Act also extended the federal government's responsibility for mental health by subscribing to a theory of psychological environmentalism. The legislation was premised on the idea that the general environment could lead to either healthy or unhealthy individuals and that the federal government had a responsibility to assist communities coping with the psychological effects of various social problems. As one proponent testifying before Congress explained, the community mental-health centers would help localities solve social problems "through the training of ministers, of social workers, of teachers, of police officers, of juvenile court representatives in the community in order that mental health will be promoted."[18] The Community Mental Health Centers Act therefore not only embraced an expanded vision of the federal government's responsibility but also incorporated a grander vision of mental health, one that included the entire community. Now communities whose mental health was lacking could expect direct federal assistance.

Discontent at Home and Abroad

To the suggestion that America needed to win the hearts and minds of the Vietnamese people, President Lyndon B. Johnson famously retorted, "When you've got 'em by the balls, their hearts and minds will follow." Yet, despite the skepticism implicit in this retort, American policymakers in the 1960s increasingly turned to the psychological profession to understand and to resolve America's dilemmas both at home and abroad.

The concept of psychological warfare was not without precedent; propaganda had been used in both world wars. However, propaganda had previously been regarded as essentially a catalyst of military success. A country whose morale had been weakened, it was thought, would succumb more readily to force. During the cold war, military psychologists began to challenge that view, particularly with respect to internal military conflicts. "Few insurgencies," they argued, "have been won or lost by large, decisive military battles." Indeed, the military scorecard was only one factor in the eventual outcome: "much of the political leverage involved in favorable settlements is derived from underground psychological operations."[19] In the view of psychologists, the goal was to convince the enemy that they were losing; actual military victory was only one means to that end and perhaps not even the most effective one.[20] With this in mind, the American military in Vietnam spent vast resources on psychological warfare. In one month in 1969 alone the military dropped 713 million leaflets from the air and broadcast two thousand hours of propaganda.

But there was a second, even more crucial difference in the role psychology would ultimately play. Psychological warfare had previously been viewed as a weapon much like many others in the military's arsenal, a means of damaging and weakening the enemy. In the 1950s and 1960s military psychologists envisioned a far different role. First, they increasingly believed that the political behavior of foreign countries could be understood—and predicted—through the use of psychological tools. By understanding how people in other countries felt and thought, it was believed, it would be possible to predict and contain their revolutions. Toward this end the Department of Defense (DOD) commissioned a vast number of psychological studies of developing nations. More than 7,500 such studies were done in the sixties and early seventies. By 1973 they accounted for 12 percent of the DOD's research budget.[21]

These studies were performed by private research organizations as well as public and private universities. One prominent example was the Special Operations Research Organization at American University (SORO).[22] SORO was headed by Theodore Vallance, a psychological researcher whose initial experience had been gained in World War II. Vallance conceived of these studies of countries as case studies. Using this approach, SORO created the most comprehensive database in the world on the psychological state of developing nations. SORO, renamed CRESS (Center for Research in Social Systems) in 1966, published vast amounts of this psychological information in the *Annotated Bibliography of CRESS Publications* (1969).

The challenge facing these researchers was how to apply psychological methods and insight to mass communications. To achieve this goal, SORO and other institutions turned, interestingly, to methods of motivation research developed by the advertising profession in the 1950s. SORO researchers believed that political behavior was not fundamentally different from consumer behavior and that motivation research methods could therefore be readily applied to discover "what circumstances and reasons motivate [persons in foreign nations] to become part of an illegal, subversive movement?"[23] Researchers found that like consumers, insurgents were not always motivated by "rational" reasons. The thesis that revolutionaries were motivated by poor economic conditions was "not substantiated by the data." Rather, to understand why some countries experienced revolution, one needed to understand the "personal needs" of revolutionaries. In short, political problems could be understood as psychological problems.

The most ambitious attempt to understand the political in psychological terms was undertaken in Vietnam. The DOD commissioned the Rand Corporation to find out "who are the Vietcong and what motivates them." Rand's effort, dubbed the Viet Cong Motivation and Morale Project, produced more than sixty-two thousand pages of interviews with National Liberation Front prisoners and defectors. In what must have seemed a bizarre ritual to the Vietcong ready to be interrogated on military secrets, researchers asked questions such as "What sports did you like best?", "Could you give us an example of the poems you like best?" and "Before you became active in the Liberation Front, how did you feel about your life. . . . Why were you dissatisfied?"[24]

Psychologists' success in convincing the State Department and the DOD to use their services was in part due to their ability to address American anxiety concerning the cold war. American leaders, firmly convinced of the superiority of America's economic and political order, were perplexed and disturbed by the unrest in many countries with U.S.-supported leaders, and they were disturbed by the tendency of many emerging nations to gravitate toward the Soviet model. Psychologists promised that explanations for why such nations tended to "become unhappy" and take "actions which might tend to upset established order"[25] could be found in developmental psychology:

> Like our young Americans in their late adolescent years, people in developing countries do not really know what they want to be. They are in the process of growing up. They are searching frantically for a purpose in life and a reason in the things they do, believe and want. But they do not really know what they should do or want except that, in a vague way, they want to be strong, successful, great, happy, and prosperous. They are confused.[26]

Thus, psychologists provided the welcome news that rather than reflecting a fundamental break with the U.S. model, unrest in developing nations was like youthful rebellion, a phase that would surely pass if properly treated.

The proposed treatment involved focusing on nations' psychological needs rather than simply their economies. In reality, military psychologists argued, "the new countries of Asia have had more difficulties with the psychological than with the objective economic problems: a vicious circle somehow seems to develop in transitional societies: fears in the adventure of nation building create deep anxieties, which tend to inhibit effective action; thus imagined problems become real and fears of failure become the realities of failure; and these failures further heighten anxieties."[27]

Since the political problems of developing countries were fundamentally psychological, so too was the solution. Destructive revolutionary activity could be avoided only if the citizens of those nations were helped to find their identity and a sense of self-respect. To accomplish this, the United States needed to take "therapeutic measures" to address the problems of developing nations, to "help them grow, help them see and understand the meaning of things they wonder about. In short to help them discover themselves."[28]

In addition, foreign nations, again like errant youths, were in need of programs of "mass treatment" or "catharsis" to siphon off "aggression" and "frustration" that fed revolutionary and destructive political behavior in poor countries. To accomplish this, youth activities and entertainment were provided to lessen tension, and morale was improved by building bridges and schools. Such programs also had the added benefit of increasing people's positive attitudes toward local military forces, as well as the U.S. Army and government. In undertaking such programs, military psychologists played a far broader role than they had played in the past. The focus was no longer merely on direct military conflict, on the morale of U.S. and enemy soldiers, but on the more general problem of revolution in developing nations.

In many respects the war in Vietnam represented the perfect opportunity for psychological researchers. Not only did it promise enormous resources, as wars always did, but it seemed to be a war designed to put the services of military psychologists at the fore. Because Vietnam was in large measure an internal battle, traditional military evaluations could not accurately gauge who was winning the war. Instead, psychological evaluations were needed to understand accurately what the South Vietnamese people believed and to gauge accurately the strength of the Vietcong.

Unfortunately, however, while the methods of psychological researchers may have differed from those of other military analysts, their conclusions seemed ultimately to flow from the same misguided hubris and contempt for their enemy. Researchers with the Viet Cong Motivation and Morale Project were convinced that the Vietcong's "ego-tripping cadres" had incurred the resentment of South Vietnamese villagers and that their "self-confidence" had been shaken by their recent failures. Reports from the morale project "indicated a decline in the morale of the enemy and a belief that the communist forces have lost the Vietnamese War. . . . The findings of the survey supported allied military tactics in almost every respect, and gave an encouraging overall picture of the progress of the ground war."[29] Of course, these assessments proved to be dead wrong. The resentment felt by South Vietnamese villagers was directed not at the Vietcong but at the brutal and corrupt South Vietnamese army and government. In addition, the Vietcong would not exhibit the lack of resolve or declining morale that military psychologists believed they had detected (though such problems could soon be found in the United States and its troops). Military psychologists seemed incapable of accurately gauging the sentiments of Vietnamese people or of the Vietcong, and they advised that with increased military activity, including extensive bombing, the Vietcong would soon crumble.

In July 1965 President Johnson decided to escalate the war in Vietnam, utilizing the powers he had obtained from the Gulf of Tonkin resolution passed by Congress the year before. Johnson assigned 180,000 Americans to Vietnam, increasing more than tenfold Kennedy's commitment of 17,000 "advisers" there. A year later Johnson doubled his commitment, bringing the total number of Americans in Vietnam to 385,000.

* * *

While Johnson was mobilizing American troops to fight insurgents in Vietnam, American cities themselves appeared to come under attack. A month after Johnson made the fateful decision to dramatically increase the American presence in Vietnam, riots erupted in Los Angeles. Thirty-four people died, and more than a thousand were injured. Property damage climbed to millions of dollars as looting and burning destroyed large portions of the city. The National Guard was called in, and fifteen thousand guardsmen and police officers intervened, making more than four thousand arrests in what came to be known as the Watts Riots.

The unrest seemed to spread like wildfire. Detroit exploded in the summer of 1967, resulting in forty-three dead, seventy-two hundred arrested, and $40 million in property damage. Two weeks later it was Newark. Soon riots occurred in Tampa, Cincinnati, Atlanta, and New Brunswick. Between 1966 and 1968 riots took their toll on more than 150 cities.

Today it is difficult to imagine the shock that Americans felt at this violence. Americans had been enjoying a golden age of prosperity and world leadership. Suddenly, seemingly without warning, the dream seemed to be disintegrating before their eyes, and for reasons they simply did not understand. Two weeks after the Detroit riots, in an attempt to understand better what was going on, President Lyndon Johnson set up the National Advisory Commission on Civil Disorder, which came to be known as the Kerner Commission, after its chairman, Otto Kerner, the governor of Illinois.[30] In his address to the American public Johnson charged the commission with producing "a profile of the riots—of the rioters, of their environment, of their victims, of their causes and effects."[31]

To coordinate its research effort, the commission turned to Robert Shellow, a social psychologist who had previously been with the NIMH. The commission's report, which contained some fifteen thousand pages of data, set forth views that would profoundly influence how poor minority communities would be seen in the ensuing decades. The report described communities plagued by rage. "At the center of racial disorder," the Kerner Commission reported, were social conditions that were "the source of the deepest bitterness." While for most Americans the strong economy was cause for celebration, for "the Negro poor and the jobless ghetto youth" the "affluence flaunted before the[ir] eyes" led to anger and hostility. Their "frustrated hopes" were a major cause of the riots.

Perhaps most interesting was the commission's disinclination to see either the problem or its solution in entirely economic terms. The report emphasized that two basic needs of Blacks—the material and "inner resources which give life meaning"—were not being met.[32] The result was alienation and hostility. Applying a psychological standard, researchers found that Blacks were in need of mass treatment.

The Kerner Commission's study was hardly the only psychological effort to understand urban unrest. Numerous studies of urban disorder were commissioned by the federal government as well as by state and city governments. The NIMH alone commissioned more than fifty studies of mass violence.

Like the studies of counterinsurgency in developing nations, domestic studies of urban riots set out to produce a psychological profile of the rebellious and document the underlying causes of rebellion. These studies found a direct relationship between the rioter's state of mind and his behavior. One psychological researcher explained that this relationship "appears to be as fundamental to understanding civil strife as the law of gravity is to atmosphere physics."[33]

Some thought the studies had gone too far. Interesting was the reaction of Kenneth Clark, who testified before the commission on 13 September 1967. In Brown v. Board of Education Clark had used psychological concepts as a powerful tool to attack segregation. But in Clark's view, the Kerner Commission was being distracted by its psychological investigation. The search for a "diagnosis" had been excessive, when the problems was obvious and well known: "Psychological experts and policy-makers alike understood exactly what sort of 'treatment' was needed to cure cities and turn them into environments conducive to human development rather than violence."[34] But while Clark thought excessive attention had been given to diagnosis, he did not mean to say that a diagnosis was not in order. He too believed that economic and political deprivation had harmed Blacks' sense of identity and that this was an appropriate topic for governmental concern and action.

Identity politics provided a powerful explanation of what was wrong and what needed to be done. Indeed, it was invoked not only by social-policy experts but also by local community leaders. One Black minister from Watts, for example, offered in less academic language the standard psychological interpretation of the riots: "Here's a man who doesn't have any identity. But *to-night* he has the Los Angeles Police Department and the Los Angeles Fire Department upset. He has the National Guard called out. Tonight he is somebody."[35] This "I need to be somebody" theory of rioting was widely subscribed to. It turned out that rebels at home, like those abroad, were struggling to express themselves. As one DOD-sponsored study concluded, there was "a common psychological dynamic shared by African-American rioters, striking French farmers, Guatemalan guerillas, and Indonesian rioting students—most are frustrated in the pursuit of their goals which angers them and they are acting on that anger."[36] According to psychologists and psychiatrists, good domestic policy required an understanding of those in the urban ghetto just as good foreign policy required an understanding of people in developing countries.

The Black Panthers

In 1965 Eldridge Cleaver was sent to California's Soledad prison for rape. Much like Malcolm X, Cleaver entered prison a poorly educated common criminal and left dramatically changed by what he had read. In Cleaver's case, the book that transformed him was by a French-educated Black man by the name of Frantz Fanon. Fanon had worked with the Algerian rebels in the war for national liberation. He saw the struggle of African indigenous groups in different terms. Before Fanon, revolutionaries had perceived the greater political and economic might of the European nations as the chief obstacles. But Fanon saw a psychological obstacle: he believed that Europeans had instilled in native Africans a "colonized personality,"[37] whose features he would describe in a book titled *Wretched of the Earth*. Europeans had instilled in native Africans an "inferiority complex" that made them believe that their position of political subjugation was both deserved and inevitable. Thus, Fanon believed that a necessary step in political revolution was an internal psychological revolution, "the liberation of the man of color from himself." It was toward this liberation that Fanon devoted his intellectual efforts. Ironically, Fanon believed that it could only be accomplished through a European tradition. "Only a psychoanalytic interpretation of the black problem can lay bare the anomalies of affect that are responsible for the structure of the [inferiority] complex."[38]

As Fanon's ideas developed, it became increasingly clear that the psychological revolution was not merely a means to a political revolution but a goal in its own right. The challenge was to undo the harmful psychological effects of colonialism: "Because it is a systematic negation of the other person and a furious determination to deny the other person all attributes of humanity, colonialism forces the people it dominates to ask the question constantly: 'In reality, who am I?'" Through this process, he wrote in *Black Skins, White Masks* the Black had acquired a psychological need to be white; he had experienced a "collapse of the ego" and felt that only the Other (the White) "can give him worth."[39] Fanon sought to restore to Blacks their sense of worth and identity.

When Cleaver read Fanon, it did not simply strike a cord; it seemed to unlock a puzzle. "The feelings and thoughts and passions that were wracking us," wrote Cleaver, "were incoherent and not connected until we read Fanon."[40] Although Fanon was writing about European colonies halfway around the world, Cleaver believed the exact same phenomenon was taking place in the United States. The problems of American Blacks were the result of a type of repression. "Oppressed people feel an uncontrollable desire to kill their masters. But the feeling itself gives rise to myriad troubles, for the people when they first become aware of the desire to strike out against the slave master shrink from this impulse in terror. . . . Intimidated by the superior armed might of the oppressor, the colonial people feel that he is invincible and that it is futile to ever dream of confronting him."[41]

Moreover, Cleaver added a crucial piece to the puzzle. Cleaver was surrounded by Black men who had committed crimes, many against their fellow Blacks. Cleaver saw a crucial connection between Fanon's ideas and the pathological and self-destructive behavior that surrounded him and to which he himself had succumbed. Blacks in the United States who could not strike back at their oppressors "kill each other and do all the things they would, in fact, like to do to the master."[42]

Upon leaving prison in December 1966, Cleaver joined the Black Panther Party and soon became its minister of information. He spread his ideas, as well as Fanon's, in the bestselling book *Soul on Ice* (1968) and as a presidential candidate of the Peace and Freedom Party. Largely as a result, Fanon's book became widely influential among Black leaders and was dubbed the handbook of the Black revolution. Among those who acknowledged its influence were Stokely Carmichael and James Foreman, a founding member of the Student Nonviolent Coordinating Committee (SNCC), who became an ardent

Black Nationalist. Foreman said that "there was no real division between the sugar cane fields of Martinique and the cotton fields of the American South, between the mental colonization that Fanon fought and the psychological oppression of Black Americans."[43]

Cleaver's influence on the Black Power movement was fundamental. As he himself put it, he made psychology "the new black Bible."[44] This sharply distinguished it from the civil-rights movement that had preceded it. Martin Luther King's focus had in large measure been outward: on convincing the society as a whole to grant Blacks their civil rights. The Black Power movement was much more inwardly focused. Black leaders sought to eliminate the negative self-image promoted by White culture by raising Blacks' awareness of their history and culture. They sought to reverse self-hatred by directing Black rage toward what they believed was the appropriate target, namely, racism and the White society that cultivated it. Taking a stand against police brutality was not just aimed at eliminating it. Rather, it was a personal affirmation of belief that one had a right not to be brutalized.

Interestingly, Cleaver's observations were similar in some respects to those of Kardiner and Ovesey a decade earlier. They had concluded that the "Negro Personality" was fundamentally damaged by Blacks' subjection to "hostile stimuli" and "the necessity to curb aggressive response."[45] Cleaver simply took this observation one step further, albeit a radical step. If restraining the natural response to hostile treatment, that is, violence, was psychologically harmful, then a hostile response was psychologically healthy. Thus, the therapeutic gospel had far different implications for Blacks than for society as a whole. Normally, violence was associated with mental illness and abnormality; however, Cleaver believed that for Blacks precisely the opposite was true. The failure of Blacks to respond violently to their treatment was pathological, while a violent response was normal.

The Black Panthers embraced Cleaver's idea. Originally known as the Black Panther Party for Self-Defense, the party was founded in the fall of 1966 by Huey Newton and Bobby Seale. The choice of the black panther as an image came from an earlier struggle in Lowdes County, Mississippi, where the local all-white Democratic party used a white rooster as its mascot and SNCC adopted the black panther as a symbol for its candidates. The Black Panthers later named their movement after the black panther because it was a "bold, beautiful animal, representing the strength and dignity the black demands today."[46]

The Black Panther Party grew out of the Community Action Patrol (CAP), an antipoverty program funded by the federal government whose function was to protect Blacks from police harassment. This Los Angeles organization encouraged residents of Watts (the place of the infamous riots) to call CAP when they saw the police stopping someone Black. CAP would immediately dispatch a patrol car to the scene to observe and record what happened as well as to inform the person being interrogated or arrested of his rights.

Increasingly, however, encounters between CAP and the police took on elements of political theater, albeit of a dangerous type. Huey Newton and Bobby Seale would deliberately provoke police attention by driving around in a car, Newton dressed in a beret, black leather jacket, and dark sunglasses and armed with a gun, a lawbook, a tape recorder, and a camera. Inevitably, the police would stop them. If the police asked, "What are you doing with those guns?" Newton would respond, "What are you doing with your gun?" If asked if he was a marxist, Newton would ask if the policeman was a fascist.

Newton's defiance would often lead the officer to radio for help, and as the patrol cars surrounded the scene a crowd would develop, which was the goal. Surrounded by witnesses, Newton would play his cards even more boldly. In one incident Newton pointed to a man who was walking away and shouted, "Don't turn your back on these backshooting motherfuckers!" Seething with anger at Newton's disrespect, a police officer unstrapped his gun. Newton walked toward him, staring him down and taunting him, "What's the matter, you got an itchy finger?" "You want to draw your gun?" "You big fat racist pig, draw your gun! Draw it you cowardly dog!"

To the Blacks watching, these encounters were truly remarkable. Until then, Blacks had generally avoided standing up to the police, much less taunting them as openly as Newton was. To an outsider, Newton's antics might seem silly and ineffective compared with the NAACP's carefully planned legal assault on segregation or Martin Luther King's political assault on it. King and the NAACP sought to work within the existing political and legal structure, King's peaceful protests were carefully constructed to appeal to the nation's conscience. By contrast, the Black Panthers' methods seemed calibrated precisely to alienate the mainstream. Elements of their platform were preposterous, including, for example, such demands as "freedom for all black men held in federal, state, county, and city prisons and jails" and a "United Nations–supervised plebiscite to be held throughout the black colony in which only black colonial subjects will be allowed to participate, for the purpose of determining the will of black people as to their national destiny." Clearly, it would be silly to interpret the Black Panthers' activities as seeking to achieve concrete goals of the type envisioned by the civil-rights movement. Rather, the Black Power movement was political drama with a therapeutic goal. The Black Panthers believed that it was good for the Black community to see a Black man stand up publicly to the police and declare himself unwilling to be subjected to wrongful treatment. It helped to assuage two centuries of mistreatment. It was, in a sense, a treatment for the afflictions of the Black personality identified by Kardiner and Ovesey more than a decade earlier.[47]

Counterculture and the Therapeutic Gospel

The student movement of the 1960s was initially a political movement. Students threw themselves behind the civil-rights movement. Hundreds participated in the Mississippi Freedom Summer in 1964. Simultaneously, the free-speech movement blossomed at the University of California at Berkeley. Then came the mass protests against the Vietnam War. Yet alongside this political activity another type of movement developed, a movement that was more about culture than about politics.

Those involved in this other movement were dubbed "hippies" by the media, "the counterculture" by later, more sympathetic chroniclers. Their lives were dramatically different than those of mainstream Americans in almost every way, in how they ate, dressed, lived, spoke, and groomed themselves. These long-haired men and braless women, with their vegetarianism, herbal teas, and communes, seemed to want to make everything different. Yet perhaps the most radical aspect of the counterculture was its devotion to what it called "alternative consciousness."

In 1963 a Harvard psychology professor named Timothy Leary was fired for his drug-induced experiments with cosmic consciousness. From Harvard he went on to found the League for Spiritual Discovery. Leary soon hooked up with Ken Kesey, author of *One Flew over the Cuckoo's Nest*, who had worked as a psychiatric aid at a Veterans Administration hospital. Among the mind-expanding drugs they promoted was LSD. When California outlawed its use in 1966, Leary, Kesey, and others put their philosophy into a document, which they modeled after the Declaration of Independence.

When in the flow of human events it becomes necessary for the people to cease to recognize the obsolete social patterns which have isolated man from his consciousness and to create with the youthful energies of the world revolutionary communities of harmonious relations to which the two-billion-year-old-life process entitles them, a decent respect to the opinions of mankind should declare the causes which impel them to this creation. We hold these experiences to be self-evident, that all is equal, that the creation endows us with certain inalienable rights, that among these are: the freedom of body, the pursuit of joy, and the expansion of consciousness, and that to secure these rights, we the citizens of the Earth declare our love and compassion for all conflicting hate-carrying men and women of the world. We declare the identity of flesh and consciousness; all reason and law must respect and protect this holy identity.[48]

Leary attended many of the pageants, festivals, and events that were central to the counterculture. One of the most significant took place in Golden Gate Park in the summer of 1967, the so-called Summer of Love. Its organizers called it a "Human Be-In"; its goal was to orchestrate "a new concert of human relations." At this event Leary proclaimed that people should "Turn On, Tune In, Drop Out," which would become a counterculture refrain. Leary's statement reflected a faith in a pursuit of consciousness that was independent of conventional material possessions. Counterculturists rejected the consumption obsession that had seemingly enveloped the United States. As one counterculturist explained, "Why should we work 12 or 16 hours a day . . . ? For a color TV? For wall-to-wall carpeting? An automatic ice-cube maker?" Counterculturists like Leary wanted Americans to drop out of the consumption rat race, open themselves up to new experiences, and tune in to the new radio stations that promoted the new rock music of the 1960s.[49]

Radical alternatives, conterculturists believed, were a necessity. According to them, reality was, as the saying goes, a nice place to visit, but you wouldn't want to live there. In their view, the world did not make sense and therefore nonsense was a perfectly legitimate response to the senselessness they saw all around them. As Tim Leary said, "It becomes necessary to go out of our minds in order to use our heads." To him and many others, "LSD made more sense than LBJ."[50]

Perhaps no counterculturist made better use of the senselessness of American culture than Abbie Hoffman. Hoffman attended Brandeis College, which had been founded in 1948 by a group of wealthy Jews in part to hire

Jewish intellectuals who could not get jobs at other universities because of quotas and to educate Jewish students who could not get the education they deserved for the same reason. Brandeis attracted a stellar faculty during the cold-war years that included Herbert Marcuse, Philip Reiff, Irving Howe, Lewis Coser, Max Lerner, and Philip Rahv. The faculty member who made the largest impression on Hoffman, however, was Abraham Maslow.

Hoffman came across Maslow in his introductory psychology class, a requirement at Brandeis. Maslow fascinated Abbie. Early on in the course, for example, he said that it would be alright to use words like *fuck* in his courses. Maslow's point apparently was that there was nothing inherently obscene in the word; it was what was imputed to the word that made it so. (This point about subjectivity and the whole issue of obscenity would be major themes of the radicalism of the 1960s.)

Maslow inspired Hoffman to become a psychology major (disappointing news to his parents, who hoped their son would become a doctor). In 1954 Hoffman attended a conference organized by Maslow that brought together the leading luminaries in the newly formed field of humanistic psychology, including Gordon Allport, Eric Fromm, Kurt Goldstein, Paul Goodman, Carl Rogers, Erik Erikson, and Rollo May. But it was Maslow himself who would have the most profound impact on Hoffman: "Most of all, I loved Professor Abe Maslow," he would later write. "There was something about his humanistic psychology (considered radical at the time) that I found exhilarating amidst the general pessimism that pervaded Western thought."

Maslow charged that psychology focused on the "darker, meaner aspects of human nature, on man's shortcomings, illnesses, his sins," while ignoring the more positive side, man's "potentialities, his virtues, his achievable aspirations . . . his psychological height." Maslow developed the concept of the hierarchy of man's needs. After the need to satisfy one's hunger and thirst, man needed love, belongingness, self-esteem, and ultimately self-actualization.

Hoffman would later say that "Maslowian theory laid a solid foundation for launching the optimism of the sixties. Existential, altruistic, and up-beat, his teachings became my personal code." Hoffman believed that self-expression was the highest aim. He rejected politics as it was currently practiced for its convention and restrictiveness. In Hoffman's words, "Politics is like going to Shul. It's what you have to do. But what I really want to be is an outlaw."[51]

He was certainly one of America's funniest social critics. He was also thoroughly immersed in the psychological thinking of the day. But he is best known for his political antics. Perhaps the only American radical to be influenced by a comedian, Hoffman was a great admirer of Lenny Bruce. His showmanship skills were masterful, and his political acts were like stand-up routines. He used these abilities to promote a variety of activities. He co-founded with Jerry Rubin, for example, an organization called the Youth International Party, or Yippies, which was meant to mock political organizations. Hoffman once commented that Yippies was really another name for Jewish hippies. Their philosophy was eclectic and absurd. Yippie slogans included "Don't grow up. Growing up means giving up your dreams"; "Free speech is the Right to Shout 'Theater' in a Crowded Fire"; and "Amerika says: Don't! The Yippies say Do It!" Yippies were against "pay housing, pay media, pay transportation, pay food, pay education, pay medical help, and pay toilets." They also believed strongly that "people should fuck all the time, anytime, whomever they wish." Not surprisingly, Hoffman entitled his political manifesto, *Revolution for the Hell of It and the Fuck the System Manual.*[52]

Hoffman first gained national attention at the New York Stock Exchange, where he and some friends threw paper money from the visitors' gallery and watched with glee as traders down below scrambled for the floating money. Through such showmanship, Hoffman exposed the greed of Wall Street. He also dramatized contradictions. For example, Hoffman founded a store called Free Store, where payment was discouraged. Parodying capitalist ethics, he also took the Free Store to Macy's, where he stood in the middle of the floor and announced that all items were now free.

Hoffman was a master at creating a show with political commentary. In 1967 he requested a permit to levitate the Pentagon three hundred feet above the ground. When his requests were denied, he offered a compromise: if the Pentagon would give him a permit, he and his fellow Yippies would levitate the five-sided building only ten feet off the ground. Hoffman explained his politics this way: he "believed in the violation of every law, including the law of gravity."[53] When news spread that the police would use Mace to subdue any attempts to surround the Pentagon, Hoffman called a press conference to explain that fire would be fought with fire. The police should be prepared for Lace, the protesters' secret weapon of defense. Lace was made, Hoffman claimed, of LSD and was a secret skin-penetrating agent that would make the police sexually excited.

Perhaps Hoffman is best known for his activities at the Democratic National Convention in Chicago in 1968, at which Hoffman nominated a pig named Pigasus for president. The Yippies explained the nomination this way: "They nominate the president and he eats the people. We nominate a president and the people eat him." Pigasus's platform was straightforward and simple: "garbage." Hoffman also orchestrated the Festival of Life in Chicago's Lincoln Park as a sideshow of the Democratic Convention. The hope of the festival was that "people would get out of their angry paranoid winter roles into the gentle playful roles of their fantasies." The revolution was "living the life you dream of living."[54] As at sixties be-ins, the counterculture emphasized that in a healthy society everyone "did their own thing." Violence eventually broke out, and mayhem followed. Abbie was ultimately arrested on obscenity charges: he had written the word *fuck* across his forehead.

At the trial of the Chicago Seven, the seven Yippies' conspiracy trial for their role in demonstrations at the convention, Hoffman continued his antics. He challenged Mayor Daley to a fight, dressed up in different costumes, and refused to play by the normal rules of legal process. At one point in the trial, for example, Hoffman greeted a surprised judge with what sounded to many in the room as gibberish. He was actually speaking Yiddish. Gesticulating and shouting, he said to the judge, "You Schtunk. Schande vor de goyim, huh?" No one in the room seemed to understand him. For the press he translated what he had said: "You front man for the Wasp power elite." Though he claimed with typical irreverence that his political commitments were formed "out of left-wing literature, sperm, licorice, and a little chicken fat," he was greatly influenced by professional psychology.[55]

Feminism and the Therapeutic Gospel

In May 1970 radical feminists took over a key session at the annual meeting of the American Psychiatric Association in San Francisco. Carrying signs reading "Are you a male chauvinist?" and "Down with sexism!" and chanting slogans such as "The Psychiatric Profession Is Built on the Slavery of Women," they held a surprised and slightly baffled group of psychiatrists hostage to the din of feminist protest. The women's list of demands included putting an end to blaming mothers for society's ills, providing legal assistance so that women could sue abusive clinicians, and placing a ban on sexist advertising in professional journals. For those who were sympathetic to the feminist cause, they circulated a list of suggested activities, including "compiling a list of psychiatrists in every city who are willing to back women filing malpractice suits against psychiatrists who have fucked them over" and "trashing" exhibits "that are oppressive to women."[56]

Feminist of the late 1960s and early 1970s not only took direct action against the psychological professions but also filled their writings with critiques of current psychological thinking. From Betty Friedan to radical feminists like Kate Millett, Robin Morgan, and Meredith Tax, feminists blamed psychological experts for women's false consciousness. They also directly attacked what they saw as an ideology of fulfillment, which demanded that women find psychological satisfaction in femininity conventionally defined. Wanting no part of it, they condemned the logic as a product of male-supremacist culture.

Despite their hostility toward psychological experts, feminists were actually highly indebted to therapeutic thinking. Indeed, central to most feminist arguments were the key concepts of identity and fulfillment. To feminists, the private sphere was a place not of fulfillment but of emotional pain and suffering. They found women living a psychological nightmare. Feminists of this generation also focused on the psychological nature of women's oppression. The colonization they discovered was interior. The psychological tyranny women experienced required a new form of consciousness, one that could help women identify and overcome the oppression subjugating them. Women activists turned to feminism as that ideological and psychological tool.

That the women's movement relied so heavily on the therapeutic gospel in their quest for gender equality and a more women-friendly society is really not so surprising. The postwar culture, as I have shown, was infused with a strong faith in the psyche. The cold-war American culture offered American women its own brand of identity politics. Women were told repeatedly that they were to find fulfillment in their identity as women. Added to this legacy was that of the civil-rights movement and the New Left. Emphasizing the sacredness of subjectivity, these movements too embraced the therapeutic gospel. They celebrated personal experience over the wisdom of experts. They maintained that the psychic integrity of man was being destroyed by the racism, militarism, and poverty that plagued society. The dehumanization they saw around them, however, did not include the oppression of women. Sexism did not appear on the radar screen of 1960s activists until women demanded that it be put front and center.

Women made such demands because they became increasingly fed up with the way they were treated in activist circles. Despite the calls for social justice and tirades against dehumanization, women were marginalized in the New Left and subject to innumerable slights. A pamphlet published by the Students for a Democratic Society (SDS), for example, advised critics of "the system" that "the system is like a woman; you've got to fuck it to make it change." When women complained about their treatment, one Berkeley activist responded, "Let them eat cock!" Such responses led radical women to work independently of the various other social movements. And so they did, declaring in the words of the radical feminist Shulamith Firestone, "Fuck off left, . . . we're starting our own movement."[57]

For many Americans, the women's movement proved to be the most unsettling of the social movements of the sixties, for feminists sought to flout not only the rules of political etiquette but also the norms of womanhood. As their stage, radical feminist organizations used the streets, courts, and corporate offices, as well as such symbols of American power and culture as Wall Street, the Miss America pageant, and Arlington Cemetery. Their political theater sought to commemorate the death of an old social and symbolic order and to orchestrate the birth of a new one.

One of the earliest feminist demonstrations was a funeral at Arlington Cemetery in January 1968 for "traditional womanhood." Organized by New York Radical Women (NYRW), the funeral protested not only traditional conceptions of womanhood in society generally but their use by the antiwar movement as well. Thus, the funeral protest was itself inspired by the all-women antiwar Jeannette Rankin Brigade protest. NYRW criticized the organizers of the brigade protest for coming "as wives, mothers, and mourners: that is as tearful and passive reactors to the actions of men rather than organizing as women to change the definition of femininity." The funeral procession included a gigantic dummy of a woman transported on a bier displaying the signs of hyperfemininity: a blank face and blond curls. Draped from the bier were Green Stamps, curlers, garters, and hairspray. The funeral party carried banners urging women, "Don't cry: Resist."

In outrageousness, no group outdid an organization named the Women's International Conspiracy from Hell (WITCH). WITCH was formed after a decision by the House Un-American Activities Committee (HUAC) to investigate the 1968 demonstrations at the Democratic National Convention.

HUAC subpoenaed such prominent male radicals as Dave Dellinger, Abbie Hoffman, Jerry Rubin, and Tom Hayden. New York feminists, who considered themselves the "real subversives, the real witches," were angered that they were not called to testify. In response, on Halloween a group of thirteen "heretical" women gathered in New York City to form WITCH. Soon, "Covens" sprang up in Boston, Chicago, San Francisco, Portland, Austin, and several other cities. WITCH claimed to be "a total concept of revolutionary female identity." It also claimed that 9 million witches had been burned at the stake because they were the "original guerrillas and resistance fighters against oppression" and "bowed to no man."

WITCH's targets were "whatever is repressive solely male-oriented, greedy, puritanical, or authoritarian." Its weapons were "theater, satire, explosions, magic, herbs, music, costumes, cameras, masks, chants, stickers, stencils, paint, films, tambourines, bricks, brooms, guns, voodoo dolls, cats, candles, bells, chalk, nail clippings, hand grenades, poison rings, fuses, tape recorders, incense, your own self as a woman." WITCH sponsored "hexings" of various institutions and entities, including the financial district (which was reportedly accompanied by a drop in stock-market prices); the United Fruit Company, for "slave labor practices abroad and sex discrimination practices at home"; and the University of Chicago's sociology department, for its firing of a radical feminist professor.[58]

Perhaps WITCH is best remembered for its February 1969 protest of a bridal fair in Madison Square Garden. Wearing "Buy Me" stickers and dressed in black veils or veils made of dollar bills, WITCH members descended on the bridal fair singing, "Here come the slaves, off to their graves," to the tune of "Here comes the bride." They also released white mice in the aisles. Similar protest actions were soon staged at bridal fairs around the country.

Other institutional sources of women's oppression also came under attack. On 13 September 1969 a group of radical feminist led by Ti-Grace Atkinson stormed the New York City Marriage License Office and charged officials "with fraud, with malicious intent against the women of the city." The protesters argued that women had been duped into believing "the conditions of the marriage contract to be positive and reciprocal feelings between the two parties," while in fact the marriage contract "legalized and institutionalized the rape and bondage of women." They therefore charged the Marriage License Office with failing "to list the terms of that contract, a failure which would automatically nullify the validity of any other important contract." They also confronted Mayor Lindsay, whom they regarded as "the official representative of male society which uses force to suppress women into monogamous relationships dangerous to their individual identities."[59]

Perhaps what most successfully brought radical feminism into the limelight was the protest at the Miss America pageant in Atlantic City on 7 September 1968. The protest was inspired by Gunvor Nelson's mid-1960s experimental feminist film *Schmearguntz,* which contained footage of a Miss America pageant. Protesters descended upon Atlantic City carrying signs that read "Up Against the Wall, Miss America" and "Miss America Is a Big Falsie" and chanting "Ain't She Sweet, Making Profit Off Her Meat" and "No More Miss America."

In addition, inspired by the Yippies, who the previous week had nominated a pig for the presidency at the Chicago Democratic Convention, protesters crowned a sheep to symbolize the way in which participants in the pageant were "appraised and judged like animals at a county fair." Protesters chained themselves to life-size Miss America puppets to dramatize women's enslavement to beauty standards and created the famous Freedom Trash Can, into which were thrown large quantities of various "feminine" articles, including high-heeled shoes, bras, girdles, typing books, curlers, false eyelashes, and copies of *Playboy, Cosmopolitan,* and *Ladies' Home Journal.* (Contrary to conventional wisdom, bras actually were not burned because a city order prohibited the lighting of fires and because public officials were ostensibly concerned about burning down the boardwalk.)

The Miss America protest in turn inspired more protests. Any institution seen as contributing to women's oppression, particularly those responsible for the production of dominant images of womanhood, might be a target. One of the most hated sources of such imagery was women's magazines. The Freedom Trash Can was by no means the first assault on these magazines. Betty Friedan had attacked them in 1963, and the National Organization for Women had denounced them at an "apron burning" gathering in 1968. Finally, in 1970, feminists opted for a direct assault.

On 18 March 1970, after three months of planning, a group of seventy-five feminists led by Susan Brownmiller assembled at the corner of Lexington Avenue and 54th Street at 8:45 A.M. They then marched toward the building that housed the offices of the *Ladies' Home Journal,* one of the most popular women's magazines in the country. Carrying protest signs and large mock-ups of the magazine that read *Women's Liberation Journal,* they entered the building. They walked straight to the office of John Mack Carter, the editor in chief, and promptly occupied it. Carter was presented with a lengthy list of demands, including that he be replaced by a woman; that all editorial, sales, and advertising personnel be women; that Black editorial workers be hired in proportion to the Black readership; that a daycare center be established on the premises for working mothers, that the magazine "eliminate all degrading and useless advertising . . . and focus on the real issues facing women today"; and that an issue be published on women's liberation written by members of the movement.[60]

Sometimes feminist meetings themselves became targets of protest and political theater. On 1 May 1970 three hundred women had gathered in the auditorium of an intermediate school to participate in the second annual meeting of the Congress to Unite Women. Right before the meeting was supposed to come to order the lights suddenly went out. Chairs were moved, shouts were heard, people moved toward the stage, and when the lights came on the women "found themselves in the hands of the Lavender Menace."[61]

The invaders were a group of lesbians garbed in T-shirts emblazoned with the name of their organization. For more than two hours they held the floor and recounted their stories about what it was like to be a lesbian in a heterosexist culture. They also distributed a list of resolutions that included the following: (1) women's liberation is a plot against lesbians; (2) they would affirm rather than deny the label "lesbian" when it was used against the movement collectively; (3) in discussions of birth control they would include homosexuality as a legitimate method of contraception; and (4) all sex education curricula must include lesbianism as a valid, legitimate form of sexual expression or love.

Feminists borrowing from the theatricality of the counterculture put their outrageous acts in the service of radical feminist ideals. Their outrage, however, owed a debt to the therapeutic gospel. Beginning with Betty Friedan and up through such actions as the takeover of the offices of the *Ladies' Home Journal,* the New York City Marriage License Office, and the Miss America protest, feminists relied on the ideology of fulfillment to make their case against the sexism of American culture.

Betty Friedan was perhaps the first feminist to put women's psychological identity front and center in American public debate. She was also the first to directly attack the ideology of fulfillment, calling its bluff. Challenging what she saw as the conventional wisdom about women's happiness, she surveyed her Smith College classmates and found them to be resoundingly miserable. Friedan relied on the therapeutic gospel to refute the "happiness thesis."

Applying the psychological standard of happiness to women had explosive effects. In *The Feminine Mystique* Friedan argued that the social conventions limiting women's place to the home had an adverse effect on women's state of mind. Friedan identified a pathological tendency in American culture to deny women a sense of identity, offering a profound indictment of domestic ideology. She urged women to reject "the feminine mystique," which she believed prevented women from gratifying "their basic need to grow and fulfill their potentialities as human beings." She also insisted that only an entirely new understanding of themselves and their roles as women would enable women to develop "a new sense of identity" and to live with "the enjoyment, the sense of purpose that is characteristic of true human health."[62]

Embracing key tenets of the therapeutic gospel, Friedan emphasized the psychological damage done by domesticity and the importance of self-fulfillment. She defined in largely psychological terms "the problem that has no name." Friedan identified the injustice done to women as the myth of the fulfilled woman and blamed popular culture and experts for these distortions. Friedan was outraged that while women "suffer from a feeling of desperation," "a strange stirring sense of dissatisfaction," a feeling that "there's nothing to look forward to," the image of women that pervaded American popular culture and the social-science literature was that of the "happy housewife." She argued that such misrepresentation denied women the capacity to address their unhappiness and seek fulfillment outside the domestic realm. It also denied women a "firm core of self." Friedan urged women to shun definitions of themselves that "do not demand or permit, realization of women's full abilities." She urged women to "unequivocally say no" to images of womanhood "that do not provide adequate self-esteem, much less pave the way to a higher level of self-realization."[63]

For Friedan, the injustice to American women was not the denial of economic and political sources of power but rather the obstruction of women's achievement of personhood. She asked, "Why, with the removal of all the legal, political, economic, and educational barriers that once kept woman from being man's equal, a person in her own right, an individual free to develop her own potential, should she accept this new image which insists she is not a person?"[64] American culture's denial to women of an appropriate self-image formed the centerpiece of Friedan's political commentary.

Friedan found no conceptual tradition that women could draw upon to challenge this denial. In fact, she urged women to acknowledge that the problem facing women "cannot be understood in the generally accepted terms by which scientists have studied women, doctors have treated them, counselors have advised them, and writers have written about them." Friedan rejected expertise in favor of personal experience. She believed that by ignoring expert advice and listening to "that voice inside" themselves, women could eliminate the obstacles to their self-development. According to Friedan, experts were of no help because although women were consumed by "a strange stirring, a sense of dissatisfaction, a yearning" that would not go away, "in the millions of words written about women, for women, in all the columns, books, articles by experts, there was no word of this yearning."[65]

Friedan's investigation of women's lives and her conclusions about domesticity were clearly innovative. Injecting an unprecedented drama into the public discussion of women's roles, Friedan turned womanhood and domesticity into matters of intense public controversy. But while her views were striking and novel, her use of psychology was not. She relied on the psychological wisdom of the era in her critique of American society. Friedan's reliance on the therapeutic gospel is not surprising given her educational background and work experience. Betty Friedan majored in psychology as an undergraduate at Smith College; spent summers studying with Kurt Lewin at the University of Iowa; studied as a graduate student with Erik Erikson at the University of California at Berkeley; underwent psychoanalysis in New York City, where she began, she said, to focus on her rage; and worked for a while at the Westchester mental-health facility.[66] She was thoroughly involved in the humanistic psychology of her day.

In the late 1960s radical feminists extended Friedan's critique in fundamental ways. They politicized more areas of everyday life, finding that sexual intercourse, marriage, and even love contained political relationships. In ferreting out the politics behind the most intimate activities of the personal sphere, radical feminists discovered a whole system of oppression. Only seven years after Betty Friedan wrote about the mystique of femininity, for example, Anne Koedt wrote "The Myth of the Vaginal Orgasm." While Friedan wrote in the early sixties about hyperdomesticity and how it left women numb, Germaine Greer wrote in the early 1970s about the ultrafeminine's castrating effect on women.[67]

Out of their own experience of oppression feminists hoped to unlock the secret of male tyranny and rebuild gender relations from the ground up. Feminists believed that what made their politics revolutionary was that it was "the first radical movement to base its politics—in fact, create its politics—out of concrete personal experiences."[68] As the feminist Katie Sarachild explained, "We always stay in touch with our feelings. Our feelings revolve around our perceptions of our self-interest. We assume that our feelings are telling us something from which we can learn . . . that our feelings mean something worth analyzing . . . that our feelings are saying something political."[69] Despite their claim to be drawing simply on raw experience, the experience on which feminists drew was in reality highly filtered through the lens of the therapeutic gospel. Psychological values influenced the stories of oppression they told as well as the solutions they offered.

Feminists embraced "consciousness-raising" as a key tactic in their struggle to end the oppression of women. The idea was that all women had to do to develop political theories was talk to one another. Their own personal experience of oppression was enough for them to generate their analysis of women's plight. Out of these informal conversations about their feelings would come feminist theory and action. Consciousness-raising was also a political tactic based on the idea that a key to changing women's position in society was changing their understanding. In other words, consciousness was seen as half, if not more, of the battle. Since patriarchy was a kind of interior colonization, feminists had to fight fire with fire. They had to undo years of teaching that women found fulfillment in femininity conventionally defined. Reversing this teaching, feminists preached that women should use the standard of fulfillment to judge all institutions—marriages, motherhood, the workplace—and reject those that in any way compromised their full human potential. Through consciousness-raising sessions, feminists promoted the psychological yardstick for measuring women's experience.

In feminists' hands the therapeutic gospel had a radical effect on American society. The most sacred institutions of American life came under attack. Marriage, motherhood, and even sex became subject to the gospel of fulfillment, and in this light all three fell short. According to radical feminists, not only did domesticity and traditional notions of femininity not fulfill women but they obliterated their identity. In order for women to discover their own identity, they had to throw off all of the cultural chains that bound them to conventional conceptions of womanhood. And throw them away they did. In addition to taking over bridal fairs, the *Ladies' Home Journal,* and the Marriage License Office and fighting for reproductive rights and equal pay for equal work, they rejected the idea that the professions were a male prerogative and entered the fields of law, medicine, and business with a vengeance.

* * *

The therapeutic gospel's important role in the social movements of the 1960s and early 1970s is really not that surprising. After all, the therapeutic gospel had been expanding exponentially since the mid-nineteenth century. Its growth after World War II, however, was particularly dramatic. In the 1950s popular culture became saturated with therapeutic messages. The number of psychological professionals also shot up; between 1945 and 1970 the number of psychiatrists increased from about 3,600 to 18,400. The percentage of Americans who consulted psychological professionals also increased dramatically. Surveys indicate that between 1957 and 1976 the percentage of Americans who sought therapeutic assistance increased from 14 percent to 26 percent.[70]

In the 1960s the federal government also got into the act. Both domestic and foreign policy were increasingly shaped by the dictates of the therapeutic gospel. The forces of both counterinsurgency and insurgency increasingly drew on identity politics to justify their actions. But it was the activists of the late sixties who took their therapeutic views to the streets. They fought against racism, militarism, and sexism in the name of the human personality. They sought to reform American society and liberate the self. In the place of dehumanizing, bureaucratic institutions, they hoped to create caring ones that celebrated human potential. Their social protests had a therapeutic mission.

7 FEELiNGS

1970–1980

In a high-school auditorium on Manhattan's Upper East Side more than fifteen hundred people gathered to attend the first Awareness Extravaganza. The year was 1978. The event sold out, with tickets ranging from thirty to sixty dollars. Self-discovery celebrities spoke and led participants in a series of awareness exercises. Lining the walls outside the auditorium were vendors selling a dazzling array of self-actualization, self-enhancement, self-assertion, and self-treatment aids. One handout at the Extravaganza summed up the event's ethos: "You just need to be who you really are and who you are is whoever you are when you stop doing all the things you do to be someone other than who you are because you're so afraid who you really are may not be all right."[1]

In the 1970s many Americans became preoccupied with their identity. They sought to uncover their true selves and to eliminate their "hang-ups." Self-awareness became the new religion; trust, intimacy, and communication, the gospel. In this religion, all institutions, social mores, or actions that blocked awareness came under attack, and all those that promoted self-realization and emotional honesty were praised. Feelings became a matter of national concern. Indeed, in 1977 President Jimmy Carter set up a national commission to study the nation's state of mind. The Commission on Mental Health concluded that a quarter of all Americans suffered from bad feelings and that up to 32 million Americans were in need of psychological help.[2]

The identity politics of the 1960s laid the ground for America's obsession with feelings in the 1970s. The New Left contributed to the so-called me decade not only by blending the personal and the political but also by offering

Americans a highly psychologized vision of liberation. Turning away, however, from the decade's political agenda, many Americans began to preach emotional honesty. They saw self-expression as the answer to all problems, both personal and political ones. Liberation of the self came increasingly to be defined outside of the hierarchies—gender, racial, sexual, and economic—that the social movements of the 1960s had been concerned with. Instead, self-liberation was simply defined as a matter of freeing one's emotions. Focusing on "inner ghettos," they worried about the "bad neighborhoods" that existed in people's heads.

To this generation, the battle cry became "getting one's head together," fighting against being "uptight" or "hung up," the emotional states responsible for the loss of human potential. And for Americans in the seventies there could be no greater loss. The me generation thus waged a campaign against all that prevented emotional candor, intimacy, and self-awareness. Expressing feelings was akin to godliness. Salvation lay in openness and communication.

The commitment to self-expression and the development of each individual's psychological potential took a variety of forms. The era produced a host of new therapeutic products. Indeed, the self-discovery services and products were so numerous that they were catalogued. Such books as *The Whole Soul Catalogue* and *A Catalogue of the Ways People Grow* provided consumers with a comprehensive list of the facilities available for learning to express one's real and deepest feelings.[3] The therapeutic gospel was also promoted through the genre of self-help books. Although America has a long tradition of do-it-yourself psychological literature dating back to the time of Phineas P. Quimby and the mind-cure movement, the genre achieved a new status in the 1970s. Self-help books dominated the bestseller lists; indeed, bookstores created a special section—self-help—to accommodate this consuming reading interest. In addition, the 1970s contributed "encounter" groups, where small groups of people got together to confront and explore their feelings. By the mid-1970s it was estimated that close to 6 million Americans were "encountering." Never before had so many people tried to express how they really felt and rid themselves of their psychological "baggage."[4]

The Feel Wheel and Other "Let It All Hang Out" Products

The me generation of the 1970s found fault with America's antiexpressive culture. In their view, mainstream American culture condemned true self-expression, which it considered obscene, if not un-American. It was this reign of emotional inhibition that the me generation sought to overthrow. Their revolution, however, would not take place in the streets. Rather, it would take place in their heads and yet would be more subversive than other revolutions. For the me generation, there was nothing more radical than changing the way human beings felt about themselves or related to one another. Their revolution was also radical because it could be practiced anytime, anyplace.

It was perhaps this supreme domestication that characterized the me generation's contribution to America's obsession with the psyche. In the 1970s an increasing number of people came to believe that the notion that psychological attention was warranted only in the therapist's office or when a person's mental health was threatened was far too narrow and in fact contributed to the psychological damage they saw around them. For the me generation, exploring the psyche became quite literally an everyday affair. Their goal was to promote self-awareness everywhere—at home, at work, in bed, even on the tennis court. (The 1970s was, of course, the era that produced the concept of inner tennis.) While experts could and certainly did guide this effort, the emphasis was on self-help, that is, helping oneself to express one's feelings in the ordinary course of living.

Only such an era could have produced products like the Feel Wheel, a noncompetitive board game designed to help players discover how and why they felt the way they did. It was based on the premise that most people were unselfconscious, not aware of their feelings. At any given moment they had no idea how they felt deep down, so they certainly could not communicate their feelings to others. Worse than their ignorance, however, was that people were often brought up to hide their true feelings. The idea behind the Feel Wheel was that within the structured setting of a game players would learn true self-expression and interpersonal communication.

The Feel Wheel created "encounters." The wheel itself was divided into rings. The outermost ring was divided into sections representing loneliness, joy, hate, anger, fear, strength, and unfulfillment. Players placed tokens in the areas that best described their feelings. Although expressing one's feelings was the object, players could choose temporarily not to express their feelings. They could move into the Sanctuary, in the center of the wheel, or take the less drastic step of moving into Transition. According to the game's instructions, one should "use Transition when you begin tentatively to feel like going into or coming out of sanctuary. You may feel pushed too hard by the full encounter around the Wheel. Say why. Or you may be tempted to come out of Sanctuary because of something you want to deal with. Say why. You are inviting someone to invite you into involvements." To ease the initial pain of encountering, the game built in "safe havens" for the emotionally skittish.

Each player was given a certain number of personal tokens. To express a feeling toward a particular person, the player placed one of his or her tokens under the other person's token. In addition, "to identify the feeling that seems to be coming to you from another participant lay one of his or her tokens over one of yours. Talk it through. Put a token down to express how you feel about it." When a player's feelings changed, he or she was to move his or her tokens to reflect that change. This call to take one's emotional inventory was a hallmark of the me generation, for whom knowing at all times how one felt became paramount.

The Feel Wheel was a therapeutic product that could indeed be used to ease tensions in any context, whether between colleagues, family members, or guests at a dinner party. It could be carried to work or stored in a kitchen drawer or in the drawer of a night table, next to a couple's bed. The idea was to have it always within reach so that it could be taken out whenever "a hidden emotional agenda generates confusion and rigidity." It could be placed on the floor or a table or on the wall, and as many as thirteen persons could participate at one time.

One San Diego family frequently resorted to the Feel Wheel to monitor the feelings of its members. The Feel Wheel was hung on the kitchen wall so that it could be immediately available whenever the family needed it. It also provided a useful record of the day's emotional encounters: "The father, coming home from work, takes in the emotional landscape at a glance. If the senior son has driven the mother into Sanctuary again, that's priority number one. But if her tokens stand in the softer emotions (the strength of the emotions a person experienced were reflected in the colored wedged sections for each emotion. Hues and emotions got stronger the closer one got to the center of the Wheel), or in the Free Zone, the father knows that the evening may take a pleasant turn." In the seventies, taking the family's emotional temperature took precedence over finding out about the day's activities or accomplishments.[5]

The Feel Wheel was not designed by an entrepreneur on the margins of American culture. Indeed, it was developed under the auspices of the Center for Studies of the Person in La Jolla, California, a psychodynamic institute associated with Carl Rogers. Rogers, who was considered the founder of client-centered therapy, was a major figure in American psychology. He lent his full support to "encountering," which he called "the most significant social invention of [the twentieth] century."[6] Rogers considered achieving personhood or acquiring one's true identity to be the major goal of the twentieth century. For psychologists like Rogers as well as self-help experts of the era the question of identity was not an abstract one. It could be discovered through interpersonal encounters, but direct encounters were seemingly difficult to come by.

American culture discouraged such directness. In the view of the me generation, Americans had been taught to use their heads instead of their hearts, so it was difficult for them to know how they felt. Intellect often got in the way of emoting; even talk could be a barrier to communication. The me generation thus emphasized nonverbal communication. To help them learn this kind of communication, psychologists created the game Body Talk. Also developed by the Center for Studies of the Person, Body Talk was an "experience in nonverbal sharing of feelings" that allowed participants to give themselves "fully to an emotion, feel it in each muscle group, and let your body speak to you."

Unlike with the noncompetitive Feel Wheel, in Body Talk there were winners. Those who could "read" the emotions of others and express their own emotions had a competitive advantage. But "encounters" between two participants were not simply a matter of listening and being listened to. Participants had to be able to explain why they misread or misinterpreted the emotions of others: "If two players constantly misread each other they need to get at the source of their misunderstanding." Such conversations, the instructions noted, "[lead] the players toward openness which is one purpose of the game."[7]

In the 1970s a host of products and services designed to facilitate openness and interpersonal communication were created. The me generation assumed that most Americans had trouble being emotionally direct and instead, whether out of ignorance or an inability to confront their feelings, played psychological "mind games" with one another. Capitalizing on this trend were such psychiatrists turned entrepreneurs as David Viscott. Viscott founded Sensitivity Inc., which created the most commercially successful products of the self-discovery movement. Within a year of introducing his Sensitivity Inc. greeting cards, for example, Viscott sold 25 million cards. Each card featured a Rorschach-like inkblot and a statement; for just thirty-five cents Viscott had a solution for the "hung up" or "uptight." Among the bestsellers were cards with such statements as "Thank you for giving when I couldn't ask," and "I think you use being hurt as a weapon against me." As he explained in an interview with *Newsweek*, "People have a need to reach out and say why they're reaching out . . . but most people who feel these things have difficulty expressing them." The irony of solving the problem of personal expression with prepackaged, mass-produced cards appears to have escaped their makers. In true encounter spirit, Viscott saw himself as helping individuals learn to identify and express their true feelings with "card encounters."

For these non-face-to-face emotional meetings Viscott developed four categories of cards: my hang-ups (which had such statements as "Sometimes I act the way I do because I think I have to"); your hang-ups ("I could give more if I knew you could accept it"); mutual hang-ups ("You don't listen to me and I suspect I don't listen to you"); and no hang-ups ("These are our beautiful years"). Viscott also developed a line of relatively successful napkins and party glasses to facilitate interpersonal communication. On the glasses were printed such statements as "Tell me something about yourself you've never told anyone else before" and "Whom would you like to meet here? I'll go over and introduce you." Viscott also developed "ego-supportive" posters, which featured a Rorschach inkblot and a statement such as "I am trying hard. I wish you'd notice." Viscott also developed a specialized series of posters for adolescents. Addressing the conflicts and confrontations between alienated youths and their parents, these posters carried such statements as "Grades don't measure everything," "People who argue better aren't always right," and "My experience has taught me things too."

To Viscott, the success of his products was quite simple. As he explained about the cards, "These cards are the absolute essence of what conversations build up to but often don't reach, because people's defenses keep them from coming to the point . . . the cards acts as a wedge to get people to talk directly to one another."[8] The "emotional" products of the seventies were designed to teach people how they felt. More importantly, they were designed to teach people the process of discovering one's feelings. Only when everyone knew the methods of self-realization would humans be restored to their full humanity.

The turn inward brought with it the sixties' emphasis on equality. The me decade placed its faith in the democratization of human potential. Seeking to level the emotional playing field, it found the means in the therapeutic ethos. In typical 1970s fashion, David Viscott explained: "What I'm saying is that no one has ever come out with this stuff so clearly or simply that a fucking truck driver can pick [it] up and say 'Aha! When I'm angry, it's because someone has hurt my feelings!'"⁹ In this therapeutic version of equality, everyone had the right to psychological insight and the opportunity to explore their true feelings.

Self-Help Books and the Me Generation

The 1970s initiated an unprecedented expansion of the self-help book market. Indeed, during that decade more than 15 percent of all bestseller books were self-help books, a larger percentage than in any previous decade.¹⁰ During these years Americans purchased hundreds of millions of self-help books. Their appetite was seemingly endless for books with titles such as *The Language of Feelings, How to Be Awake and Alive, It's Me and I'm Here! When I Don't Like Myself, Assert Yourself! How To Be Your Own Person,* and *I Ain't Much Baby—But I'm All I've Got.*

Sales for many of these books were as high as 3 million copies each, putting them on the bestseller list for three to four years. Publishers promised great things from such books. For example, a *Publishers Weekly* ad for *Do-It-Yourself Psychotherapy* read: "This book will save you thousands of dollars and give you control of your own life and your best self. No More Paid Advisors, Sex Hangups, Feeling of Inferiority, Psychosomatic Illness, Guilt. Enjoy More Personal Power, Boundless Sensual Pleasure, New Found Self-Reliance, Your Birthright of Health, New Life Styles."¹¹ Self-help books promised nothing less than the fast and cheap release of human potential.

The self-help book that perhaps most revolutionized America's relationship with the psyche was Thomas A. Harris's *I'm OK—You're OK.* Published in 1967, it was not until the mid-seventies that it became a bestseller, with sales reaching 6 million copies. *I'm OK—You're OK* introduced the American public to transactional analysis, or TA. One contemporary commentator called TA "the most widely used and fastest growing form of treatment for emotional distress in the world." Another explained that "Tom Harris has done for psychotherapy the same thing that Henry Ford did for the automobile: made it available to the average person." Indeed, it was the potential to develop "a therapy for the people" that led Harris to leave the sanctuary of private practice and enter American public debate.

Harris, a psychiatrist, studied with Henry Stack Sullivan. He received his early training at St. Elizabeth's Hospital, in Washington D.C. During World

War II he served as a Navy psychiatrist, and in 1947 he was appointed the Navy's Chief of the Psychiatric Branch. In 1956 he entered private practice in Sacramento, California. In the 1960s, however, Harris became impatient with both the approach and the effects of psychoanalysis and psychotherapy as they were currently being practiced. "After about five years in psychoanalysis," he explained, "you get a ton of garbage and an ounce of usable material." By contrast, in TA "we go after the usable material right away."[12]

TA was a "here and now" therapeutic method. It was based on concepts developed by Eric Berne, who called himself a "cowboy therapist." Born in Canada as Eric Leonard Bernstein, he got his medical degree from McGill University and had a psychiatric residency at Yale University. Faced with anti-Semitism at Yale, he changed his name to Berne. When he completed his residency, he got a position at Mt. Zion Hospital in New York and began training at the New York Psychoanalytic Institute. He underwent analysis with Paul Federn, a former colleague of Freud's. But when America got involved in World War II Berne joined the fight against the Nazis. As it was for so many others, the war was a professionally transforming experience for Berne. It led him to rethink his formal academic and psychoanalytic training. As part of the Army Medical Corps, Berne practiced group therapy. The war required him to make quick diagnoses, which Berne believed actually improved his therapeutic judgment and treatment ability. Out of necessity during World War II he adopted a "get well first, analyze later" attitude that would carry over into his postwar private practice.

After the war, Berne settled in Carmel, California, where he wrote his first book, *A Layman's Guide to Psychiatry and Psychoanalysis*. He took a position with Mt. Zion Hospital in San Francisco, resumed his psychoanalytic training, this time with Erik Erikson, and opened a private practice. It was during the fifteen years following the war that Berne developed the fundamental principles of TA, which he articulated in the *Transactional Analysis Bulletin*. But it was not until 1964, when he published *Games People Play*, that his ideas became known to a broader public. This book gained almost immediate fame and reached the top of the bestseller list in 1965, 1966, and 1967. It remained popular well into the seventies, selling more than 3.5 million copies by 1977.[13]

According to Berne, instead of dealing directly and honestly with one another, most people interacted through "games" or "unconscious destructive behavior." Berne described these games as characterized by four different life positions: I am OK—You are not OK; I am not OK—You are OK; I am not

OK—You are not OK; and I am OK—You are OK. Berne considered only the last position a sound basis for an interpersonal relation.

Harris, who attended a series of seminars conducted by Berne, was greatly influenced by his method of TA and his concept of the four life positions. So much so that his first two books used them in the title, *I'm OK—You're OK* and *Staying OK*. For Harris, the therapeutic goal was to help people become open and develop self-accepting emotional postures. The problem was that most people suffered from the feeling that they were "not OK." Indeed, Harris can be credited with introducing millions of Americans to the concept of the universality of the inferiority complex. While psychiatrists like Alfred Adler had put forth the notion of a universal "inferiority feeling," Harris popularized the concept.

According to Harris, low self-esteem was not something suffered only by the mentally ill or even the neurotic: 96 percent of Americans suffered from feelings of inferiority, or what he called the "I'm Not OK" state of mind. Not only was it universal but it appeared to be present from birth. Harris explains that "right from birth, life is pretty rugged. The child almost immediately develops 'not OK' feelings."[14] The goal of TA was to instill "I'm OK—You're OK" feelings. Harris combined the gospel of self-esteem with a nonjudgmental approach. In the 1970s version of the therapeutic gospel, feeling good about oneself was as important as not putting others down; in fact, the problem was that they went hand in hand.

In Harris's view, their connection was most evident in the "transactions," or interpersonal relations, of everyday life. It was here that an individual's feeling of low self-worth could be seen. According to Harris, all transactions were determined by three ego states, the Parent (P), the Adult (A), and the Child (C). TA materials regularly advised readers to "listen to the voices within you and you will 'hear' your Parent, Adult, and Child." The parent in us represents our shoulds and don'ts. The child in us wants to play, loves sex, but also suffers from feelings of inferiority. The adult mediates between the claims of parent and child. Only the adult can achieve self-esteem and trust, or "I'm OK—You're OK" feelings.[15]

Most of the time, however, transactions are marred by "cross-transactions" and "games people play." The case of John and Barbara is typical. These two adults (but not, to use TA vocabulary, Adults) are at a party. Both are having fun and therefore are in their Child ego state. When John suggests that they have another drink, however, Barbara for some reason moves into her Adult ego state and says to John, "You always drink too much at parties." John responds, "You know very well that I don't always drink too much at parties, and furthermore you said you'd drive us home, and furthermore, if I'm hung over tomorrow it's my hangover and not yours, and anyway it's Sunday." John's Adult in this case is addressing Barbara's Adult. However, a cross-transaction has occurred. Harris explains that "when stimulus and response cross on the PAC [Parent-Adult-Child] transactional diagram, communication stops." That is, real communication or emotional honesty stops, and repetitious patterns of name-calling escalate into a shouting match. At the bottom of such a match is the fact that both husband and wife suffer from feelings of low self-worth. As Harris explains, the "origins of the non-Adult responses is the NOT OK position of the Child."[16]

To undo such repetitions or counteract cross-transactions, Harris recommends "positive strokes," such as caresses, smiles, and words of acceptance. Good therapeutic feedback becomes essential to self-realization. What became apparent in the 1970s was that while therapists can teach the tools to avoid problems like cross-transactions, most of the malfunctioning of the ego states comes from within, so individuals must learn to stroke themselves.

This concept was epitomized in the bestselling book *How to Be Your Own Best Friend*. This fifty-six-page invitation to self-love assumes that feeling OK about oneself is an endangered state of mind. This book, written by husband and wife psychoanalysts Mildred Newman and Bernard Berkowitz, reached the bestseller list in 1973 and had sold over 2 million copies by 1977. Like the authors of many other popular self-help books of that decade, these authors were university-trained and part of the psychological establishment. Berkowitz had been educated at City College, Columbia University, and received his Ph.D. from New York University. He had attended the Alfred Adler Institute and the Postgraduate Center for Mental Health. Mildred Newman had a master's degree in psychology from Hunter College and had trained psychoanalytically with Theodore Reik as well as the National Psychological Association for Psychoanalysis. Both practiced psychoanalysis in New York City, where they were known as "analysts to the stars"; the patients giving testimonials for their new book included Rex Reed, Dick Benjamin, Anthony Perkins, Neil Simon, Nora Ephron, Dan Greenberg, and Liz Smith.

How to Be Your Own Best Friend was hailed from New York City to Oakland as a life-changing book. The *New York Times* called it "a kind of psychiatric pep talk . . . directed at people who hate or despise themselves . . . people who have the patience to learn how to operate a car but won't be bothered learning how to operate themselves." The *Detroit Free Press* noted that Americans now had a book that showed them how to "stop messing up your adult life with inappropriate emotional responses carried over from childhood, and stop putting yourself down." The *Oakland Tribune* reported that Newman and Berkowitz had "devised a formula to help people live more meaningful lives and give them the courage in overcoming the hang-ups that keep them from being happy." Even the reading public in smaller cities learned about the dramatic insights that could be gained from *How to Be Your Own Best Friend*. The *Hartford Courant* recommended reading it "over and over. It's truly enjoyable, leaving the reader with a sense of relief, knowing there is a logical reason for anxiety and frustration." The *Pensacola News* noted that "it's important to listen to ourselves and if we become our own best friends we can be happy. This is an excellent book of advice."[17]

Like other self-help books of the time, *How to Be Your Own Best Friend* has as its central premise that human potential is unfulfilled. Berkowitz and Newman addressed themselves not to the mentally ill or even the neurotic but to people who were simply missing "a sense of zest in their daily lives." This new standard for therapeutic intervention foreshadows Prozac and its new cosmetic psychopharmacology. In the brave new world of antidepressants, psychological dullness alone is adequate reason for therapeutic intervention. Of course, *How to Be Your Own Best Friend* sees the cure as not a pill but a new self, one capable of being a person's best friend. Those who could not find this friend or could not allow themselves to offer love and support so that they could truly enjoy life were in need of therapeutic help. The authors urged readers to take their lack of happiness seriously and do something about it. To "tap into your potential" and "feel all you can feel" were the goals. The obstacles were "within."

How to Be Your Own Best Friend maintains that the reader is his or her "own worst enemy." This failure to "be on your own side" or your "own best friend" leaves one without advocates, lonely, and depressed. The challenge of life, according to the authors, was "finding the things about yourself that make you feel good about yourself." The major problem was that "we all fail to appreciate ourselves enough." Developing a therapeutic attitude toward the self was essential to emotional well-being and happiness. To accomplish this it was necessary to undo "negative self-hypnosis." According to Berkowitz and Newman, most people spent their emotional energy convincing themselves that "I a) am a terrible person, b) always do awful things, c) can't possibly do better." Positive self-hypnosis was needed to get away from this kind of thinking. "Everytime you catch yourself putting yourself down, just stop and push yourself up." Readers were told to become their own friends— to say nice, encouraging things, to be sympathetic and empathetic, not to punish but to accept themselves. Sounding close to the New Thought of the late nineteenth century, the self-help of the seventies was radically optimistic. Its proponents were convinced that a simple fifty-six-page book could help a person repossess his or her human potential.

"Fuck You, I'm Me": New Therapies and New Groups

Never had there been so many ways of "getting one's head together." There were therapies, workshops, "awareness events," and labs, including, "intimacy labs," "stranger labs," "nonverbal labs," "risk-taking labs," "creative-divorce labs," and "creative-aggression labs." But the small group most emblematic of the 1970s was the encounter group. Encounter groups were designed to help overcome the devastating effects of an antiexpressive culture. One commentator described such groups as a

> gathering for a few hours or a few days of twelve or eighteen personable, responsible, certifiably normal and temporarily smelly people. Their destination is intimacy, trust, and awareness of why they behave as they do in groups; their vehicle is candor. . . . In many instances they have never even met before, but, like the proverbial strangers on a train, quickly talk of their deepest emotions. Sometimes they use gadgets and exercises and props; sometimes they don't. Some of them shout, seethe, sob, attack and eventually embrace each other.[18]

The idea behind such groups was that the interactions and confrontations within a small group of people brought together to work on personal issues would force participants to recognize their hang-ups and uncover their true feelings.

The first so-called encounter group was offered at the Esalen Institute in Big Sur, California. Esalen was founded in 1962 by Michael Murphy and Richard Price. Murphy had studied spiritualism and comparative religion at Stanford and had lived at an ashram in India for a few years. Price had studied psychology at Stanford and then had begun graduate study in clinical psychology at Harvard. A few years later he had entered the Air Force, where he had what the military considered a nervous breakdown but what Price considered an "ecstatic" experience. After stays in various hospitals, Price moved to San Francisco, where he waited "for the world to come around." During this time he met Michael Murphy, who suggested that they look at some property his family owned with the thought of opening up some sort of center for the study of psychology, philosophy, and spirituality.

Murphy's grandfather, who was a doctor, had originally purchased the land with the idea of some day opening a health spa. He had gotten as far as building bathhouses. The spot was named Esalen, after the Esalen Indians, who had bathed for centuries there in the hot mineral water. To Murphy and Price it seemed like a perfect place for a kind of psychological spa. Encouraged by a number of friends and spiritual advisers, including Aldous Huxley, Murphy and Price went to see Murphy's grandmother. In her eighties but strong and mentally sharp, she was not easily convinced. Her weak spot, however, was that it had been her late husband's dream to open up a European spa on the property. Perhaps Murphy and Price did not go into all the details of exactly what kind of spa they envisioned, but slowly she warmed to the idea.

In 1962 Esalen opened its doors. Price was in charge of the administrative side of the operation, while Murphy handled programming and marketing, lining up during the first year such key figures as Alan Watts, Arnold Toynbee, Ken Kesey, Paul Tillich, Gray Snyder, Norman O. Brown, Rollo May, Carl Rogers, and Carlos Castaneda. The first program consisted of four seminars entitled "The Human Potentiality." In 1962, not long after Esalen opened, Abraham Maslow, considered the father of humanistic psychology, accompanied by his wife, happened upon Esalen and became a lifetime friend and participant in the Esalen project. Murphy and Price had wanted to meet Maslow but had not had the chance. One foggy night, however, Maslow and his wife knocked on the door looking for lodging. They introduced themselves, and Murphy, Price, and others at Esalen who had read and discussed Maslow's work were thrilled. Maslow, who would return again and again to lecture and lead seminars, called Esalen "the most important educational institution in the world."[19]

During the first year four thousand people visited Esalen to get what Tom Wolfe called "a lube job for the personality."[20] When Esalen opened a San Francisco office, eight thousand people attended programs during the first three weeks. At its height Esalen attracted twenty-five thousand people a year. Esalen participants paid $220 a week to experiment with what Michael Murphy described as "new methods of personal and interpersonal relations." Murphy saw Esalen as offering what amounted to courses and workshops in "non-verbal humanities." In the words of one brochure, at Esalen a person would find "a tool kit of non-verbal and sensory experiences" that would help him or her "know what it is to be human."[21] Expanding the traditional notion of the humanities (and radically departing from it in the process), the curriculum at Esalen emphasized learning through direct experience. It also redefined the meaning of the humanities, which were viewed not as mankind's cultural legacy but as its sensory and sensual grandeur here and now. Feelings in the present replaced knowledge of the past as the core curriculum.

A would-be humanities student at Esalen was likely to see a person blindfolded being led around silently by a group member in order to "restore the individual's sense of touch and to give the experience of dependency." Or you might see a group of five to eight pairs of people staring intently at each other. "Eye-a-logues" were exercises in which group members practiced conversing with their eyes, "cutting through society's excessive verbalism to authentic feelings." Promoters of encounter groups maintained that people did not need talk to understand one another's feelings; in fact, talk often obscured rather than revealed. In the 1970s a premium was placed on interpreting body language because the body did not lie. In contrast, the mind played all sorts of games. Even unintentionally, indeed unconsciously, people said things that did not represent how they really felt. But a person's eyes, especially, communicated his or her true feelings.

Jane Howard, a reporter for *Life* magazine, wrote some of the earliest stories about Esalen. As she explains in a book about her experience, "I had never heard of any of this until a little before January 27, 1968 when *Life* magazine sent me to Big Sur, California." Her job was to report on a five-day Advanced Encounter Workshop. "I had never heard of an 'Advanced Encounter Workshop' much less been to an elementary one, nor had I even much idea of what one was. But I had done risky things before, Had I not skipped fifth grade. . . . Had I not on one foolhardy occasion leaped from a plane with a parachute? Perhaps now, with a similar combination of luck and chutzpah, I could fake it and 'encounter'—whatever encountering was—in a passably advanced manner."

The first meeting of the group took place in the Maslow Room, named for Abraham Maslow. The group was led by Dr. William Schutz, author of the popular book *Joy* and director of the Group Process Section of the Albert Einstein School of Medicine in New York City. Schutz asked the members of the group, who had already achieved a certain success in "emotionally letting go," to provide a brief account of the problem they had come to work on. After everyone had been given an opportunity to "talk" about their "hurts," it was time to "feel" and "experience." Howard characterized the group's task as "interpersonally relating, interacting, honing, and venting our feelings about one another, psychically unmasking ourselves and one another, and equipping one another with generous doses of what to me was a new currency: the gift of seeing ourselves as others see us, technically known as feedback." In the 1970s, holding up a psychological mirror became a national pastime. Esalen was one of the earliest organizations to institutionalize this practice using the small group.

What participants mainly discovered through the process of encountering was emotional pain. Indeed, the unspoken motto at Esalen was, "I hurt, therefore I am." No one in the 1970s capitalized more on the idea of emotional pain as the central fact of man's existence than Arthur Janov, founder of the Primal Scream Institute. Janov believed that most people lived in a "Primal Pool of Pain." His technique for evaporating it was screaming. For six thousand dollars he promised to take people through a rigorous therapeutic encounter that would help them "to achieve the Absence of Significant Blocking Pain." His therapeutic aim was to bring the "inner ghetto" of pain, rage, and fear out into the open. Like many others in the therapy business, Janov believed that Primal Therapy was uniquely effective because it got to the root cause of the problem. Unlike the host of short-term therapies that might sand off the rough spots, Primal Therapy got to the decay. To become truly "Post Primal," Janov believed, one had to confront the pain that was in each of us. As he explained in an interview, "I believe the only way to eliminate neurosis is with overthrow by force and violence." He claimed a 95 percent cure rate.[22] Within the first six months of its existence the institute had three thousand requests for therapy.[23]

Janov, like so many others promoting popular therapies during the 1970s, was a professional psychologist. Using a Navy scholarship, he had studied psychiatric social work at UCLA and then earned his Ph.D. in psychology from the Claremont Graduate School. He went into private practice in the sixties, and it was then that he discovered Primal Therapy. In 1967 a twenty-two-year-old patient whom Janov calls Danny Wilson described a one man show he had attended in which the actor had dressed in diapers and paced the

stage shouting "Mommy!" "Daddy!" At the conclusion, the actor had vom-
ited and then handed out plastic bags and invited the audience to join him.
As Janov tells the story, his patient was fascinated by the show, and so Janov
encouraged Danny to call out for his parents. After initially refusing, Danny
agreed to try it. The patient became increasingly upset, angry, and volatile. Indeed, at one point Danny writhed on the floor seemingly in incredible pain.
But the finale came when Danny let out a piercing scream unlike Janov had
ever heard before. When it was over, Danny reported a transforming experience: "I made it!!! I don't know what, but I can feel."

The experience of regaining their feelings or ridding themselves of anesthetized feelings was common for Janov's patients. One businessman, for example, said that when he first visited Janov, he was unhappy. No matter how
much money he made or how big his company got, "it was never enough."
"The truth was I didn't want to build circuit boards that became the backbone
of guidance systems that went into Polaris missiles. I no longer wanted to
manufacture and sell 'the world's thinnest billfolds' that could carry up to 48
credit cards." So he decided to sign up for intensive Primal Therapy. In language that any other businessman could understand, he described the ar-
rangement and its effects: "In 1971 I made a business deal with a man in
which I agreed to pay him some money and he agreed, in effect, to teach me
how to feel." The price was well worth the results: "It gave me something I
had no way of imagining—it gave me Me, and I'm worth every nickel." In the
1970s many Americans wanted their selves back. Believing that they had lost
a sense of who they were, they paid others to help locate the "me" in them.

Primal Therapy became so popular that other organizations began to offer
this unique kind of therapy. There were even Primal communes. Some also
taught themselves by practicing Self Primal. Janov became increasingly concerned about quality control; at one point he warned potential patients that
"the only person qualified to practice Primal Therapy is someone with a cer-
tificate and approval as a Primal Therapist from the Primal Foundation in Los
Angeles."[24]

There were indeed rivals. Dr. Daniel Casriel, however, maintained that he
had discovered scream therapy completely independently of Janov. Casriel,
like Janov, had substantial professional training. He had received a medical
degree from the University of Cincinnati College of Medicine and then spent
four years in training at Columbia University's Psychoanalytic Institute for
Training and Research. Casriel also served in the U.S. Army as a psychiatrist.

In 1953 he opened a private practice in New York City. During the next ten years Casriel became increasingly involved in the problem of drug addiction. As a consultant and part of the mental-health staff of a high school for delinquent youth, he worked with addicts. In 1962 Casriel visited Synanon, an experimental therapeutic community for drug addicts. Encounter groups were standard fare there. Enormously impressed by what he saw, Casriel wondered whether such a method could be successfully used with nonaddicts, for they too had built up enormous defenses. Confrontation and forcing group members to express how they really felt might prod patients out of their state of emotional alienation.

When Casriel returned to New York, and before he had a chance to think about how encounter groups might be applied to private patients, he was asked to become involved in an experimental drug treatment program called Drug Addicts Treated on Probation, or Daytop. Slowly Casriel began to modify the group process to which he had first been exposed at Synanon and which he had then used at Daytop. According to Casriel, he "discovered" screaming accidentally. In one group-therapy session that he was leading a woman in the hot seat began to talk about her fear. She talked and talked but apparently did not express this feeling. As group members prodded her to tell them how she really felt, the woman became increasingly angry and insisted that she felt fear. Suddenly she broke down and began screaming, "I'm afraid!, I'm afraid!" Eventually her screams became incomprehensible, and she just let out a series of piercing shrieks. "Through such one-at-a-time occurrences," Casriel explained, "it became clear that *words alone* were often a defense which insulated many persons from actually experiencing the emotions they were talking about."[25] Screaming, however, was a pure, genuine expression of emotion.

The screaming sometimes led to visits from the police. When Casriel set up his private practice in a townhouse on Manhattan's fashionable Upper East Side, neighbors who heard the screams sometimes thought that someone was getting beat up and called the police. Eventually Casriel was forced to install soundproofing so that he could continue to help his clients.

According to Casriel, clients often had trouble expressing their feelings because they did not feel entitled to feel the way they really did. To address this issue, Casriel had group members practice looking one another in the eye and saying, "I'm entitled." Indeed, he believed that such an utterance must be preceded by an even more dramatic gesture: taking Harris's "I'm OK—You're

OK" philosophy to new levels, group members shouted at one another, "Fuck you! I'm Me" and "Fuck You! I'm Entitled." Casriel explained that in the English language *fuck* is "the most visceral statement." After group members had established their right to feel the way they did and to be themselves the real screaming got under way. Each group member was asked to find his or her emotional "note" and convert it into a scream; he or she was then asked to find it again and scream longer and louder.

Once the group had reached a crescendo of noise, Casriel or a trainer offered each group member an embrace. Scream Therapy sessions often ended in tears, with group members sobbing inconsolably. For those who needed more work or individual attention there was individual Scream Therapy. But whether dealing with an individual or a group, for Casriel the advantage of Scream Therapy was that it "removes [patients'] fear of emotions and permits them to show anger while not fearing that they will go crazy; to show their need and not feel defeated."

Screaming was necessary because society "anesthetized feelings." This charge against society differed significantly from earlier complaints. Before the 1970s society was often castigated for creating mental illness or neurosis. But for the me generation the problem was that society "blocked" everyone from "experiencing" feelings or developing "emotional resonance." According to Casriel, Americans had become "alienated" from their feelings. The neurotic was actually better off than most Americans, for "neurotics feel their fear, their pain, their anger. They may have trouble expressing it (especially in a healthy way), but they *experience* it, nevertheless."[26]

The "emotionally discomforted" had trouble even achieving "emotional contact"; they simply could not feel true emotions. According to Casriel, almost everyone was "out of contact with his basic feelings." It was for this reason that a radical approach was necessary. Screams, according to Casriel, "can express or uncover emotions that cannot easily be put into words." In Scream Therapy the "stress is on showing feelings, not talking about them." Casriel also emphasized the importance of doing this in the group context. "My patients faced [in a group] accusations I could never have offered. They confronted each other about behavior and attitudes, often with more anger than anyone deserved. They were screamed at for being emotionally dishonest; loudly admonished when they withdrew emotionally from the group. And they were challenged to give up their destructive symptoms."[27]

Casriel's Scream Therapy was considerably cheaper and less time-consuming than Primal Therapy, and unlike Primal Therapy, it did not focus exclusively on pain. Rather it was a "feeling therapy" that sought to put people in touch with pleasure and love. According to Casriel, getting group members to feel pain was easy; "the hard part is to get them to feel entitled to pleasure. We want the patients to recondition themselves through emotional experience to gain new identity—one in which they see themselves as adequate, lovable human beings who can get their needs met if they put effort into it. But now I am convinced that can happen only by learning to feel."[28] By the late 1970s ten thousand people a week were learning to feel by screaming their way to happiness.

Screaming also played an important role in the wildly popular Erhard Seminars Training, or Est, founded in 1971 by Werner Erhard (born Jack Rosenberg). In its first year of operation Est "graduated" eighty-three thousand people in twelve cities. Borrowing from scientology, psychoanalysis, humanistic psychology, TA, and various Eastern religions, Est, like many other self-help programs of the seventies, aimed to transform "your ability to experience living." For a cost of $250 for sixty hours of training, plus more for followup work, Est participants were guaranteed that they would not simply understand but experience, in Erhard's words, that "there's nothing to get." "What is is," said Erhard, "and what ain't ain't."

Erhard apparently came to this profound insight while driving on a California freeway, where he had a life-transforming experience. Erhard, however, is quick to correct this misimpression: "To relate what I experienced to time is a true lie. It did not happen in time. . . . It didn't happen in some place. I wasn't on the freeway in my wife's car on the way to the city. Yet to put it in language I must locate it for you. But that does damage to it. . . . There were no words attached to it. No feelings, no attitudes, no body sensations." What Erhard experienced was "getting it," the "it" being unmediated experience. In Erhard's own words, "IT is you experiencing yourself without any symbology or any concept. Normally, I experience myself through my thoughts; I think who I am. Sometimes I experience myself through my body; I sense who I am. Sometimes I experience myself through my emotions; I feel who I am. Well, IT is you experiencing you directly without any intervening system."[29]

Selling various products, including the experience of "getting it," was also fundamental to his personal history. Erhard was born John Paul Rosenberg in Philadelphia, where his father owned a restaurant. After high school Rosenberg married his high-school sweetheart. Under the name Jack Frost he ran an automobile dealership until 1960, when, at the age of twenty-five, he deserted his wife and four children. He fled to the West Coast with a woman he eventually married. In California he called himself Werner Erhard after reading two articles in *Esquire* magazine, one about Werner Heisenberg and another about Ludwig Erhard, the German chancellor of the exchequer. As Werner Erhard he got a job in the late 1960s training encyclopedia salesmen, and in 1971 this supersalesman turned to selling "getting it." In 1975 Est grossed $9.5 million.[30]

Like many other self-help programs in the seventies, Est emphasized experience, authenticity, and emotional honesty and deemphasized intellectualizing. But it pursued its goals not within the touchy-feely context of the small group but in the "mass group," a far more combative and authoritarian context. These mass-group exercises were like a psychological basic training. Trainees were frequently called "assholes." They were required to "suspend judgment." As one trainer explained, "judgment is a voice in the back of my head and it still goes on but I don't allow it to affect my relationships."[31] In addition to suspending judgment, participants were supposed to suppress their hunger, their urge to go to the bathroom, or their desire to smoke a cigarette. There were strict rules and few bathroom, smoking, or eating breaks. And Est training seminars were large, with between 250 and 2,500 attendees.

A typical training would begin at 8:30 A.M. in a hotel convention hall. As participants filed into the cavernous room lined with folding chairs, they were greeted by cheerful Est volunteers and trainers. It was the last bit of cheerfulness they would experience. Once the trainees had taken their seats, instructions were barked from a raised platform with microphones: "No eating except at times specified. Is that clear? No one leaves his seat without permission. Is that clear? If you are sitting next to a friend, change seats. All time pieces surrendered. All pens and pencils surrendered. No notes."[32] The trainees were informed that they not only could but should share their immediate feelings and experience. They just had to stand up, and a microphone would be brought to them.

One weekend Est training session held in New York City was led by Ron, an Est trainer from California. This deeply tanned blond-haired man in his early thirties leapt onstage and announced that everyone there was an "asshole." He explained that now that everyone's fees had been collected, neither he nor any of the trainers care about the 250 people sitting quietly in their folding chairs. He had their money, and it was up to them to get what they wanted.

He said that they were there because their lives did not work. A young woman named Wendy stood up, and when a microphone was brought to her, she insisted that her life did work, that she had come directly from transcendental meditation, and that she was attending simply to get more enlightenment. Ron responded, "She's full of shit," and then he launched into a ten-hour lecture on epistemology that was periodically interrupted by members of the audience.

"Most of what we know consists of received ideas and secondhand experiences. We see the world through a glaze of beliefs and ideas. Thinking is crap—the yammering in the back of our heads." After such declarations, Ron interrupted his lecture to ask the audience, "How many of you believe what I've said?" When a number of audience members raised their hands, Ron told them: "Then your assholes." He advised Est participants not to believe or disbelieve but just to "get it." Skeptical audience members who stood to speak were told to "come off your act." In Est, as in other self-help programs, there was practically nothing worse than an "act" or "emotional dishonesty." Starting at about 9:00 P.M. Ron conducted exercises for a few hours so that Est trainees could "experience" their boredom, anger, and headaches and then "digest" them. Finally, at 11:30 the Est seminar ended and the audience was told to return at 10:15 the next morning.

The next day, after Est trainees reported on their experience of the previous day, there was a three-hour "letting go" exercise. For this exercise all 250 seminar members lay on the floor with their eyes closed. Ron instructed everyone to experience the troubling items in their lives, such as anger, loneliness, or joy. The trainees were expected to "Let go, let it all out!" through their bodies and voices. A deafening sound of screams, moans, and shouts emerged, accompanied by limbs flailing all about.

In an Est seminar led by Werner Erhard himself things unfolded in much the same way. Held in a San Francisco convention hotel, the seminar began with Est philosophy, whose essential tenet was that only that which is experienced personally is true and satisfying. The only way to get trainees to give up their "acts" was to confront and exhaust them and to restrict their food, drink, and bathroom privileges. After Erhard lectured the audience for hours in a mostly incomprehensible way, punctuated by calling Est trainees assholes, an outraged trainee named Walter stood up. When a microphone was brought to him, in a booming voice he accused Erhard of being the asshole. Erhard applauded him and said, "Thank you Walter." Then Erhard started to shout at the audience: "You Turkeys! Everything I've said is lies! Walter has the guts to share how he feels about this. I'm a liar! Only an asshole would try to understand lies!!" Then Erhard resumed his lecture. "The real self is actually satisfied," he said. "If you think you need something out there to be satisfied, you're in the wrong context." After hours of such psychobabble, Est trainees reported a feeling of catharsis.[33]

What screaming was to Werner Erhard, Arthur Janov, and Daniel Casriel, regurgitation was to Francis I. Regardie, the inventor of Active Psychotherapy. This form of therapy used tongue depressors and a kidney pan to rid the patient of his inhibitions and get to his "real self." Regardie's procedure was

> to let him gag anywhere up to a dozen times, depending on the time of response. In itself, the style of gagging is an admirable index of the magnitude of the inhibitory apparatus. Some gag with finesse, with delicacy, without noise. These are, categorically, the most difficult patients to handle. Their character armor is almost impenetrable, and their personalities rigid almost to the point of petrification. They require to be encouraged to regurgitate with noise, without concealment of their discomfort and with some fullness. Others will cough and spit, yet still remain unproductive.[34]

In this era of feelings no technique, no matter how forceful (or disgusting), was considered too extreme.

Most encounters were orchestrated without the use of tongue depressors. One kinder, gentler, approach to feeling that became popular in the seventies was Co-Counseling. This consisted in working in pairs, "listening and be listened to." The goal was "Zest," and the way to achieve it was through "appreciation." As one commentator explained, "Zest is to co-counseling what the Absence of Significant Blocking Pain is to Primal Therapy and original sin is to a good Catholic—it is the natural feeling of a human being." To recover Zest, participants in Co-Counseling needed to engage in the "Complete Appreciation of Oneself Without Reservation." The founder of Co-Counseling, Harvey Jenkins, said that this was to be accomplished through "appreciative, positive words," a "proud exultant posture," and "a pleased, happy expression."[35]

The lengths to which Co-Counseling was willing to go in applying the I'm OK—You're OK" philosophy was made evident at one Co-Counseling workshop in June 1973 when the question of how to appreciate Richard Nixon came up. The facilitator responded: "You remember that the person is okay, but let him know that what he is doing is not all right. Let him know that he needs to cut out the stupid things he is doing; that isn't validating him. We have inherent affection for other human beings, but don't mince around with the patterns."[36]

The issuing of positive feelings that all the therapies of the 1970s recommended was made difficult by the existence of bad feelings, believed to be deeply ingrained. Most therapeutic methods saw them as fundamental or primal. But none located them as specifically as Rebirthing Therapy. Rebirthers believed that bad feelings originated at birth and that only by reliving that experience could adults be cured of the low self-esteem that plagued them.

Leonard Orr, the founder of Rebirthing, invented "Happy Birth," a rebirthing process involving a hot tub of water, a snorkel, and nose clips. Comparing Rebirthing to Primal Therapy, advocates of the "Happy Birth" saw clear advantages in their therapy: "In Primal Therapy you're supposed to reexperience every little thing, not just your birth. In rebirthing, though, you just let go of the Big Feeling. It's a lot quicker."[37] The "Big Feeling" was a central concept in Rebirthing. The fundamental or original bad feeling that one acquired at birth stemmed not only from the trauma of being expelled from the womb but also from the cutting of the umbilical cord. According to Rebirthers, infants felt intense loss when they had suddenly to leave the womb and learn to live on their own. For the rest of their lives, unless the problem was dealt with therapeutically, adults experienced this pain and an ambivalence about being in the world. Rebirthing addressed this problem by helping one let go of the Big Feeling. Orr describes the Big Feeling as the fundamental feeling that affects all people from their earliest moment of existence, a sadness or feeling of worthlessness, a feeling that "you're not important enough to take up anybody's time. Sometimes, just before the baby's born it can get the feeling that the doctor is in a big hurry to get out of the delivery room and screw the head nurse, for instance. So you grow up with this feeling that everyone's got more important things to do than listen to you."[38]

Orr initially worked for Est, which he described "as a good warmup" for Rebirthing. By 1977 there were twenty-nine Rebirthing centers in the United States, with more than ten thousand graduates of "Happy Birth" and two hundred Rebirthers. Orr discovered Rebirthing accidentally in the sixties, when he was spending time with members of metaphysical societies in San Francisco and looking for the truth. He noticed that he became anxious just before and after getting out of a hot tub, and by experimenting with his feelings during long hours in the bath he developed his unique therapeutic process.

Those interested in letting go of the Big Feeling were not allowed to immediately re-create their birth experience. First they had to attend a rebirthing seminar, at which the theory behind "Happy Birth" was explained and they underwent a dry run. The dry run cost thirty-five dollars, and the wet run, fifty. At the wet run the patient took off his or her clothes and got into a hot tub along with the rebirthing therapist. The temperature of the water was supposed to match the temperature of the amniotic fluid. With snorkel and nose clips the client put his face down into the water. He was held or suspended by the therapist, who taught the client how to breathe. The rebirther also provided reassurance through affirmations such as "You have survived your birth so you have a right to be here" and "You have time to take a deep breath of air." Patients reported feeling a variety of sensations and memories during this stage. At a certain point they usually panicked. Orr calls this primal panic "the creeping crud," a reliving of the original birth trauma. As soon as the client panicked, he was removed from the water and put on a table, where he was toweled dry, massaged, and generally comforted. Many patients had to undergo the treatment several times before they were "totally free of birth trauma."[39]

While some tried to free themselves of the trauma of birth through Rebirthing, others tried to temporarily return to the unclothed status at birth through nude encounter groups. The pioneer of such groups was Paul Bindrim, according to whom "clothing means we really don't trust each other. There's so much bullshit about an American's home being his castle, and such a fetish about privacy. After all, you were born nude, weren't you?"[40] Bindrim ascribed to nudity the power "to increase interpersonal transparency, remove inhibitions in the area of physical contact, decrease the sense of personal isolation and estrangement, and culminate in a feeling of freedom and belongingness."

He discovered the power of nude encounter groups while earning a living leading clothed weekend therapy marathons. Toward the end of one such marathon group members spontaneously stripped and jumped into the pool. They reported experiencing intense feelings of catharsis. Many also said that for the first time they felt like themselves. Indeed, many group members went running around the pool naked shouting, "Look! It's me." And in the 1970s version of the therapeutic gospel nothing was more sacred then being oneself or being one's own best friend.

For Bindrim's basic, twenty-four-hour nude group marathons (as opposed to his advanced nudity marathons) participants paid forty-five dollars. Bindrim said that this was a particularly good deal given that most members stood "a good chance of having a peak experience," a Maslowian term that referred to the highest emotional experience a person could have. He used his own house in Hollywood Hills or borrowed a friend's house. When group members arrived, they were asked to go back out to their cars and scatter them so that neighbors would not get suspicious. Each group member was asked to bring along several peak stimuli, "things in this world you like very most to see, to hear, to smell, to taste, and to touch." Bindrim promised that he would take members back to primitive times, "when we were not vexed, harried, over-civilized human beings, but free and happy animals." Group members' mass regression would take place in a "womb pool."

Before undressing, those gathered would form a group and talk about what they had come "to work on." Each member was given three minutes. Next the group members were to stare intently into one another's eyes, and then each one was to state the feelings this had generated in him or her. With these introductions to feelings out of the way, they were sent to undress for the womb pool. Once in the pool, Bindrim led the group in a "trust exercise." Each member of the group was passed around to all the others. Everyone was asked to talk about how the experience made him or her feel. After several hours of working on their "trust issues," Bindrim reminded group members that "we are land-based animals. We want to learn to be free in an air and ground atmosphere as well as in water." For this reason more than half of the twenty-four-hour nude marathon was conducted on land.

This land part resembled other types of encounter groups except that everyone was nude. In one session, for example, a group member named Lloyd experienced his anger, which initially expressed itself through tears. When Lloyd first burst into tears, Bindrim instructed him to "stay with the tears!" "Feel them," he was ordered. Bindrim detected that Lloyd had not gotten at the real emotion that was afflicting him. "Who are you angry at," demanded Bindrim. Lloyd blurted out "It's—it's Miss Cavanaugh." Miss Cavanaugh had been Lloyd's first-grade teacher, who he had hated. Asked to imagine her, Lloyd saw her kicking him out of her classroom for no reason. When Bindrim urged Lloyd to tell Miss Cavanaugh what he thought of her, Lloyd shouted, "You goddam bitch! You're punishing me for no reason! I'd like to tear your hair out by the roots!" Bindrim then dashed across the room and grabbed a Sears catalog, which he handed to Lloyd. "Here's her hair," Bindrim told him.

"Tear it up." Lloyd made confetti out of the catalog. Bindrim explained to the group that everyone has his or her own way of expressing anger, but the idea is "to regress, if possible, to the trauma that caused the distortion. That's the way to start a peak experience."

Bindrim accused American culture of ignoring fantasy and its role in making a person whole. American culture also ignores the crotch area, he said. "Genitally speaking, we're so terribly negatively conditioned. After all, where would your head end be without your butt end?" Apparently no one could argue with that, and Bindrim led the group in a "crotch-eyeballing" exercise. He began slowly with Lorna. First she was asked to stand in front of a full-length mirror, while the group looked on. Bindrim asked her not to censor herself and to simply share with the group her thoughts about what she saw. Lorna apparently considered herself too thin and her thighs too far apart. Disappointedly, she explained, "You can see the air between them." After Lorna's feelings and the group's generally supportive reaction were processed, Bindrim moved on to the heart of the exercise. Lorna was asked to lie down. Bindrim took one of Lorna's ankles in each hand, raising her legs straight up in the air. The mirror was brought closer, and Lorna was directed to look at her crotch. Bindrim exclaimed, "This is where it's at. This is where we are so damned negatively conditioned." Lorna was then asked to name the person in the group whom she would least like to have look at this area of herself. In a feeble voice Lorna named Katy. Bindrim removed the mirror and asked Lorna and others to eyeball Lorna's crotch. Bindrim instructed Lorna to "tell Katy . . . what things happen in your crotch. Say 'Katy, this is where I shit, fuck, piss, and masturbate.'" Looking from her rather unusual vantage point at all the eyes fixed on her, Lorna said, "I think that Katy already knows that." After a number of others had undergone the "crotch-eyeballing" exercise, there was praise all around for its effects. Maxine, for example, proclaimed that the exercise had "done more for me than three years of therapy." Another expressed the regret that "my daughters have to wait until they're twenty-one to be straightened out by Paul Bindrim."[41]

Some "encountering" enthusiasts blamed the only partial success of the social movements of the 1960s for their turn away from politics. Many asked what the point was of critiquing a system so thoroughly corrupt. They decided to seek personal empowerment instead of political empowerment, and freeing themselves of their emotional "baggage" became their preoccupation.

Others saw turning inward as a natural extension of New Left philosophy.

If the personal was political, then it made sense that in order to change the world they first had to find out who they were. Identity, as I have shown, has always been a critical part of movement rhetoric, whether it was the civil-rights movement, the women's movement, or the antiwar movement. The me generation took the 1960s emphasis on identity one step further (or backward, depending upon one's perspective).

For the me generation, self-awareness was not simply a means to an end; it was the end itself. They began by questioning the values underlying the American way of life and ended by asking, Who am I? The sixties emphasis on direct experience as a valid source of knowledge developed into an emphasis on experience as the only true way of knowing. In the 1970s feelings were the barometer of truth. Everything that obstructed their expression was condemned, and everything that facilitated their expression was celebrated.

In this struggle to feel, advocates of the therapeutic gospel wavered between optimism and pessimism. On the one hand, members of the me generation were certain that intimacy, communication, and self-awareness could be achieved, and by all. On the other hand, they were apocalyptic about the antiexpressive forces dominating American life. They saw conspiracies to keep Americans from feeling everywhere. They also viewed Americans as nearing emotional death. The goal of the encounter-group movement was to keep them alive.

* * *

There's a joke about the 1970s:

> Q: How many people did it take to screw in a light bulb?
> A: Four: one to screw it in and three to share the experience.

The primacy placed on feelings and self-expression in the seventies was unprecedented. Never before had such a premium been placed on intimacy, trust, and self-awareness. The sin of ignorance of the self and the gospel of self-discovery fueled the encounter-group movement. This emphasis on self-discovery would, however, ultimately be dwarfed by the recovery movement of the 1980s and 1990s. The me generation's mantra to share experiences was not fully taken up by most Americans until "support groups" swept the country. The encounter groups of the seventies were still a semi-countercultural phenomenon. By the 1990s recovering by sharing stories of addiction, however, had become mainstream.

PERSONAL
8 PROBLEMS

and Public Debate

In 1982 Bob Morris, a commission sales representative for CompCare Publishers, convinced two major bookstores, B.Dalton and Walden, to radically change the layout of their stores. Morris convinced these bookstores not to scatter books about recovering in the psychology, sociology, and even self-help sections but to locate them in a single "recovery" section, today the largest section of most bookstores. According to Morris, bookstores were initially afraid of alienating their customers by prominently displaying books that openly addressed addictive behavior.[1] But as it turned out, the risk produced large dividends. When bookstores like B.Dalton consolidated their recovery materials in one section, sales for these books increased four to seven times.

Today it is hard to believe that bookstores or any other institutions of American life would be reticent about personal problems. Indeed, the public debate in America has become so filled with the intimate details of people's lives and the afflictions they suffer from that it is difficult to imagine a time when it was any other way. Perhaps ZipperGate, the scandal involving sexual relations between the White House intern Monica Lewinsky and President Bill Clinton, represented an apex. Day in and day out, in every media market in the country, the details of their affair were made public.

During the 1980s and 1990s all prohibitions against publicizing private or intimate matters seem to have been declared null and void. Not only did it become commonplace for personal problems to be publicly announced but the number of problems one might have rose meteorically. There were the relatively familiar problems of alcohol and drug addiction and depression, anxiety, and mood disorders. But in the 1980s there emerged such specialized problems as "identity disorder," defined by the *Diagnostic and Statistical Manual of Mental Disorders* as "severe subjective distress regarding inability to integrate aspects of the self into a relatively coherent and acceptable sense of self." The manual explained further that for persons with this disorder "there is uncertainty about a variety of issues relating to identity, including long-term goals, career choice, friendship patterns, sexual orientation, and behavior, religious identification, moral value systems and group loyalties. . . . Frequently, the disturbance is epitomized by the person asking 'Who am I?'"[2] Although the me generation in the 1970s urged Americans to ask, Who am I? they clearly never imagined that asking would be described as an official disorder. Nor did they imagine that its treatment was potentially reimbursable by insurance companies.

This chapter asks why and how it became commonplace not only to have so many afflictions but to make them public as well. Clearly, the recovery movement and its extensive campaign played a key role. The creation of television talk shows was also important. With the birth of *The Oprah Winfrey Show,* confessing one's personal problems truly became a subject of mass entertainment. Finally, the Internet provided a brand-new forum for the promotion of personal problems as public debate. When the therapeutic gospel went online, the possibilities for "public" conversations about personal problems became infinite.

Addiction as Identity

A 1990 notice posted in a Colorado church listing support groups meeting in the coming week read as follows:

Sunday

12:00 NOON—Cocaine Anonymous, Main Floor
5:30 pm—Survivors of Incest, Main Floor
6:00 pm—Al-Anon, 2nd Floor
6:00 pm—Alcoholics Anonymous, Basement

Monday

5:30 pm—Debtors Anonymous, Basement
6:30 pm—Codependents of Sex Addicts Anonymous, 2nd Floor
7:00 pm—Adult children of Alcoholics, 2nd Floor
8:00 pm—Alcoholics Anonymous, Basement

8:00 pm—Al-Anon, 2nd Floor
8:00 pm—Alateen, Basement
8:00 pm—Cocaine Anonymous, Main Floor

Tuesday

8:00 pm—Survivors of Incest Anonymous, Basement

Wednesday

5:30 pm—Sex & Love Addicts Anonymous, Basement
7:30 pm—Adult Children of Alcoholics, 2nd Floor
8:00 pm—Cocaine Anonymous, Main Floor

Thursday

7:00 pm—Codependents of Sex Addicts Anonymous, 2nd Floor
7:00 pm—Women's Cocaine Anonymous, 2nd Floor

Friday

5:30 pm—Sex & Love Addicts Anonymous, Basement
5:45 pm—Adult Overeaters Anonymous, 2nd Floor
7:30 pm—Codependents Anonymous, Basement
7:30 pm—Adult Children of Alcoholics, 2nd Floor
8:00 pm—Cocaine Anonymous, Main Floor

Saturday

10:00 am—Adult Children of Alcoholics, Main Floor
12:00 pm—Self-Abusers Anonymous, 2nd Floor
Sunday

In this Colorado town there is a twelve-step program for everyone; those suffering from a range of problems can find help seven days a week. Under the auspices of the church, members and nonmembers alike practice the gospel of recovery. Participants confess the sin of addiction and accept that salvation lies in recovery. As part of the twelve-step program they must also accept that healing has no end: their faith in recovery has to be continually renewed. Throughout this difficult process the support group stands ready to help, as well as ready to expose the evils of denial.[3]

During the 1980s, twelve-step and other types of recovery programs proliferated. Today, there are more than 3 million recovery groups in the United States. In New York City alone there are four thousand self-help meetings a week. In Los Angeles nearly five thousand support groups cater specifically to women's needs. The phenomenon is not confined to the coasts: research shows that in most cities with populations of more than fifty thousand there are six hundred support-group meetings per week.[4]

An estimated 40 percent of Americans, or approximately 75 million adults, attend such meetings. Participants insist that support groups help them cope with the problems that afflict them. Jeffry Ahorn, for example, recounts how the local chapter of California's Pet Loss Support Group helped him deal with the death of Fred, his twenty-pound boa constrictor, whereas outside the group "no one understood what Fred had meant to me." Jennifer Stratford credits her nail-biters support group for helping her overcome her habit. She proudly announces that she can finally wear neon orange nail polish "without feeling foolish."[5] Janet Damon, of a compulsive shoppers support group, overcame her compulsion to buy as many as 130 pair of pantyhose at a clip.[6]

The support groups that Americans join range from therapy groups to Bible support groups to groups fitting specific problems or circumstances, such as Women and Their Cheating Husbands, or WATCH; Banana Splits, a support group for children whose parents have divorced; and Graceworks, a support group for clergy members in recovery. They run the gamut from the credible to the incredible. Channelers, for example, a support group for psychics struggling to communicate with the dead, is probably among the more bizarre. On the third Thursday of every month thirty or so psychics meet to gain support for pursuing mental telepathy. As Lenny Rawls, a twenty-eight-year-old Air Force veteran who has been receiving visitations from outer space explained, "I tried telling my friends about it, but they just thought I was crazy." He finally found support when he joined Channelers, which "helped me to understand that I wasn't the only one with these abilities." Another regular attendee of the support group, Frank Friel, a local police chief who uses psychics to solve murder cases, reports that Channelers provides him with the support he needs to pursue his forensic tactics.[7]

The proliferation of support groups is a critical chapter in the story of the therapeutic gospel. Millions of people who had been affected in only a general way by therapeutic thinking came into direct contact with it through their participation in support groups. America certainly has come a long way since the encounter-group movement of the 1970s, when participation in small groups was limited largely to those who embraced an alternative culture. Not only did participation in groups skyrocket during the 1980s but it became mainstream. Of course, the character of America's group participation changed too. Instead of encounter groups in which a premium was placed on new experiences generated through interpersonal confrontation, Americans in the eighties and nineties joined groups in which the emphasis was on support. Group members came together to help one another acknowledge their problems and find salvation in healing.

The story of the recovery movement begins in 1935, with the creation of what must be considered the original twelve-step program, Alcoholics Anonymous (AA). Just two years after Prohibition ended, Bill Wilson, a New York stockbroker and an alcoholic, founded AA. Wilson first belonged to the Oxford Group, a Protestant organization whose goal was spiritual renewal. This group provided Wilson with the initial encouragement to stop drinking. Once, on a business trip to Akron, Ohio, he found himself tempted to drink. The impulse was slight at first, but it then became overwhelming. Uncertain what to do or where to turn, he thought that if he could talk with another alcoholic he might be able to resist the temptation. So he looked up the local head of the Oxford Group and made an unusual request: he wanted to meet with a fellow alcoholic.

Wilson was taken to meet Robert H. Smith—Dr. Bob, a prominent physician who was an alcoholic. As the story goes, they talked and talked and talked. The fellowship Wilson found in communicating with a another alcoholic helped him remain sober and renewed his faith in his ability to overcome his alcoholism. The experience was so powerful that Wilson and Dr. Bob decided to create a group whose sole purpose was to help and support other alcoholics.

Breaking away from the Oxford Group, in early June 1935 Wilson and Dr. Bob created AA, though it was not called that at the time. Alcoholics Anonymous emerged as the fellowship's official name only in 1939, when Wilson and Smith published their first statement of purpose and principles under the title *Alcoholic Anonymous,* which stuck as the name of the new movement. A rash of publicity shortly after the book was published provided the initial boost to membership. AA had been seeking a way to spread the word, or in AA lingo, to "pass it on." It finally got the chance when the *Saturday Evening Post* did a story on AA in 1941, "Alcoholics Anonymous—Freed Slaves of Drink, Now They Free Others." Explaining the organization's mission and methods, the story highlighted the power of talk and fellowship in treating alcoholism: "A bridge of confidence is thereby erected, spanning a gap which has baffled the physician, the minister, the priest, or the hapless relatives.

Over this connection, the troubleshooters convey, bit by bit, the details of a program for living which has worked for them and which, they feel, can work for any other alcoholic."[8] The article concluded with the AA mailing address.

The article had the desired effect. As AA's founder, Bill Wilson recalled, "By mail and telegram a deluge of pleas for help and orders for the book, 'Alcoholics Anonymous' first in hundreds and then in thousands, hit Box 658." AA responded by putting into action a plan that had been months in the making. All AA members who were women and wives of members who could use a typewriter were rounded up, an emergency headquarters was created, and each appeal for help was personally responded to. Every person asking for help was given the nearest local contact. Between 1941 and 1942 AA membership grew from two thousand to eight thousand.

World War II also considerably boosted membership. In order to communicate with AA members in the armed forces, AA began publishing *A.A. Grapevine*. This newsletter and soldiers' own grapevine introduced others to this first twelve-step program. By the end of the war fifteen thousand Americans belonged to AA. AA had only three hundred thousand members as late as 1971 and not more than five hundred thousand in the early 1980s. Between 1985 and 1995, however, AA became a household word, and today there are more than 2 million members.

Clearly, AA was ahead of its time. In 1935 the gospel of recovery did not resonate with large numbers of Americans. For the first few decades of AA's existence most Americans still considered admitting personal problems to be a sign of weakness, not strength. Denial was expected, perhaps even required. Personal problems were not appropriate topics for public debate. Alcoholism was a private matter that most Americans believed should be handled privately. To the extent that it was viewed as a real problem, the immediate family was supposed to handle it as quietly as possible.

AA took an entirely different approach. It not only embraced admission but insisted on the public nature of this admission. In front of a group of fellow alcoholics who would bear witness, the alcoholic was supposed to confess. The first of the twelve steps is to admit the affliction. Hence, the opening statement, "Hi, I'm ———— and I'm an alcoholic." Of course, AA made this confession more acceptable by emphasizing anonymity. Last names are not used in AA. AA also made confession easier because it treated alcoholism as a disease. As such it required treatment, not condemnation.

Embracing the tenets of the therapeutic gospel, AA promoted the view that talk is the first step in the cure. Its version of the talking cure was not secular, however. AA promoted the idea of a higher power, insisting that salvation lay only in recovery. Turning the addiction of alcoholism into a new form of religion, AA promoted the gospel of recovery.

This new blend of religious medicine was relentlessly promoted. The twelve-step method was applied to other problems besides alcoholism. Narcotics Anonymous was founded in 1953, followed by Gamblers Anonymous in 1957, Debtors Anonymous in 1968, and Emotions Anonymous in 1971. The year 1976 was somewhat of a watershed year, for it was the year when Adult Children of Alcoholics (ACOA) was founded. Before ACOA, twelve-step programs were limited to recovery programs designed to alleviate specific addictions or compulsions. With the creation of ACOA, the twelve-step ideology became radically inclusive. General problems of living that could be attributed to being the child of an alcoholic were now fair game for treatment.

During the 1980s there was a veritable explosion of twelve-step programs. This growth contributed to an unparalleled diseasing of America. Twelve-step programs turned everyday behaviors into diseases to be treated. For example, it was in the 1980s that eating became a form of disease, with anyone who had repeatedly attempted to diet considered a food addict. According to the Overeaters Anonymous (OA) literature, "Compulsive overeating is a progressive illness . . . one that, like alcoholism and some other illnesses can be arrested." Like other illnesses, overeating has symptoms. According to OA, anyone who has repeatedly tried diets or who has ever experienced "the despair of feeling fat" is a candidate for an eating-disorder group.[9]

In the new therapeutic order one could be addicted not only to food, alcohol, and drugs but also to activities like sex. For this affliction there were such groups as Sex Addicts Anonymous, Sex and Love Addicts Anonymous, and Sexaholics Anonymous. Another such group, Sexual Compulsives Anonymous, for example, describes itself as a fellowship whose purpose is to help participants remain "sexually sober and to help others achieve sexual sobriety."[10] For the uninitiated who might be confused about which group to attend and the differences among them, a veteran provides limited guidance. He explains that he goes to Sex Addicts Anonymous for his "core physical addiction" and to Sex and Love Addicts Anonymous for his addiction to romance.

As in all twelve-step programs, participants in sex and love addiction groups are expected to begin with admission. Thus, a newcomer to Sex Addicts Anonymous declared, "My name is Jeanie and I'm a sex addict." This forty-four-year-old woman confessed to getting "loaded" on sex. "I'd spend my time and money on alcohol, drugs, and sex toys. I'd spend the rest of my time fantasizing and recuperating from those acts." As of 1992 there were more than six thousand groups for sex, love, or romance addicts.[11]

Twelve-step programs exist not only for those suffering from compulsive physical desire but also for those simply addicted to relationships. Women, in particular, are "men junkies." Relationship Anonymous, which caters to this constituency, defines an addictive relationship as one "in which we rely on someone to fulfill our unmet needs from childhood, to escape our own inner sadness, turmoil, and pain, to heal us and 'save' us through their attention and love, and to make us feel 'whole.'"[12] It is ironic that this definition is regarded as a negative one. It might be said that it describes the majority of relationships. After all, significant others often give their partners what their parents did not give them and serve to make them feel complete.

Broader still is the twelve-step program for those simply suffering from emotional distress. Emotions Anonymous describes itself as a fellowship "composed of people who come together in weekly meetings for the purpose of working toward recovery from emotional difficulties. . . . The only requirement for membership is a desire to become well emotionally." With more than fifteen hundred groups nationwide, Emotions Anonymous claims to have worked "miracles in the lives of many who suffer from problems as diverse as depression, anger, broken or strained relationships, grief, anxiety, low self-esteem, panic, abnormal fears, resentment, jealousy, guilt, despair, fatigue, tension, boredom, loneliness, withdrawal, obsessive and negative thinking, worry, compulsive behavior, and a variety of other emotional illnesses." In typical AA fashion, Emotions Anonymous meetings begin with the admission that "we are powerless over our emotions—that our lives have become unmanageable."[13]

More specialized twelve-step groups exist for those suffering from intense emotional difficulties, such as Trauma Anonymous for those recovering from posttraumatic stress disorder, or PTSD (Post-traumatic Stress Disorder) Anonymous. Participants in either of these groups must begin with admission. A newcomer therefore declares, "Hello my name is ———, and I am a survivor of a traumatic event in my life that led to PTSD."[14] The proliferation of twelve-step programs itself seems to have created a new kind of emotional trauma: many who have been unsuccessful at recovering via such programs have experienced repeated devastation. Recovery Anonymous, designed for such persons, is, according to its mission statement, "especially for those who have searched for recovery in other programs, but have thus far not found it, as well as for those who may have found some recovery, but are frustrated by the endless discussion of, and focus upon, self-destructive behavior and personal problems."[15]

Today there are more than 260 twelve-step programs in America.[16] They include programs for nail-biters, those traumatized by religious fundamentalism, debtors, compulsive shoppers, and workaholics. It seems that almost every activity can become addictive and require a twelve-step program to alleviate it. One of the most recent additions to the litany of afflictions is information addiction. "Dataholics" crave information; they walk around with pagers or cell phones and are constantly e-mailing or accessing information online. One dataholic explained, "I have to be reachable 24 hours a day."[17] Fortunately, dataholics can find fellowship and support in Dataholics Anonymous.

Twelve-step programs seem to exist not only for every conceivable affliction but also for every conceivable class of people. There are twelve-step groups for gays and lesbians, Jews and Christians, women, Blacks, teens, the elderly, and the middle-aged. There are special programs for parents, wed and unwed, batterers, and child abusers, and the victims of child abuse. Professionals too have specialized groups tailored to their particular needs. There are twelve-step programs for doctors, clergy, prostitutes, and artists, such as A.R.T.S Anonymous (Artists Recovering in the Twelve Steps), for "poets, painters, singers, instrumentalists, composers, dollmakers," and other artists. The purpose of the fellowship is to "share their experience, strength and hope with each other that they may recover from their common problem and help others to surrender their creativity." The first step for artists who want to deal with the emotional handicaps that are "deadly to the creative soul" is to admit that "we are powerless over our creativity—that our lives have become unmanageable." How artists can "surrender their creativity" and still be artists was not explained.[18]

Clearly, the specialization of twelve-step programs is a product of the identity politics that emerged in the 1960s and 1970s. The social movements of that period made identity central to politics. Whether one was Black or White, male or female, straight or gay, Catholic or Jewish, mattered. They became key categories in American public debate. But the recovery movement also rejects aspects of this kind of politics and the fragmentation it involves, since on some level the recovery movement recognizes only one kind of identity, that of the addicted.[19] As an AA pamphlet explains, "We in A.A. believe alcoholism is a disease that is no respecter of age, sex, creed, race, wealth, occupation, or education. It strikes at random."[20] Of course, the statistics for such disorders as drug addiction, alcoholism, weight problems, and physical and sexual abuse show that class does indeed matter. For example, poor people are disproportionately plagued by alcohol and drug addiction.

The point is that twelve-step programs subscribe to a kind of universalism that is grounded in psychology. Twelve-step programs insist, for example, that while the Black lesbian Catholic alcoholic may be different in certain respects from the straight Jewish white male alcoholic, both are fundamentally similar because both live addictive lives. To overcome their addiction, they must first admit fellowship in the addicted community. The public ritual of disclosure in which the alcoholic introduces him- or herself is meant to establish this fundamental identity. Twelve-step literature warns, "Don't compare, identify." And those who do not identify with their addiction or dependency are considered to be "in denial."

The popularity of twelve-step programs may stem in part from the specific form of fellowship it offers. They offer an alternative to American culture's recent emphasis on difference and diversity. Rejecting the identity politics of the sixties and seventies, the twelve-step philosophy embraces a universal perspective in which the only identity that matters is one of addiction and dysfunctionality. In this new form of identity politics the autobiographical story that counts is the story of addiction and recovery. This, of course, begs the question of how a whole society came to embrace this kind of autobiography. How did our lives get boiled down to stories about dysfunctionality? How did addiction become our primary badge of identity? How did denial of illness become morally taboo? When did we come to apply a "psychologically correct" standard?

For AA and other twelve-step groups to be successful, Americans had to believe that the problem of addiction applied to more than a small unfortunate number. Indeed, during the 1980s the nation "discovered" a virtual epidemic of addiction. Not only had the number of possible addictions increased but estimates of how many people suffered from any particular one went through the stratosphere. And such discoveries were not made by lone experts peddling recovery treatments. Prominent psychologists, psychiatrists, and hospital administrators of leading treatment facilities concurred with the recovery movement's estimates. The psychology industry's bible, the *Diagnostic and Statistical Manual*, is evidence of this explosion: between 1980 and 1990 the number of disorders increased by close to 300 percent.[21]

But it was not simply that there were more maladies. The estimated numbers of people suffering from these increasingly widespread emotional disorders are staggering. For example, reportedly 10 percent of Americans, or 20 million, suffer from alcoholism. And this 20 million is small compared with the 80 million made codependent by their familial association. The number of gamblers is estimated at 20 million, matching the number of alcoholics. Compulsive eaters number some 30 million, 80 million if the obese are included. Sex addiction apparently plagues 25 million Americans. The compulsive-shopping population is estimated at 15 million, or 40 million when those afflicted with overspending are included. For depression and anxiety, the most widely cited figure is 50 million. Even the figures for such specialized kinds of dysfuntionality as clergy in need of recovery are staggering. The twelve-step group for clergy members, Graceworks, estimates that more than 25 percent of the clergy have engaged in inappropriate sexual behavior and need help.[22]

The discovery of new addictions, disorders, and compulsions and their seeming ubiquity has become a staple of our daily news. In the fall of 1988, for example, a NIMH study revealed that obsessive-compulsive disorder, previously thought to be rare, was horrifyingly widespread afflicting 3-6 million. In the early 1990s the prevalence of seasonal affective disorder, or SAD, became front-page news. Dr. Norman Rosenthal, a NIMH psychiatrist specializing in the disorder explained that "winter after winter, these people experience lethargy and fatigue, sadness and despair." SAD "disrupts personal relationships, causes victims to overeat, gain weight, and become indifferent toward their jobs." Studies revealed that during the winter season approximately 35 million Americans were afflicted.[23]

The discovery of a virtual epidemic of psychological maladies leads naturally to the question whether there really are more afflictions or whether there is simply more information about them. While this chicken-and-egg question may never be resolved, the forces promoting a therapeutic vision are conspicuous; that is, a number of interests were selling, and others were lobbying for, the diseasing of America.

During the 1980s and 1990s what might be called the therapeutic-advocacy community exploded. Unlike the therapeutic professions, including psychiatrists, psychologists, and social workers, who also, of course, lobby for the expansion of the psychology industry, the new advocacy community of interested associations went directly to the people. Such organizations as the Depression and Related Affective Disorders Association, the Anxiety Disorders Association of America, the Shyness Institute, the National Association for Christian Recovery, the National Association on Sexual Addiction Problems (one of five such national clearinghouses), and the National Council on Compulsive Gamblers emerged to educate the public about particular emotional maladies or problems. The mission of the National Council on Codependence, for example, is to "provide education, referral, and advocacy to the general public about codependence."[24] The National Association of Self-Esteem describes itself as an organization "committed to integrating self-esteem into the fabric of our society."[25] The National Association for Christian Recovery provides educational materials to those directly affected. Its books and audio tapes include *Recovery from Addiction, Recovery from Guilt, Recovery from Abuse, Recovery from Spiritual Abuse, Recovery from Distorted Images of God, Recovery from Workaholism, Recovery from Shame, Recovery from Codependency, Recovery from Bitterness, Recovery from Broken Relationships,* and *Recovery from Family Dysfunctions.* Other organizations educate by sponsoring actual events. The National Depression Screening Day, for example, sets aside one day a year to focus the American public's attention on this problem. In 1998 it held events at three thousand sites across the country.[26]

Even the federal and state governments got involved in raising Americans' consciousness of emotional problems. In 1970 the federal government established the National Institute on Alcohol Abuse and Alcoholism, or NIAAA. By the early 1980s most states had state divisions of alcoholism and alcohol abuse. These agencies conducted intensive public-information campaigns warning of the dangers of abuse. They also offered treatment programs and referral services for the addicted.

Pressures from another direction also got governments involved in the recovery movement. Fiscal pressures of the 1970s forced state and local governments to look for cheaper ways of handling a variety of social problems. Just as middle-class consumers found recovery cheaper than therapy, states saw potentially huge savings in substituting recovery programs for more costly social services. Between 1976 and 1996 there was, for example, a dramatic expansion in court referrals to AA. Prisons too found AA meetings a cost-effective way of handling the social needs of inmates, for such treatment requires minimal therapeutic supervision.[27]

The private sector also got into the act, and today there is a veritable treatment industry. There has been a virtual explosion in private residential treatment programs. Between 1978 and 1984 the number of residential treatment centers increased by 350 percent, and the caseloads at these centers expanded by 400 percent. The private sector has also realized tremendous profits from recovery literature and other recovery goods. Recovery products can be found at recovery stores. A glance at any of the recovery newspapers or magazines, such as *Sober Times* and *Recovering*, reveals how extensive and influential these stores have become. "The old concept of a 12 Step shop as being primarily a drug and alcohol recovery shop is vanishing," said one recovery-business owner. "More people want to find out what's wrong with them, and they no longer have to be alcoholics and drug addicts."[28]

Pharmaceutical companies have realized the greatest profits from the spread of emotional afflictions. Eli Lilly leads the way with its bestselling antidepressant, Prozac. Prescriptions of this product, introduced in 1987, have doubled every year since 1990. Currently, 25 million prescriptions for Prozac are issued per year. Eli Lilly's success stems in part from the revolution in health care. Psychopharmacology has directly benefited from managed care's domination of the health-care market. Drugs are clearly cheaper than traditional therapy. Most insurance companies reimburse 80 percent of prescription costs but only 50 percent of the costs for psychotherapy visits. Lilly also undertook an unprecedented advertising campaign. Until Lilly's campaign, most prescription drugs were not marketed directly to consumers. Medical advertising was limited to persuading physicians to prescribe a particular drug. Lilly leapfrogged over the doctor and went directly to the customer, advertising in mainstream newspapers and magazines.[29]

The initial major advertising campaign for Prozac consisted of a two-page color advertisement depicting a dark rain cloud followed by a bright sun. The caption under the dark cloud read, "Depression Hurts," and that under the bright yellow sun read, "Prozac Can Help," followed by the phrase "Welcome Back." The ad agency came up with this add after working with focus groups and extensive interviews with more than nine hundred people suffering from depression. Toby Sachs, the account director for Prozac, explained that "we asked them [focus group members] to draw their depression using colored crayons and one woman stood out in all our minds. After three minutes she turned and said, 'Is there any more black?'" Lilly believed it had the answer to this profound desperation.

Using the "Welcome Back" ads, Lilly marketed Prozac in more than twenty consumer magazines, including *Newsweek, Time, Cosmopolitan,* and *Marie Claire.* The ads sought to get patients to diagnose themselves as depressed and then to ask their doctors for a prescription. Eli Lilly's director of marketing, Andrew Hodgekiss, justified this radically new approach by citing the number of Americans suffering from depression who were not getting help, which he maintained was a third of the approximately 20 million Americans suffering.[30] This was not the case in what has come to be known as Prozacville, USA. In the conservative farming town of Wenatchee, in Washington State, a psychologist named Jim Goodwin put seven hundred of his patients on Prozac because "there is a huge amount of unrecognized depression out there. . . . I was just a little bit early in making the diagnosis." Perhaps since the Jim Goodwins of the world were few and far between, Eli Lilly mounted a massive ad campaign to reach "people who may be suffering and not know that they have depression."[31]

Lilly's plans to increase its $2 billion–a–year business included marketing to the potentially 3 to 4 million child and teen consumers. To increase its market share, Lilly has created a liquid mint Prozac. Soon after its introduction, Lilly was selling its new product to 580,000 children. Other companies, such as those that produced Zoloft and Paxil, have also begun to offer fruit-flavored versions of their antidepressants.[32] There is also Prozac for pets, which comes, for example, in fish shapes for cats. Depressed dogs apparently can also benefit from Prozac. The *Los Angeles Times* warned, however, in an article about Prozac for animals that humans "should never share your medicines with anyone in your family including your pet."[33] Pets must be diagnosed by a veterinarian, who should prescribe the drug for them.

Just as the major drug companies were celebrating the success of their close to $11 billion industry, competition came from a completely unexpected corner. Natural alternatives to drugs like Prozac, Zoloft, and Paxil are fast becoming the new rage. The most popular natural antidepressant is St. John's wort. This ancient natural remedy is believed to provide measurable relief for people with mild and moderate depression without side effects. First marketed by Licht Wer Pharma, a small company in Berlin, Germany, this drug outsells Prozac by four to one in Germany.[34] Since 1997 the drug has become increasingly popular in the United States. There are now twelve websites where users exchange information about this new alternative to Prozac. One website on herbal antidepressants receives four thousand to six thousand hits per day.[35] There is also a host of other kinds of natural antidepressants, including the new Celestial Seasonings tea Mood Mender.

Clearly, the psychology industry, twelve-step programs, and the recovery movement have exaggerated the extent of mood disorders and other such afflictions. Epidemiological researchers find much lower levels of alcoholism, drug addiction, and sexual abuse, estimating, for example, that only 1 percent of the population fits their clinical definition of alcoholism.[36] The broad definition of the addicted embraced by twelve-step programs—that everyone is in need of therapeutic help—is conspicuously imperialistic.[37]

But regardless of motivation, the really interesting question is, Why in the 1980s and 1990s did it make sense to millions of people that families are dysfunctional and there are emotional issues that must be resolved through therapy, support groups, or self-help books? Fifty, even twenty-five years ago the popularity of therapeutic treatment would have seemed absurd. Then the addicted person would not have been lionized but pitied or shunned, whereas today the person who admits to an addiction or emotional affliction is a hero. We relish disclosure and the story of recovery. Those who need healing and those who have been healed absorb us nationally. Their stories are told, repeated, and retold.

America's faith in healing has a long, venerable history. Our nation is unique in turning emotional healing into a national pastime. We have been soul-doctoring for more than 150 years. Since the days of Phineas P. Quimby we have preached the gospel of recovery and practiced the therapeutics of happiness. Administering to the soul appears to be one of our particular specialties. All of this does not, however, explain why suddenly in the 1980s healing personal problems came to dominate our public debate.

One institution that played a critical role in this transformation was television. Capitalizing on and adding to the success of the recovery movement, the television industry discovered the talk show and the profits to be made from this new form of entertainment. Bringing the language of recovery out of the church basement and into American living rooms and offices, talk shows dissolved the distinction between personal problems and public debate once and for all. Television talk shows made it possible for literally millions of people to simultaneously participate in a form of the "talking cure." Oprah,

Geraldo, Sally Jessy Raphael, and even more recently Ricki Lake, Montel Wil-
iams, and Jerry Springer created a kind of public therapy in which guests talk
about their personal problems (and sometimes yell, scream, punch, or throw
chairs) while so-called psychological experts guide them to recovery.

TV's Talking Cure

You can no longer just put prostitutes on. It has to be prostitutes who are sex
addicts.   Ed Glavin, a *Donahue* producer

It's not enough to have a husband and the wife he cheated on. You've got to have
the mistress, maybe her boyfriend. You take things as far as they go.
     Laura Wiley, a *Geraldo* producer

The origins of the talk-show format can be traced to Monday, 6 November
1967, at 10:30 A.M. Eastern Standard Time, when Phil Donahue introduced
his first guest on his first TV talk show for the local station in Dayton, Ohio.
It was a dramatic entrance into the world of television. Not only did his talk-
show format dispense with the traditional band, but his content was shocking and personal. Madalyn Murray O'Hare, an Irish Catholic, revealed her
atheism. Not only did O'Hare not believe in God but she believed that religion "breeds dependence." While a far cry from the disclosures of the nineties,
in which ministers confessed to pedophilia and women confessed that they
had slept with their daughters' boyfriends, O'Hare's revelation created quite a
stir in Dayton, Ohio, in 1967.

Airing shocking material in a personal way became a Donahue hallmark.
Donahue also departed from the talk-show format by getting out of his interviewing chair. He took his microphone directly into the audience and involved
the audience in the discussion of the controversial topic. This had an electrify-
ing effect on the audience, the viewers, and, of course, the advertisers.

The rest of *Donahue*'s first week included some equally shocking shows.
On the third day a Dayton obstetrician was featured and viewers saw a film of
the birth of a baby. Never before had such material been so publicly and
graphically shown. The premiere week's show that received the most attention, however, was the Friday show, when Donahue brought onstage an an-
atomically correct male doll, which he then proceeded to undress. Holding
the doll up to the camera, Donahue asked viewers to vote on whether the toy
was objectionable for children. Separate phone numbers were given for yes

and no votes. The response was immediate and overwhelming, so much so that the phone lines in Dayton became jammed and Ohio Bell pleaded with the studio to end the poll. When pleading didn't work Ohio Bell threatened to cut off the station lines so that fire and police calls could get through.

The ratings for the premiere week indicated that Donahue had hit upon something. The show had a fifteen-point rating, which meant that half of all television sets in Dayton were tuned in to *Donahue*. The closest competition, a game show called *Concentration*, only attracted 23 percent of the Dayton households. How had Donahue hit on such a winning formula? As he explains it in his autobiography, "The show's style developed not by genius but by necessity. The familiar talk-show heads were not available to us in Dayton, Ohio. Although we were able to attract a Phyllis Diller or a Paul Lynde during the summer months when the 'Hollywood stars' worked the Kenley Theatre circuit in Ohio after the biggies left town we were left with a lot of dates to fill. The result was improvisation."

Unable to get the famous, Donahue was forced to feature the ordinary. But he turned this necessity into an asset. He did it by finding extraordinary examples of ordinary people and experiences. He also personalized public debate. Individuals like Madalyn Murray O'Hare represented important questions of public debate. Audience involvement also brought home the topic and engaged viewers in a personal way with broader topics. As Donahue himself explained it, "We were forced to get by with issues. Issues are what saved us. We discovered women were out there in the daytime and dying for this kind of program. There was tremendous sexism among decision makers. They thought women cared only about covered dishes and needlepoint." Of course, Donahue redefined issues. He turned adultery, marriage, homosexuality, mother-daughter relationships, to name only a few, into issues. In one show, for example, he explored promiscuity by interviewing Sabrina Aset, plumbing the psyche that led her to have sexual relationships with 2,686 men. Critics chastised Donahue for featuring "freaks" on his show, but Donahue defended his selections by saying that "somebody's freaky is another person's personal problem." The audience obviously agreed.[38]

Once *The Phil Donahue Show* went national and moved to Chicago, the problem of securing stars as guests was no longer a problem. By the mid-1970s Donahue featured a variety of big-name stars, including Dolly Parton, Sammy Davis Jr., John Wayne, and Gregory Peck, as well as more controversial public figures such as Gloria Steinem, Jerry Rubin, Bella Abzug, Anita Bryant, and

David Duke. But having hit upon the enormously successful talk-show formula of featuring ordinary people and their problems and turning them into public debate, Donahue continued to build on his success. Among his most popular shows were ones that would become the staple of later talk shows, including shows featuring lesbian mothers who had won custody of their children, mistresses who discussed the pain of dating married men, William Masters and Virginia Johnson discussing Americans' sexual practices and problems, a film of an actual abortion, parents of gays, and penal implants. Donahue explained his influence this way: "Years ago, when we were doing stories on date rape, artificial insemination, homophobia, sex bias crimes, and spousal abuse, serious news programs wouldn't touch them."[39]

While Donahue deserves credit for pioneering the talk-show format and masterfully using television to personalize public debate, his innovations look tame in comparison with the changes wrought by Oprah Winfrey. Dispensing with all vestiges of public-affairs programming, Oprah went personal. She aired increasingly intimate topics, taking her guests, audience members, and millions of viewers down the therapeutic path. These public therapy sessions mesmerized the nation. She also got personal herself, revealing that she herself was a victim of child sexual abuse. By the mid 1990s she had confessed to having a food compulsion and having in her past been addicted to cocaine. It was not simply that Oprah was more personal than Donahue: Oprah eviscerated all remaining barriers between personal problems and public debate. More than any other single force in America, *The Oprah Winfrey Show* and the millions of dollars it generated fundamentally reconstituted public debate, making stories of addiction, denial, and recovery the story of America. Oprah brought the extraordinary psychodramas of ordinary people into the living rooms and offices of 20 million viewers every day.

The story of how Oprah came to emcee such stories of hurt, pain, and recovery begins in Baltimore in 1976. As local stations across America were lengthening their local news programs from a half hour to a full hour, Baltimore's WJZ-TV was looking for a coanchor for its evening news show. At the same time the Federal Communications Commission began to pressure TV stations to diversify. Not only did Oprah have a great voice and television presence but she was both black and a woman. She had gained some basic broadcast experience in Nashville, where as a student at Tennessee State University she had secured her first full-time television position anchoring the local news.

Within a year of arriving in Baltimore, however, Oprah was pulled off the air. There were several problems, among them her tendency to ignore the TelePrompTer and ad lib. But the final blow came when Oprah was covering a tragic house fire in which a woman lost all of her seven children. Rather than conducting an interview, Oprah talked with the mother about her pain. On the air, Oprah wept as the woman talked. For her unprofessional conduct, Oprah was forced to go on the air the next day and apologize. That was 1976, before talk shows and news itself had come to valorize intimacy and emotional pain above all else.

Because Oprah had a six-year contract and was clearly talented, the station manager did not fire her. Instead, he came up with a new role for her, one that suited her spontaneity and her ability to draw people out emotionally: Oprah became the cohost of *People Are Talking*. Many at the station thought the show was doomed to fail. Its time slot was the same as that of *Donahue*, which at the time had the highest ratings of all talk shows in the country. But even opposite Donahue, Oprah was an instant success; in fact, Oprah consistently beat him in the ratings.

Oprah's success was part substance and part style. Boldly focusing on such personal topics as love, romance, betrayal, adultery, sex, obesity, suicide, and incest, Oprah drew an immediate and mesmerized audience. Oprah asked her guests the kinds of questions everyone wanted answered but only Oprah dared ask. As one observer explained, "When Donahue interviews a hooker who services twenty men a night, he wants to know how much money she makes, Oprah wants to know if she's sore."[40] Another commentator described Oprah as "every woman's friend. The kind of brassy neighbor who barges into your house and immediately goes to your refrigerator for a little Cheese Whiz and bacon dip. And you love her for it. Because when you tell her your husband is bisexual, she understands. When you tell her you were molested by your doctor or you haven't spoke to your mother in a year, she understands" (54). After seven years of intimate questions and emotional closeups on local TV, Oprah got a chance to promote her new talk-show format in a larger market.

AM Chicago was in trouble. Competing against Donahue, its ratings were terrible. To fix the situation, a new producer, Debra DeMaio, and host, Robb Weller, were hired. Shortly after DeMaio arrived from Baltimore, where she had been the assistant producer for *People Are Talking*, Weller left for bigger and better things in New York. DeMaio went to her boss, Dennis Swanson, and suggested Oprah for the job. It was Labor Day weekend. Oprah flew to Chicago that weekend to audition. Swanson recalls, "Sitting in my office, watching this audition, I said, Holy smokes. This is something. I had looked at tapes for years, but never had I seen anything like Oprah. She is a unique personality. So up. So effervescent. So television. So spontaneous and unrehearsed. She was not like anyone else on the tube" (74). Swanson signed a four-year deal with Oprah for $200,000 a year. That was 1984. By 1986 Oprah had gone national and was making $30 million a year.

Oprah's phenomenal success was due in part to the King brothers, Roger and Michael, of King World. They had no equals in sales of syndicated TV. Their company, built by their father, Charlie King, had made its initial fortune by selling *Little Rascals*. Roger and Michael had added *Wheel of Fortune* and *Jeopardy*. By the mid-eighties King World was grossing more than $60 million a year. Studying the ratings books, the King brothers were fascinated by Oprah's ability to beat Donahue's ratings. They went to Chicago to talk to Oprah and her lawyer, Jeffrey Jacobs. Though other syndicators had approached Oprah, the King brothers impressed her most with their strategy. They believed that the show had to be heavily promoted to station managers in advance and that topics had to be thoroughly researched to ensure drawing power.

Roger and Michael King went on the road to promote Oprah sixteen hours a day, seven days a week. Oprah's ability to beat Donahue was their major selling point. They contrasted his cerebral approach with her ability to touch people emotionally. In their sales presentation they always tried to ensure that there was a woman in the room. They often encouraged the general manager's secretary to sit in on the taping. As one King World executive recalled, "They knew it was very difficult for a lot of male, fifty plus general managers to really look at an Oprah who went against every stereotypical personality on television and say, 'Yeah she's a hit'" (111). A Black, overweight woman was not what general managers thought of as the perfect icon of American culture. Yet, on 8 September 1986, when *The Oprah Winfrey Show* went national, it had been picked up by 138 stations.

Oprah's phenomenal success was also due to her talent for managing the exposure of emotional trauma in front of a national audience. Provocative and personal, her shows featured pornography addicts, women whose husbands cheated on them, women hearing the biological clock, women who hired hit men to kill their sons, Casanovas and women who loved them, ugly people, celebrity mothers, ministers who sinned, and women who gave up men and became lesbians. Her topical shows, in which she focused on such problems as monogamy, teenage pregnancy, child abuse, domestic violence, depression, overeating, and addiction, drew equally large numbers of viewers.[41]

Even when she focused on celebrities, it was Oprah's personal questions and the celebrities' experience of emotional trauma that animated the interview. In her world-famous interview with Michael Jackson, for example, which drew the largest audience in television history (approximately 62 million viewers), the focus was on his personal history, his own experience of child abuse, and his current emotional state. For all his fame, Jackson summed up his life for Oprah this way: "I am one of the loneliest people on this earth. I cry sometimes because it hurts. It does. To be honest, I guess you could say it hurts to be me" (291). In her interview with Rod Steiger she focused on his depression, and in her interview with Angie Dickinson she focused on the emotional effects of being the daughter of an alcoholic. It was this kind of pageant of emotional pain that made Oprah famous.

Oprah's popularity stemmed not only from her willingness to probe what others had previously considered private but also from her own admissions of deep-seated emotional problems. Oprah was personal in a way that no talk-show host before her had been. *Chicago* magazine observed that "the Oprah Winfrey Show has been one of the true astonishments of television. Single-handedly, she and it have revolutionized talk shows and rendered the notion of Mid-western reticence quaint and obsolete. No one else on television has been so open as Oprah. Within months of coming to Chicago, she'd told viewers about her troubles with men, and the terrifying history of her childhood sexual abuse. She told them they could take control of their life and energies . . . [and] she gave them the practical means of doing so" (82).

The admission that probably interested viewers the most was Oprah's confession that she had a food addiction. In Oprah's words, "I was a total compulsive eater for most of my life. That's how I worked out my junk and other people work it out through alcohol or drugs or just bad relationships. So that's not my problem. You know mine, you know it comes out in my hips. For me the weight is me trying to protect myself or feeling fearful or not being all that I really could be" (226). Whether Oprah was announcing a dramatic weight loss or a dramatic gain, her admission was always put in the therapeutic terms of overcoming a personal problem.

The cycle of dramatic announcements began on the show on 15 November 1988. On the show "Diet Dreams Come True," Oprah announced that she had lost sixty-seven pounds by dragging behind her a little red wagon containing sixty-seven pounds in animal fat. Oprah celebrated her confrontation of a psychological problem and her ability to overcome it. Forty-five percent of viewers in America were mesmerized by her performance. But her announcement did not exactly come as a surprise: viewers had received almost daily updates on her medically supervised diet. Her success in licking her compulsion was one that millions of dieting women could identify with. When Oprah in front of that little red wagon proclaimed, "Right now I feel about as good as you can feel and still live," many of her viewers understood her elation.

Of course, her joy was only temporary. What Oprah insisted was her "single, greatest achievement in my life" ended up being an ephemeral one. On national TV five days a week Oprah could hardly hide her ballooning figure. Though initially angered by the skeptics, Oprah not only regained the sixty-seven pounds but a few years later would host shows on food addiction weighing more than 230 pounds. What is interesting about her anger at the skeptics is the therapeutic terms of her reaction. Affronted by a question about whether she could keep the weight off, Oprah responded indignantly, "Asking me if I'll keep the weight off is like asking 'will you ever be in a relationship again, where you allow yourself to be emotionally battered?' I've been there and don't intend to go back" (227). Any twelve-stepper could have told her that that is what all addicts think. Oprah would eventually admit how wrongheaded she had been to think that she could once and for all overcome her addiction. It would be a constant struggle.

On the show "Pain of Regain," Oprah confessed to having dieted most of her adult life and admitted that "the reason I fail is that diets don't work . . . now I'm trying to end a way of life in a world with food without being controlled by it, without being a compulsive eater" (307). Advising her viewers that weight is not simply a physical thing but stems from an emotional problem, she insisted that fears and low self-esteem must be dealt with if the weight issue was to be successfully addressed. To bring home the point of food as an emotional problem, Oprah did several shows on her private diary that revealed an agonizing struggle with weight. The frustration, self-hate, and pain of weight was disclosed in its intimate and gory detail.

A master in orchestrating disclosure, Oprah combines the stories of ordinary people and expert testimony. Psychotherapists, clinical psychologists, and recovery gurus are a staple of The Oprah Winfrey Show. Geneen Roth, a diet expert and author of *When Food Is Love* and *Feeding the Hungry Heart,* for example, has been a frequent guest on the show. "Secrets from the Past," a series of shows about guests whose secrets have unexpectedly come to light, featured a psychotherapist who offered strategies for coping with exposure. On one show, for example, about a happily married father who has achieved a middle-class standard of living but who in his youth had prostituted himself with men in order to earn money, the therapist commented on the toxicity of secrets and the healing that comes with finally revealing them. With the help of representatives from the mental-health industry, Oprah preaches the therapeutic gospel. The show establishes the virtues of revelation and the sins of keeping secrets. Not only is talk cathartic but it cleanses the soul.

At the height of her popularity, in 1990, 19 million viewers a day in sixty-four countries tuned in to experience Oprah's talking cure. But by May 1994 Oprah's ratings had dropped by 7 percent overall and by 11 percent among women viewers aged 18 to 49, the critical advertising audience. Shortly before Oprah's decline *Donahue* went off the air. It was not that America was losing interest in TV's talking cure but that the proliferation of talk shows had given viewers many more options. Next to the newer, racier talk shows, like *Ricki Lake* and *Jerry Springer, Donahue* and even *Oprah* seem staid and dull. Viewers of the new talk shows were entertained by not mere talk but scenes of intense emotional combat that sometimes turned physical.

A year after Oprah went national she faced competition from other talk shows. In 1987, for example, Geraldo arrived, and the following year came Sally Jessy Raphael. By 1993 there were sixteen nationally syndicated television talk shows. Sally was not worried: "There's not too many talks shows any more than there are too many pubs in London," she told advertisers. "Americans like to share stories and that's what talk shows do" (263). Sally was both right and wrong. The nation's appetite for talk or emotional wrestling, which it increasingly has become, does seem endless. On the other hand, *Oprah* has lost its share in the therapeutic-gospel market to more outrageous shows. In 1998 *Jerry Springer* was the number one television talk show.

The talk shows that followed *Oprah* built on its formula but introduced a new level of sensationalism. Geraldo led the way. The psychological problems he featured were outrageous. His so-called ordinary guests actually suffered from extraordinary problems. In one of his early shows, for example, Geraldo featured women who had married their rapists. This typical show began with Geraldo striding quickly down the center aisle of the studio to thunderous applause. Onstage in a semicircle facing the audience were three guests and a therapist. Geraldo began by discussing the shocking biographies of the three guests. Then, microphone in hand, he introduced the therapist: "Dr. Stuard Fishoff, a clinical psychologist from Los Angeles, is here to help us answer the $64,000 question: Why would a woman marry her rapist?" Even the titles of his shows, such as "Women Who Have Taken Back Their Lying, Cheating Dog of a Husband," reveal their sensationalism.

But it gets worse. Focusing almost exclusively on interpersonal conflict, the TV talk shows of the nineties have upped the emotional ante. Sobbing, screaming, and even physical combat have become part and parcel of the new talk shows' psychodramas. Jerry Springer, for example, once presided over a food fight that broke out among family members at the dinner table. In another televised family breakdown Springer successfully revived a mother who had collapsed from shock after her daughter's accusation that "she doesn't even know who my father is!" As Springer recounted his attempt to revive the mother backstage while cameras rolled, "For a few moments there I thought we were losing her. I couldn't feel a pulse at all."[42]

Ricki Lake, which premiered in 1993, was perhaps most responsible for introducing the no-holds-barred format of TV talk shows. Gail Steinberg, the executive producer of the show, recalled the decision to focus on young people. "We saw no reason why [a youthful approach] couldn't be successful in daytime and a lot of people didn't agree. They said these people aren't home to watch daytime TV. They said it would never work. . . . You can't be a better 'Oprah.' She is the best. So we decided we wouldn't even try. We would carve out a new niche for ourselves." This niche was women aged 18 to 34, and emotional confrontations were staged at a breakneck pace. Twenty-six-year-old Ricki Lake was found to host the show.

With shows like "Listen Family, I'm Gay . . . It's Not a Phase . . . Get Over It!" "Girl You're Easy Because You're Fat . . . Respect Yourself ASAP," "Yeah Mom, I'm 13 . . . But I'm Going to Make a Baby," and "Yeah Mom/Dad, I'm Marrying That Jerk . . . Whether You Come to the Wedding or Not," *Ricki Lake* was an instant success. In less than four months' time the show was being aired on 212 stations, breaking Oprah's record of 179.[43] Catering to a young audience, Ricki developed a raw therapeutic style. For example, a show on unwed mothers began with prerecorded statements by the family of Danielle, who with her boyfriend Max had had a baby. Family members said things like "I hate Max." The camera focused on Danielle, who supposedly was learning for the first time what her family thought of her, her boyfriend, and the fact that she was an unwed mother. Her feelings of anguish and anger were palpable. Ricki began by asking the question around which the show revolved: "Danielle, how does that make you feel to hear them say what they have to say?" Like a circus ringmaster, Ricki orchestrated the emotional combat.

Ricki credits her producer Gail Steinberg with inventing the confrontational format. It brought a kind of drama to the show that compelled viewers to watch. In Ricki's own words, "The idea of having somebody onstage telling their side of the story, and having the other person behind the stage . . . so that you can see the reaction as the other person is, like, dissing them, or doing something to them . . . does so much for the energy of the show."[44]

Trying to out-Ricki Ricki became the goal of the new talk shows of the mid-nineties. In 1995 more than ten new talk shows aired on TV. Those that made it include *Carnie, Tempestt, Charles Perez, Gabrielle, Danny!* and *Mark*. A study conducted by the Kaiser Family Foundation found that these new talk shows focused on family, relationships, and sex. Of the average of nine disclosures per hour, five were of a sexual nature and four revolved around an addiction, compulsion, disorder, or health issue. While such disclosures were by no means new to TV talk shows, the 1990s ushered in a brand-new kind of disclosure. This new kind of disclosure, which came to be known in the industry as "ambush disclosure," involved a guest surprising a family member, friend, or acquaintance with some dark secret. A typical show might involve a daughter who learned that her mother had been sleeping with her fiancé or a woman who learned from her lover's previous girlfriends that he had cheated on every woman he had ever been involved with. The person causing emotional pain was then called to task for hurting another and for not being open, though the codependent did not escape scrutiny.

Watching people confess, feel, or disclose hurt and pain on television in front of millions of viewers became a national pastime in the 1980s and 1990s. TV's talking cure began with Phil Donahue's relatively serious-minded but personalized explorations. With the creation of *The Oprah Winfrey Show* talk TV became public therapy. By 1994 revenues from *Oprah* had reached $180 million. The booming talk-show market would spawn more than fifteen other shows. By 1995 this new genre had ended the near fifty-year reign of soap operas as the most popular form of daytime television. Apparently, the real-life psychodramas held more interest than fictionalized domestic disputes and, less surprisingly, public affairs.[45]

Cybertherapy, or the Therapeutic Gospel Goes Online

However large the market for talk found on daytime TV, it is small compared with the new seven-days-a-week, twenty-four-hours-a-day online market. Worldwide the possibilities seem endless. As a public arena for conveying private pain, the Internet may surpass even television. Today users can do electronic therapy, find virtual support groups, visit advice sites, and participate in therapeutic news groups and chat rooms. There are, for example, more than five thousand online support groups.[46] The mental-health website that provides the most comprehensive list of such groups gets more than thirty thousand hits a day. A personal-growth site created in 1998 was accessed by 365,161 people in its first year, and approximately 5,000 new people visit it each day.[47]

Catering to users' appetite is the cybertherapeutic community. These certified on-line therapy practitioners offer a variety of services, such as individual and group therapy, as well as marriage counseling, family counseling, pastoral counseling, recovered-memory counseling, and even biblical counseling, whose goal is to "change the counselee's focus on the false self, a self of lusts and appetites to a realization of his true self, a self in union with Christ."[48] There are also such specialized services as online hypnotherapy and dream therapy. DreamLink, DreamMosaic, and DreamWave, for example, offer dream analysis.

Online therapists work both alone and as part of a counseling service. Individual therapists, whose number is seemingly infinite, may or may not have a degree. Bernard Hansen, who provides relationship counseling, is somewhat typical of individual therapists who do not have a degree. His expertise stems from direct experience, and his own litany of afflictions serves as a recommendation rather than a deterrent for would-be clients. As he explains, "In our marriage, we discovered that we were dealing with much more than two people who saw things differently. When our marriage almost completely self-destructed over 6 years ago—after 4 affairs (3 mine, 1 Lynda's)—the confusion, pain, despair, we both felt led to us discovering that we had brought much more baggage into the relationship than we had ever realized. Combined we were dealing with long-buried issues involving past sexual abuse (including rape), chronic depression, workaholism, computer addiction, and a real scarcity of helpful relationship support services."[49] Hansen is one of thousands who hope to reduce this scarcity by hanging up his online shingle.

Many who put up their shingles on the Internet, however, emphasize their academic credentials. Ph.D.'s, master's degrees in social work, and Ed.D.'s abound. There are therapists with degrees from Harvard and ones from universities that few will have heard of. Blake Westley, for example, who offers individual counseling, got his master's degree in marriage and family counseling from Loma Linda University and is currently completing his doctorate in psychology at the United States International University. While Blake handles the usual emotional problems in his practice, including marriage and family problems, sexual abuse, and adolescent problems, he also claims expertise in helping those suffering from "fire setting." Whatever their problem, it seems, online clients can find a therapist that is right for them.

Personal therapeutic styles also vary. The businesslike cybershrink David Sommers, who has a Ph.D. in clinical psychology, can be visited at his Mental Health Cyber Clinic for $1.50 per minute. Sommers urges clients to "open up about their past and talk about their biggest challenges."[50] Julie Keck, another Ph.D., takes a more touchy-feely approach at her site, Counseling Café. Keck views her therapeutic café as "a place where you can become happier, change your life, and understand yourself more." Keck promises that all you have to do is "pour yourself a cup of coffee, fill out the information form and I will e-mail you back with a direction toward solving any conflict." To Keck, having a personal counselor is "like having a personal trainer for your life," someone who "assists you to move your life forward toward your dreams and goals and away from emotional pain."[51]

Those suffering from emotional pain can also get help at online counseling services. These sites have multiple cybershrinks to choose from, so for one to two dollars per minute users can shop around for the therapist they like best. Or they can use different therapists for different problems. Among the best-known counseling services are WebAccess Counseling, The Counselors.com, CounseLine (with the motto "Helping You to Put the Pieces Together"), Netpsych, Cyberpsych, Headworks, and TherapyOnLine. Here one can log on and hook up with a therapist who can do everything from "brief therapy" in a single session to longer-term counseling. The Therapy Network (TTN), for example "offers online multifaceted approach to emotional well-being through various avenues of inter-personal growth." The site lists its particular areas of expertise as "abandonment issues, anger—dealing with it constructively, anxiety, assertiveness training, ADD, child development and parenting, codependency, death, dying, and grief, depression and hopelessness, dieting and weight loss, divorce, gambling, goal setting, love, intimacy, romance, and marriage, men's issues, relatives and friends of addicts and substance abusers, self-esteem, sexuality, step families, and women's issues."[52]

Another service, Miracle Counseling, which caters to an equally broad range of users, offers "confidential counseling rooms." In the privacy of home or office online clients can get the therapeutic help they need simply by typing in their problems. This site instructs clients "to type in as much information as you wish regarding your particular situation, background, and needs. Relax. Don't worry about typos or grammar; this is your opportunity to write about your problem in a safe place, with time to think. You can change your mind at any time, clear the form with the 'Clear Form' button below, start over, or erase or say anything you need to say. This is your session. No one is judging you."[53] Clearly, the therapeutic gospel, with its ethic of nonjudgmentalness, rules cyberspace no less than it rules the rest of the world.

The central tenets of the therapeutic gospel can also be found on the more than five thousand online support groups. Users can follow a twelve-step program in even more permutations than in the "real" world. All the usual twelve-step groups can be found on the Internet, along with support groups specific to the web, such as Free to Be/Break the Silence, a website for the abused, Another Empty Bottle, a website for codependents of alcoholics or members of alcoholics' families, and The Healing Club, a website for those who have suffered physical, sexual, or emotional abuse. Graceworks, the online service for clergy in recovery, announces that "if you are a pastor, missionary, religious professional or spouse of one and you need help . . . we hope that this site will be helpful to you and that your time here will guide you towards a saner and more grace-full style of life. Welcome home. We have been waiting for you."[54]

Those who attend "virtual" support groups do so for a variety of reasons. Time constraints is one of the most common motivations. For example, John M., from Orange County, New York, used to spend four nights a week away from his family because he was attending AA meetings. Through Compuserve he now "attends" two online meetings a week and has more time with his family.[55] Alison takes part in an online support group because "I do shift work and can't always make regular meetings, which might be a more normal way of doing these things."[56] Others simply find that online sessions are convenient, meeting the full range of their physical and emotional needs. J. D. Mang, a forty-five-year old horticulturist from Pennsylvania, explains that "my previous support groups online were for agoraphobia, mitral valve prolapse and hyperglycemia, all of which I'm in the process of overcoming or controlling." About her various support groups she says that "we have had so many wonderful conversations concerning disorders" and that she finds real comfort "in chatting with many people suffering from what I've gone through and what I continue to deal with on a daily basis."[57]

It is perhaps the need to chat about one's personal problems that is best fulfilled by the Internet. Therapeutic e-mail lists, news groups, and chat rooms serve those with an immediate problem or those who simply want to stay in therapeutic contact with others when the need arises. These e-mail lists or what are called server lists range from the very general to the highly specific, for example, Alt.support.loneliness, Alt.support.shyness, Alt.support.anxiety, Alt.support.frustration, Alt.support.depression, and Alt.support.badfeeling.

More general chat rooms include The Self-esteem Chat Room and The Suffering and Recovery Chat Room. One of the most general and most popular therapeutic chat rooms is the Feelings Forum Chat Room, which offers "the opportunity to connect with others and participate in the all important sharing that is sometimes so lacking in our daily lives."[58] Visitors are welcomed, but they are reminded that since this is a forum for expressing feelings, it is imperative that all visitors be "sensitive, considerate, and caring" in their responses to one another. In fact, visitors are required to sign a Feelings Forum Agreement, which regulates conduct in the chat room. Violations will result in the termination of the visitor's account.

Among topics handled recently at the Feelings Forum Chat Room were "Tired of Fears (Anonymous)," "Mostly Unhappy (Anonymous)," "Emotionally Unavailable Men(nykitkat)," "How to Leave My Wife (Luke)," "Help (Anonymous)," "Living with a Passive-Aggressive Spouse (Alyssa)." One chat, initiated by "Feeling Pretty Lonely," produced a torrent of responses. Seventy-nine people visited the conversation, commenting on the emotional pain of Feeling Pretty Lonely and offering their own tales of emotional woe. Feeling Pretty Lonely was emotionally overwhelmed and suffering from a chest so tight that she took Vicodin. She was married to a "passive-aggressive" from a dysfunctional family, and her own family also suffered from dysfunctionality. The main problem, however, was that her husband refused to talk to her. "Every day some issue is arising and my husband will not talk to me. This morning is a perfect example." Feeling Pretty Lonely narrated a long story about how her husband and son, who were to leave the house at 5:00 A.M., had taken the dogs out, and the dogs were barking loudly. She had gotten up because she was worried about disturbing the neighbors. She also felt that it was inconsiderate of her husband to let the dogs bark while she was trying to sleep. Feeling Pretty Lonely concluded with a desperate plea for help and advice. She said she must "alleviate this pressure I am feeling."

Luke, who had put out his own call for help ("How to Leave My Wife?"), sympathized with Feeling Pretty Lonely. He too was from a dysfunctional family and knew how difficult it could be. About the dog incident he advised, "I don't think you should get too upset . . . most people are pretty cranky, when they get up earlier than normal. Try to give him the benefit of the doubt." He acknowledged, however, that the overall pattern of behavior she described was "rather worrisome." Feeling Pretty Lonely also received a response from an anonymous reader who also came from a dysfunctional family and apparently had a dysfunctional marriage. She knew exactly what Feeling Pretty Lonely was going through because her husband too was a wall of silence, heavy sighs, and angry looks. Her advice to Feeling Pretty Lonely was to keep her self-esteem intact and recognize that her husband was probably an "emotional dyslexic."[59] Such chat rooms promote national and potentially transnational conversations about the psyche. They allow participants to publicly air their private pain. That so many people feel completely miserable at 2:00 A.M. and have the need to communicate with equally troubled strangers around the globe is clearly sad and troubling. Chat-room providers argue, however, that the inadequacy of the therapeutic infrastructure makes their service not only necessary but also highly beneficial. Of course, as this book demonstrates, there is hardly a shortage of forums. Still, the appetite for this kind of exchange appears to be insatiable. Via the Internet this appetite can now be satisfied twenty-four hours a day, and a wider range of anonymous supporters can be called upon for their therapeutic input. As Peggy, an incest survivor with suicidal tendencies, explains about her use of Silent No Longer, an e-mail list for people who have been abused: "If I'm having a bad night, I can post a message at 3 am and know I'll be getting some kind of response soon."[60]

Virtual support can, however, create its own problems. Recently, psychologists and recovery experts have discovered a new disorder, Internet Addiction Disorder (IAD). The official diagnosis defines IAD as a "maladaptive pattern of Internet use, leading to clinically significant impairment or distress." Its symptoms include "a need for markedly increased amounts of time on the Internet to achieve satisfaction" and "markedly diminished effect with continued use of the same amount of time on Internet." Withdrawal symptoms are also an indication of IAD. According to the official definition, these include developing within several days or a month after withdrawal "psychomotor agitation," "anxiety," "obsessive thinking about what's happening on Internet," "fantasies or dreams about Internet," and "voluntary or involuntary typing movement of the fingers."[61]

Dr. Kimberly Young is the world's leading expert on IAD and the author of *Caught in the Net: How to Recognize the Signs of Internet Addiction and a Winning Strategy for Recovery.* Her Center for On-Line Addiction at the University of Pittsburgh provided the material for her book. As the book jacket indicates, the book "reveals why a growing number of people are losing their jobs, families, and finances because of their out-of-control online habits and what can be done to stop them." Young insists that IAD is "as serious a problem as alcoholism or chemical dependency." She predicted that by the year 2000, 8.1 million people would be addicted to the Internet.[62]

One New York lawyer who eventually went to see Dr. Kimberly Young at the Center for On-Line Addiction got his addiction trying to solve his alcohol problem. He was attending AA a couple of times a week, but it was taking up too much of his time. AA members recommended that he attend virtual AA meetings. He had never used the Internet but decided to give it a try. Before he knew it, he was spending more than seventy hours a week on the Internet and needed help for his new addiction.[63] Those suffering from IAD often spend considerable sums of money to support their addiction. The majority have tried unsuccessfully to cut back their usage.

Dr. Maressa Orzack specializes in IAD in Massachusetts, where the number of sufferers is above the national average. About her practice she says, "I see students, professionals, housewives, the retired, everyone. Computer addicts can be people who are depressed, lonely, afraid to go out, in high family conflicts, and generally people in trouble, because they can't leave their computers. They are men, women, and children."[64] The inability to disconnect is coming to be recognized as a serious problem. James Fearing, president of the National Counseling Intervention Services in Minneapolis, stated that "we haven't even seen the tip of the iceberg yet . . . for some people there is a loss of control. There's an inability to turn it off." Surveys conducted by Fearing's organization revealed that more than 54 percent of Internet users regularly reported feeling euphoric when they found what they'd been seeking electronically.[65]

Men outnumber women in the IAD community, leaving a trail of "cyber-widows" behind. One women recounted the pain she experienced as a result of her husband's Internet addiction: "My name is Ellen and I live in Pittsburgh. Today, my husband of 15 years told me he's leaving to go live with a woman in Australia whom he met on the Internet three months ago. I am shocked. They have never met in person. My husband has never been out of the country. Now she's finding him a job in Australia, he's got a plane ticket, and he's going tomorrow. How could this have happened? What do I do?" According to IAD experts, those who are dependent on the Internet spend as many as eighty hours a week on it, ruining their non-Internet relationships. Dr. Young concludes that "internet abuse has created millions of online addicts who suffer withdrawal symptoms when they switch off their computer and have anxiety and panic attacks if they have no email. They suffer cyber shakes and screen sickness and are more likely to have terminal love or virtual affairs with strangers than talk to their partners."[66] Moreover, IAD experts maintain that it is the world's fastest-growing addiction.

Young does not recommend going cold turkey as a way of getting over IAD. The afflicted need to develop "healthy, positive alternatives" and will have to suffer some withdrawal symptoms. But Young does not believe that IADers have to give up the Internet entirely. Her strategies for recovering include waiting until after breakfast to check e-mail, setting time limits for online usage, and moving the computer to a more public location. She also insists that it is crucial to recognize "denial symptoms." Ultimately, a real addict will need face-to-face therapy. A number of therapists specialize in treating the disorder. There are also support groups and twelve-step programs—both online and offline—for those suffering from a compulsion to log on. The most well-known support groups are Netaholics Anonymous, Internet Addiction Support Group, and Weboholics Anonymous.

* * *

Calls to air personal problems have a long history. In the 1850s Phineas P. Quimby called upon his fellow Americans to examine the false ideas that made them sick at heart. In the 1920s Progressive-era reformers urged Americans to "look within" for answers to the social problems that plagued the nation.

During the 1920s and 1930s the newly emerging marriage-counseling profession warned of the dire consequences of ignoring the problem of marital discord. In World War II the military made the soldier's psyche a key part of its military strategy for the first time. The military establishment set up a whole system of addressing the soldier's personal problems, from publishing pop psychology books to creating mental-hygiene units. With the rise of the cold war, the therapeutic gospel was applied to the American housewife. Women's magazines encouraged women to scrutinize themselves and evaluate their happiness. In the 1950s their so-called personal problems became a matter of public debate. During the sixties, a new form of politics, often called "personal politics," was celebrated. This "personal" politics broadened the definition of what counted as political. For example, feminists, with whom the term is most closely associated, argued that housework, marriage, and even sex were political issues that had to be publicly debated. Moreover, identity became a key battleground, with students, Blacks, and women arguing that the dominant institutions of American life severely limited human potential. "Personal politics" also referred to a style of politics. It called for personal acts of commitment and change. Blurring the boundaries between public and private, the liberation movements of the sixties sought a more organic approach.

Dissolving this distinction even further, the me generation of the 1970s turned "getting one's head together" into a major public campaign. This campaign domesticated as it had never quite been before the religion of self-awareness. With simple principles like "I'm OK—You're OK," it was imagined that, in the words of David Viscott, a designer of therapeutic products, even "a fucking truckdriver can pick [self-awareness] up and say 'Aha! When I'm angry, it's because someone has hurt my feelings."[67]

The intersection of personal problems and public debate reached a new level in the eighties and nineties. The recovery movement, TV talk shows, and the Internet raised the therapeutic ante. Awash in personal problems, the country struggled to "recover." But when Bill Clinton declared in 1992 that "I feel your pain," the core concepts of the therapeutic gospel and its 1990s spin reached the highest echelons of power. ZipperGate was in many ways just a continuation of the recovery presidency. In the summer of 1998, when the impeachment hearings were under way, Clinton acknowledged, in the language of AA, that "by not confronting problems early you end up making things worse." Both Clinton's exposure and his survival can be explained by

America's recent obsession with addiction and denial and public disclosure. If Americans had not been accustomed to airing their personal problems in public à la Oprah, it would have been hard to imagine ZipperGate.

On the other hand, Clinton survived in large part because of the belief that everybody has problems. For most Americans, Clinton's worst sin was denial. Healing and recovering demand that one admit one's guilt, which Clinton eventually did, thereby satisfying the majority of Americans, who are versed in the therapeutic gospel. Typical of those practicing this therapeutic analysis was Jerome D. Levin, the author of *The Clinton Syndrome: The President and the Self-Destructive Nature of Sexual Addiction*. According to Levin, Clinton was an ordinary American suffering from a grave but treatable personal problem. The electorate, on the other hand, was codependent, guilty of "enabling" Clinton's self-destructive behavior: "If the President were to drop his denial and get appropriate help, then I think the public would finally come to realize that in supporting him, whatever other valid reasons we might have had for that support, we were in fact enabling his behavior in a way similar to a wife who stays in a destructive relationship with an alcoholic."[68] Reducing the presidency to a destructive relationship could only have happened in a country in which personal problems had become a national obsession.

EPiLOGUE

Between the mid-nineteenth century and the late twentieth century, Americans developed an intense preoccupation with psychological well-being. Today this obsession knows no bounds. All the institutions of American life—schools, hospitals, prisons, courts—have been shaped by the national investment in feelings. Devotion to personal happiness and self-realization has also shaped American rhetoric. Personal problems dominate public debate. This intense concern with the psyche is unique historically as well as culturally. No other nation in the world puts so much faith in emotional well-being and self-help techniques.

Where does this lust for the therapeutic come from? What are the causes of this rage for psychological remedies? Put another way, why do other countries not produce television talk shows, with their "ambush disclosures," or have "recovery" sections in bookstores? What accounts for America's unique obsession with soul-doctoring?

There are many possible explanations. America's long-noted individualism and optimism account in part for the national investment in the psyche. As Tocqueville observed firsthand, Americans attributed tremendous agency to the self but also obsessively joined associations to fix problems deemed self-made. This essential contradiction has many variations. Although Americans are known for their rugged individualism, they are plagued by self-doubt and therefore turn constantly to quick and easy solutions. America's optimism, which may stem from its material prosperity, seems continually undermined by consumerism. America's consumer culture markets psychological ill-being. Products and, now, the act of purchasing itself are the cure.

The decline of religion may also account for the devotion to the psyche. As Americans began to lose faith in salvation from above, they put more faith into self-glorification. This new psychological gospel insisted on scrutiny of the psyche and devotion to personal happiness. New "soul" doctors emerged to lead congregants in their quest for emotional health. Phineas P. Quimby was clearly such a doctor. His "mind cure" was one of many new solutions to the old-age problems of sickness and sin. America's penchant for religious experimentation in part accounts for its enthusiasm for psychological cures.

Institutional experimentation also allowed for the growth of the therapeutic gospel. In the early twentieth century, builders of the welfare state incorporated psychological services as a major part of their initiative. Similarly, from the onset of World War II psychological services were incorporated into the military-industrial complex.

The dynamic nature of America's cultural economy also explains the place of therapeutic thinking. In a relatively short time period, for example, America had four successive bestselling magazines: *Life, People, Us,* and *Self.* As America's focus shrank at an increasingly rapid rate in the post–World War II era, cultural entrepreneurs capitalized on the diminishing expectations. Time and again America has created new cultural products reflecting and further expanding America's devotion to the psyche.

Another perspective on America's obsession with the psyche emphasizes the economic factors. The short explanation is that only the wealthiest country in the world could become so focused on psychological or nonmaterial concerns. A Marxist interpretation emphasizes that just as capitalism took production out of the hands of workers, creating the proletariat, so too did capitalism result in the proletarianization of parenthood: how to bring up one's children and avoid dysfunctional families becomes a new area of expertise. With the rise of corporate capitalism, reproduction as well as production became a vehicle of social control.

While some find economic explanations most powerful, others turn to cultural, social, or political ones. Clearly, all these theories of why the therapeutic gospel is such a fixture of American life have some merit. But the search for causes should not obscure the incredible and unpredictable confluence of events that led to the therapeutic gospel.

America's fascination with feeling management began in the 1850s with the mind-cure movement. Before that time medicine had both a spiritual and a somatic orientation, but treatment was not conceived of psychologically.

While there were numerous quick cures, they were not "mind cures." With the emergence of Phineas P. Quimby's "science of happiness," America began its journey toward the therapeutic altar, never to turn back.

Without the rise of the mass media, however, this fateful investment would not have been very significant. Quimby, after all, directly affected only a small number of patients who came personally to call on him. But his writings were reproduced and popularized by the emerging mass media. By 1910 a column in the mainstream *Good Housekeeping* magazine was devoted to New Thought, the movement that popularized many of Quimby's ideas, and the concepts of mental health and healing had a foothold in America's consciousness.

But these concepts remained largely absent from America's social, economic, and political life. The expansion of higher education and the birth of the helping professions changed that. In the second decade of the twentieth century, experts in the fields of psychiatry, psychology, social work, education, and criminology embraced a therapeutic agenda. Working to better the lives of the poor and to correct what they saw as their "abnormalities," they discovered the importance of the psyche and treatment. Their discovery became a critical weapon in their battle to construct the welfare state. Finding the answer to social problems in psychological remedies, they launched a campaign to establish psychological services at hospitals, courts, prisons, schools, and social-welfare agencies. While they were partially successful in obtaining the resources and institutional infrastructure, they fell far short of their goals.

With the birth of marriage counseling, psychological professionals turned their attention away from the poor and their attendant social problems. Its new science of personal relations gave the therapeutic agenda a whole new cast. The "marriage repairmen" made marital happiness among the middle class their mission, thereby broadening the therapeutic constituency as well as therapeutic goals. In the midst of the nation's most severe economic depression they insisted that marital happiness was the nation's number one problem. Once again, while marriage counselors established a body of marriage research and were able to gain a foothold in the university, many of their elaborate plans did not come to fruition. In 1942, when the American Association of Marriage Counselors was formally established, most middle-class Americans were familiar with neither the array of psychological problems that might afflict them nor the range of treatments available to them.

World War II significantly changed that. Total war made many of psychological professionals' therapeutic fantasies come true. For the first time in U.S. history a wide swath of American society was exposed to key psychological concepts and psychodynamic methods of treatment. At the end of the war this psychological machinery was put in the service of returning soldiers. No sooner had the war ended than psychological professionals began once again to expand their scope to include veterans and even their wives.

Just as low morale had affected the soldier, said psychological professionals, it also afflicted the housewife. Laying claim to a new realm, the home, America's psychological faith domesticated terms like *ego, inferiority complex,* and *self-esteem.* Women's magazines were a primary vehicle for this domestication. It turned out that stories about women's unhappiness sold magazines. Month after month, therefore, women's magazines recounted in gruesome detail the marital and personal travails of women trying to live by the standard of domestic bliss. While their intention was probably to show women how to meet this standard, at best they showed that it was a constant struggle for women to be happy.

The social movements of the 1960s drew heavily upon the psychological legacy of the cold war. Feminism, the civil-rights movement, and even the student movement relied upon therapeutic standards of integrity, development, freedom, and justice. Measuring social evil with a psychological yardstick, social activists condemned gender relations, race relations, university and student relations, and the relationship between the government and citizens. Respect for the individual psyche was at the heart of much of their social criticism.

Turning away from this explicitly political agenda, promoters of the me generation in the seventies urged Americans to practice emotional honesty. They saw stripping the self of artifice as the answer to both political and personal problems. "Getting one's head together" became the first and necessary step toward the release of any and all human potential. The me decade found salvation in emotional openness and communication. Encountering became the means of this new religion of self-awareness. With slogans such as "I'm OK—You're OK" the me generation sought to remake America.

By the 1980s the optimism of the sixties and seventies seemed to have dissipated. Rather than focusing on human potential, promoters of the therapeutic gospel focused on psychological vulnerabilities. Advocates of the therapeutic gospel found Americans suffering from a host of afflictions and addictions. Guilty of denial, the nation had to learn to admit its psychological sins. This transformation can be seen in the response in the 1960s and the 1990s to the issue of identity. While for the me generation Who am I? was a universal question that should be asked by everybody, by the 1990s those who asked such a question often suffered from an "identity disorder." But in many ways the recovery movement, with its emphasis on public consumption of personal pain, was a continuation of the seventies religion of self-awareness. In the 1990s *The Oprah Winfrey Show* and online support groups and chat rooms took the seventies call for emotional honesty to new levels. "Ambush disclosures" displayed on national TV contestants' psychological baggage.

From one perspective we have reached an absurd point in our history. On *Ricki Lake, Geraldo, Jenny Jones,* and *Montel Williams* we consume scenes of emotional wrestling. To confess or disclose hurt and pain in front of millions of viewers has become commonplace. It is bizarre and radical. Of course, from another perspective, our nation has a long history of zany psychological fads. For more than 150 years we have embraced forms of public therapy. With each new generation the forms have changed, but the emphasis on quick and easy steps remains the same. In some ways the mind cure of the 1850s is not very different from the cybertherapy offered online.

The persistence of Americans' faith in psychological happiness is troubling. No matter what the age or particular circumstances, Americans seem reflexively to turn to psychological cures. And rather than offering real psychological insight, these cures are vapid therapies. There is little rigorous psychological thinking in our culture. Rather, we embrace fast, simple, and often mindless solutions.

While I have no argument with psychological contentment as an important standard for individuals and no argument with in-depth psychological investigation as a means, when a whole society makes happiness and self-realization its rallying cry, clearly something is lost in the process. Time and again throughout our history our emphasis on the individual psyche has blinded us to underlying social realities. When, for example, therapeutic reformers during the Progressive era found that young, female delinquents needed psychological treatment, they appeared to forget that what made the girls "abnormal" was at least in part their scant economic resources. Often their so-called pathology stemmed from the failures of the market economy. Similarly, in World War II when psychotherapists examined the psyches of soldiers and traced their problems back to their psychodynamic relationships with their mothers and fathers, they appeared to forget the massively violent context in which soldiers lived. Psychological interpretations tend to crowd out social, economic, and political ones.

The other main problem with the therapeutic gospel is that the emphasis on individuals and mental healing often comes at the expense of considerations of the larger public good. There is clearly a civic cost to our obsession with the psyche. In the late twentieth century, while we worried about self-esteem, the children in America who died from gunshots outnumbered the American soldiers who died in the Vietnam War. Internationally, the contrast is even bleaker. Starvation, illness, and warfare ravage the world while we obsess about anxiety, shyness, and denial. We must somehow shift our outlook so that we may be socially responsible.

The therapeutic agenda has not always been devoid of such responsibility, however. During the Progressive era and the 1960s, social activists used the therapeutic gospel to overturn injustices, inequalities, and deprivations of freedom. During these times the concern with the poor and disenfranchised was real. The faith in the psyche and the sacredness of the human personality, for example, was an important impetus behind the civil-rights movement. The problem, perhaps demonstrated most clearly by the women's movement, is that psychological standards are insufficient to overturn the exigencies of class, race, and gender. While feminism's emphasis on women's failure to be happy in the home was helpful for upper-middle-class White women, its limitations for women of color and poor women who had already worked outside the home quickly became evident.

We need a politics and a therapeutics that are not mutually exclusive. But this appears difficult if not impossible to achieve. We cannot go back to a pretherapeutic era. Yet we fail to grapple with domestic and international social responsibilities at great cost to posterity. There are no simple answers to this dilemma. We must be wary of vapid public therapies offered while remaining open to the possibilities of a therapeutic politics that enhances social life. At the same time, we must remain critical of a therapeutics that easily displaces real solutions to pressing social problems. At a minimum we must continue to confront both the professional and popular therapeutic communities and the public at large with our quagmire.

Notes

INTRODUCTION   The Therapeutic Gospel

1. Ben Yagoda, "I'm Upset. Quote Me," *New York Times,* 14 January 1995.

2. Nancy Wartik, "Is Everybody Happy?" *American Health* 14 (May 1995): 38.

3. Office of the Surgeon General, *Mental Health: A Report of the Surgeon General* (Washington, D.C.: National Institute of Mental Health, December 1999).

4. Elizabeth Barnett, *Practical Metaphysics or the True Method of Healing* (Boston: H. H. Carter & Karnck, 1889), 49.

5. Oprah Winfrey, quoted in Howard Kurtz, *Hot Air: All Talk, All the Time* (New York: Random House, 1996), 71.

6. See the bibliography for existing secondary literature on the nation's interest in psychological interpretations. While this body of work is extensive and many historians and social critics have made important contributions to our understanding of the phenomenon, the origins of the therapeutic gospel and its complex history during the course of the twentieth century have yet to be fully understood. The existing literature tends to focus on a limited historical period, such as the Progressive era or the postwar years. It also focuses on key figures, professions, or core concepts. This book tells the story of a set of ideas—the therapeutic gospel—and their institutionalization over the course of the twentieth century. Each chapter draws upon the body of existing secondary literature but is also based on primary research.

7. Lech Choroszucha, interview by author, New York City, June 1994.

8. David D. Burns, *The Feeling Good Handbook* (New York: Plume, 1999).

9. John Cowan, *The Science of a New Life* (New York: Cowan, 1871), 397.

CHAPTER ONE   Illness

1. My description of the early history of mind cure relies heavily on Horatio Dresser's account, *A History of the New Thought Movement* (New York: Crowell, 1919); for the first announcements of Quimby's new medicine, see 105–6.

2. For the earliest press reports of mind cure, see ibid., 58–66.

3. Phineas P. Quimby, *Science of Health and Happiness*, ed. E. S. Collie (New York, 1939), 2–3.

4. Ibid., 3. My source for the next several paragraphs is ibid., 14–34.

5. Quimby, quoted in Dresser, *History of the New Thought Movement*, 49.

6. Quimby, *Science of Health and Happiness*, 151.

7. Dresser, *History of the New Thought Movement*, 244.

8. Ibid., 175–76.

9. John Higham, "The Reorientation of American Culture in the 1890s," in *Writing American History: Essays in Modern Scholarship,* ed. John Higham (Bloomington: Indiana University Press, 1970), 73–102.

10. *Journal of Practical Metaphysics*, no. 3 (December 1897): 86.

11. This quotation and those in the following paragraphs are from Helen Bigelow Miriam, *What Shall Make Us Whole* (Boston: Cupples & Herd, 1898), 36–49.

12. Henry Wood, *Edward Burton* (New York: Dillingham, 1890), 70, 74.

13. Cassins MacDonald, "Metaphysical Terminology," *Mind,* October 1897, 43.

14. Henry Wood, *Ideal Suggestions Through Mental Photography, A Restorative System for Home and Private Use* (Boston: Lee & Shepard, 1893), 54.

15. Edward A. Pennock, "Storm-Centres," *Journal of Practical Metaphysics,* no. 1 (October 1997): 14.

16. "Notes from the Journal of a Truth Seeker," ibid., no. 4 (January 1898): 109–10.

17. George Beard, *American Nervousness: Its Causes and Consequences* (New York: Putnam, 1881), 7.

18. Miriam, *What Shall Make Us Whole,* 22.

19. Clara Elizabeth Choate, "Committing Sickness," *Nautilus* 8 (December 1905): 15.

20. Clara Elizabeth Choate, "The Potency of Good Thinking," *Journal of Practical Metaphysics,* no. 2 (November 1898): 43.

21. "Magic of Mood," ibid., no. 1 (October 1897): 20.

22. Choate, "Potency of Good Thinking," 43.

23. Elizabeth Barnett, *Practical Metaphysics or the True Method of Healing* (Boston: H. H. Carter & Karnck, 1889), 47.

24. Ibid., 16.

25. Wood, *Ideal Suggestions Through Mental Photography,* 79.

26. Horatio Dresser, "The Failure of the New Thought Movement," *Journal of Practical Metaphysics,* no. 4 (January 1898): 97.

27. Barnett, *Practical Metaphysics or the True Method of Healing,* 49.

28. "Magic of Mood," 18.

29. Choate, "Potency of Good Thinking," 44.

30. Henry Wood, "Auto-Suggestion and Concentration," *Arena* 12 (March 1995): 142.

31. "Concentration," *Journal of Practical Metaphysics*, no. 1 (October 1897): 11.

32. Wood, *Ideal Suggestions Through Mental Photography*, 24.

33. Wood, "Auto-Suggestion and Concentration," 142–43.

34. Barnett, *Practical Metaphysics or the True Method of Healing*, 23.

35. Wood, "Auto-Suggestion and Concentration," 141–44.

36. "Family Counsel," *Nautilus* 8 (December 1905): 29.

37. Ibid.

38. "Happiness and Health," *Good Housekeeping* 50 (April 1910): 470–72.

39. George M. Gould, "A Pathological View of the 'New Thought' as a Form of Mania," *Current Literature* 546 (January 1909): 97–98.

40. Richard Cabot and Hugo Munsterberg, quoted in Richard Weiss, *The American Myth of Success: From Horatio Alger to Norman Vincent Peale* (New York: Basic Books, 1969), 199–201.

CHAPTER TWO   Poverty

1. Ellen Fitzpatrick, *Endless Crusade: Women Social Scientists and Progressive Reform* (New York: Oxford University Press, 1990), 116.

2. Sarah Lederman, "From Poverty to Philanthropy: The Life and Work of Mary Richmond" (Ph.D. diss., Columbia University School of Social Work, 1994), 42.

3. Lederman, "From Poverty to Philanthropy," 101.

4. S. Humphreys Gurteen, *A Handbook of Charity Organization* (Buffalo, N.Y.: privately printed, 1882), 22.

5. Josephine Shaw Lowell, *Public Relief and Private Charity* (New York: G. P. Putnam's Sons, 1884), 58, 92–93.

6. Ibid., 55–61. Lowell reports on her colleagues' thoughts about the dole and its negative effect on poverty.

7. Mary Richmond, *Friendly Visiting among the Poor* (New York: Macmillan, 1903), 37–47.

8. Robert Brenner, *American Philanthropy* (Chicago: University of Chicago Press, 1988), 94.

9. John Boyle O'Reilly, quoted in James Leiby, *A History of Social Welfare* (New York: Columbia University Press, 1978), 116.

10. George Washington Plunkitt, quoted in Walter Trattner, *From Poor Law to Welfare State: A History of Social Welfare in America* (New York: Free Press, 1979), 85.

11. Mary Richmond, *Social Diagnosis* (New York: Russell Sage Foundation, 1917), 4.

12. Ibid., 66.

13. Gurteen, *Handbook of Charity Organization*, 30.

14. Edward Devine, "The Value and Danger of Investigation," *Proceedings of the National Conference of Charities and Corrections* 24 (1897): 195.

15. Leiby, *History of Social Welfare*, 109.

16. John W. Kramer, *A Manual for Visitors of the Poor* (New York: Appleton, 1876), 13, 15.

17. Richmond, *Friendly Visiting among the Poor*, 201.

18. Kramer, *Manual for Visitors of the Poor*, 12–13.

19. Ibid., 128.

20. Ibid., 128–29.

21. Trattner, *From Poor Law to Welfare State*, 84.

22. Ibid., 174–76.

23. Kramer, *Manual for Visitors of the Poor*, 27–42.

24. Richmond, *Friendly Visiting among the Poor*, 68–78.

25. Lowell, *Public Relief*, 94.

26. Ethel Drummer, quoted in Miriam Van Waters, *Youth in Conflict* (New York: Republic, 1925), ix.

27. Miriam Van Waters, "Youth in Conflict," in *The Child, the Clinic, and the Court,* ed. Jane Addams (New York: New Republic, 1925), 20.

28. William Healy, "The Application of Mental Tests in Family Case Work," *The Family* 2 (July 1921): 97.

29. Edith R. Spaulding, *An Experimental Study of Psychopathic Delinquent Women* (New York: Rand McNally, 1923), 51–52.

30. See, e.g., Augusta F. Bonner, *A Comparative Study of the Intelligence of Delinquent Girls* (New York: Teachers College, Columbia University, 1914), 86–87.

31. Richmond, *Social Diagnosis*, 107.

32. Ibid., 39–40.

33. William Healy, *Individual Delinquent: A Textbook of Diagnosis and Prognosis for All Concerned in Understanding Offenders* (Boston: Little, Brown, 1915), 25.

34. Richmond, *Social Diagnosis*, 110.

35. Bernard Flexner, Reuben Oppenheimer, and Katherine F. Lenroot, *The Child, The Family, and the Court* (Washington, D.C.: U.S. Government Printing Office, 1931), 116.

36. Clifford Beers, *A Mind That Found Itself: An Autobiography* (New York: Doubleday, 1908), 3.

37. Adolf Meyer, quoted in David Rothman, *Conscience and Convenience: The Asylum and Its Alternatives in Progressive America* (New York: HarperCollins, 1980), 320.

38. Elizabeth Lunbeck, *The Psychiatric Persuasion: Knowledge, Gender, and Power in Modern America* (Princeton, N.J.: Princeton University Press, 1994), 177–80.

39. Ibid., 135.

40. Robert M. Mennel, *Thorns and Thistles: Juvenile Delinquents in the United States, 1825–1940* (Hanover, N.H.: University Press of New England, 1973), 130.

41. Jane Addams, *My Friend, Julia Lathrop* (New York: Macmillan, 1935), 133.

42. Jane Addams, "Organization of Family Courts," in Addams, *The Child, the Clinic, and the Court,* 263.

43. Van Waters, *Youth in Conflict,* 198.

44. Ibid., 153.

45. Ibid., 11.

46. Sophonisba P. Breckinridge and Edith Abbott, *The Delinquent Child and the Home: A Study of the Delinquent Wards of the Juvenile Court of Chicago* (New York: Russell Sage Foundation, 1917), 43.

47. Mennel, *Thorns and Thistles,* 133.

48. James Bennett, *Oral History and Delinquency: The Rhetoric of Criminology* (Chicago: University of Chicago Press, 1981), 107–8.

49. Judith Sealander, *Private Wealth and Public Life: Foundations, Philanthropy, and the Reshaping of American Social Policy* (Baltimore: Johns Hopkins University Press, 1997), 10.

50. Brenner, *American Philanthropy,* 100.

51. Bennett, *Oral History and Delinquency,* 112.

52. Ibid., 114.

53. George E. Gardner, "William Healy," *Journal of Child Psychiatry* 11 (January 1972): 12–13.

54. Bennett, *Oral History and Delinquency,* 114.

55. Estelle Freedmen has written an outstanding biography of Miriam Van Waters, a model of historical scholarship. While Freedmen's book is not explicitly concerned with the therapeutic gospel, her account shows Van Waters to have been one of the premier advocates of therapeutic reform. I relied heavily on her work for information about Van Waters's life. See Estelle Freedmen, *Maternal Justice: Miriam Van Waters and the Female Reform Tradition* (Chicago: University of Chicago Press, 1996), 63.

56. Van Waters, *Youth in Conflict,* 199.

57. Bernard Flexner and Roger N. Baldwin, *Juvenile Courts and Probation* (New York: Century, 1914), 6.

58. Van Waters, *Youth in Conflict,* 9, 198.

59. Freedmen, *Maternal Justice,* 63.

60. For description of cases see Van Waters, *Youth in Conflict,* 23–35.

61. Jane F. Cuh, "The Public School as Little Used Social Agency," *National Conference of Social Work Proceedings* 20 (1921): 95.

62. Van Waters, *Youth in Conflict,* 91.

63. Frankwood E. Williams, "The Significance of Mental Hygiene for the Teacher," *National Committee for Mental Hygiene Proceedings* 17 (1928): 359.

64. Mary B. Sayles, *The Problem Child in the School: Narratives from Case Records of Visiting Teachers* (New York: Commonwealth Fund, 1927), vii.

65. Julius John Oppenheimer, *The Visiting Teacher Movement* (New York: Public Education Association, 1924), 26.

66. "How Mental Hygiene May Help in the Solution of the School Problem," *National Conference of Social Work Proceedings* 20 (1921): 398.

67. "Elementary School and the Individual Child," ibid., 353.

68. Van Waters, *Youth in Conflict*, 98-99.

69. Oppenheimer, *Visiting Teacher Movement*, 10.

70. Sayles, *Problem Child in the School*, 6.

71. For an interesting analysis of how the visiting teacher became the school psychologist see Thomas K. Fagan, "Compulsory Schooling, Child Study, Clinical Psychology, and Special Education: Origins of the School Psychologist," *American Psychologist* 47 (February 1992): 236-43.

72. Jane F. Cuh, "A Factor in the Treatment of the Socially Handicapped Child," *National Conference of Social Work Proceedings* 22 (1922): 35.

73. William A. White, quoted in Van Waters, *Youth in Conflict*, ix.

74. Ethel S. Dummer, quoted in ibid., vi.

75. Joanna Colcord, *Broken Homes: A Study of Family Desertion and Its Social Treatment* (New York: Russell Sage Foundation, 1919), 30-31, 66.

76. Van Waters, "Youth in Conflict," 222.

77. Ibid., 65-76.

78. Helen L. Myrick, "Personality and Family Social Work," *The Family* 6 (May 1925): 64.

79. "The Story of One Family," ibid. 6 (June 1925): 110.

80. Spaulding, *Experimental Study*, 145.

81. Van Waters, *Youth in Conflict*, 86-87.

82. Colcord, *Broken Homes*, 19.

83. Myrick, "Personality and Family Social Work," 64-70.

84. Mary Christine Shea, "The Ideology of Mental Hygiene: The Emergence of the Therapeutic Liberal State" (Ph.D. diss., University of Illinois, Champaign-Urbana, 1980), 52.

85. Jennifer Gennari Shepard, "Tower Room Talk: Friendship, Expertise, and Gender in *Woman's Home Companion*, 1909-1936" (M.A. thesis, University of Virginia, 1990).

86. James Hay Jr., *Mrs. Marden's Ordeal* (Boston: Little, Brown, 1918), 2-3.

87. Healy, *Individual Delinquent*, 66.

88. Julia Mathews, "A Survey of 341 Delinquent Girls in California," *Journal of Delinquency* 3 (1923): 226.

89. Spaulding, *Experimental Study*, 151.

90. Ibid., 145.

91. Ibid., 173.

92. Augusta Scott, "Three Hundred Psychiatric Examinations Made at the Women's Day Court, New York City," *Mental Hygiene* 7 (April 1922): 362.

93. Mathews, "Survey of 341 Delinquent Girls," 209.

94. Breckinridge and Abbott, *Delinquent Child and the Home,* 37–38.

95. Mary W. Dewson, "Probation and Institutional Care for Girls," in *The Child in the City,* ed. Sophonisba P. Breckinridge (1912; reprint, New York: Arno, 1970), 358.

96. Mathews, "Survey of 341 Delinquent Girls," 205–7.

97. Nellie L. Perkins, "Mental and Moral Problems of the Woman Probationer," *Mental Hygiene* 8 (April 1924): 509.

98. Spaulding, *Experimental Study,* 89.

99. Ibid., 14–36.

100. Rothman, *Conscience and Convenience,* 133–35.

101. Sealander, *Private Wealth and Public Life,* 145–51.

102. William Logie Russell, *The New York Hospital: A History of Psychiatric Service, 1771–1936* (New York: Columbia University Press, 1945), 415.

103. *New York Times,* 19 March 1920, 6.

104. Freedmen, *Maternal Justice,* 134–35.

105. Spaulding, *Experimental Study,* 32.

106. It is important to understand, however, that resistance by female delinquents was directed not only against therapeutic reformers but also against parents. In a substantial number of cases parents went to the police and asked that their daughters be arrested. See Mary Odem, "Delinquent Daughters: The Sexual Regulation of Female Minors in the United States, 1880–1920" (Ph.D. diss., University of California, Berkeley, 1989), 307–50.

107. William I. Thomas, *The Unadjusted Girl: With Cases and Standpoint for Behavior Analysis* (Boston: Little, Brown, 1928), 177.

108. Scott, "Three Hundred Psychiatric Examinations," 354–63.

109. Spaulding, *Experimental Study,* 95.

CHAPTER THREE   Marriage

1. Oliver Butterfield, "To Live Happily Ever After," *Reader's Digest,* May 1936, 27.

2. Roy E. Dickerson, "Prepare Them for Marriage," *Parents Magazine,* December 1937, 24.

3. Paul Popenoe, "The Marriage Clinic," ibid., May 1932, 60.

4. L. B. Day, "The Development of the Family Court," *Annals of the American Academy of Political and Social Science* 76 (March 1928): 105–11.

5. Jonah J. Goldstein, *The Family in Court* (New York: Clark Boardman, 1934), 76.

6. Ralph P. Bridgman, "Guidance for Marriage and Family Life," *Annals of the American Academy of Political and Social Science* 160 (March 1932): 157.

7. Goldstein, *Family in Court,* 47.

8. Ibid., 80.

9. Harriet Mowrer, "Domestic Discord, Personality Adjustment, and the Court," *The Family* 15 (June 1934): 106.

10. Bridgman, "Guidance for Marriage and Family Life," 157.

11. Ernest R. Groves, "Mental Hygiene and Marriage," in *Readings in Mental Hygiene,* ed. Ernest R. Groves and Phyllis Blanchard (New York: Henry Holt, 1936), 221.

12. Raymond Royce Willoughby, "Neuroticism in Marriage: The Problem and Its Significance," *Journal of Social Psychology* 5 (February 1934): 4.

13. Paul Popenoe, *Conservation of the Family* (Baltimore: Williams & Wilkins, 1926), quoted in Linda Gordon, "The Politics of Population: Birth Control and the Eugenics Movement," *Radical America* 8 (1974): 69.

14. Marie E. Kopp, "Development of Marriage Consultation Centres," *American Journal of Obstetrics and Gynecology* 26 (July 1933): 176.

15. Popenoe, "Marriage Clinic," 15.

16. Paul Popenoe, quoted in *Current Biography,* ed. Anna Rotner (New York: H. W. Wilson, 1946), 487.

17. Newell W. Edson, "Family Adjustments through Consultation Service," *Journal of Social Hygiene* 18 (April 1932): 200.

18. Emmet Crozier, "Why Marriages Go Wrong," *American Magazine,* June 1933, 61.

19. Popenoe, "Marriage Clinic," 15.

20. Popenoe, "A Family Consultation Service," *Journal of Social Hygiene* 18 (June 1931): 310.

21. Paul Popenoe, "The Institute of Family Relations," *Eugenics* 3-4 (1930-31): 135.

22. Popenoe, "Family Consultation Service," 313.

23. Ibid.

24. Crozier, "Why Marriages Go Wrong," 110.

25. Ibid., 112.

26. Paul Popenoe, "Marital Counseling with Special Reference to Frigidity," *Mental Hygiene* 4 (August 1937): 38.

27. Paul Popenoe, "Marital Happiness in Two Generations," ibid. 4 (June 1937): 218-23.

28. "Scholarship Loans Held Marriage Back," *New York Times,* 17 July 1931, 16.

29. George K. Pratt, "Doctors of Matrimony," *Survey Graphic* 67 (January 1932): 359.

30. "Emily Mudd," in *Current Biography,* ed. Anna Rotner (New York: H. W. Wilson, 1956), 455.

31. Emily Mudd, in "Brief Descriptions of Typical Marriage and Family Counseling Services," *Parent Education* 3 (April-May 1936), 18.

32. Rev. Edwin T. Dahlberg, quoted in "Marriage Lessons Urged for Church," *New York Times,* 5 July 1935, 6.

33. *New York Times,* 10 April 1933.

34. Bridgman, "Guidance for Marriage and Family Life," 148.

35. Edson, "Family Adjustments through Consultation," 198.

36. Mowrer, "Domestic Discord, Personality Adjustment, and the Court," 106.

37. Meyer F. Nimkoff, "Education for Marriage," *Birth Control Review* 15 (September 1931): 246.

38. Robert G. Foster, "Servicing the Family through Counseling Agencies," *American Sociological Review* 2 (October 1937): 764.

39. Norman E. Himes, *Your Marriage: A Guide to Happiness* (New York: Farrar & Rhinehart, 1940), 7.

40. The Marriage Study Association of New England's marriage-consultation bureau is described in Mary S. Fisher, "The Development of Marriage and Family Counselling in the United States: A Critical Interpretation," *Parent Education* 3 (April–May 1936): 9.

41. Paul Popenoe, quoted in Crozier, "Why Marriages Go Wrong," 113.

42. "Training for Marriage," *Literary Digest* 114 (26 November 1932): 15.

43. Popenoe, "Social Life," *Journal of Social Hygiene* 20 (May 1934): 245.

44. Crozier, "Why Marriages Go Wrong," 113.

45. Popenoe, "Social Life," 248.

46. Groves also institutionalized the field of family sociology. In 1924 he established a section on the family as part of the American Sociological Society. Groves also initiated in 1928 and then edited the section on marriage and the family in the journal *Social Forces.* Finally, he played a leading role in the establishment of a professional journal of marriage counseling, *Marriage and Family Living,* founded in 1939.

47. Ernest R. Groves, "Sociology and Psycho-analytic Psychology," *American Journal of Sociology* 23 (1917–18): 107; idem, *Introduction to Mental Hygiene* (New York: Holt, 1930); idem, *Marriage* (New York: Holt, 1933).

48. Sherman Gwinn, "Thousands Bring Their Troubles to This Quiet Man," *American Magazine* 52 (November 1926): 143–48.

49. Groves, *Marriage,* viii.

50. Groves recounts his own involvement with marriage education in Ernest R. Groves, "Teaching Marriage at the University of North Carolina," *Social Forces* 16 (October 1937): 95.

51. "Co-educational Course at Iowa University Deals with Marital Affairs," *New York Times,* 6 January 1935.

52. "Butler University Offers Course in Marriage," ibid., 31 December 1932.

53. Ernest R. Groves, in "Brief Descriptions of Typical Marriage and Family Counseling Services," *Parent Education* 3 (April–May 1936): 24.

54. Flora M. Thurston, "A Course on Family Relationships for College Men," ibid. 2 (May 1935): 19.

55. Malcolm S. Maclean, "The Program at an Experimental College," ibid., 21.

56. Thurston, "Course on Family Relationships," 20.

57. Maclean, "Program at an Experimental College," 21.

58. Charles Philbower, quoted in "Wants High School to Teach How to Pick Husband and Wife," New York Times, 12 November 1930.

59. Lemo Dennis Rockwood, "The Development of Education in Family Life in the United States," in Groves and Blanchard, Readings in Mental Hygiene, 264.

60. Popenoe, "Social Life," 246.

61. Dora S. Lewis, "Education for Family Life in Washington State," Parent Education 2 (May 1935): 26.

62. Sadie J. Swenson, "Teaching Family Relationships in a City High School," in Groves and Blanchard, Readings in Mental Hygiene, 249.

63. "Advises Marriage Course," New York Times, 9 January 1928.

64. Clifford Kirkpatrick, "Techniques of Marital Adjustment," Annals of the American Academy of Political and Social Science 160 (March 1932): 180.

65. Himes, Your Marriage, 79.

66. Hornell Hart and Ella B. Hart, Personality and the Family (Boston: Heath, 1935), 56.

67. Ibid., 154.

68. Meyer F. Nimkoff, The Family (New York: Houghton Mifflin, 1934), 382.

69. Emily Mudd, in "Brief Descriptions of Typical Marriage and Family Counseling Services," 19.

70. Hornell Hart, Chart for Happiness (New York: Macmillan, 1940), 88–96.

71. Ibid., 160.

72. Himes, Your Marriage, 64.

73. Hart and Hart, Personality and the Family, 134.

74. Ibid., 14.

75. Ibid., 79.

76. Ibid., 151.

77. Ibid., 215.

78. Valeria Parker, "The Influence of Sex in Family Life," Mental Hygiene 18 (January–October 1934): 267.

79. Popenoe, "Marriage Counseling with Special Reference to Frigidity," 36–46.

80. For a review of the literature see Leonard Ferguson, "Correlates of Woman's Orgasm," Journal of Psychology 6 (1938): 295–302.

81. George Pratt, "Some Problems of Modern Marriage," American Sociological Society Publications 25 (May 1931): 226.

82. Popenoe, "Marriage Counseling with Special Reference to Frigidity," 38.

83. Paul Popenoe, "Acquaintance and Betrothal," *Social Forces* 16 (1937-38): 552.

84. Popenoe, "Marriage Counseling with Special Reference to Frigidity," 45.

85. Ibid., 46.

86. Himes, *Your Marriage*, 55.

87. Hart and Hart, *Personality and the Family*, 312.

88. Himes, *Your Marriage*, 277.

89. Paul Popenoe, quoted in Hart and Hart, *Personality and the Family*, 113.

90. Hart and Hart, *Personality and the Family*, 113.

91. Hart, *Chart for Happiness*, 116.

92. Hart and Hart, *Personality and the Family*, 132-46.

93. Himes, *Your Marriage*, 49.

94. Hart and Hart, *Personality and the Family*, 135.

95. Ibid., 335.

96. Ernest R. Groves, "Emotional Immaturity," in Groves and Blanchard, *Readings in Mental Hygiene*, 222-24.

97. Meyer F. Nimkoff, "A Family Guidance Clinic," *Sociology and Social Research* 18 (1933-34): 239.

98. Harriet Mowrer, *Domestic Discord* (Chicago: University of Chicago Press, 1928), 51.

99. Hart and Hart, *Personality and the Family*, 329.

100. Paul Popenoe, "Personal and Family Counseling," *Journal of Social Hygiene* 22 (January 1936): 18.

CHAPTER FOUR War

1. See R. Elberton Smith, *The Army and Economic Mobilization* (Washington, D.C.: U.S. Government Printing Office, 1959), 77.

2. Eli Ginzberg, "Logistics of the Neuropsychiatric Problem in the Army," *American Journal of Psychiatry* 102 (May 1946): 731.

3. Bailey Pearce, *The Medical Department of the U.S. Army in World War*, vol. 10 (Washington, D.C.: U.S. Government Printing Office, 1929), 58.

4. L. G. Rowntree, "Eliminating Registrants Mentally Unfit for Service," *Michigan Society of Neuropsychiatry*, 25 March 1943, 79.

5. Ginzberg, "Logistics of the Neuropsychiatric Problem in the Army," 730.

6. William C. Menninger, *Psychiatry in a Troubled World* (New York: Macmillan, 1948), 125.

7. U.S. Army, Office of the Surgeon General, "Disposition of Individuals with Neuropsychiatric Disorders," letter 194, 3 December 1943.

8. U.S. Army, War Department Technical Bulletin, Medicine, 21 (April 1944).

9. For a more detailed discussion of this process see, e.g., H. H. Goldstein and W. Rottersman, "Induction Psychiatry," *American Journal of Psychiatry* 101 (September

1944): 210–15. For the way the process worked at an individual induction center see, e.g., W. Bloomberg and R. W. Hyde, "A Survey of Neuropsychiatry Worst at the Boston Induction Station," ibid. 99 (July 1942): 23–28.

10. Menninger, *Psychiatry in a Troubled World*, 279.

11. Harry Solomon, ed., *Manual of Neuropsychiatry* (Philadelphia: W. B. Saunders, 1945), 45.

12. Menninger, *Psychiatry in a Troubled World*, 287.

13. Geoffrey Perret, *There's a War To Be Won: The United States Army in World War II* (New York: Ballantine, 1991), 72.

14. Ibid., 42–43.

15. M. H. Maskin and L. L. Altman, "Military Psychodynamics: Psychological Factors in the Transition from Civilian to Soldier," *Psychiatry* 6 (August 1943): 266.

16. I. L. Janis, "Psychodynamic Aspects of Adjustment to Army Life," ibid. 8 (May 1945): 165.

17. Menninger, *Psychiatry in a Troubled World*, 48.

18. Janis, "Psychodynamic Aspects of Adjustment to Army Life," 159.

19. Menninger, *Psychiatry in a Troubled World*, 64.

20. Ibid., 187. For an analysis of the soldier and alcoholism see S. A. Callman and M. Moore, "The Soldier Who Drinks Too Much," *Military Surgeon* 91 (December 1942): 648–50.

21. Janis, "Psychodynamic Aspects of Adjustment to Army Life," 162.

22. Menninger, *Psychiatry in a Troubled World*, 157.

23. Ibid., 211–12.

24. Janis, "Psychodynamic Aspects of Adjustment to Army Life," 167.

25. Leon J. Saul, "Psychological Factors in Combat Fatigue," *Psychosomatic Medicine*, September 1945, 257.

26. Menninger, *Psychiatry in a Troubled World*, 113.

27. Margaret D. Craighill, "Psychological Aspects of Women Serving in the Army," *American Journal of Psychiatry* 104 (October 1947): 229.

28. Menninger, *Psychiatry in a Troubled World*, 113–18.

29. Craighill, "Psychological Aspects of Women Serving in the Army," 230.

30. Maskin and Altman, "Military Psychodynamics," 267.

31. Menninger, *Psychiatry in a Troubled World*, 117.

32. Harry L. Freedman, "The Role of the Mental-Hygiene Clinic in a Military Training Center," *Mental Hygiene* 27 (October 1943): 83.

33. John W. Appel, "Psychology and Morale," in *Manual of Neuropsychiatry*, 474.

34. Sam H. Kraines, "Adviser System," *Mental Hygiene* 27 (October 1943): 595.

35. Ibid., 592–607.

36. U.S. Army, War Department Technical Bulletin, Medicine, 12 (22 February 1944).

37. Menninger, *Psychiatry in a Troubled World,* 83.

38. Arnold Eisendorfer, 74. See also "Extramural Psychiatry in Army," *War Medicine* 5 (March 1944): 146–49.

39. U.S. Army, War Department Technical Bulletin, Medicine, 21 (15 March 1944), 11.

40. M. S. Guttamacher, "Army Consultation Services," *American Journal of Psychiatry* 102 (May 1946): 737.

41. U.S. Army, War Department Technical Bulletin, Medicine, 21 (15 March 1944), 2.

42. Menninger, *Psychiatry in a Troubled World,* 66.

43. Freedman, "Role of the Mental-Hygiene Clinic," 85.

44. Max Deutscher, "The Clinical Psychologist in an AAF Mental Hygiene Unit," *Psychological Bulletin* 141 (1944): 545.

45. M. A. Seidenfeld, "The Clinical Psychological Program in the Army," *Bulletin of the Menninger Clinic* 8 (September 1944): 513.

46. Jules D. Holzberg, "Projective Techniques in Military Clinical Psychology," ibid. 9 (May 1945): 91.

47. Ibid., 96.

48. Guttamacher, "Army Consultation Services," 745.

49. Frank T. Groving and Myron Rockmore, "Psychiatric Case-work as Military Service," *Mental Hygiene* 29 (July 1945): 453.

50. Menninger, *Psychiatry in a Troubled World,* 63.

51. Groving and Rockmore, "Psychiatric Case-work as Military Service," 500; Freedman, "Role of the Mental-Hygiene Clinic," 102.

52. Albert Preston, "The Mental-Hygiene Unit in WAC Training Center," *Mental Hygiene* 30 (June 1946): 376.

53. Freedman, "Role of the Mental-Hygiene Clinic," 105–7.

54. Menninger, *Psychiatry in a Troubled World,* 254.

55. Guttamacher, "Army Consultation Services," 742.

56. Menninger, *Psychiatry in a Troubled World,* 37.

57. Ibid., 84.

58. Appel, *Manual of Neuropsychiatry,* 469.

59. Menninger, *Psychiatry in a Troubled World,* 70.

60. Appel, *Manual in Neuropsychiatry,* 477.

61. John A. Clausen, "Research on the American Soldier as a Career Contingency," *Social Psychology Quarterly* 47, no. 2 (1984): 208.

62. Samuel A. Stouffer, *The American Soldier: Adjustment during Army Life* (Princeton, N.J.: Princeton University Press, 1949), 12.

63. Jean M. Converse, *Survey Research in the United States: Roots and Emergence, 1890–1950* (Berkeley: University of California Press, 1987), 167.

64. "Influencing Attitudes with Information," *What the Soldier Thinks* 9 (20 January 1945): 2.

65. Peter Buck, "Adjusting to Military Life: The Social Sciences Go to War," in *Military Enterprise and Technology* (Cambridge: MIT Press, 1985), 219.

66. Menninger, *Psychiatry in a Troubled World*, 579.

67. Stouffer, *American Soldier*, 85.

68. Menninger, *Psychiatry in a Troubled World*, 91-99.

69. Craighill, "Psychological Aspects of Women Serving in the Army," 229.

70. Menninger, *Psychiatry in a Troubled World*, 72.

71. Perret, *There's a War To Be Won*, 469.

72. Ibid., 461-69.

73. Menninger, *Psychiatry in a Troubled World*, 66.

74. Perret, *There's a War To Be Won*, 485.

75. Menninger, *Psychiatry in a Troubled World*, 50.

76. Perret, *There's a War To Be Won*, 375.

77. Donald S. Napali, "The Mobilization of American Psychologists, 1938-1941," *Military Affairs* 42-43 (1974): 32.

78. Perret, *There's a War To Be Won*, 195.

79. R. Sobel, "The Battalion Surgeon as Psychiatrist," in *Combat Psychiatry: Experiences in the North African and Mediterranean Theaters of Operation, American Ground Forces, World War II*, ed. Fred Hanson (Washington, D.C.: U.S. Government Printing Office, 1949), 37-41.

80. Fred Hanson, "Psychiatry at Division," in ibid., 51.

81. Philip. S. Wagner, "Psychiatric Activities during the Normandy Offensive, June 20th-August 20th, 1944," *Psychiatry* 9 (November 1946): 342.

82. Menninger, *Psychiatry in a Troubled World*, 143.

83. A. O. Ludwig, "Neurosis Occurring in Soldiers after Prolonged Combat Exposure," *Bulletin of the Menninger Clinic* 11 (January 1947): 17.

84. Wagner, "Psychiatric Activities during the Normandy Offensive," 345.

85. Ginzberg, "Logistics of the Neuropsychiatric Problem in the Army," 728-31.

86. Menninger, *Psychiatry in a Troubled World*, 309.

87. Fred D. Kartchner and Ija N. Korner, "The Use of Hypnosis in the Treatment of Acute Combat Reactions," *American Journal of Psychiatry* 103 (March 1947): 631.

88. Ibid., 631-34.

89. Fred Hanson, "Psychiatry at the Army Level," in *Combat Psychiatry*, 86.

90. Perret, *There's a War To Be Won*, 239-45.

91. Theodore Lidz, "Psychiatric Casualties from Guadalcanal," *Psychiatry* 9 (August 1946): 200-203.

92. Theodore Lidz, "Nightmares and the Combat Neuroses," ibid. 9 (February 1946): 39–48.

93. Albert N. Mayers, "Dug-Out Psychiatry," ibid. 8 (November 1945): 384.

94. Smith, *Army and Economic Mobilization*, 306.

95. Fanny Amster and Samuel Amster, "Spot Therapy (Short-Term) for the Soldier and the Implications for Long-term Treatment," *American Journal of Orthopsychiatry* 14 (June 1944): 505.

96. Donald W. MacKinnon, *Assessment of Men: Selection of Personnel for the Office of Strategic Services* (New York: Rinehart, 1948), 2–9.

97. Ibid., 33–65.

98. J. M. Schneck, "Neuropsychiatry at a Separation Center," *Military Surgeon* 100 (March 1947): 232–33.

99. Irwin L. Child and Marjorie Van de Water, eds., *Psychology for the Returning Serviceman* (New York: Penguin, 1945), 2–23.

100. Menninger, *Psychiatry in a Troubled World*, 296–98.

101. "Formative Influence in the First Half of the Twentieth Century: The First Historical Period," *Counseling Psychologist* 12 (fall 1985): 9.

102. Jacob S. Kasanin, "The Organization of a Veteran's Rehabilitation Clinic," *American Journal of Orthopsychiatry* 9 (1945): 123.

CHAPTER FIVE Home

1. GAP mission statement, quoted in Gerald N. Grob, *From Asylum to Community: Mental Health Policy in North America* (Princeton, N.J.: Princeton University Press, 1991), 32.

2. Ibid., 36.

3. Albert Maisel, "Bedlam, 1946: Most U.S. Mental Hospitals Are a Shame and a Disgrace," *Life*, May 1946, 102–10.

4. See Albert Deutsch, *The Shame of the States* (New York: Harcourt Brace, 1948); and Lincoln Steffans, *The Shame of the Cities* (New York: Hill & Wang, 1904).

5. *National Medical Health Act*, Public Law 487.

6. *National Medical Health Act*, quoted in Grob, *From Asylum to Community*, 53.

7. Ibid., 100, 106.

8. Robert Felix, quoted in ibid., 55.

9. Council of State Governments, *The Mental Health Programs of the Forty-eight States: A Report to the Governors' Conference* (Chicago, 1950).

10. *Joint Commission on Mental Illness and Health* (New York: Basic Books, 1961).

11. Grob, *From Asylum to Community*, 173–85.

12. Quotations are from Vance Packard, *The Hidden Persuaders* (New York: D. McKay, 1957), 21–23.

13. *Wall Street Journal,* 13 September 1954, 45; *Sales Management,* 15 February 1955, 22.

14. For a contemporary explanation of this new approach to advertising, see Joseph W. Newman, "Looking Around: Consumer Motivation Research," *Harvard Business Review* 33 (January-February 1955): 135.

15. Penn Stryker, "Motivation Research," *Fortune,* June 1956, 147.

16. George Fredrick, *Introduction to Motivation Research* (New York: Basic Books, 1957), 7.

17. George Smith, *Motivation Research in Advertising and Marketing* (New York: McGraw-Hill, 1954), 10.

18. Packard, *Hidden Persuaders,* 85–87.

19. Ibid., 49.

20. Louis Cheskin and L. B. Ward, "Indirect Approaches to Market Reactions," *Harvard Business Review,* 25 September 1948, 572–80.

21. James Vicary, "How Psychiatric Methods Can Be Applied to Market Research," *Printer's Ink,* April 1950, 30–38.

22. Packard, *Hidden Persuaders,* 70–78.

23. R. Graham, "Adman's Nightmare: Is the Prune a Witch?" *Reporter* 9 (13 October 1953): 27–31.

24. Packard, *Hidden Persuaders,* 137–39.

25. Ibid., 6.

26. I first challenged the conventional wisdom about women's magazines in "'It's Good to Blow Your Top': Women's Magazines and a Discourse of Discontent, 1945–1965," *Journal of Women's History* 8 (fall 1996): 66–98.

27. Betty Friedan, *The Feminine Mystique* (New York: Dell, 1963), 30.

28. Sara Evans, *Personal Politics: The Roots of Women's Liberation in the Civil Rights Movement and the New Left* (New York: Vintage, 1979), 213; Glenna Matthews, *"Just a Housewife": The Rise and Fall of Domesticity in America* (New York: Oxford University Press, 1987), 212; William L. O'Neil, *Feminism in America: A History,* 2nd ed. (New Brunswick, N.J.: Transaction, 1989), 308.

29. David Halberstam, *The Fifties* (New York: Fawcett Columbine, 1994), 588.

30. A. Mulcahey, "How Emotions Cause Unnecessary Surgery," *Cosmopolitan,* November 1955, 20.

31. James F. Bender, "What Sends People to Reno?" *Ladies' Home Journal,* April 1948, 296.

32. "What Makes Wives Unhappy," ibid., January 1949, 26.

33. Barbara Benson, "Would You Marry Your Husband Again?" ibid., February 1947, 26.

34. Marynia Farnham, "Women and Wives," *McCall's,* October 1945, 60.

35. Dorothy Thompson, "Occupation: Housewife," *Ladies' Home Journal,* March 1949, 11.

36. Jacques W. Bacal and E. B. Foskett, "Divorce—the Lonesome Road," *McCall's*, December 1945, 103.

37. Karl Huber, "Crying as Catharsis," ibid., November 1960, 46.

38. Clifford R. Adams, "Making Marriage Work: Is It You or Your Marriage That Is Getting Out of Hand?" *Ladies' Home Journal*, January 1948, 26.

39. David Mace, "Marriage Is a Private Affair," *McCall's*, October 1960, 34.

40. Clifford R. Adams, "Making Marriage Work," *Ladies' Home Journal*, September 1949, 26.

41. Kate Holliday, "It's Good to Blow Your Top," *McCall's*, January 1950, 4.

42. David Mace, "Marriage Is a Private Affair," ibid., October 1957, 97.

43. D. G. Cooley, "What's Your Emotional Breaking Point?" *Cosmopolitan*, February 1955, 12.

44. "Are You an Everyday Neurotic?" ibid., April 1957, 25.

45. Mulcahey, "How Emotions Cause Unnecessary Surgery," 24.

46. Clifford R. Adams, "Making Marriage Work," *Ladies' Home Journal*, June 1954, 26.

47. H. Hart, "Autoconditioning Can Make You a Happy Person," *Cosmopolitan*, January 1956, 18.

48. "Are Marriage Counselors Any Good?" ibid., January 1953, 105.

49. Adams, "Making Marriage Work: Is It You or Your Marriage That is Getting Out of Hand?" 26.

50. David Mace, "Marriage Is a Private Affair," *McCall's*, April 1959, 36.

51. Clifford R. Adams, "Making Marriage Work," *Ladies' Home Journal*, March 1950, 26.

52. "Can This Marriage Be Saved?" ibid., February 1953, 134.

53. Betty Friedan Papers, Schlesinger Library, Radcliffe College, Cambridge, Mass., box 744. The quotations in the remainder of this paragraph are from boxes 743, 744, 741, 742, 745, 744, 741, and 742, in that order.

CHAPTER SIX   Social Protest

1. Theodore Adorno, *The Authoritarian Personality* (New York: American Jewish Committee, 1950), v.

2. Abram Kardiner and Lionel Ovesey, *The Mark of Oppression: A Psychological Study of the American Negro* (New York: Norton, 1951), 302–38.

3. For my understanding of the damage theory, I relied on the most insightful book on this subject, Daryl Scott's *Contempt and Pity: Social Policy and the Image of the Damaged Black Psyche, 1880–1996* (Chapel Hill: University of North Carolina Press, 1997).

4. Bruno Bettelheim, *Dynamics of Prejudice: A Psychological and Sociological Study of Veterans* (New York: Harper, 1950); Gordon Allport, *The Nature of Prejudice* (Boston: Beacon, 1954); Kenneth B. Clark, *Prejudice and Your Child* (Boston: Beacon, 1955).

5. The information in this paragraph and the next several pages is from Richard

Kluger's *Simple Justice: The History of Brown v. Board of Education and Black America's Struggle for Equality* (New York: Knopf, 1976), 316–24, provides a fascinating account of the use of social science testimony in the NAACP's legal strategy in the 1950s.

6. Ibid., 423.

7. "Appendix to Appellants' Brief: Statements by Social Scientists," reprinted in *Social Problems* 227 (1955): 228.

8. Paul D. Rosen, *The Supreme Court and Social Science* (Urbana: University of Illinois Press, 1972), 140.

9. *Brown v. Board of Education of Topeka*, 347 U.S. 483, 489 (1954).

10. Ibid.

11. I am indebted to Daryl Scott's excellent book *Contempt and Pity* for this point; see 125–28 there.

12. Rosen, *Supreme Court and Social Science*, 145.

13. James Reston, column, *New York Times*, 18 May 1954, 14.

14. James F. Byrnes, "The Supreme Court Must Be Curbed," *U.S. News and World Report* 40 (1956): 54.

15. See Rosen, *Supreme Court and Social Science*, 176–77.

16. William C. Menninger, *A Psychiatrist for a Troubled World; Selected Papers* (New York: Viking, 1967), 795–97.

17. John F. Kennedy, *Memorable Quotations of John F. Kennedy*, comp. Maxwell Meyersohn (New York: Thomas Crowell, 1965), 230–34.

18. Grob, *From Asylum to Community*, 230.

19. Andrew R. Molnar, Jeryy M. Tinker, and John D. LeNoir, *Human Factors: Considerations of Underground Insurgencies* (Washington, D.C.: American University, Center for Research in Social Systems, 1966), 8.

20. Peter Watson, *War on the Mind: The Military Uses and Abuses of Psychology* (New York: Penguin, 1980), 307.

21. Ibid., 25.

22. Ellen Herman provides a thoughtful analysis of SORO's importance in *The Romance of American Psychology: Political Culture in the Age of Experts* (Berkeley: University of California Press, 1995), 168–70.

23. Molnar, Tinker, and LeNoir, *Human Factors*, 69.

24. David Landau, "Behind the Policy Makers: Rand and the Vietnam War," *Ramparts*, November 1972, 28–36.

25. Theodore Vallance, "Project Camelot," *American Psychologist* 21 (May 1966): 470.

26. Frederick Yu, a DOD-hired psychologist, quoted in Herman, *Romance of American Psychology*, 175.

27. Charles Windle and Theodore Vallance, "The Future of Military Psychology: Paramilitary Psychology," *American Psychologist* 19 (February 1964): 124.

28. Ibid., 129.

29. Landau, "Behind the Policy Makers," 52.

30. For a more extended discussion of the Kerner Commission and the profession of psychology, see Herman, *Romance of American Psychology,* 208–13.

31. U.S. Kerner Commission, *Report of the National Advisory Commission on Civil Disorder* (New York: Bantam Books, 1968), 537.

32. Ibid., 203–4.

33. Ted Gurr, "Urban Disorder: Perspectives from the Comparative Study of Civil Strife," *American Behavioral Scientist,* March–April 1968, 50.

34. Kenneth Clark, quoted in Herman, *Romance of American Psychology,* 221.

35. Terry Anderson, *The Movement and the Sixties* (New York: Oxford University Press, 1995), 135.

36. Gurr, "Urban Disorder," 50.

37. Frantz Fanon, *Wretched of the Earth* (New York: Grove, 1963), 250.

38. Frantz Fanon, *Black Skins, White Masks* (New York: Grove, 1952), 12.

39. Ibid., 154.

40. Micheline Rice-Maximin, "Frantz Fanon and Black American Ideologists in the 1960s," *Contemporary French Civilization* 5, no. 3 (1981): 372.

41. Fanon, *Black Skins, White Masks,* v.

42. Eldridge Cleaver, *Soul on Ice* (New York: Laurel, 1968), 19.

43. Rice-Maximin, "Frantz Fanon and Black American Ideologists in the 1960s," 369–79.

44. Eldridge Cleaver, "The White Race and Its Heroes," *Psychology Today* 6 (June 1968): 3.

45. Kardiner and Ovesey, *Mark of Oppression,* 332.

46. Hugh Pearson, *The Shadow of the Panther: Huey Newton and the Price of Black Power in America* (Reading, Mass.: Addison-Wesley, 1994), 96.

47. Ibid., 114–16.

48. Mission statement, League for Spiritual Discovery, quoted in James Ferrel, *The Spirit of the Sixties* (New York: Routledge, 1997), 211.

49. Anderson, *The Movement and the Sixties,* 172.

50. Ibid., 262–63, 172.

51. Marty Jezer, *Abbie Hoffman: American Rebel* (New Brunswick, N.J.: Rutgers University Press, 1992), 22–28.

52. Ferrel, *Spirit of the Sixties,* 219.

53. Stephen J. Whitfield, "The Stunt Man: Abbie Hoffman," *Virginia Quarterly Review* 66 (autumn 1990): 570.

54. Jezer, *Abbie Hoffman,* 131.

55. Ibid., 145.

56. Lenore Tiefer, "A Brief History of the Association for Women in Psychology, 1969-1991," *Psychology of Women Quarterly* 15 (December 1991): 635-49.

57. Much of the material for my analysis of feminism and the women's movement is drawn from Eva S. Moskowitz, "A Short History of Uppity Women and Outrageous Acts," *P-form*, no. 35 (spring 1995): 8-10.

58. Robin Morgan, *Sisterhood Is Powerful: An Anthology of Writing from the Women's Liberation Movement* (New York: Vintage, 1970), 604-6.

59. Alice Echols, *Daring To Be Bad: Radical Feminism in America, 1967-1975* (Minneapolis: University of Minnesota Press, 1989), 170.

60. The event is recounted in Marcia Cohen, *The Sisterhood: The Inside Story of the Women's Movement and the Leaders Who Made It Happen* (New York: Fawcett Columbine, 1989), 185.

61. Echols, *Daring To Be Bad*, 196-215.

62. Friedan, *Feminine Mystique*, 69, 281.

63. Ibid., 11-24 and 293-304, passim.

64. Ibid., 61.

65. Ibid., 22, 26, 11.

66. Cohen, *Sisterhood*, 63.

67. Anne Koedt, "The Myth of the Vaginal Orgasm," in *Notes from the Second Year*, ed. Shulamith Firestone and Anne Koedt (Wooster, Ohio: Bell & Howell, 1972), 37; Germaine Greer, *The Female Eunuch* (New York: Bantam, 1972).

68. Morgan, *Sisterhood Is Powerful*, xx.

69. Katie Sarachild, "A Program for Feminist 'Consciousness Raising,'" in Firestone and Koedt, *Notes from the Second Year*, 78.

70. Joseph Veroff, Elizabeth Douvan, and Richard Kulka, *The Inner American: A Self-Portrait from 1957-1976* (New York: Basic Books, 1981); idem, *Mental Health in America: Patterns of Help-Seeking from 1957-1976* (New York: Basic Books, 1981); Joseph Veroff, Gerald Gurin, and Sheila Field, *Americans View Their Mental Health* (Ann Arbor: Institute for Social Research, 1957).

CHAPTER SEVEN   Feelings

1. "In New York: Much Ado about 'It,'" *Time*, 4 December 1978.

2. Thomas O'Toole, "U.S. Panel Urges Overhaul Mental Health Services," *Washington Post*, 28 April 1978, A1.

3. Eleanor Criswell and Severin Peterson, *The White Soul Catalog* (San Francisco: CRM Books, 1972); Severin Peterson, *A Catalog of the Ways People Grow* (New York: Ballantine, 1971).

4. "Survey of Encounter Group Movement," *New York Times*, 13 January 1974, 1.

5. Anthony L. Rose, "The Feel Wheel," *Psychology Today* 5 (May 1972): 45-48.

6. C. A. Weber, "Carl Rogers on Encounter Groups," *Commonweal* 95 (November 1971): 136.

7. Layne E. Longfellow, "Body Talk—A Game," *Psychology Today* 4 (October 1970): 45.

8. "The Hang-Up Card," *Newsweek*, 7 September 1970, 88.

9. R. D. Rosen, *Psychobabble: Fast Talk and Quick Cure in the Era of Feeling* (New York: Atheneum, 1977), 35.

10. Steven Starker, *Oracle at the Supermarket: The American Preoccupation with Self-Help Books* (New Brunswick, N.J.: Transactions, 1989), 120.

11. Rosen, *Psychobabble*, 14.

12. "T.A.: Doing OK," *Time*, 20 August 1973, 44.

13. Starker, *Oracle at the Supermarket*, 115.

14. Thomas A. Harris, quoted in Martin Gross, *The Psychological Society* (New York: Random House, 1978), 287.

15. TA brochure, quoted in ibid., 290.

16. Thomas A. Harris, *I'm OK—You're OK: A Practical Guide to Transactional Analysis* (New York: Harper & Row, 1969), 80.

17. All reviews are quoted from Mildred Newman and Bernard Berkowitz, *How to Be Your Own Best Friend* (New York: Ballantine, 1971).

18. Jane Howard, *Please Touch: A Guided Tour of the Human Potential Movement* (New York: McGraw-Hill, 1970), 3.

19. Michael Murphy, "Esalen: Where It's At," *Psychology Today* 1 (January 1967): 39.

20. Tom Wolfe, "The Me Decade," *New York Magazine*, 23 August 1976, 33.

21. Howard, *Please Touch*, 9–11.

22. "The Screaming Cure," *Newsweek*, 10 July 1978, 39.

23. Sam Keen, "Janov and Primal Therapy: The Screaming Cure," *Psychology Today* 5 (February 1972): 46.

24. Rosen, *Psychobabble*, 147.

25. Daniel Casriel, *A Scream Away from Happiness* (New York: Grosset & Dunlap, 1972), 60.

26. Ibid., 3.

27. Ibid., 55.

28. Daniel Casriel, interview by Martin Gross, quoted in Gross, *Psychological Society*, 284.

29. Werner Erhard, quoted in Rosen, *Psychobabble*, 63.

30. "Getting Your Head Together," *Newsweek*, 6 September 1976, 58.

31. Adelaide Bry, *Est: Sixty Hours That Transform Your Life* (New York: Harper & Row, 1976).

32. "Pay Attention Turkeys!" *New York Times Magazine*, 2 May 1976, 46.

33. Mark Brewer, "Erhard Seminar Training: We're Gonna Tear You Down and Put You Back Together," *Psychology Today* 9 (August 1975): 35–39.

34. Rosen, *Psychobabble,* 148.

35. Ibid., 83.

36. Ibid., 85.

37. Ibid., 119.

38. Ibid., 123–24.

39. Ibid., 123–31.

40. Howard, *Please Touch,* 87.

41. Paul Bindrim, "A Report on a Nude Marathon," *Psychotherapy* 5 (fall 1968).

CHAPTER EIGHT   **Personal Problems and Public Debate**

1. Margaret Jones, "The Rage for Recovery," *Publishers Weekly,* 23 November 1990, 16–24.

2. *Diagnostic and Statistical Manual of Mental Disorders,* 3rd ed., rev. (Washington, D.C.: American Psychiatric Association, 1987).

3. Charles J. Sykes, *A Nation of Victims: The Decay of American Character* (New York: St. Martin's, 1992), 135–36.

4. Robin Room, "'Healing Ourselves and Our Planet': The Emergence and Nature of a Generalized Twelve-Step Consciousness," *Contemporary Drug Problems,* winter 1992, 717–40.

5. "Some Folks Find That Elvis Makes Their Spirits Rise—A Support Group for Psychics," *Wall Street Journal,* 20 October 1992, A1.

6. www.compulsiveshoppers.anonymous.com.

7. "Some Folks Find That Elvis Makes Their Spirits Rise."

8. *"Pass It On": The Story of Bill Wilson and How the AA Message Reached the World* (New York: AA World Services, 1984), 248.

9. www.overeaters.anonymous.org.

10. www.sca-recovery.org.

11. B. J. White and E. J. Madara, eds., *The Self-Help Sourcebook* (Denville, N.J.: American Self-Help Clearinghouse, 1992).

12. webmaster@bewebbed.com.

13. www.mtn.org/EA.

14. www.bein.com/trauma/news.html.

15. www.R-A.org.

16. Vince R. Miller, "The Twelve Steps: Meeting the Challenge of Our Success," *Recovering,* January 1991, 1, 9.

17. Stephanie Armour, "Technically, It's an Addiction Some Workers Finding It Hard to Disconnect," *USA Today,* 21 April 1998, B1.

18. www.pagehost.com/arts/12steps.htm.

19. I am indebted to the insightful article by Robyn R. Warhol and Helena Michie for helping me to clarify my thoughts on this point. See their "Twelve-Step Teleology: Narratives of Recovery / Recovery as Narrative," in *Getting a Life: Everyday Uses of Autobiography*, ed. Sidonie Smith and Julia Watson (Minneapolis: University of Minnesota Press, 1996), 338.

20. AA pamphlet, quoted in ibid.

21. On the origins of the *Diagnostic and Statistical Manual*, see Gerald N. Grob, "The Origins of DSM-I: A Study in Appearance and Reality," *American Journal of Psychiatry* 148 (April 1991): 421–31.

22. www.alcoholics.anonymous.org; www.codependents.org; www.gamblers.anonymous.org; www.overeaters.anonymous.org; www.sexaddiction.anonymous.org; www.compulsiveshoppers.anonymous.com; www.depression.org; www.christianrecovery.com/graceworks.shtml.

23. "35 Million Afflicted by Winter Blues," *Chicago Tribune*, 10 December 1993, 3.

24. www.nccod.netgale.net/index.html.

25. www.self-esteem-nase.org.

26. www.nmisp.org.

27. For governmental uses of twelve-step philosophies and programs, see J. P. Takala and G. Hunt, eds., *Cure, Care, or Control: Alcoholism Treatment in Sixteen Countries* (Albany: State University of New York, 1992), 87–109.

28. I. D. Zedaker, "Booming New Industries Serve Millions in Recovery," *Sober Times*, October 1989, 23–24.

29. James Talan, in *St. Louis Post-Dispatch*, 1 September 1997, E4.

30. "Sun Rises on Prozac-Popping America: Ads Directed at Depressed Are Condemned," *Guardian* (London), 4 July 1997, 1.

31. "Prozacville, USA," *Psychology Today* 28 (January 1995): 16.

32. "Minty Liquid Prozac," *Rolling Stone*, 21 August 1997, 70.

33. "Don't Give Prozac to Mopey Pooch," *Los Angeles Times*, 27 April 1998, 8.

34. "Special Report: Herbal Remedy Takes on Prozac," *Denver Post*, 9 September 1997, A2.

35. redbeet.dyn.ml.org/geninfo.htm.

36. Stanton Peele, *Diseasing of America: How We Allowed Recovery Zealots and the Treatment Industry to Convince Us We Are Out of Control* (New York: Lexington Books, 1995), 2.

37. One student of Prozac has called the trend "cosmetic psychopharmacology" (Peter D. Kramer, *Listening to Prozac* [New York: Viking, 1993]). The idea behind Prozac is that our therapeutic goals have changed. We are no longer simply aiming for emotional health; now we want to improve our personalities and enhance our emo-

tional potential. Taking our cues in an odd way from the human-potential movement but adding a nineties twist, we want to achieve our emotional potential artifi-
cially with drugs. In the brave new world of Prozac the question becomes, If by increasing seratonin levels, people can increase their ability to enjoy life, why not
prescribe Prozac?

38. Phil Donahue, *Donahue: My Own Story* (New York: Simon & Schuster, 1979),
98–100.

39. Howard Kurtz, *Hot Air: All Talk, All the Time* (New York: Random House, 1996),
50–54.

40. George Mair, *Oprah Winfrey: The Real Story* (Birch Lane Press, 1994), 52.

41. Ibid., 289.

42. Kurtz, *Hot Air,* 61.

43. Jane M. Shattuc, *The Talking Cure: TV Talk Shows and Women* (New York: Routledge,
1997), 147–48.

44. Kurtz, *Hot Air,* 66.

45. Shattuc, *Talking Cure,* 113.

46. "Some Find Path to Recovery on the Net," *Denver Post,* 20 February 1998, A21.

47. In addition to providing links with relevant sites, Self-Improvement offers viewers
inspirational quotes, a complete directory of self-improvement topics, relevant associations and organizations, self-help magazines, a list of self-help gurus, emotional tests, and a list of relevant newsgroups.

48. www.immanuels.org/bc/bc_goal.htm.

49. www.nsonline.com.counselling.

50. "Cyberpsychology: Therapy for the 1990s," MSNBC TV, 29 May 1997.

51. www.counselingcafe.com/ser_info.htm.

52. www.thetherapynetwork.com.

53. www.miraclescounseling.com/question.htm.

54. www.christianrecovery.com/graceworks.shtml.

55. "Self-Help Groups Thrive on Information Highway," *New Orleans Times-Picayune,*
26 March 1995, A22.

56. "Internet: Care in the (Virtual) Community," *Guardian,* 16 March 1995, 4.

57. "Shrinks Aplenty Online," *New York Times,* 7 November 1997.

58. www.thetherapynetwork.com.

59. Ibid.

60. "Some Find Path to Recovery on the Net."

61. www.iucf.indiana.edu.

62. "Apples and Oranges and Computer Chips," *Computing Canada,* 27 April 1998, 49.

63. "Web of Intrigue," *Guardian,* 3 February 1998, T15.

64. "An Internet Addict Confesses," *New Statesman,* 19 June 1998, 26.

65. "Technically, It's an Addiction."

66. "Web of Intrigue."

67. David Viscott, quoted in Rosen, *Psychobabble*, 35.

68. Jerome D. Levin, *The Clinton Syndrome: The President and the Self-Destructive Nature of Sexual Addiction* (Rocklin, Calif.: Forum, 1998).

Bibliography

This book is based on a wide array of primary sources. It also draws extensively on the large body of secondary literature that covers the history of pop psychology as well as such related topics as science and pop culture, the history of the professions, the development of the welfare state, the military-industrial complex, the history of gender politics, and the history of television and talk shows. The serious student of America's obsession with the psyche will not want for books or articles. For the benefit of those doing research, a chapter-by-chapter discussion of primary and secondary sources is included.

General

The literature on the general phenomenon of America's obsession with the psyche is extensive. It was first explored with great interest in the 1970s by a range of social critics. Tom Wolfe, for example, in his essay "The Me Decade and The Third Great Awakening," which first appeared in *The Critic*, May–June 1973, was one of the first to address the psychologization of American society. Other social critics followed. See, for example, Martin Gross, *The Psychological Society* (New York: Random House, 1978); Russell Jacoby, *Social Amnesia* (Boston: Beacon, 1975); Richard D. Rosen, *Psychobabble: Fast Talk and Quick Cure in the Era of Feeling* (New York: Atheneum, 1977); and perhaps most well known, Christopher Lasch, *The Culture of Narcissism* (New York: Norton, 1979). Feminists had their own slant on the nation's obsession with the psyche. Beginning with Betty Friedan, feminists criticized the psychologists and other members of the helping professions for their bias against women. For a more contemporary account see Barbara Ehrenreich and Diedre English, *For Her Own Good: One Hundred Fifty Years of Experts' Advice to Women* (New York: Anchor, 1979). See also Eva S. Moskowitz, "Naming the Problem: How Popular Culture and Experts Paved the Way For 'Personal Politics'" (Ph.D. diss., Johns Hopkins University, 1991).

Concerning the historical question when and why Americans turned to psychological interpretations, there are two seminal works. Anyone interested in the subject should turn first to Warren Susman's famous essay "Personality and the Making of Twentieth Century Culture," in *New Directions in American Intellectual History* (Baltimore: Johns Hopkins University Press, 1979). Historian Jackson Lears, picking up where Susman left off, wrote the first history of the "therapeutic ethos," a phrase he coined. Lears explored the spiritual malaise that led Americans to the therapeutic altar in the late nineteenth century and documented the role of advertising in promoting a new commitment to the therapeutic. While his work is tremendously useful, Lears's interest lies in the socioeconomic causes of malaise and advertising's role in creating a new therapeutic ethos. See Lears's "From Salvation to Self-Realization: Advertising and the Therapeutic Roots of the Consumer Culture, 1880–1930," in *The Culture of Consumption: Critical Essays in American History, 1880–1980,* ed. Richard Wrightman Fox and T. J. Jackson Lears (New York: Pantheon, 1983), 3–38.

Other historians have focused on the role of such key figures as Freud, William James, George Mead, and G. Stanley Hall, as well as such less well-known figures as John Watson, Hugo Munsterberg, and Adolph Meyer. See, for example, Nathan G. Hale, *Freud and the Americans: The Beginnings of Psychoanalysis in the United States, 1876–1917* (New York: Oxford University Press, 1971); Dorothy Ross, *G. Stanley Hall: The Psychologist as Prophet* (New York: Cambridge University Press, 1972); Daniel Bjork, *The Compromised Scientist: William James in the Development of American Psychology* (New York: Columbia University Press, 1983); Gary Cook, *George Herbert Mead: The Making of a Social Pragmatist* (Urbana: University of Illinois Press, 1993); Ruth Leys, "Types of One: Adolf Meyer's Life Chart and the Representation of Individuality," *Representations* 34 (spring 1991): 1–28; and Matthew Hale, *Human Science and Social Order: Hugo Munsterberg and the Origins of Applied Psychology* (Philadelphia: Temple University Press, 1980). Still others have explored the history of the professions of psychology and psychiatry and the practice of psychotherapy. For psychology and psychotherapy see, for example, Albert R. Gilgen, *American Psychology since World War II: A Profile of the Discipline* (Westport, Conn.: Greenwood, 1982); Elizabeth Scarborough, *Untold Lives: The First Generation of American Women Psychologists* (New York: Columbia University Press, 1987); Robert I. Watson, *The Great Psychologists: A History of Psychological Thought* (New York: HarperCollins, 1991); John O'Donnell, *The Origins of Behaviorism: American Psychology, 1870–1920* (New York: New York University Press, 1985); Eric Caplan, *Mind Games: American Culture and the Birth of Psychotherapy* (Berkeley: University of California Press, 1998); and John C. Burnham, *Paths into American Culture: Psychology, Medicine, and Morals* (Philadelphia: Temple University Press, 1988). For psychiatry see, for example, Gerald N. Grob, *The Innerworld of American Psychiatry, 1890–1940* (New Brunswick, N.J.: Rutgers University Press, 1985); Henri Ellenberger, *The Discovery of the Unconscious: The History and Evolution of Dynamic Psychiatry* (New York: Basic Books, 1970). Among works that document the history of psychiatry during the period 1890–1930 one of the most important to date is Elizabeth Lunbeck's *The Psychiatric Persuasion: Knowledge, Gender, and Power in Modern America* (Princeton, N.J.:

Princeton University Press, 1994). For the postwar period there is the important work of Ellen Herman, who explores the ways psychological knowledge has been used to promote political, social, and cultural goals. See Ellen Herman, *The Romance of American Psychology* (Berkeley: University of California Press, 1995).

There are also general works that focus on such aspects of the therapeutic gospel as the self, the unconscious, or emotional maturity. See, for example, Philip Cushman, *Constructing the Self, Constructing America* (Boston: Addison-Wesley, 1995); William Graeber, "Coming of Age in Buffalo: The Ideology of Maturity in Postwar America," *Radical History Review* 34 (1986): 53–74; Jan Lewis, "Mother's Love: The Construction of an Emotion in Nineteenth Century America," in *Social History and Issues in Human Consciousness,* ed. Andrew Barnes and Peter N. Stearns (New York: New York University Press, 1989); and Carol Zisowitz Stearns and Peter N. Stearns, *Anger: The Struggle for Emotional Control in America's History* (Chicago: University of Chicago Press, 1986). There is also a wonderful collection of essays called *Inventing the Psychological: Toward a Cultural History of Emotional Life in America,* ed. Joel Pfister and Nancy Schnog (New Haven: Yale University Press, 1997).

CHAPTER ONE Illness

The research for this chapter is based on Phineas P. Quimby, *The Quimby Manuscripts Showing the Discovery of Spiritual Healing and the Origin of Christian Science,* ed. Horatio Dresser (New York: Crowell, 1921), and New Thought books and periodicals, as well as contemporary accounts of the mind cure and New Thought movements. For Quimby's own writings see Phineas P. Quimby, *The Science of Health and Happiness by P. P. Quimby: The Unpublished Writings of P. P. Quimby, Copied from the Original Quimby Manuscripts in the Library of Congress, Washington D.C., by E. S. Collie* (New York, 1939). For nineteenth- and early-twentieth-century accounts of Quimby and mind cure see Julius A. Dresser, *The True History of Mental Science: The Facts Concerning the Discovery of Mental Healing* (Boston: Ellis, 1887); Annetta Gertrude Dresser, *The Philosophy of P. P. Quimby: With Selections From His Manuscripts and Sketch of His Life* (Boston: Ellis, 1895); Horatio Dresser, *The Quimby Manuscripts Showing the Discovery of Spiritual Healing and the Origins of Christian Science* (New York: Crowell, 1921); and Frank Podmore, *Mesmerism and Christian Science: A Short History of Mental Healing* (London: Methuen, 1909).

The New Thought periodicals I examined for this study include *Arena, Christian Metaphysician, Harmony, Higher Law, Ideal American, Immortality, Journal of Practical Metaphysics, Library of Health, Mental Science Monthly, Nautilus, New Thought, Realization, and Success Magazine.* I also examined dozens of New Thought self-help manuals. Finally, I examined New Thought novels. The largest collection of New Thought material is located at the Bridwell Library, Southern Methodist University, Dallas. For the best contemporary account of New Thought see Horatio Dresser, *A History of the New Thought Movement* (New York: Crowell, 1919).

The secondary literature on America's first steps down the therapeutic aisle comprises works on such related topics as mesmerism, phrenology, and spiritualism. On mesmerism see Robert Darton, *Mesmerism and the End of the Enlightenment* (Cambridge: Harvard University Press, 1968); and Robert C. Fuller, *Mesmerism and the American Cure of Souls* (Philadelphia: University of Pennsylvania Press, 1982). For an analysis of American literature and mesmerism see Samuel Coale, *Mesmerism and Hawthorne: Mediums of American Romance* (Tuscaloosa: University of Alabama Press, 1998). For studies of phrenology see John D. Davies, *Phrenology, Fad, and Science* (New Haven: Yale University Press, 1955); Madeline B. Stern, *Heads and Headlines: The Phrenological Fowlers* (Norman: University of Oklahoma Press, 1971); and Charles Colbert, *A Measure of Perfection: Phrenology and the Fine Arts in America* (Chapel Hill: University of North Carolina Press, 1997). For a discussion of spiritualism and American culture see Howard Kerr, *Mediums, and Spirit-Rappers, and Roaring Radicals: Spiritualism in American Literature, 1850–1900* (Urbana: University of Illinois Press, 1972); R. Lawrence Moore, *In Search of White Crows: Spiritualism, Parapsychology, and American Culture* (New York: Oxford University Press, 1977); Anne Braude, *Radical Spirits: Spiritualism and Women's Rights in Nineteenth-Century America* (Boston: Beacon, 1989); and Michael O'Sullivan, *A Harmony of Worlds: Spiritualism and the Quest for Community in Nineteenth-Century America* (New York: 1981).

Another relevant body of work comprises studies on the history of religion and the history of medicine during this critical period in the history of pop psychology. In terms of religion, America went through a period of intense anticlericalism that led to the proliferation of self-appointed healers. For a discussion of these themes see, for example, Jay Fliegelman, *Prodigals and Pilgrims: The American Revolution against Patriarchal Authority, 1750–1800* (Cambridge: Harvard University Press, 1982); Gordon S. Wood, "The Democratization of Mind in the American Revolution," in *Leadership in the American Revolution* (Washington, D.C.: Library of Congress, 1974); and Nathan O. Hatch, *The Democratization of American Christianity* (New Haven: Yale University Press, 1989). Medically, America's therapeutic revolution coincided with the rise of soul doctoring. The best book documenting changing medical ideas and practices during the birth of mind cure is John H. Warner's *The Therapeutic Perspective: Medical Practice, Knowledge, and Identity in America* (Cambridge: Harvard University Press, 1986).

For histories of Christian Science see Stewart W. Holmes, "Phineas Pankurst Quimby: Scientist of Transcendalism," *New England Quarterly* 17 (1944): 356–80; Charles Braden, *Spirits in Rebellion: The Rise and Development of New Thought* (Dallas: Southern Methodist University Press, 1963); Stephen Gottschalk, *The Emergence of Christian Science in American Religious Life* (Berkeley: University of California Press, 1973); and Stuart Knee, *Christian Science in the Age of Mary Baker Eddy* (Westport, Conn.: Greenwood, 1994). For histories of mind cure and New Thought see Gail Thain Parker, *Mind Cure in New England* (Hanover, N.H.: University Press of New England, 1973); Donald Meyer, *The Positive Thinkers: Religion as Pop Psychology from Mary Eddy*

Baker to Oral Roberts (New York: Pantheon, 1965); Jay Watson Fay, *American Psychology before William James* (New Brunswick, N.J.: Rutgers University Press, 1939); J. Stillson Judah, *The History and Philosophy of the Metaphysical Healing Movement in America* (Philadelphia: Westminster, 1967); and Norman Gevitz, *Other Healers: Unorthodox Medicine in America* (Baltimore: Johns Hopkins University Press, 1988).

CHAPTER TWO Poverty

The research for this chapter was based on accounts and personal memoirs of what might be called "poverty workers," those who worked with the poor. For the pretherapeutic period I relied heavily on books by several leading poverty workers, including Reverend S. Humphreys Gurteen, Josephine Shaw Lowell, and John W. Kramer. See Reverend S. Humphreys Gurteen, *A Handbook of Charity Organization* (Buffalo, N.Y.: privately printed, 1882); Josephine Shaw Lowell, *Public Relief and Private Charity* (New York: G. P. Putnam's Sons, 1884); and John W. Kramer, *A Manual for Visitors of the Poor* (New York: Appleton, 1876). For the period of what I call therapeutic reform I examined the leading social-science and reform journals of the day, including *Family, Journal of Delinquency, National Conference of Social Work Proceedings, Mental Hygiene,* and *Journal of Abnormal Psychology.* I also examined the published works of leading therapeutic reformers, including William Healy, Augusta Bonner, Miriam Van Waters, Julia Mathews, Katherine Davis, Mary Richmond, Jane Addams, Bernard Flexner, Roger Baldwin, Mary Sayles, Julius Oppenheimer, William White, Joanna Colcord, Edith Spaulding, Jessie Taft, Sophonsiba Breckinridge, and William Thomas.

Over the last twenty years or so there has been an explosion of studies documenting the birth and course of the welfare state. See, for example, Edward Berkowitz, *Creating the Welfare State: The Political Economy of Twentieth-Century Reform* (New York: Praeger, 1980); Mimi Abramovitz, *Regulating the Lives of Women: Social Welfare Policy from Colonial Times to the Present* (Boston: South End, 1988); Linda Gordon, ed., *Women, the State, and Welfare* (Madison: University of Wisconsin Press, 1990); Daniel Levine, *Poverty and Society: The Growth of the American Welfare State in International Comparison* (New Brunswick, N.J.: Rutgers University Press, 1988); John F. McClymer, *War and Welfare: Social Engineering in America, 1890-1925* (Westport, Conn.: Greenwood, 1980); James Leiby, *A History of Social Welfare* (New York: Columbia University Press, 1978), and William Trattner, *From Poor Law to Welfare State: A History of Social Welfare in America* (New York: Free Press, 1979).

Although this work has made a substantial contribution to our understanding of the development of the welfare state, the importance of the therapeutic gospel to these developments has been generally ignored. For a few exceptions see Mary Christine Shea, "The Ideology of Mental Hygiene: The Emergence of the Therapeutic Liberal State" (Ph.D. diss., University of Illinois, Champaign-Urbana, 1980); and Andrew Joseph Polsky's excellent book *The Rise of the Therapeutic State* (Princeton, N.J.: Princeton University Press, 1991). Polsky identifies the institutionalization of therapeutic thinking as a critical moment in American history. A political scientist, his main interest lies in the political effects of the new therapeutic state.

Scholars interested in the historical processes underlying the introduction of therapeutic thinking and techniques have tended to focus on particular institutions, such as courts and hospitals. Indeed, one of the best recent studies, Lunbeck's *Psychiatric Persuasion,* tells the story of one particular hospital, the Boston Psychopathic Hospital. Using this hospital's records, Lunbeck traces the transformation of psychiatry from a discipline concerned with custodial care to one addressing the problems of everyday life. An earlier study examined the history of New York Hospital: William Logie Russell, *The New York Hospital: A History of Psychiatric Service, 1771-1936* (New York: Columbia University Press, 1945). Scholars interested in medical and reform history focus more generally on the introduction of therapeutic services into hospital care. See, for example, David Rothman's pathbreaking *Conscience and Convenience: The Asylum and Its Alternatives in Progressive America* (New York: HarperCollins, 1980). Other important works include Gerald N. Grob, *The Mad among Us: A History of the Care of America's Mentally Ill* (New York: Free Press, 1994); and idem, *Mental Illness and American Society, 1875-1940* (Princeton, N.J.: Princeton University Press, 1983).

The transformation of the criminal-justice system was a critical part of the psychologization of American society. In particular, the creation of juvenile justice played a key role in introducing therapeutic thinking into the American welfare state. For information about the history of the juvenile courts see Steven L. Schlossman, *Love and the American Delinquent: The Theory and Practice of "Progressive" Juvenile Justice, 1825-1920* (Chicago: University of Chicago Press, 1977); Robert M. Mennel, *Thorns and Thistles: Juvenile Delinquents in the United States, 1825-1940* (Hanover, N.H.: University Press of New England, 1973); Elizabeth Clapp, *Mothers of All Children: Women Reformers and the Rise of the Juvenile Courts in Progressive Era America* (University Park: Pennsylvania State University Press, 1998). Perhaps the best book on criminal justice in the Progressive era is a new biography of Miriam Van Waters, a key figure in the juvenile-justice movement. I relied heavily on Estelle B. Freedmen's wonderful book *Maternal Justice: Miriam Van Waters and the Female Reform Tradition* (Chicago: University of Chicago Press, 1996). Although this book does not aim to describe the institutionalization of therapeutic thinking, it sheds much light on how one individual reformer brought psychological concepts to her work with poor youth.

Gender figures prominently in the story of the psychologization of American society and the institutionalization of therapeutic thinking into the welfare state. For pathbreaking work on the general topic see Steven L. Schlossman and Stephanie Wallach, "The Crime of Precocious Sexuality: Female Juvenile Delinquency in the Progressive Era," *Harvard Educational Review* 48 (February 1978): 65-95; Barbara Brenzel, "Domestication as Reform: A Study of the Socialization of Wayward Girls, 1856-1905," ibid. 50 (May 1980): 196-213; George Chaucy, "From Sexual Inversion to Homosexuality: Medicine and the Changing Conceptualization of Female Deviance," *Salmagundi*

58–59 (fall–winter): 114–46; Michael W. Sedlack, "Young Women and the City: Adolescent Deviance and the Transformation of Educational Policy, 1870–1960," *History of Education Quarterly* 23 (spring 1983): 1–28; Joan Brumberg, "'Ruined Girls': Changing Community Responses to Illegitimacy in New York, 1890–1920," *Journal of Social History* 18 (winter 1984): 247–72; Elizabeth Lunbeck, "'A New Generation of Women': Progressive Psychiatrists and the Hypersexual Female," *Feminist Studies* 13 (fall 1987): 513–43; Mary E. Odem and Steven Schlossman, "Guardians of Virtue: The Juvenile Court and Female Delinquency in Early Twentieth-Century Los Angeles," *Crime and Delinquency* 37 (April 1991): 186–203; Ruth M. Alexander, "'The Only Thing I Wanted Was Freedom': Wayward Girls in New York, 1900–1930," in *Small Worlds: Children and Adolescents in America, 1850–1950*, ed. Elliot West and Paula Petrik (Lawrence: University of Kansas Press, 1992), 275–95; Carol Groneman, "Nymphomania: The Historical Construction of Female Sexuality," *Signs* 19 (1994): 337–67; and Regina G. Kunzel, *Fallen Women, Problem Girls: Unmarried Mothers and the Professionalization of Social Work 1890–1945* (New Haven: Yale University Press, 1994).

CHAPTER THREE Marriage

My exploration of the rise of the marriage-counseling profession began with the profession's own internal histories. Encyclopedias and other reference books provided the best starting point, though the information contained within is cursory. The most helpful of these was *Fifty Years of Marital and Family Therapy*, ed. William C. Nichols (Washington, D.C.: American Association for Marriage and Family Therapy, 1992). Key figures involved in the formation of the American Association of Marriage Counselors were also a critical source of information. While there are no published biographies of these figures, biographical reference books as well as encyclopedias of the helping professions and social sciences provided much useful information. See, for example, *Encyclopedia of Psychology*, ed. Raymond J. Corsini, 7th ed. (New York: Wiley-Interscience, 1984); William I. Trattner, ed., *Biographical Dictionary of Social Welfare in America* (Westport, Conn.: Greenwood, 1986). One of the early presidents of the American Association of Marriage Counselors, Ernest Groves, created the first graduate program in the field, and his papers are housed at the University of North Carolina at Chapel Hill. He also created the section on marriage and the family in the journal *Social Forces*. Finally, he played a leading role in the establishment of a professional journal of marriage counseling, *Marriage and Family Living*, which was founded in 1939.

In terms of primary sources, there is also the enormous body of work published by early participants in the profession. I systematically reviewed all social-science and helping-profession journals that included information about marriage counseling. The ones I found to be most helpful include *The Family*, the *American Journal of Sociology*, *Annals of American Political and Social Science*, the *Journal of Social Psychology*, *Mental Hygiene*, the *Journal of Social Hygiene*, *Eugenics*, the *American Sociological Review*, the

Journal of Home Economics, Social Forces, Birth Control Review, and the *American Journal of Public Health.* In the 1930s there was a veritable explosion in what I call marriage research. Almost all major universities had academics specializing in the topic. This cottage industry produced hundreds of studies, which I reviewed.

For typical examples of this quantitative approach to marital happiness and adjustment see, for example, Lewis M. Terman, *Psychological Factors in Marital Happiness* (New York: McGraw-Hill, 1938), Leonard Ferguson, "Correlates of Marital Happiness," *Journal of Psychology* 6 (1938): 285; G. W. Hartmann, "Personality Traits Associated with Variations in Happiness," *Journal of Abnormal and Social Psychology* 29 (1934): 202–12; Winifred B. Johnson and Lewis M. Terman, "Personality Characteristics of the Happily Married, Unhappily Married, and Divorced Couples," *Character and Personality* 3 (1935): 290–311; Paul Popenoe, "Marital Happiness in Two Generations," *Mental Hygiene* 4 (1937): 218–23; P. M. Symonds, "Happiness as Related to Problems and Interests," *Journal of Educational Psychology* 36 (1937): 290–94; Walter B. Pitkin, *The Psychology of Happiness* (New York: Simon & Schuster, 1929); Richard O. Lang, "The Rating of the Degree of Happiness or Unhappiness in Marriage" (master's thesis, University of Chicago, 1933); Clifford Kirkpatrick, "Techniques of Marital Adjustment," *Annals of the American Academy of Political and Social Science* 160 (March 1932): 178–83; E. T. Krueger, "A Study of Marriage Incompatibility," *The Family* 9 (April 1928): 53–60; Lewis M. Terman and Paul Buttenwieser, "Personality Factors in Marital Compatibility," *Journal of Social Psychology* 6 (1935): 143–71; and Jessie Bernard, "Factors in the Distribution of Success in Marriage," *American Journal of Sociology* 40 (1934): 49–60;

The popular media had a special interest in this academic research. Using the *Reader's Guide to Periodical Literature,* I comprehensively examined this coverage. Most of it can be found in a few popular magazines, including *Reader's Digest, Parent Magazine, American Magazine,* and *Parent Education.* The *New York Times* also covered some of the profession's new theories that would interest its middle-class readership.

For the role of the courts in the birth of the marriage-counseling profession see Joanna Colcord, *Broken Homes: A Study of Family Desertion and Its Social Treatment* (New York: Russell Sage Foundation, 1919); idem, "Remedial Agencies Dealing with the American Family," *Annals of the American Academy of Political and Social Science* 160 (March 1932): 124–34; idem, "The Matrimonial Advice Bureau," *The Family* 5 (May 1924): 61–63; Harriet Mowrer, *Domestic Discord* (Chicago: University of Chicago Press, 1928); Bernard Flexner, Reuben Oppenheimer, and Katherine F. Lenroot, *The Child, the Family, and the Court* (Washington, D.C.: U.S. Government Printing Office, 1931); L. B. Day, "The Development of the Family Court," *Annals of the American Academy of Political and Social Science* 126 (March 1928): 105–11; and P. J. Shelly, *The Social and Economic Value of the Family Court* (Albany: State Department of Corrections, 1929).

Schools also played a critical role in the expansion of the marriage-counseling profession. In the 1930s and early 1940s they became important disseminators of marriage education. Although high schools for some time had offered girls courses in home economics that dealt with budgeting, maternal health, and childrearing, in the 1930s new courses on marriage and family relations were added to the curriculum or psychological material was added to the older field of home management. See, for example, Ruth Strang, *Personal Development and Guidance in College and Secondary School* (New York: Harper, 1934); Mildred Thurow Tate, "What the Teacher Can Accomplish in Education for Family Life," *Journal of Home Economics* 28 (February 1936): 73; Lemo Dennis Rockwood, "The Development of Education in Family Life in the United States," in *Readings in Mental Hygiene,* ed. Ernest Groves and Phyllis Blanchard (New York: Henry Holt, 1936), 264; Dora S. Lewis, "Education for Family Life in Washington State," *Parent Education* 2 (May 1935): 26; and Sadie J. Swenson, "Teaching Family Relationships in a City High School," in Groves and Blanchard, *Readings in Mental Hygiene,* 249. For a detailed survey of marriage education in secondary schools see Lemo Dennis Rockwood, "History and Status of the Movement for Education in Family Life at the High School and College Levels," *Parent Education* 2 (May 1935): 10–16, 47.

To date there have been no scholarly histories of the marriage-counseling profession. The only students of American culture and history to undertake a related investigation have been Michael Gordon, Beth Bailey, and Ronald Howard. Gordon and Bailey focus on marriage education. With a broad chronological focus, Gordon investigated marriage-education literature between 1830 and 1940 for its message about sex. More recently, Beth Bailey wrote a short essay about the incorporation of marriage into the higher-educational curriculum. See Michael Gordon, "From Unfortunate Necessity to a Cult of Mutual Orgasm: Sex in Marital Education Literature, 1830–1940," in *Sociology of Sex,* ed. James Henslin and Edward Sagarin (New York: Schocken, 1978), 53–77; and Beth Bailey's "Scientific Truth . . . and Love: The Marriage Education Movement in the United States," *Journal of Social History* 20 (summer 1987): 711–32. Howard explored the history of family sociology in America. See Ronald L. Howard, *A Social History of American Family Sociology, 1865–1940* (Westport, Conn.: Greenwood, 1981).

CHAPTER FOUR War

My portrait of the psychological front relies heavily on participants' personal accounts and internal army histories. There are several key books, including U.S. Army, Medical Department, *Neuropsychiatry in World War II,* ed. Albert J. Glass, 2 vols. (Washington, D.C.: Office of the Surgeon General, Department of the Army, 1966); Eli Ginzburg, *The Ineffective Soldier,* 3 vols. (New York: Columbia University Press, 1959); N. A. Levy, *Personality Disturbances in Combat Fliers* (New York: Josiah Macy Foundation, 1945); D. G. Wright and B. C. Glueck, *Psychiatric Experience in the Eighth Air Force* (New York: Josiah Macy Foundation, 1944); Roy Grinker and John P. Spiegal, *War Neuroses* (Philadelphia: Blakiston, 1945); idem, *Men under Stress* (Philadelphia: Blakiston, 1945); J. R. Rees, *The Shaping of Psychiatry by War* (New York: Norton, 1945); E. D. Cooke, *Psychia-*

try at the Fox Hole Level (Washington, D.C.: Infantry Journal Press, 1946); Association for Research in Nervous and Mental Disease, *Military Neuropsychiatry* (Baltimore: Williams & Wilkins, 1946); Frederick R. Hanson, ed., *Combat Psychiatry among American Ground Forces in the Mediterranean* (Washington, D.C.: U.S. Government Printing Office, 1947); Charles M. Wiltse, ed., *Medical Supply in World War II* (Washington, D.C.: Office of the Surgeon General, 1968); Emmanuel Miller, ed., *Neurosis in War* (New York: Macmillan, 1944); and William C. Menninger, *Psychiatry in a Troubled World* (New York: Macmillan, 1948).

There was also a steady stream of articles published during the war or immediately afterward. During the years 1941–47 the major psychological journals were filled with articles documenting the "psychological front." I examined the following periodicals: *Psychiatry,* the *American Journal of Psychiatry,* the *Journal of Orthopsychiatry,* the *Psychological Bulletin,* the *Bulletin of the Menninger Clinic, Mental Hygiene,* the *Bulletin of the U.S. Army, Medical Department, Military Surgeon,* the *New York State Journal of Medicine, Mental Hygiene News,* the *Journal of Nervous and Mental Diseases, Medical Reports on Morale and Psychiatry, Psychosomatic Medicine,* the *New England Journal of Medicine,* the *American Journal of Sociology, War Medicine,* the *Journal of Military Medicine in the Pacific,* and the *Journal of Consulting Psychology.*

The first historian to document the psychological front was Albert Deutsch in "Military Psychiatry: World War II, 1941–1943," in *One Hundred Years of American Psychiatry* (New York: Columbia University Press, 1944), 426. More recently, there have been several important studies of the role of psychological professionals in the war effort. See, for example, Rebecca Greene, "The Role of the Psychiatrist in World War II" (Ph.D. diss., Columbia University, 1977); James Capshew, "Psychologists on the March" (Ph.D. diss., University of Pennsylvania, 1986); and Albert Gilgen, *Soviet and American Psychology during World War II* (Westport, Conn.: Greenwood, 1997). Other works that touch upon aspects of the story include Herman, *Romance of Psychology;* Donald S. Napoli, *Architects of Adjustments: The History of the Psychological Profession in the United States* (Port Washington, N.Y.: National University Publications, 1981); and Peter Buck, "Adjusting to Military Life: The Social Sciences Go to War," in *Military Enterprise and Technology* (Cambridge: MIT Press, 1985), 205–52. But these studies focus on the psychological professions and their growth. What interests me about World War II is its contribution to the therapeutic gospel and how the war institutionalized a new version of this religion.

There is an extensive body of literature on World War II. The literature most familiar to historians of America deals with the home front and foreign policy and strategy. Usually only war buffs concern themselves with actual military history. But an understanding of exactly how the war was prosecuted, of the logistics and battles themselves, is critical to understanding the war as a force in our cultural and social history.

The best history of the operations and logistics of World War II is Geoffrey Perret, *There's a War to Be Won: The United Sates Army in World War II* (New York: Ballantine,

1991). Other useful works include Richard M. Leighton and Robert W. Coakley, *Global Logistics and Strategy, 1940-1943* (Washington, D.C.: Office of the Chief of Military History, Department of the Army, 1955); Constance M. Green et al., *The Ordnance Department: Planning Munitions for War* (Washington, D.C.: Office of the Chief of Military History, Department of the Army, 1955); Blanche D. Coll et al., *Corps of Engineers: Troops and Equipment* (Washington, D.C.: Office of the Chief of Military History, Department of the Army, 1958); Harry C. Thomson and Lida Mayo, *The Ordnance Department: Procurement and Supply* (Washington, D.C.: Office of the Chief of Military History, Department of the Army, 1960); Robert R. Palmer, Bell I. Wiley, and Kent R. Greenfield, *The Organization of Ground Combat Troops* (Washington, D.C.: Historical Division, Department of the Army, 1947); Joseph Bykofsky and Harold Lawson, *The Transportation Corps: Operations Overseas* (Washington, D.C.: Office of the Chief of Military History, Department of the Army, 1957); Wiltse, *Medical Supply in World War II*; Mark S. Watson, *Chief of Staff: Prewar Plans and Operations* (Washington, D.C.: Historical Division, Department of the Army, 1950); and Roland Ruppenthal, *Logistical Support of the Armies* (Washington, D.C.: Office of the Chief of Military History, Department of the Army, 1953). For a history of the Women's Army Corps (WAC) see Mattie E. Treadwell, *The Women's Army Corps* (Washington, D.C.: Office of the Chief of Military History, Department of the Army, 1954).

CHAPTER FIVE Home

My exploration of the "unhappy" home and the psychologization of American society during the cold war relies on the three women's magazines having the largest circulation—*McCall's*, *Ladies Home Journal*, and *Cosmopolitan*. For the response to Betty Friedan, I examined the collection of letters to her housed at the Schlesinger Library at Radcliffe College, Cambridge, Mass.

The literature that traces the origins of the women's movement back to the unhappy housewife comprises essentially all the literature on recent feminism. I know of no published works (other than my own) that dispute this connection between the image of women as unhappy and feminist action. For accounts that rely on the conventional interpretation about women's unhappiness see Sara Evans, *Personal Politics: The Roots of Women's Liberation in the Civil Rights Movement and the New Left* (New York: Vintage, 1979); Glenna Matthews, *"Just a Housewife": The Rise and Fall of Domesticity in America* (New York: Oxford University Press, 1987); William L. O'Neil, *Feminism in America: A History*, 2nd ed. (New Brunswick, N.J.: Transaction, 1989); and David Halberstam, *The Fifties* (New York: Fawcett Columbine, 1994).

I first made the argument that pop culture prominently figured in women's unhappiness in my dissertation, "Naming the Problem," in 1991. A few years later I published a more extensive study of my findings. See Eva S. Moskowitz, "'It's Good to Blow Your Top': Women's Magazines and a Discourse of Discontent, 1945-1965," *Journal of Women's History* 8 (fall 1996): 66-98. The one other scholar who has sought to reevaluate women's magazines is Joanne Meyerowitz. In her study "Beyond the Feminine Mystique: A Reassessment of Postwar Mass Culture, 1946–1958," *Journal of American History* 79 (March 1993): 1455–82. Meyerowitz examines issues of eight popular magazines, including three women's magazines, for the purpose of "testing generalizations about postwar mass culture." Meyerowitz takes issue with the view that popular magazines were uniformly critical of women's role outside the home. She disputes the claim that these magazines never presented positive images of politically active women. I do not address this issue; rather, I take up the claim that women's magazines represented women as blissfully happy while they suffered from the severe constraints of postwar domestic ideology. I conclude that this view of women's magazines is inaccurate. Women's unhappiness was indeed represented, even though the solutions offered were at worst antifeminist and at best unhelpful.

The most comprehensive survey of mental-health policy is Gerald N. Grob, *From Asylum to Community: Mental Health Policy in America* (Princeton, N.J.: Princeton University Press, 1991). See also Alex Sareyan, *The Turning Point: How Men of Conscience Brought about Major Change in the Care of the Mentally Ill* (Washington, D.C.: American Psychiatric Press, 1994); Don Martindale, *Mental Disability in America since World War II* (New York: Philosophical Society, 1985); Murray Levine, *The History and Politics of Community Mental Health* (New York: Oxford University Press, 1981).

Vance Packard's *Hidden Persuaders* (New York: D. McKay, 1957), probably the best-known exposé of advertising in the 1950s, is the most comprehensive study of motivation research to date. For other works that investigate the innovations in advertising in the postwar period see, for example, Stephen Fox, *The Mirror Makers: A History of American Advertising and Its Creators* (New York: Morrow, 1984); Michael Schudson, *Advertising, the Uneasy Persuasion: Its Dubious Impact on American Society* (New York: Basic Books, 1984); Roland Marchand, *Advertising the American Dream: Making Way for Modernity, 1920–1940* (Berkeley: University of California Press, 1985); idem, *Creating the Corporate Soul: The Rise of Public Relations and Corporate Imagery in American Big Business* (Berkeley: University of California Press, 1998); Stanley C. Hollander, *Was There a Pepsi Generation before Pepsi Discovered It?* (Chicago: American Marketing Association, 1992); Julian Sivulka, *Soap, Sex, and Cigarettes: A Cultural History of American Advertising* (Belmont, Calif.: Wadsworth, 1998); and Edd Applegate, *Personalities and Products: A Historical Perspective on Advertising in America* (Westport, Conn.: Greenwood, 1998).

CHAPTER SIX Social Protest

To identify the therapeutic strains of radical thought and action in the 1960s I relied on radicals' own accounts. See, for example, Alfred E. Young, ed., *Dissent: Explorations in the History of American Radicalism* (DeKalb: Northern Illinois University Press, 1968); Masimo Teodori, *The New Left: A Documentary History* (Indianapolis, Ind.: Bobbs-Merrill, 1969); Stokely Carmichael and Charles Hamilton, *Black Power: The Politics of*

Liberation in America (New York: Random House, 1967); Richard E. Flacks, "The Liberated Generation: An Exploration of the Roots of Student Protest," *Journal of Social Issues* 23 (1967): 52–75; Hal Draper, *Berkeley: The New Student Revolt* (New York: Grove, 1965); Walt Anderson, ed., *The Age of Protest* (Pacific Palisades, Calif.: Goodyear, 1969); Alice Lynd, ed., *We Won't Go: Personal Accounts of War Objectors* (Boston: Beacon, 1968); and Theodore Roszak, *The Making of a Counterculture* (New York: Anchor, 1969).

To trace the influence of psychological thinking on foreign policy, which, as I show, in turn influenced domestic policy, I examined government studies. See, for example, J. E. Uhlaner, ed., *Psychological Research in National Defense Today* (Washington, D.C.: U.S. Army Behavioral Science Research Laboratory, June 1967); William Lybrand, ed., *The U.S. Army's Limited War Mission and Social Science Research* (Washington, D.C.: Special Operations Research Office, 1962); John C. Flanagan, ed., *Psychology in the World Emergency* (Pittsburgh: University of Pittsburgh Press, 1952); D. M. Condit et al., *Challenge and Response in Internal Conflict*, 3 vols. (Washington, D.C.: American University, Center for Research in Social Systems, 1968); Ted Gurr with Charles Ruttenberg, *Cross-National Studies in Civil Violence* (Washington, D.C.: American University, Center for Research in Social Systems, 1969); and Andrew R. Molnar, Jeryy M. Tinker, and John D. LeNoir, *Human Factors: Considerations of Underground Insurgencies* (Washington, D.C.: American University, Center for Research in Social Systems, 1966).

There have, however, been a number of good studies of government funding of the social sciences in the postwar era and of how the cold war shaped the social-science agenda. See, for example, Harry Alpert, "Congressmen, Social Science, and Attitudes toward Federal Support of Social Science Research," *American Sociological Review* 23 (December 1958): 682–86; and idem, "The Government's Growing Recognition of Social Science," *Annals of the American Academy of Political and Social Science* 237 (January 1960): 59–67. Since then it has also been a concern of a number of scholars. See, for example, Gene M. Lyons, *Uneasy Partnership: Social Science and the Federal Government in the Twentieth Century* (New York: Russell Sage Foundation, 1969); David Halberstam, *The Best and the Brightest* (New York: Penguin, 1969); Fred R. Harris, ed., *Social Science and National Policy*, 2nd ed. (New Brunswick, N.J.: Transaction, 1973); David Cohen, ed., *The Power of Psychology* (London: Croom Helm, 1987); Otto Larsen, *Milestones and Millstones: Social Science at the National Science Foundation, 1945–1991* (New Brunswick, N.J.: Transaction, 1992); Robert F. Arnore, *Philanthropy and Cultural Imperialism* (Bloomington: Indiana University Press, 1980); Elizabeth T. Crawford and Albert D. Biderman, eds., *Social Scientists and International Affairs* (New York: Wiley, 1969); and Mark Solovey, "The Politics of Intellectual Identity and American Social Science, 1945–1970" (Ph.D. diss., University of Wisconsin at Madison, 1996). An excellent source of information on developing-world insurgencies and American psychology is Peter Watson, *War on the Mind: The Military Uses and Abuses of Psychology* (New York: Penguin, 1980).

Most recent chroniclers of the 1960s ignore that decade's therapeutic elements. I first explored this theme in my dissertation, on the intellectual origins of recent feminism, "Naming the Problem." More recently, Ellen Herman in her article "Being and Doing: Humanistic Psychology and the Spirit of the 1960s," in *Sights on the Sixties*, ed. Barbara Tischler (New Brunswick, N.J.: Rutgers University Press, 1992), 87–101, discussed the influence of Carl Rogers and Abraham Maslow on sixties thought. In her more recent work, *The Romance of American Psychology*, Herman analyzes the rise and fall of Project Camelot. This secret study of Latin America funded in 1963 was designed to provide social-science information that would aid U.S. counterinsurgency efforts. Had it not been canceled shortly after its creation, it would have been the largest behavioral-research project in U.S. history. This $4–6 million contract was to be the Manhattan Project of the social sciences. James Farrell, taking a different tack, emphasizes the influence of "personalist philosophy" on sixties radicalism. See Farrell, *The Spirit of the Sixties: Making Postwar Radicalism* (New York: Routledge, 1997). To my knowledge, no one has tried to link the civil-rights movement, the student movement, the counterculture, and feminism to the therapeutic gospel.

The literature on the civil-rights movement is substantial. Good general histories include Aldon D. Morris, *The Origins of the Civil Rights Movement* (New York: Free Press, 1984); Walter Jackson, *Gunnar Myrdal and America's Conscience: Social Engineering and Racial Liberalism, 1938-1987* (Chapel Hill: University of North Carolina Press, 1990); and Mark Tushnet, *Making Civil Rights Law: Thurgood Marshall and the Supreme Court* (New York: Oxford University Press, 1994). There are also a number of excellent studies on the desegregation movement. A few scholars have included as part of a larger inquiry important information about the role of the social sciences in this struggle. Two excellent studies are Richard Kluger, *Simple Justice: The History of Brown v. Board of Education and Black America's Struggle for Equality* (New York: Knopf, 1976); and Paul L. Rosen, *The Supreme Court and Social Science* (Urbana: University of Illinois Press, 1972). A pathbreaking work that addresses the psychological elements of the civil-rights movement is Daryl Scott's *Contempt and Pity: Social Policy and the Image of the Damaged Black Psyche, 1880-1996* (Chapel Hill: University of North Carolina Press, 1997).

For good general accounts and interpretations of the 1960s see Morris Dickstein, *Gates of Eden: American Culture in the Sixties* (New York: Basic Books, 1977); Maurice Isserman, *If I Had a Hammer. . . : The Death of the Old Left and the Birth of the New Left* (New York: Basic Books, 1987); Allen Matusow, *The Unraveling of America: A History of Liberalism in the 1960s* (New York: Harper & Row, 1984); William O'Neil, *Coming Apart: An Informal History of America in the 1960's* (New York: Times Books, 1971); Todd Gitlin, *The Whole World Is Watching* (Berkeley: University of California Press, 1980); S. Robert Lichter, *Roots of Radicalism: Jews, Christians, and the New Left* (New York: Oxford University Press, 1982); Wini Breines, *Community and Organization in the New Left, 1962-1968: The Great Refusal* (New Brunswick, N.J.: Rutgers University Press, 1982); Clayborne Carson, *In Struggle: SNCC and the Black Awakening of the 1960s* (Cambridge: Harvard University Press, 1981); David R. Farber, *The Age of Great Dreams: America in the 1960s* (New York: Hill & Wang, 1994); Tischler, *Sights on the Sixties;* Edward Morgan, *The 60s Experience: Hard Lessons about Modern America* (Philadelphia: Temple University Press, 1991); and James Miller, *Democracy in the Streets* (New York: Simon & Schuster, 1987). Most recently, see, Douglas C. Rossinow, *The Politics of Authenticity: Liberalism, Christianity, and the New Left in America* (New York: Columbia University Press, 1998); Terry Anderson, *The Movement and the Sixties* (New York: Oxford University Press, 1995); and Farrell, *Spirit of the Sixties.*

CHAPTER SEVEN   Feelings

The 1970s produced both an explosion of self-help philosophies and works criticizing "psychobabble." Therefore, the sources of my research and the literature are often one and the same. But it was during this era that brand-new vehicles for chronicling new self-help techniques were created, probably the most important being the magazine *Psychology Today.* I relied heavily on this magazine in my effort to chronicle all new feeling-management techniques. I read all the self-help books that appeared on the *New York Times* bestseller list. I also found helpful, however, the many journalistic accounts of the human-potential movement. See, for example, Jane Howard, *Please Touch: A Guided Tour of the Human Potential Movement* (New York: McGraw-Hill, 1970); and Rosen, *Psychobabble.*

Other works address more generally the influence of psychology on American culture in the 1970s. Tom Wolfe, for example, in his essay "The Me Decade" was one of the first to comment upon the narcissism and obsession with the self in American society. Other social critics followed. See, for example, Gross, *Psychological Society;* Jacoby, *Social Amnesia;* and perhaps most well known, Lasch, *Culture of Narcissism.* Feminists had their own slant on the nation's obsession with the psyche. Beginning with Betty Friedan, they spoke out against experts' psychological portrait of women. For a more contemporary account see Ehrenreich and English, *For Her Own Good.*

CHAPTER EIGHT   Personal Problems and Public Debate

Much of the information in this chapter is based on Internet research. I visited as many websites as I could find (and there are thousands more than I ever wanted to visit). I was interested in sites that claimed to help Internet users with personal and psychological problems. I examined on-line support groups, psychotherapy services, and what are called "feeling chatrooms." I also examined popular periodicals for information on the intersection of personal problems and public debate. I conducted research on television talk shows by simply turning on my television and watching (once again) more episodes than I ever wanted or intended to of *Oprah, Ricki Lake, Jerry Springer,* and so on. There are also a number of reference books that shed light on the issue, such as the *Diagnostic and Statistical Manual of Mental Disorders* (Washington, D.C.: American Psychiatric Association, 2000); and Barbara J. White and Edward J.

Mudara, eds., *The Self-Help Sourcebook* (Denville, N.J.: American Self-Help Clearing-house, 1992).

For additional insight on Americans' current obsession with recovery see Charles J. Sykes, *A Nation of Victims: The Decay of American Character* (New York: St. Martin's Press, 1992); Robert Wuthrow, *Sharing the Journey: Support Groups and America's Quest for Community* (New York: Free Press, 1994); Wendy Kaminer, *I'm Dysfunctional; You're Dysfunctional* (New York: Vintage, 1993); Jane M. Shattuc, *The Talking Cure: TV Talk Shows and Women* (New York: Routledge, 1997): Stanton Peele, *Diseasing of America: How We Allowed Recovery Zealots and the Treatment Industry to Convince Us We Are Out of Control* (New York: Lexington Books, 1995); Gerald N. Grob, "The Origins of DSM-I: A Study in Appearance and Reality," *American Journal of Psychiatry* 148 (April 1991): 421–31; Robyn R. Warhol and Helena Michie, "Twelve-Step Teleology: Narratives of Recovery / Recovery as Narrative," in *Getting a Life: Everyday Uses of Autobiography,* ed. Sidonie Smith and Julia Watson (Minneapolis: University of Minnesota Press, 1996); Elizabeth Wurtzel, *Prozac Nation* (New York: Riverhead, 1995); and Richard Kramer, *Listening to Prozac* (New York: Viking, 1993).

index